Liverpool   9

The Mediterranean Passage
Migration and New Cultural Encounters in Southern Europe

LIVERPOOL STUDIES IN EUROPEAN REGIONAL CULTURES
Series Editors: Ullrich Kockel and Máiréad Nic Craith

The series presents original research on the regional dimension of Europe, with special emphasis on regional culture, heritage and identity in the context of socio-economic development. It offers an interdisciplinary and comparative perspective on the management of cultural resources, examining the diversity and similarity of regional cultures in Europe, and identifying potentials for inter-regional co-operation and experience interchange.

OTHER TITLES AVAILABLE IN THIS SERIES

Culture, Tourism and Development: The Case of Ireland
ed. Ullrich Kockel, Volume 1, 1994, ISBN 0-85323-369-1

Landscape, Heritage and Identity: Case Studies in Irish Ethnography
ed. Ullrich Kockel,Volume 2, 1995, ISBN 0-85323-500-7

Borderline Cases: The Ethnic Frontiers of European Integration
Ullrich Kockel, Volume 3, 1999, ISBN 0-85323-520-1

Watching One's Tongue: Issues in Language Planning
ed. Máiréad Nic Craith, Volume 4, 1996, ISBN 0-85323-611-9

Watching One's Tongue: Aspects of Romance and Celtic Languages
ed. Máiréad Nic Craith, Volume 5, 1996, ISBN 0-85323-621-6

The Irish Border: History, Culture, Politics
ed. Malcolm Anderson and Eberhard Bort, Volume 7, 1999, ISBN 0-85323-951-7

Networking Europe: Essays on Regionalism and Social Democracy
ed. Eberhard Bort and Neil Evans, Volume 6, 2000, ISBN 0-85323-941-X

THE MEDITERRANEAN PASSAGE

Migration and New Cultural Encounters in Southern Europe

edited by

Russell King

Liverpool University Press

First published 2001 by
Liverpool University Press
4 Cambridge Street
Liverpool L69 7ZU

Copyright © 2001 Liverpool University Press

British Library Cataloguing-in-Publication Data
A British Library CIP Record is available.

ISBN 0-85323-646-1

Printed and bound in the European Union by
Alden Press Limited, Oxford

Contents

Preface and Acknowledgements

I should like to open these prefatory remarks by thanking Ulrich Kockel, series editor for the 'Liverpool Studies in European Regional Cultures', for the invitation to put this book together. It was after hearing a paper which I delivered on the 'Mediterranean Río Grande' at a conference on European frontiers held at the University of Edinburgh's International Social Sciences Institute in 1997 that Ulli asked me to enlarge the paper into a book-length project. This I was pleased to do, drawing into the project contributions from a number of mostly young researchers, including several current and recent doctoral students whom it had been my good fortune to supervise, work with or meet through the workshop and networking activities of the Sussex Centre for Migration Research. As founder and co-director of this Centre, it has been one of my objectives to create regular workshops and conferences where young scholars can present and share their ongoing research findings. Given the strong interest in southern Europe amongst many members of the Sussex migration group, myself included, it was easy to gather together in this volume what I hope is a stimulating and balanced selection of recent research on this region.

My second debt of thanks therefore is to the chapter authors for agreeing to contribute to the book, for showing such enthusiasm and commitment to delivering their essays on time, and for being so ready to carry out whatever revisions I asked them to do in order to make the book an integrated account made up of complementary contributions. They may find it difficult to appreciate how much pleasure and satisfaction I have derived from working closely with them in the preparation of this volume – so let me acknowledge this publicly. It is the younger generation of researchers who are producing most of the fresh and innovative research on European migration nowadays, and this volume is, I think, the perfect answer to a story I heard very recently about a publisher turning down a volume on a not dissimilar topic on the grounds that none of the contributors was a well-known author.

Thirdly, I gratefully acknowledge the unstinting editorial assistance provided by Jenny Money of the School of European Studies at Sussex. From polishing the English and checking references through to the preparation of the camera-ready copy, her help has been invaluable.

Finally a few words on how the book has evolved at a conceptual level. The original working title of the volume was 'Europe's Río Grande: Migration and the Mediterranean Frontier'. This reflected common interests shared by the series editor and myself in boundaries and frontiers as friction planes of political conflict, border crossings and socio-cultural contact. Sometimes completely porous, sometimes hermetically sealed, but more often something in between, frontiers represent and create a fascinating array of cultural and geographical phenomena such as frontier regions, trading and smuggling, and various forms of demarcation, separation and interaction. On further reflection, however, I became increasingly uneasy about the Río Grande metaphor when applied to the Mediterranean. It seemed to me that the very use of the term – especially in the title of a book – might be seen as a legitimation of the concept and therefore of the European Union's strategy of drawing a Schengen-line through the Mediterranean Sea, with all this implies in terms of a discourse of 'us' and the 'others', behind which lies a more sinister Eurocentrism which contrasts the 'desirable, developed, democratic, Christian' Europeans with the 'undesirable, backward, undemocratic, Islamic outsiders'. Such a discourse violates the historic role of the Mediterranean as a theatre of migration and travel amongst peoples who have a common cultural heritage which, objectively, is at least as strong as the cultural bond which supposedly unites all (Western) Europeans.

Wishing to reflect this ideal of the Mediterranean Basin as a 'shared space' with multiple forms of relatively unfettered mobility around and between its shores, I changed the title of the book to *The Mediterranean Passage*. This may seem like a utopian concept at a time when, every day and night, armed patrol boats play cat-and-mouse with rubber dinghies laden with migrants, and the corridors of EU and national political power are filled with animated discussion (and eventually legislation) on the so-called 'threat' of mass immigration. So, to some extent, the title does not accurately reflect the migration *realpolitik* of Schengen, Amsterdam and the Euro-Mediterranean partnership. On the other hand, for the migrants themselves, the Mediterranean is very definitely a sea of passage. The crossings may be short – across the Gibraltar Strait between Morocco and Spain, or between Tunisia and Sicily, or Albania and Puglia – but they are dangerous, and uncounted migrants pay the ultimate price. If successful they move from the poor to the rich world, although subsequently delusion may set in when the harsh realities of life as a socially-excluded migrant labourer became apparent. Nevertheless, signs of optimism and progress, especially at the individual and local level, abound. Community organisations are taking root, bridges are being built, close cross-national friendships are forged, families are being formed, some of them based on inter-marriage, and the beginnings of genuinely pluralistic societies can just about be discerned.

Ranging across Portugal, Spain, Italy and Greece, this book tells the stories of the migrants who have taken the Mediterranean Passage, from shores near and far, and who have begun new lives in the now-wealthy societies of southern Europe. They come from an extraordinary variety of countries – amongst those treated in the book are Cape Verde, Senegal, Sierra Leone, Nigeria, Morocco, Tunisia, Albania and the Philippines. What emerges is an overall picture which is both diverse and rapidly evolving, with cultural encounters which are both enriching and depressing. At the same time, the variety and depth of the material and of the methodological approaches adopted in the chapters of this book bear witness to the vitality of the field of European migration studies at the turn of the millennium.

Russell King
University of Sussex

List of Contributors

Maria José Caldeira is Lecturer in Social Sciences, Minho University, Portugal

Faïçal Daly is Post-Doctoral Research Fellow and Lecturer in Research Methods and Social Science in the School of Applied Science, South Bank University

Alessandra Di Maio is Assistant Professor of Italian at Smith College, Northampton, Massachusetts

Alina Esteves is Researcher in the Centro de Estudos Geográficos, University of Lisbon

John Foot is British Academy Research Fellow in the Centre for Italian Studies, University College London

Mariagiulia Grassilli is doing a DPhil in Geography at the University of Sussex

Russell King is Professor of Geography and Dean of the School of European Studies at the University of Sussex

Maria Koumandraki is a Research Assistant and PhD Student in the Department of Politics, University of Dundee.

Gabriella Lazaridis is Lecturer in Gender Studies and European Studies in the Department of Politics, University of Dundee

Nicola Mai is doing a DPhil in Media Studies at the University of Sussex

Cristóbal Mendoza is Research Fellow in the Department of Population Studies, El Colegio de la Frontera Norte, Tijuana, Mexico

Ricard Morén-Alegret is Researcher in the Department of Geography, Universitat Autónoma de Barcelona, and Research Associate in the Centre for Research in Ethnic Relations, University of Warwick

Davide Però is a Marie Curie Post-Doctoral Research Fellow in the Department of Geography, Universitat Autónoma de Barcelona

Natalia Ribas-Mateos is Lecturer in Sociology at the Universitat Autónoma de Barcelona

Elisabetta Zontini is doing a DPhil in Contemporary European Studies at the University of Sussex

1

The troubled passage: migration and cultural encounters in southern Europe

Russell King

Introduction

The subject and scope of this book are clear from its title: the Mediterranean as a new (as well as an old) migration space across which many migration flows have developed, leading to new cultural encounters in the now-prosperous countries of southern Europe, above all the four southern EU states of Italy, Greece, Spain and Portugal. The objective of the volume is to present thoroughly-researched case-studies of these encounters, based on fieldwork carried out in recent years in the four above-mentioned countries as well as in some countries of migrant origin, such as Morocco, Tunisia and Albania. Most of the contributions come from geography, anthropology and sociology – the social science disciplines which are most concerned with the study of human migration – but all are written from the general perspective of migration studies, an interdisciplinary (some would say post-disciplinary) field of enquiry which has grown significantly in recent years.[1] As for the definition of 'cultural encounter', this is left deliberately vague and therefore open for individual chapter authors to define or conceptualise within the context of the material they are presenting or the type of analysis they are carrying out. Hence the contributors examine cultural encounters based on conflict, cooperation or syncretism; at a variety of scales ranging from the individual and the family to the institutional and political; and in a variety of comparative settings – across generations, between migrant groups and between destination countries. In some chapters there is a strongly foregrounded spatial setting – a town or some fragment of urban space, or a rural or tourist environment.

Changing patterns and conceptualisations of trans-Mediterranean migration

In the not-too-distant past the whole of the Mediterranean Basin was a reservoir of migrants who, between the early 1950s and the mid–1970s, headed to northern Europe in their millions. At that time most countries of the Mediterranean region were united in their poverty and relative overpopulation: emigration was seen as a desirable solution, quite apart from satisfying the demands of postwar Europe for extra labour to rebuild and develop industrial economies. The chief migrant-sending countries were the four southern European countries which have since become immigration countries and which are the subject of this book, plus Yugoslavia, Turkey, Morocco, Algeria and Tunisia. Most of the source countries had preferential destinations: Portuguese and Spanish migrants went mainly to France; Yugoslavs, Greeks and Turks migrated mainly to West Germany. Italians had a wider spread of principal destinations – France, Belgium, Germany and Switzerland, as well as overseas to North America and Australia. During these decades the small Mediterranean island countries of Malta and Cyprus also witnessed intense emigration, almost entirely to England and other anglophone countries such as Australia and Canada. Algerians and Tunisians migrated mainly to France; Moroccans to France, Belgium and the Netherlands. Many migrants from North Africa crossed the Mediterranean Sea to southern France, Spain and Italy, using these countries as transit routes to their final destinations in the big cities and major industrial towns of northern Europe.

Old migrations

The function of the Mediterranean countries as a reservoir of migrants for the labour needs of industrial Europe can be compared to Mediterranean migration patterns both before and since these early postwar decades. Fernand Braudel's (1972, 1973) seminal account of the historical geography of the Mediterranean provides abundant if scattered evidence of the way in which the peoples of the Mediterranean were historically prone to migrate around and between its coasts. The sea functioned as a 'common space', not only for trade, warfare, colonisation and exile, but also for more free-willed migration, exemplifying Braudel's conceptualisation of 'the Mediterranean as a human unit' (1972, pp. 276–352). To the millennial land-based mobilities of transhumance, nomadism and rural–urban migration were added maritime passages that linked shore with shore, city with city, mainland with island.

Let us select just a few examples of the historical pattern of intra-Mediterranean migration (Braudel 1972, pp. 158–60, 335–7, 415–16; 1973, pp. 802–26). Virtually all the islands of the Mediterranean have a tradition of exporting their people. Corsicans, emigrators *par excellence*, went to Marseilles, Genoa, Venice, Algiers and Constantinople; before long, there were more islanders living off the island than on it – a condition which still holds today. Most major Mediterranean cities were full of immigrants, who were necessary to sustain and develop urban populations and economic activities. Venice in the sixteenth century had a polyglot population: *Furlani* from the nearby mountains of Friuli, Albanians, Greeks, Turks, Armenians and Jews – 'indispensable immigrants' who were not only labourers and artisans but also merchants, artists and scholars. Seventeenth-century Lisbon was also a place of immigrants, including many black slaves who constituted 15 per cent of the city's population in 1633 and who were the forerunners of late-twentieth-century African migrations from Cape Verde, Angola and elsewhere. Then there is the case of the Jews, reluctant but creative Mediterranean migrants, expelled from just about every Mediterranean city, often moving on only to be expelled again. Finally we may note some wider-scale migrations: the Moorish colonisation of much of the Iberian peninsula and Sicily; and the nineteenth- and early-twentieth-century French, Italian and Spanish colonial settlements in North Africa. Both these latter movements illustrate the ebb and flow of populations across the Basin; both resulted ultimately in *reconquista* and repatriation.

The examples given above – and many more could have been added – are sufficient to confirm the long tradition of pan-Mediterranean mobility. One obvious consequence of this historic, structural mobility of the Mediterranean population is 'the extraordinary ethnic variety of the Mediterranean coastlands' (Horden and Purcell 2000, p. 40).

Transitional migrations

Mediterranean migration patterns after the 1970s became more complex and variegated than those of the 1950s and 1960s, when there was a dominant northward emigration from most parts of the Basin. For a time, return migration became an important trend, as Mediterranean migrants, especially those who had been taken on as temporary 'guest-workers', returned home in the wake of the oil crisis of the early–mid 1970s, or for personal reasons to rejoin their families and native communities (King 1984). But this was only one trend. Another was the development of new trans-Mediterranean migration flows eastwards to the oil-rich states of the Gulf and to Libya. Egyptians, Tunisians, Turks and Portuguese were some of the groups most affected by these migrations, which were not only of unskilled labourers but also involved technicians and managers. By and large, this was short-term contract migration linked to the oil sector and its associated industries of downstream processing, construction and service provision, and concerned overwhelmingly a male migrant labour force. A final type of migration which operated during this transition period of the 1960s and 1970s saw northward flows resulting from decolonisation and nationalism in several African countries. In the early–mid 1960s up to 1 million *pieds-noirs* – French colonial settlers and their descendents – left Algeria for France at the time of Algerian independence. Smaller echoes of this flow took place in neighbouring Tunisia, affecting both French and Italian settlers. Further east, Greek and Italian business and administrative elites left Egypt, Ethiopia and Somalia, whilst at the other end of the Mediterranean more than half a million Portuguese *retornados* moved back to the mother country from Angola, Mozambique and other Portuguese African colonies which became independent in the mid–1970s.

New migrations

The 1980s witnessed a new configuration of Mediterranean migration, and this new pattern provides the setting for this book. Several geographical, economic, political and socio-cultural factors help to explain why the Mediterranean Sea has become an arena for renewed and intense migratory activity over the past 15–20 years.[2]

- The halt called to the recruitment of labour migrants by all the main immigration countries around 1974 led to a 'diversion effect': migrants who sought entry to France, West Germany, the Netherlands etc. looked for other European countries where immigration control policies were not yet in place and whose borders were more 'open' – Italy played a pioneering role in absorbing such migrants in the 1970s and early 1980s.

- The geographical location of Europe's Mediterranean countries as a kind of 'soft underbelly' facing many migrant source countries across the Mediterranean made them logical targets for migrants transiting the Mediterranean Sea, both from the southern shore countries and those entering the Mediterranean region from more far-flung origins such as the Middle East, Asia and sub-Saharan Africa.

- The nature of the frontiers of southern European countries – long sea coasts, many islands, mountainous external borders – makes control of migrant crossings and landings very difficult. In recent years efforts have been stepped up to patrol these frontiers more effectively but clandestine border crossings (e.g. of Albanians into Greece) and illicit landings of migrants on remote beaches continue to be a common occurrence.

- The geographical openness of southern Europe exists in another sense too: the tradition of the region in maritime trade and its vitally important tourist industry imply the continuous movement of people, goods and transport media in and out of the coutry. This makes migrants or potential migrants difficult to monitor and favours a widespread form of entry – arrival on tourist visas followed by overstaying.

- Historical connections across the Mediterranean, including commercial and former colonial relationships, have helped to shape several migration flows: from the Maghreb into France, Spain and Italy; from Egypt into Greece; from Ethiopia, Eritrea and Somalia into Italy; and, beyond the western limit of the Basin, from Portuguese former colonies in Africa to Portugal.
- Since 1989 the collapse of communist regimes in Eastern Europe has opened up new migration source countries, including Poland, Rumania, Bulgaria and Albania. Rather than 'south–north' migrations across the Mediterranean, these are 'east–south' moves, although Albanians do take the 'Mediterranean passage' across the Adriatic, as do Kosovans and other refugees from the break-up of Yugoslavia.
- The demographic contrast across the Mediterranean has sharpened in recent decades, leading to strong population push-pressures for trans-Mediterranean migration. The average family size in the southern EU countries is now slightly above one child, and the population is ageing rapidly. To the south – from Morocco round to Turkey – average family sizes are between three and six children, and population structures are much younger.
- Probably most important of all has been the changing economic context. Plentiful economic data exist to demonstrate the fast development of the southern European countries (including Malta and Cyprus) in recent decades: EU accession of Greece, Spain and Portugal in the 1980s also played a role. With increasing prosperity come rising wages and new openings for migrant workers in specific sectors of the labour market.
- Finally, some key social changes in southern Europe must be noted, among which are rising levels of formal education leading to the rejection of certain types of employment by native workers (and hence the need for migrants to do these jobs), and the increasing participation of women in the workforce, triggering a demand for 'replacement workers' to take over childcare, house management, care of elderly people etc.

Quantifying recent immigration into southern Europe

Most estimates converge on a figure of about 3 million for the total number of immigrants in the four southern EU countries in the mid–late 1990s.[3] The difficulty of being more precise relates to two issues: uncertainty over the accuracy of existing records of immigrants, which are mainly based on registers of 'legally-present foreigners'; and a more obvious lack of ability to quantify so-called illegal or undocumented migrants. In Italy, Spain and Portugal, periodic 'regularisations' or 'amnesties' of undocumented migrants have progressively reduced, but by no means eliminated, the share of 'illegal' immigration. In Greece, on the other hand, most immigrants are undocumented and hence unrecorded, leading to widely-diverging estimates of the total number of immigrants in the country. Recently some estimates have started to exceed 500,000, equivalent to 5 per cent of the population living in Greece. For the other three countries, even if we take into account what are regarded as realistic estimates for the undocumented immigrant population, the fraction barely exceeds 2 per cent.

Table 1.1 sets out the official data on legally-present foreigners in Italy, Spain and Portugal for 1997. For each country, the top dozen or so migrant nationalities are listed, above the 2 per cent threshold of the total immigrant presence. The different absolute sizes of the cut-off points for listing immigrant communities in Table 1.1 reflect the different sizes of the total population of the three countries – Italy 57 million, Spain 39 million, Portugal 10 million.

Several comments are worth making about the data in the table. Morocco is the most important immigrant nationality in both Italy and Spain, reflecting a long familiarity of Moroccan migrants with these two countries, from migrations of transit to those of permanent and semi-permanent settlement. Nevertheless Moroccans are far from numerically dominant in these two countries, accounting for only one in ten immigrants in Italy and one in seven in Spain. What is striking about Italy and Spain, and especially the former, is the large number of different immigrant communities from different regions of the world: Europe, North Africa, sub-Saharan Africa, Latin America, Asia and so on. This heterogeneity and spread of immigrant communities creates obvious possibilities, and challenges, for a diverse multiculturism.

If Italy best exemplifies this diversity, the cases of the Iberian countries are somewhat different. Spain has several important Latin-American communities, partially explained by ties of history, language and culture. But over 40 per cent of the total immigrants in Spain are from European countries, reflecting a different kind of cultural and economic proximity and the role of tourism in leading to retirement settlement (Williams *et al.* 1997). This European dimension is also present in Portugal, and for that matter in Italy too, but the most notable feature of Portuguese immigration is the key role of the lusophone former colonies, above all Cape Verde. Greece has its own unique mix of immigrant nationalities, reflecting its historical relations and geographical position in the Balkans and eastern Mediterranean. Precise figures do not exist, but it is known that the main nationalities present in Greece are Albanians (the overwhelming majority), Poles, Bulgarians, Egyptians and Filipinos (Iosifides 1997).

Table 1.1 Legally present foreign population in Italy, Spain and Portugal, 1997

Italy	no.	%	Spain	no.	%	Portugal	no.	%
Morocco	131,406	10.6	Morocco	77,189	14.3	Cape Verde	39,769	22.7
Albania	83,807	6.8	UK	68,359	12.7	Brazil	19,990	11.4
Philippines	61,285	4.9	Germany	45,898	8.5	Angola	16,296	9.3
USA	59,572	4.8	Portugal	38,316	7.1	Guinea-Bissau	12,785	7.3
Tunisia	48,909	3.9	France	33,134	6.1	UK	12,342	7.0
Ex-Yugoslavia	44,370	3.6	Italy	21,362	4.0	Spain	9,806	5.6
Germany	40,079	3.2	Argentina	18,246	3.4	USA	8,364	4.8
Romania	38,138	3.1	Peru	18,023	3.3	Germany	8,345	4.8
China	37,838	3.0	Dominican Rep.	17,845	3.3	France	5,416	3.1
Senegal	34,831	2.8	USA	15,661	2.9	Mozambique	4,426	2.5
Poland	31,329	2.5	Netherlands	13,925	2.6	São Tomé	4,304	2.5
France	28,333	2.3	Philippines	11,770	2.2	Venezuela	3,783	
Sri Lanka	28,162	2.3	China	10,816	2.0			
UK	26,771	2.2						
Egypt	26,171	2.1						
Peru	24,362	2.0						
Total	1,240,721		Total	538,984		Total	175,263	

Sources : Respective national registers, taken from Caritas di Roma (1998, p. 79); Eaton (1999, p. 365); Permanent Observatory on Immigration in Barcelona (1999, p. 40).

It is also worth adding Cyprus and Malta to the list of south European countries which have turned the tables from emigration to immigration since the 1980s. Anthias (2000, pp. 29–31) quotes figures of 27,500 legal migrants and a further 10,000 illegal immigrants for Cyprus in 1997; the main nationalities, apart from Greeks, are Bulgarians, Filipinos, Sri Lankans and Syrians. For Malta, Zammit Lupi (1997, pp. 20–6) estimates a total of around 5,000 legally-resident immigrants for 1997. Apart from long-term British settlers, the main communities comprise Italians, Libyans, Egyptians, Bulgarians, refugees from the former Yugoslavia, and Chinese.

How to interpret recent Mediterranean migration

For much of the 1980s and 1990s the dominant interpretative discourse regarding trans-Mediterranean (and other) migrations into Europe was to view these swelling migrations as a 'threat' emanating largely from the push pressures of underdevelopment and overpopulation in the source countries. At a statistical level there is no doubt that the steepness of the economic and demographic gradient across the Mediterranean increased considerably during the period between the 1960s and the 1980s: this was largely because the economic structures and indicators of Italy, Spain, Portugal and Greece became much more 'European' and less 'Mediterranean' over these two or three decades. From the early 1990s on, the Mediterranean began to be viewed as Europe's 'Río Grande' – a liquid frontier separating the rich north (Europe) from the poor south (North Africa, the 'Third World') and temptingly open to migrant crossings. Jean-Christophe Rufin was perhaps the first to use the Río Grande epithet in the context of the Mediterranean (1991, p. 172). Rufin stressed the 'demographic danger' of the southern Mediterranean countries and pointed out that, if anything, the development gap between the northern and southern shores was greater than that between the United States and Mexico. And in contrast to the relative ease with which the American Río Grande can be sealed and patrolled by frontier police, tracker dogs, fences, night-vision cameras etc., the Mediterranean is by its geographical nature a much more open and complex frontier to monitor. Subsequently the notion of the Mediterranean Río Grande was developed by Montanari and Cortese (1993) and by the author (King 1998), and it continues to be used in political debates and newspaper articles on European migration.

Now, however, I see a danger in the over-use of this term. It is, by nature, divisive and can too easily lead to a 'clash of civilisations' discourse (cf. Huntington 1993) which has been used by proponents of the 'European fortress' policy and challenged by more liberal analysts who see both the necessity and the desirability of more freedom of movement, including migration across the Mediterranean. Whilst not wanting to deny the *realpolitik* of a Eurocentric, anti-immigration rhetoric, it does contravene to a large extent both a deeper history of Mediterranean movement and identity and the experiences and aspirations of today's migrants who want to be relatively free to 'come and go' within 'their' Mediterranean space.

Moreover, the last few years have seen a reappraisal of the demographic and economic situations in both Europe and the southern Mediterranean region. A recent front cover of the *Economist* proclaimed 'Go for it! Europe needs more immigrants'; inside were articles arguing the economic and demographic case for allowing 1.6 million immigrants to enter Europe each year until 2050.[4] The case is based on the need to re-stock the labour force of ageing Europe. Particular attention focuses on the case of Italy where, if the recent extraordinary birth rate persists (there is some evidence that it will not), the country's population will shrink from the present 57 million to only 40 million by 2050. Meanwhile, on the other side of the Mediterranean, countries such as Tunisia, Morocco and Turkey are moving into their demographic transitions very quickly – faster than had been forecast just a decade or so ago (Tapinos 1996, 2000).

So, to sum up, it seems that trans-Mediterranean immigration into southern Europe can be framed at a number of levels which may be analytically distinct but in practice overlap and interact. The dynamically changing context of Mediterranean migration also needs to be constantly borne in mind: migration flows wax and wane; routes change; policies for managing migration are changing at the European, national and local levels; and the socio-economic context of migration is also in a continuous state of evolution, including the possibility of chaotic events, such as those which provoked mass departures from Albania in 1991 and 1997.

The first interpretative level is the global one, based on acknowledgement of the existence of an integrated economic system in which globally hegemonic regimes of capital accumulation and their related models of productive organisation and relations of inequality may be taken as 'structural givens' (cf. Zolberg 1989, p. 403). Southern Europe's position within this international division of labour changed dramatically between the third and fourth quarters of the twentieth century, as we have seen (King and Rybaczuk 1993). Before the first oil crisis, during the so-called 'golden age' of Fordism, southern European and other Mediterranean migrant workers were a major component of the remarkably high and consistent levels of industrial development and capital accumulation in the core economies of north-west Europe. Under Fordism, migrant workers' structural position was clear and they were specifically recruited by the industrial countries to fulfil that economic role. After the 1970s, immigration *into* southern Europe has taken place within a new regime of capital accumulation in which the monetarist responses to the crisis of profits and inflation have led to a greater centrality of private initiative, the rolling back of state regulation, the weakening of collective labour power, and an all-out attempt to minimise labour costs in an increasingly competitive global market environment. The linked processes of deindustrialisation, tertiarisation, deregulation of labour-capital relations and expansion of the informal economy have had a particular impact on the countries of southern Europe which are the subject of this book. Certainly the immigrant presence in the contemporary labour market in southern Europe has been crucial to the possibility of holding down wage levels in many employment sectors (Dell'Aringa and Neri 1989; Pugliese 1993). The illegal or semi-illegal status of many immigrants from North Africa, Albania and elsewhere renders them ineligible for social protection, leading to their 'super-exploitation' (Sivanandan 1988) in the agricultural sector, in labour-intensive industries such as construction, and in seasonal and casual work in the tourist sector.

At the next level, the Mediterranean expresses itself as an active friction plane where these global processes translate themselves into strong migration pressures at the regional scale. Within the Basin there are several 'mini-Río Grandes' where short stretches of sea separate societies with very different levels of material wealth, opportunity and quality of life. Migrant traffic, most of it clandestine, has been particularly intense across the Gibraltar Strait between Morocco and Spain, the Sicilian Channel between Tunisia and Sicily, and the Otranto Channel between Albania and the Adriatic coast of southern Italy. These short Mediterranean passages are far from comfortable journeys. The sea can often be treacherous due to storms, fierce currents and strong winds. Coastguards and maritime police are ever-vigilant. Accidents and disasters are frequent, due to the desperation of the migrants and their agents and smugglers, and the flimsy and overcrowded craft used – old fishing boats or unstable rubber dinghies. Untold numbers perish. Moreover the sea passages are often only the final leg of journeys which began far away and on which migrants have suffered incredible privations. The Strait of Gibraltar is crossed not only by Moroccans but also by migrants from West Africa, some of whom have traversed long stretches of the Sahara on foot. Albania has functioned as a rallying point for migrants originating from the Balkans, the eastern Mediterranean and beyond. Other migrants make a longer westward passage through the Mediterranean, starting from Egypt, Syria or Turkey. Geographers have yet to map the Mediterranean's new migrant passages: this book is just a beginning.

The final level is the human scale of individuals, families, social groups and communities. This is the level at which all the chapters in this book pitch their analysis, exploring the 'lifeworlds' of migrants in a variety of social, economic and spatial settings. A key focus is on migrants' variable experiences of interaction with the 'host' society; the primary emphasis is on social and cultural aspects, with only secondary emphasis on economic ones, except insofar as economic 'integration' has a bearing on social experiences. The chapters mainly employ intensive qualitative (and, in one case, literary) research methods rather than extensive demographic or statistical surveys; they explore questions of both migrant identity and how host-society identity is affected by migration; and they analyse variations in migrant experiences between countries and across migrant groups, allowing some comparative dimensions to be drawn out. Indeed one of the challenges of studying migrants in southern Europe is how to achieve a balanced evaluation between the diversity of migrant origins (including diversity *within* migrant nationalities) and the common experience derived from migrants' fundamental role as cheap labour and from their social position as – by and large – excluded 'others'. Strong regional differences are noted – for instance between Catalonia and the Algarve, or between Sicily and northern Italy. Also important is the impact of migrants on social relationships and townscapes at the very local level of the street, the quarter, or the local political forum. Examples of all these interactions, scales and comparisons will be found in the chapters which follow.

What is clear is that a new social geography and anthropology of the European Mediterranean needs to be written: again, this book is a first step. There is, of course, an established body of ethnographic literature on the Mediterranean. A critical examination of this corpus opens up several rather fundamental questions, some of which were raised some time ago by John Davis (1977). One slightly elliptical question is the extent to which the anthropology of Europe is really an anthropology of Mediterranean Europe (see Delamont 1995). A parallel question is the extent to which the anthropology of the Mediterranean is really an anthropology of the European Mediterranean (Davis 1977). This leads to yet another related question – the validity of the existence of the Mediterranean (or the European Mediterranean) as a distinct cultural region. Judging by recent debates (Goddard *et al.* 1994), the jury is still out on this issue. What is less in doubt is the past preoccupation of 'Mediterranean' anthropologists with southern European peasant societies, small villages, rural politics, familism and clientelism. Now this is changing, with urban studies and tourism receiving attention. What still seem to be lacking are studies on the new immigrants who are retexturing the erstwhile homogeneous cultural fabric (although the extent to which southern European societies, even rural ones, were homogeneous is highly debatable). Research on new migrant-centred cultural encounters in southern Europe is beginning to emerge from several doctoral and other young scholars, and this volume presents a selection of their work.

An overview of the book

In Chapter 2 Natalia Ribas-Mateos picks up the debate started above concerning the conceptualisation of the new migratory context of the Mediterranean. Following my suggestion that the term Río Grande connotes a too-brutal division, Ribas-Mateos introduces the intriguing concept of the 'Mediterranean caravanserai' – an open but bounded space for collecting, hosting and redistributing migrants moving from several countries to a variety of destinations. The caravanserai metaphor is perfectly in tune with the new flexibilities of mobility which challenge conventional definitions of migration, including the often false distinction between legal and illegal immigrants. In reality, people are moving back and forth across the Mediterranean, through and onward, stopping for shorter or longer periods of time. There is the tourist who decides to stay longer than permitted, the student who accepts a job without having a work permit or the refugee whose application for asylum has been refused and who remains in the country. More specifically, there is the Tunisian seasonal worker in Sicily, the Moroccan peddler in Spain, the illegally-employed Cape Verdean construction worker in Portugal, the Albanian domestic servant in Athens (cf. Werth and Körner 1991, p. 12).

The rest of Chapter 2 engages in a carefully structured discussion of the reception context and modes of incorporation of three migrant communities – Moroccans, Gambians and Filipinos. Following Portes and Rumbaut (1990), the reception context is analysed at three levels: host-country policies towards immigration, the conditions of the labour market, and the characteristics of individual ethnic groups. Special attention is given to the key role of the ethnic community in explaining differences in degrees and modes of incorporation of immigrants into Catalan society. Ribas-Mateos also carried out fieldwork in Morocco, the Gambia and the Philippines. She shows how social structures and changes in the countries of origin shape both the migration flows and the socio-cultural experiences of immigrants in the destination setting. Key variables include the gender balance of migration, associationism, and the intention to stay, return or shuttle back and forth as a member of a 'transnational community'.

Cristóbal Mendoza's Chapter 3 is also comparative, focussing on cultural dimensions of the labour market experiences of African migrants (from Morocco and West African countries) in Lisbon, the Algarve and the Spanish province of Girona. Each of these areas corresponds to a different job environment for immigrant workers: construction in Lisbon, tourism in the Algarve, and agriculture in Girona. Mendoza maintains that employment situations for immigrants are socially and culturally regulated rather than being the result of a simple market relationship. Important elements of this social regulation include government policies towards admitting certain immigrant nationalities for certain types of work (most obvious in Spain); employers' often stereotyped attitudes towards the employment of immigrants; the changing cultural attitudes of host-country nationals to certain types of work (seasonal agriculture or insecure construction work) which are now regarded as socially demeaning by all classes; the use of migrant social networks for accessing employment; and the role of social networks and family structures in shaping internal population mobility of immigrants within Spain and Portugal.

Mendoza highlights four conclusions from his work. The first is to contrast a more 'immigrant-friendly' Portuguese policy with the more exclusionary stance of the government in Spain, where migrants are considered as temporary workers. The fact that most immigrants in Portugal come from Portuguese-speaking former colonies is a major factor helping to explain this contrast. The second conclusion revolves around employers' beliefs and opinions about immigrants. In Spain it is clear that, whilst immigrants in general are perceived as a docile and cheap labour source (and their hard-working nature contrasted with the 'lazy' Spaniards), the use of particular types of immigrant labour is based on preconceptions rooted in prejudice and racism. The third conclusion turns the spotlight on employees' values and attitudes towards various types of paid work, noting for instance the cultural aversion of male Moroccans to certain types of work such as cleaning. Finally, Mendoza highlights the different ways in which ethnic social networks are used amongst migrant groups in the two countries. African workers in Portugal are able to use 'conventional' job-hunting channels to find work because of their familiarity with the culture and the language of the host country and perhaps also because immigrants are more 'accepted' in Portugal; in Spain, Moroccans and West Africans rely much more on friends and family networks.

Chapter 4 is about Barcelona, and the organised expressions of multiculturalism observed by Mariagiulia Grassilli in that city. Four events are described and analysed. Two are major festivals: the three-day *Festa de la Diversitat* which is the city's 'official' celebration of multicultural diversity; and the *Feria d'Abril*, the ten-day manifestation of the city's Andalusian cultural heritage reflecting the large number of internal migrants who have settled over several decades. These 'big events' are counterposed with two local-scale and more informal events: the *Setmana Intercultural*, a week-long programme of cross-cultural activities in an old *barrio* close to the city centre; and a youth sports event based on hip-hop and skateboarding in another poor inner-city district inhabited by many immigrant families. Grassilli contrasts the spontaneous and authentic collective atmosphere of the smaller-scale celebrations with the stage-managed commercialism of the centrally-organised events: in her words, the 'everyday multicultural life of the *barrio*' versus the 'ethnic performance' of specially marketed events. Beneath these four events Grassilli also detects a more hidden discourse about post-Franco Catalan identity politics. Celebrating multiculturalism and the diversity of foreign communities in Barcelona, and encouraging the use of the Catalan language both amongst these immigrants and the long-settled community of Andalusian origin is an effective mechanism for blocking the encroachment of Castilian Spanish – the real cultural enemy of Catalonia.

In Chapter 5, Alina Esteves and Maria José Caldeira examine the contribution of the Cape Verdean community to the cultural life of Lisbon. Their hypothesis is that appreciation and acceptance of immigrants' important contributions to the cultural richness of the host society will encourage people to view migrants not as 'strangers' or 'others' but as new citizens who have much to add to the cultural life of the city. The main body of the chapter consists of a discussion of several cultural elements of the Cape Verdean community in Portugal, including the Creole language, food, music and dance, literature, religious rites and the use of public space. By and large, Lisbon has proved receptive to these Cape Verdean (and wider African) influences and has successfully incorporated them into the evolving cultural mosaic of the city. But this process has not been entirely one-way. The authors give some examples of ways in which Cape Verdeans have had to abandon or renegotiate some cultural traditions and social habits.

Chapter 6 is about African immigrant organisations in Lisbon. In the first part of this chapter Ricard Morén-Alegret situates immigrant associations in their theoretical context: as intermediate institutions between the individual immigrant and the host society, and as sites of resistance where immigrants can organise their social lives in ways that reflect their dual relationship to their cultures of origin and to their new residential and economic setting. Morén-Alegret lays particular emphasis on the ways in which the balance between social principles (of cooperation, mutual aid, equality etc.) and the systemic logic of capitalism (based on competition, profit, control etc.) can be expressed and negotiated within the organisation and functioning of immigrant associations. He points out how some associations change their positions over time, moving from a social to a systemic basis.

The second part of the chapter contains the empirical results of the author's fieldwork in Lisbon. Immigrant associations can be classified by their ethnic background, class origin, gender, religion and purpose – conservation of culture, defence of human rights, mutual aid etc. Other variables include date of foundation, size of membership and location. Morén-Alegret surveys the early Cape Verdean associations, whose origins go back to the 1960s, religious associations attached to the Hindu and Islamic communities, neighbourhood associations and immigrant trade unions (both of which emerged strongly in the 1980s), the creation of a common immigrant platform in 1987, and the last generation of immigrant groups (representing new immigrant arrivals from non-lusophone countries such as Pakistan, Senegal and Rumania) in the 1990s.

After five chapters on Iberia, the next five are on Italy, followed by two on the Balkans. In Chapter 7 Alessandra Di Maio looks at the evolution of an immigrant literature in Italy during the 1990s. Using autobiography, fiction, poetry and other genres, authors originating from Morocco, Tunisia, Senegal, Cameroon, Palestine and Brazil write the 'Mediterranean passage', expressing their experiences with a mixture of pride, resignation, hope and anger. On the one hand each of the authors and pieces analysed by Di Maio reflects a personal experience and is rooted in the author's own cultural background; on the other hand the accounts all spring from the authors' (and their subjects') circumstances within Italian society, whilst at the same time addressing that society as an audience. With often dramatic effect, such authors assert for themselves the right to tell their own stories, to write the history of which they themselves are part, reclaiming the narratives that are so often written about them by others whose stance and information are based at worst on prejudice and ignorance, at best on a wide-eyed sense of exotic 'otherness'.

Chapter 8, by Davide Però, examines the contrast between the inclusionary rhetoric and the exclusionary practice of the Left administration in Bologna in its dealings with immigrants in the city. Però starts off by presenting a wide-ranging sample of policy statements and other documentary sources, including websites, of the Democratic Left administration (successor to the Italian Communist Party). At this rhetorical level there is no mistaking the inclusionary stance towards immigrants as 'new citizens' whose multicultural diversity must be welcomed and celebrated. Policy statements repeatedly speak of the need for a full social, cultural and economic integration 'which is respectful of immigrants' histories, cultural characteristics and differences'. Però then counters the official rhetoric by quoting from the voices of the migrants themselves, first via some extracts from a book written by a Moroccan living in Bologna, and secondly via his own fieldwork amongst the city's immigrants. He presents two case-studies of 'policy practices' – the shabby and inconsistent treatment of a group of Moroccans living in a temporary housing scheme, and the even more disgraceful handling of a community of Rom refugees from the former Yugoslavia. Both episodes described by Però reveal strong elements of cultural imperialism, extreme residential segregation, marginalisation, infantilisation and disempowerment. Però concludes that the new cultural encounters involving immigrants in Bologna have been a missed opportunity for the mainstream Left in one of southern Europe's supposedly most progressive cities to seriously put into practice its egalitarian scope and vision.

In Chapter 9 Faïçal Daly introduces another variant of the Mediterranean passage: the 'double passage' of Tunisians first to nearby Sicily and then onwards via the much longer overland journey to the industrial North of Italy. This double migration is both a two-stage physical movement and a stepped socio-economic and cultural transition. Daly traces Tunisian migration to Sicily from its origins in the 1960s, showing that it was a continuation of rural–urban migration prompted by the failure of the Tunisian agrarian reforms as well as a diversion of established Tunisian migration streams to France and Germany which were halted by the reception countries in the early 1970s. First-wave Tunisian emigrants to Sicily worked in farming and fishing in the western part of the island, close to their points of arrival. The second and third waves were associated with the Italian regularisations of 1986 and 1990, leading to a fourth stage of northward migration within Italy during the late 1980s and 1990s. For Tunisians, the common pattern is to arrive in Sicily or other parts of the Italian South, and spend some time there getting socially acclimatised, working in the black economy and arranging a residence permit. It is easier both to find illegal work and to get a permit in the South of Italy, where the authorities are generally more relaxed about such things. Possession of a permit is then often the trigger for the second migration to northern Italy where better and more remunerative jobs can be found in the industrial and service sectors. However there is a further contrast which Daly reveals, based on his interview and questionnaire research with Tunisian immigrants in the northern industrial town of Modena. Economic opportunities may be better in the North of Italy, but racist attitudes are more entrenched compared to the South and Sicily where, on the whole, the local populations are more welcoming, perhaps because of a consciousness of their own history of emigration and experience of racism in northern Europe.

Another northern Italian industrial city – Turin – forms the subject of Chapter 10, by John Foot. More specifically, Foot focuses on the central neighbourhood of San Salvario where, during the mid and late 1990s, the local and national media's attention was continually spotlighted on the so-called 'immigrant emergency' of the quarter, constructing it as a 'dangerous place'. After giving some facts and figures on the geography of the quarter and its history of immigration, Foot carefully unpicks the events behind the creation of San Salvario as a dangerous place, focusing on key personalities (the priest, the local politician, the vigilante), on key moments such as the organisation of demonstrations and vigilante patrols, and on the build-up of the discourse of criminalisation of the immigrants. The author argues that, objectively, San Salvario is no more dangerous than many other Turinese neighbourhoods and less dangerous, in fact, than many other Italian urban areas. He also shows that in reality it is far more dangerous for the immigrants living there than for the native residents, for the former are constantly under the surveillance of the police as well as subjected to racist attacks by right-wing thugs. Meanwhile the authorities have altered the micro-geography of the quarter to prevent immigrants from using public spaces. Seats have been removed, fences built and from time to time police blockades set up and immigrants stopped and searched. At the wider scale, Foot relates the events of San Salvario to the national debates on immigration played out daily in the newspapers and nightly on televison screens, and to the sharp decline of Turin as a manufacturing city, leading to a loss of economic and class identity for much of the local working population.

With Chapter 11, by Elisabetta Zontini, we return to Bologna and to a comparative analysis of the process of family formation amongst Filipino and Moroccan migrants. Zontini starts off by reminding us that migrations into southern Europe are sharply gendered (cf. Anthias and Lazaridis 2000). Different migration streams are either predominantly male (e.g. the Moroccan one) or predominantly female (the Filipino case), and the jobs on offer to different migrant groups are also narrowly defined with respect to gender – construction and factory work on the one hand, domestic help and cleaning on the other. Zontini's account is built around the biographies of six women matched in three pairs (each pair with a Moroccan and a Filipina): women with partners but no children, single-parent working mothers, and married women with children. Careful comparisons are drawn between the cases, drawing out both similarities and differences in terms of stages of family formation and cross-national experience. The case-studies reveal some heroic efforts of sacrifice, hard work and skilled organisation in order for immigrant women to cope with their work, their household and spousal responsibilities and their children. Often these familial relationships and responsibilities span more than one country, illustrating the special role that women play in transnationalism and migration.

One of the more shadowy aspects of the new Mediterranean migrations is the development of migrant trafficking, often linked to criminal or semi-criminal organisations based either in the countries of destination (the Italian mafia) or spawned from sending countries such as Albania. The trafficking of young women and children is a particularly tragic part of the exploitative 'business' of migration. In Chapter 12 Nicola Mai makes a critical analysis of the trafficking of Albanian teenage girls for sexual exploitation in Italy and elsewhere. The chapter is not about the mechanisms of sexual exploitation and abuse in the destination countries (on this see Campani 1998, 2000; Psimmenos 2000), but analyses the Albanian cultural background to this regrettable phenomenon. Mai enters into an extended discussion of the historical structures of patriarchy and the conditions of women in Albanian society, drawing out the linkages between Albanian customary law and gender relations from the pre-communist background, through the long communist period and into the chaotic post-communist transition of the last ten years 'when people (males) attempted a reinvention of some strategic aspects of their traditional (patriarchal) heritage in order to serve their own needs – exercise of power and acquisition of capital in a situation of mounting economic and social chaos'. As a result the phenomenon of trafficking in Albania results from the encounter between two social groups who found themselves in a situation of extreme vulnerability in the post-communist Albanian transition: young men at risk of criminal behaviour, and young women at risk of sexual exploitation.

The final chapter looks at the racialisation of ethnic minorities in Greece. Gabriella Lazaridis and Maria Koumandraki use life stories of several immigrants in Greece, mainly from Albania and West Africa, to show that racism is not just a 'black/white thing' but, in the Greek case at least, is extended also to highly racialised white migrants, demonstrating that race is both a biological and a cultural construct. Albanians, in particular, have become stereotyped as hard workers but also stigmatically labelled as vagabonds, cheats, generally untrustworthy. At the same time the authors' interviews with a Nigerian man and two Sierra Leonean women reveal explicit racism on the part of Greeks towards those with black skins. On the basis of the testimonies they have collected, Lazaridis and Koumandraki conclude that 'racism in Greece is a proven fact ... it is intricately woven in the fabric of everyday living and transcends other group divisions such as class, age and gender'. This evidence exposes the myth of Greek tolerance and hospitality towards 'strangers'. There is a sharp differentiation to be drawn between the cultural encounter between Greeks and free-spending foreign tourists on the one hand, and the much more troubled encounter between Greeks and immigrants whose contribution to the Greek economy and society may well be considerable but is apparently not recognised by the majority of Greeks.

Notes

1   See Cohen (1995, pp. 5–8) for an interesting yet tantalisingly brief discussion on the disciplinary/interdisciplinary/post-disciplinary nature of the study of migration. Symptomatic of the rise of migration studies as a major field of enquiry in the social sciences has been the flurry of books on the theme in the last few years: see, for instance, Boyle *et al.* (1998), Castles and Davidson (2000), Castles and Miller (1998), Cohen (1995), Cornelius *et al.* (1994), Faist (2000), Ghosh (1998), Hammar *et al.* (1997), Harris (1995), Massey *et al.* (1998), Papastergiadis (2000), Rapport and Dawson (1998), Skeldon (1997), Weiner (1995). This by no means exhausts the library of recent important

books on international migration, but it includes most of those which adopt a broadly global perspective.

2　Since I have written at length on these new cross-Mediterranean migratory factors elsewhere, they are summarised as a series of bullet-points here. For more detail and discussion see King (1996, 1998, 2000), King and Donati (1999), King and Konjhodzic (1995), King and Rybaczuk (1993), King *et al.* (1997).

3　For a more thorough review of data sources and trends see Baldwin-Edwards (1997), King and Konjhodzic (1995), King *et al.* (1997).

4　See the *Economist*, 6 May 2000, pp. 19–20, 25–31.

References

Anthias, F. (2000) Metaphors of home: gendering new migrations to southern Europe, in Anthias, F. and Lazaridis, G. (eds) *Gender and Migration in Southern Europe: Women on the Move*. Oxford: Berg, pp. 15–48.

Anthias, F. and Lazaridis, G. (eds) (2000) *Gender and Migration in Southern Europe: Women on the Move*. Oxford: Berg.

Baldwin-Edwards, M. (1997) The emerging European immigration regime: some reflections on implications for southern Europe, *Journal of Common Market Studies*, 35(4), pp. 497–519.

Boyle, P., Halfacree, K. and Robinson, V. (1998) *Exploring Contemporary Migration*. London: Longman.

Braudel, F. (1972, 1973) *The Mediterranean and the Mediterranean World in the Age of Philip II*. London: Collins, 2 vols.

Campani, G. (1998) Trafficking for sexual exploitation and the sex business in the new context of international migration: the case of Italy, *South European Society and Politics*, 3(3), pp. 230–61.

Campani, G. (2000) Immigrant women in southern Europe: social exclusion, domestic work and prostitution in Italy, in King, R., Lazaridis, G. and Tsardanidis, C. (eds) *Eldorado or Fortress? Migration in Southern Europe*. London: Macmillan, pp. 145–69.

Caritas di Roma (1998) *Immigrazione Dossier Statistico '98*. Rome : Anterem.

Castles, S. and Davidson, A. (2000) *Citizenship and Migration: Globalization and the Politics of Belonging*. London: Macmillan.

Castles, S. and Miller, M. J. (1998) *The Age of Migration: International Population Movements in the Modern World*. London: Macmillan.

Cohen, R. (ed.) (1995) *The Cambridge Survey of World Migration*. Cambridge: Cambridge University Press.

Cornelius, W. A., Martin, P. L. and Hollifield, J. F. (eds) (1994) *Controlling Immigration: A Global Perspective*. Stanford: Stanford University Press.

Davis, J. (1977) *People of the Mediterranean*. London: Routledge and Kegan Paul.

Delamont, S. (1995) *Appetites and Identities: An Introduction to the Social Anthropology of Western Europe*. London: Routledge.

Dell'Aringa, C. and Neri, F. (1989) Illegal immigrants and the informal economy in Italy, in Gordon, I. and Thirlwall, A. (eds) *European Factor Mobility: Trends and Consequences*. Basingstoke: Macmillan, pp. 133–47.

Eaton, M. (1999) Immigration in the 1990s: a study of the Portuguese labour markets, *European Urban and Regional Studies*, 6(4), pp. 364–70.

Faist, T. (2000) *The Volume and Dynamics of International Migration and Transnational Social Spaces*. Oxford: Clarendon Press.

Ghosh, B. (1998) *Huddled Masses and Uncertain Shores: Insights into Irregular Migration*. The Hague: Martinus Nijhoff.

Goddard, V., Llobera, J. and Shore, C. (eds) (1994) *The Anthropology of Europe: Identities and Boundaries in Conflict.* Oxford: Berg.

Hammar, T., Brochmann, G., Tamas, K. and Faist, T. (eds) (1997) *International Migration, Immobility and Development: Multidisciplinary Perspectives.* Oxford: Berg.

Harris, N. (1995) *The New Untouchables: Immigration and the New World Worker.* Harmondsworth: Penguin.

Horden, P. and Purcell, N. (2000) *The Corrupting Sea: A Study of Mediterranean History.* Oxford: Blackwell.

Huntington, S. P. (1993) The clash of civilizations? *Foreign Affairs,* 72(3), pp. 22–48.

King, R. (1984) Population mobility: emigration, return migration and internal migration, in Williams, A. M. (ed.) *Southern Europe Transformed: Political and Economic Change in Greece, Italy, Portugal and Spain.* London: Harper and Row, pp. 145–78.

King, R. (1996) Migration and development in the Mediterranean region, *Geography,* 81(1), pp. 3–14.

King, R. (1998) The Mediterranean: Europe's Río Grande, in Anderson, M. and Bort, E. (eds) *The Frontiers of Europe.* London: Pinter, pp. 109–34.

King, R. (2000) Southern Europe in the changing global map of migration, in King, R., Lazaridis, G. and Tsardanidis, C. (eds) *Eldorado or Fortress? Migration in Southern Europe.* London: Macmillan, pp. 1–26.

King, R. and Donati, M. (1999) The 'divided' Mediterranean: redefining European relationships, in Hudson, R. and Williams, A. M. (eds) *Divided Europe: Society and Territory.* London: Sage, pp. 132–62.

King, R. and Konjhodzic, I. (1995) *Labour Markets, Employment and Migration in Southern Europe.* Brighton: University of Sussex, Research Papers in Geography 19.

King, R. and Rybaczuk, K. (1993) Southern Europe and the international division of labour: from emigration to immigration, in King, R. (ed.) *The New Geography of European Migrations.* London: Belhaven, pp. 173–206.

King, R., Fielding, A. and Black, R. (1997) The international migration turnaround in southern Europe, in King, R. and Black, R. (eds) *Southern Europe and the New Immigrations.* Brighton: Sussex Academic Press, pp. 1–25.

Massey, D. S., Arango, J., Hugo, G., Kouaouci, A., Pellegrino, A. and Taylor, J. E. (1998) *Worlds in Motion: Understanding International Migration at the End of the Millennium.* Oxford: Clarendon Press.

Montanari, A. and Cortese, A. (1993) South to north migration in a Mediterranean perspective, in King, R. (ed.) *Mass Migrations in Europe: the Legacy and the Future.* London: Belhaven, pp. 212–33.

Papastergiadis, N. (2000) *The Turbulence of Migration.* Cambridge: Polity.

Permanent Observatory on Immigration in Barcelona (1999) *Foreign Immigration in Barcelona 1994–1997.* Barcelona: CIDOB Edicions.

Portes, A. and Rumbaut, R. G. (1990) *Immigrant America: A Portrait.* Berkeley and Los Angeles: University of California Press.

Psimmenos, I. (2000) The making of periphractic spaces: the case of undocumented female migrants in the sex industry of Athens, in Anthias, F. and Lazaridis, G. (eds) *Gender and Migration in Southern Europe: Women on the Move.* Oxford: Berg, pp. 81–102.

Pugliese, E. (1993) Restructuring of the labour market and the role of Third World migrants, *Society and Space,* 11(3), pp. 513–22.

Rapport, N. and Dawson, A. (eds) (1998) *Migrants of Identity: Perceptions of Home in a World of Movement.* Oxford: Berg.

Rufin, J.-C. (1991) *L'Empire et les Nouveaux Barbares.* Paris : Editions Jean-Claude Lattès.

Sivanandan, A. (1988) The new racism, *New Statesman and Society,* 4 November, pp. 8–9.

Skeldon, R. (1997) *Migration and Development: a Global Perspective.* London: Longman.

Tapinos, G. (1996) *Europe Méditerranéenne et Changements Démographiques.* Turin: Edizioni della Fondazione Giovanni Agnelli.

Tapinos, G. (2000) Migration, trade and development: the European Union and the Maghreb countries, in King, R., Lazaridis, G. and Tsardanidis, C. (eds) *Eldorado or Fortress? Migration in Southern* Europe. London: Macmillan, pp. 277–97.

Weiner, M. (1995) *The Global Migration Crisis.* New York: Harper Collins.

Werth, M. and Körner, H. (1991) Immigration of citizens from third countries into the southern member states of the EEC, *Social Europe,* Supplement 1/91, pp. 1–134.

Williams, A. M., King, R. and Warnes, A. M. (1997) 'A place in the sun': international retirement migration from northern to southern Europe, *European Urban and Regional Studies,* 4(2), pp. 115–34.

Zammit Lupi, C. (1997) *Recent Trends in Migration to Malta: Following the South European Model?* Brighton: University of Sussex, MA dissertation in Contemporary European Studies.

Zolberg, A. (1989) The next waves: migration theory for a changing world, *International Migration Review,* 23(3), pp. 403–30.

2

Revising migratory contexts: the Mediterranean caravanserai

Natalia Ribas-Mateos

Introduction: the Mediterranean caravanserai

Much has already been written about the Mediterranean as a 'common space' where economic and cultural exchanges, as well as violent confrontation, take place (Braudel 1972, 1973; Horden and Purcell 2000). Nowadays, the Mediterranean represents one of the most active friction-planes when considering North–South imbalances in the globalised world: it is the setting both for sharp socio-economic contrasts and for various kinds of migratory phenomena which derive from global inequality and instability. The origins of trans-Mediterranean disequilibrium lie in the history of past economic and political contact and power asymmetries between the two sides of the Mediterranean. The differences between the north and the south sides of the Mediterranean are very clear when we examine economic and social indicators such as the well-known index of human development (UNDP 1999). Countries like Spain, Italy and France are amongst the leaders in world rankings of human development; Portugal and Greece are not far behind. On the other hand, countries like Morocco, Tunisia, Algeria and Egypt have low or at best middle rankings in world development. Furthermore, some countries which are geographically European, such as Albania, Macedonia (FYROM) and Turkey, have middle or low-to-middle indices of human development.[1]

In virtually all regions of the world we can today observe a continuous internationalisation of migration with more and more countries becoming involved, an acceleration in the rate of mobility and a differentiation of flows (Castles and Miller 1998). Diverse categories of migrant exist, including temporary migrant workers, irregular migrants and others who migrate for family reunion. As a context in which to observe all these migratory changes, the Mediterranean illustrates very well the new challenges for the future of managing migration. Within the Basin, the countries of southern

Europe – Spain, Portugal, Italy and Greece – have witnessed a turnaround in their migration behaviour from emigration to immigration (King *et al.* 1997). Some of the causes and mechanisms of this migratory turnaround were spelt out in Chapter 1. Particularly relevant for my analysis in the present chapter is the way in which migrants from North Africa have transformed southern Europe, and especially Spain, from a transit route mainly towards France, into a new set of destination countries – even if these countries had not yet developed any policies or legislation concerning immigration. The new role of the southern European countries in relation to the other countries of the Mediterranean region is also related to important processes of social change in southern Europe, which makes it no longer necessary for their populations to emigrate to sustain their livelihood. Instead the migration frontier, which during the 1950s and 1960s ran along the Alps and the Pyrenees, now runs east–west through the Mediterranean from Istanbul to the Straits of Gibraltar (King 1998).

Migration scholars are searching for a suitable model to frame this new, yet diversified, migration phenomenon. Studies by Pugliese (1993; 1995) and King *et al.* (1997; also King 2000) have particularly focused on the characteristics of heterogeneity which can be correlated with the multiplicity of nationalities and types of migrant, as well as an important gender asymmetry depending on national origin. The economic context is also shown to be highly relevant: in spite of stringent border controls in all four southern EU countries, their important informal economies host large quantities of irregular immigrants with particularly high concentrations in certain sectors such as agriculture and construction. However, significant differences between the four new destination countries must also be taken into consideration. Some of these derive from specific historical conditions, such as the role of ex-colonial, and hence Portuguese-speaking, countries in Portuguese immigration and the status of the ethnic Greeks in immigration trends in Greece. In Spain and Italy there are different settings and experiences of immigration to be noted between northern and southern regions of those countries, which in turn derive from different historical experiences of economic and social modernisation.

Spain has been the fastest moderniser in southern Europe in recent decades, so that many of the images of the poverty and poor social conditions of the 'old Spain' – such as those documented in the films of Luis Buñuel – seem to have been quickly forgotten.[2] Meanwhile, a good example of the impact of Spanish modernisation on migration dynamics is given by an account of two trips separated by 40 years to the province of Almería, in south-east Spain, by Juan Goytisolo.[3] In 1957 he described how poor peasants were abandoning their villages in droves, most of them migrating to Barcelona, which for them symbolised a closer version of the Americas. At that time Almería province was one of the poorest areas of Europe. In 1998, in the same place, thousands of immigrants from the Maghreb and sub-Saharan Africa were working as cheap and often irregular labour in the region's phenomenally productive irrigated agriculture. Migrant workers have become an integral part of a production system which takes full advantage of the region's climate, soils and investment in irrigation, chemical inputs and plastic sheeting. Almería's agriculture is now one of Spain's leading regional export economies. But the cultural encounter between the migrant workers, most of whom are badly exploited and endure harsh working conditions and minimal social facilities, and the local inhabitants is far from harmonious. The area has a recent history of racial conflict.[4]

In this chapter I focus on the social context of trans-Mediterranean migration, looking at both sides of the migration coin – the macro-processes taking place in southern Europe and the micro-processes taking place within particular migration flows corresponding to different migrant groups. Taking as an interpretative model Portes and Rumbaut's (1990) analysis of reception contexts and modes of immigrant integration, I will examine the interaction between three contextual factors in the Mediterranean case: the policies of the receiving country's government towards immigration; the conditions of the host labour market; and the characteristics of the individual ethnic communities. The empirical evidence which is built around this conceptual framework comes from doctoral research which I carried out in the 1990s on three immigrant nationalities – Moroccans, Filipinos and Gambians – in Catalonia (Ribas-Mateos 1999a; 2000), whilst the theoretical perspective derives from ongoing post-doctoral research which is still largely at the formative stage (Ribas-Mateos 1999b).

As a final part of the introductory framing of this chapter, I want to introduce the metaphor of the Mediterranean as a *caravanserai* or 'common space' for migrant groups and flows. In its original form, dating back to the sixteenth century, the caravanserai (which comes from the Persian *karawan saray*) was a kind of inn, made up of a large quadrangular building with a spacious court in the middle. In this inner court caravans of merchants and travellers could be received and hosted, before continuing their journeys in different directions. The way in which southern Europe functions as a new reception space for 'caravans' or groups of migrants coming from the other side of the Mediterranean or further afield has obvious parallels with this earlier institution.

Migratory contexts and social change in southern Europe

Since the 1980s southern Europe has witnessed a complex set of dynamic changes as we saw in Chapter 1. Amongst the various dimensions of this multifaceted transformation are deindustrialisation, the tertiarisation and flexibilisation of the labour market, the emergence of foreign immigration, demographic trends including the future problem of the 'ultra-elderly', the restructuring of social services and the re-examination of the role of the welfare state. All these issues constitute the broad scenario for social change in Europe, especially in southern Europe, and provide part of the context within which the recent phenomenon of large-scale foreign immigration must be understood (Ribas-Mateos 1999b).

The remainder of this chapter is structured around the analytical framework proposed by Portes and Rumbaut (1990) for North American immigration, here applied to the Mediterranean case and to the social changes listed above. This approach enables us to progress beyond the one-dimensional perspective based on push–pull theories of migration and on supply–demand theories of labour. Three contexts influence the modes of incorporation of immigrants.

Government policy is put in first place because it represents the first stage of the process of incorporation; it affects the probability of successful immigration and the legal framework in which the (non-)integration of the immigrant is taking place. We will also stress the unpreparedness of the southern European countries when confronted by the reality of immigration and their failure to develop coherent policies for managing the migration flows and, in particular, for combating various forms of social exclusion.

Secondly, we can identify the labour market as a key mode of incorporation, and note the variable ability of different types of migrants to overcome labour market discrimination. By and large, immigrants in southern Europe are incorporated into the secondary segment of the labour market where racial, ethnic and gender markers indicate their vulnerability and their confinement to certain employment niches; they are not placed according to their skills and qualifications.

Thirdly – a factor which was undervalued in previous literature before the work of Portes and Rumbaut – there is the key role of the construction of the ethnic community in explaining differences in modes of incorporation. In the words of Portes and Rumbaut (1990, pp. 83, 93), what immigrants 'bring with them – motivation, knowledge and resources – is a decisive feature affecting their path of economic mobility... How they use these personal resources often depends on international political factors – where individuals have no control – and on the history of earlier arrivals and the types of communities already created.' This third dimension of the context of reception places great importance on the cultural identity and achievements of the migrant group, where family and kinship play a central role. Towards the end of the chapter I will especially focus on family, kin and gender divisions in the context of social change in the countries of origin – Morocco, the Philippines and the Gambia. I will consider the conditions of departure according to variations by social class, place of origin, and gender and family contexts. By using this micro-approach we can find alternative explanations for the analysis of international migration: alongside nation-states as actors in the migration process we can add the strategies and actions of transnational households in a globalised world.

The policy context: foreign immigration and the welfare state

The continuing growth of immigration and asylum issues and the dilemmas in the formulation of migration control models across the countries of southern Europe have posed a series of important questions both to national governments and to European Union institutions. In the 'old countries of immigration' (France, Belgium, the Netherlands, Germany, the United Kingdom etc.), rather different models of immigrant incorporation have evolved over the past 20–30 years. For all their achievements (and shortcomings), these differences raise awkward problems for the harmonisation and coordination of national policies on immigration and integration at the European level. These debates for European policy-makers become even more difficult when the complexity of the new situation in southern Europe is brought in – the novelty of the phenomenon of immigration in these countries, their incapacity in policy formulation, and the variety of immigrant types with which they are faced. The general picture is a lack of regulation in labour markets and in policies for 'dealing with' immigrants. Moreover a contradiction is evident between the restrictive border control policies (which, however, are far from effective) and emerging policies for the social integration of immigrants.

Differences in the timing of migration trends and in the evolution of migration policy amongst the southern European countries also have to be recognised. Emigration fell off earliest and quickest in Italy, which also now has the largest absolute total of recorded immigrants (see Chapter 1 for details). Italy therefore is the pioneer of southern European migration trends and can be suggested as the paradigmatic example of the southern European model of immigration. Portugal and Greece are at the other extreme: Portugal because emigration flows continued much later than the other three countries; and Greece because this is the country where the implementation of immigration policies has been the most delayed.[5]

The main instruments of immigration policy – regularisations, quotas (Spain) or *laissez-faire* (Greece)[6] – tend to shape the labour market niches in which immigrants are recruited. These niches are mainly determined by principles of substitution or complementarity with the local labour force, which tends to reject such low-status job types. Consequently, if during the 1950s and 1960s the countries of northern Europe opted for the 'return logic' (excluding, at least initially, the family dimension of immigration), we can observe that, 30 years later, the countries of southern Europe express a 'mercantile logic'.

When looking for a common context for migration policies in these countries, we can identify general features related to the types of political domination, the form and pace of economic development (or stagnation) and the system of social class relations (Giner 1995). Three of the four countries experienced harsh dictatorships which lasted into the 1970s, delaying their entry into the European Community, which eventually took place in the 1980s as the 'second enlargement'. Italy's experience of authoritarian rule was no less harsh but ended with World War Two, allowing this country to be a founder-member of the Common Market. Until recently, southern Europe seemed to be stranded mid-way between the 'advanced societies' to the north and the 'less advanced' parts of the world. The coexistence of somewhat opposing forces – tradition and modernity, democracy and authoritarianism, advanced capitalism and the informal economy – constitutes a common theme in the recent evolution of these four countries, including the development of immigration policy and of the welfare state.

Following the well-known Esping-Anderson (1990) typology, we can identify four welfare regimes in Europe: social democratic (Scandinavia), conservative (continental Europe), liberal/social democratic (UK) and the southern European. Ferrera (1995) points out some common traits of the welfare systems of Greece, Italy, Spain and Portugal: low coverage of the population, high differentiation of benefits, a massive asymmetry of expenditure alongside underdeveloped unemployment benefits and inadequate universalistic national systems. The south European model has not been adequately covered in literature on comparative welfare regimes, except possibly the Italian case which can be considered the best illustration of the clientelistic welfare state (Ferrera 1995, p. 85). Whenever the south European model is portrayed, its 'rudimentary character' is stressed, combined with the influence of Catholic ideology in programme design and reliance on the support role of the traditional family structure. However, according to Ferrera, this 'rudimentary character' cannot always be generalised and the strength of the leftist tradition also has to be recognised. In this latter sub-model, welfare services are dependent on workers' contributions; therefore the dual labour market reproduces a dual welfare system, so that immigrant workers belonging to the irregular or non-institutional sector of the labour market will have little or no welfare coverage.

An important further contribution to our analysis is the gender perspective. Sainsbury (1994) points out a major gap in mainstream research on welfare regimes which fails to examine the care and human service sector. Traditional comparative analysis concentrates on the social insurance schemes and income maintenance policies of the state–market nexus; there is little attempt to incorporate gender within an examination of wider state–market–family relationships. Social services indicators are not only useful for analysing the gendering of the welfare state but can also be seen as the matrix linking immigration, the welfare state and the family (Ribas-Mateos 1999b). In a privatised conception of social services, and thinking of the indigenous family's strategy for care, the double-earner household could be playing a reproductive role on the demand side, whilst immigrant women (who are also involved in transnational family strategies) could be seen as playing an important role on the supply side, in addition to their functions as household heads in development strategies. Accordingly, gendered family strategies and a sexual division of labour can be seen as the grounds for an ethnically gendered conception of care as well as a transnational division of female labour.

The late developers: immigration in a highly informalised market

Together with the lack of national policies towards migration and the 'rudimentary' and 'clientelistic' nature of the welfare state, we can also add to our characterisation of the new immigration countries the adjective 'late-developing' (Mingione 1995). The late-developer capitalistic model is defined by its obsolete economic structures (except some regions such as Northern Italy and Catalonia), a modernisation path which leads from a rural economy directly to one based on urban services (missing out significant industrialisation), a gender asymmetry in sectoral employment changes, and the important role of a dynamic informal sector.

Apart from the standard push factors in the sending countries, migration flows into the southern European region respond to a market for certain types of jobs (low-status, low-wage activities, primarily in the expanding informal economy) which are filled by immigrants from 'Third World' or other poor countries. On the other hand, reflecting the dualisation of the labour market, another type of labour demand is found – a professional and high-skill demand mainly satisfied by migrants from 'First World' countries. Recent studies of the interaction between labour markets and immigration in Lisbon and Catalonia have emphasised this duality of migrant types (Baganha 2000; Pascual de Sans *et al.* 2000).

The existence of a demand for low-status workers (the main sector of demand) has to be understood within the context of the socio-economic formation of southern Europe. King *et al.* (1997, p. 9) indicate key features of this formation as: processes of modernisation, urbanisation and tertiarisation; the dynamism of the informal sector;[7] the importance of small-scale enterprises; an enhanced level of education for most young people leading to the rejection of manual work;[8] and a sharply defined conception of social and family prestige reflected in attitudes towards 'acceptable' and 'unacceptable' types of work.

Mingione (1995) has outlined a labour market model which is peculiar to southern Europe; it is in this type of labour market – highly segmented, partly dualistic, dynamic, informal – that immigrants insert themselves, often in rather clearly defined employment niches. The incorporation of migrants in south European labour markets has much to do with the segmentation of those markets, as many studies have shown (Baganha 1998, 2000; Baldwin-Edwards and Arango 1999; Droukas 1998; Mingione and Quassoli 2000; Reyneri 1998; Solé *et al.* 1998), but it is also related to other characteristics of those markets such as high unemployment rates (especially in Spain and southern Italy) and the widespread presence of autonomous and irregular jobs (petty tradesmen, street-vendors etc.). Irregular work is especially concentrated in the agricultural sectors in less developed regions (southern Spain, southern Italy, northern Greece), in the construction sector, local manufacturing industries, and services to individuals and families. In the wider European Union realm, these types of irregular work are mainly found in southern Italy, Spain, Greece, Ireland and some areas of southern France (Mingione *et al.* 1990, p. 5).

The context of high unemployment and the crisis and restructuring of the welfare state favours the host society's perception of immigrants as a 'problem', even though there is a specific demand for their labour. The location of this demand in the ever-dynamic underground economy defines the character of these jobs and supports the well-known analysis of Piore (1979) concerning the dual labour market and the 'reserve army' function of immigrant workers. In southern Europe the exodus of the indigenous workforce from agriculture, the progressive tertiarisation of employment and the rise of so-called atypical jobs (temporary, part-time, casual) are parameters which are clearly reflected in the occupational structure of the immigrant labour force. Meanwhile Saskia Sassen's (1995) description of a 'degrading manufacturing sector' and burgeoning personal service sector demand in 'global cities'[9] also proves to be quite useful when analysing the incorporation of immigrants in the dozen or so big cities of southern Europe. Nevertheless, despite the attempts of economic sociologists to rationally explain and justify the presence of significant cohorts of immigrant workers in southern European society, such workers are negatively viewed by most of the inhabitants of the four countries in question, caught between the crisis of the welfare state and the re-emergence of the black economy (Solé *et al.* 1998).

Social change in the sending countries

Most of the current literature on international migration refers mainly to the reception contexts of immigration policies and labour market demand. Now we must look at the other side of the coin – how social changes in the countries of origin shape the migration flows, realising that the sending countries, too, are not monolithic societies. In another paper which looked at female migrants in Spain (Ribas-Mateos 2000), I argued that the feminisation of migration flows was to be explained not just by the interaction of the Spanish labour market and the quota system, which privileged female domestic worker migrants, but also by the emigration dynamics of the main country of origin for this type of migration. This is the case of the Philippines, where the Filipino government has discharged a strong mediating role and where family structures and strategies pushed women abroad. In the Philippines, differentiation of productive and reproductive tasks (depending on the social class of the family) defines who should help in the family/household sphere and who should migrate and be part of the specific transnational organisation of Filipino migrant families.

The analysis of the sending country context goes beyond taking into account the folkloric nature of cultures: the country of origin is taken as a whole, embracing its specific history of colonialism, its linguistic and religious characteristics, socio-political and economic features, social relations and family structures. In the analysis which follows I delineate and explore three types of reproduction – labour force reproduction, social organisation and cultural reproduction. I draw on interview material and participant observation with three groups with differing gender profiles of migration – Filipino migrants (mainly female), Moroccans (mainly male, but 'in transition' with more females migrating both through family reunion and as independent migrants) and Gambians (mostly males).[10]

Changes in the labour force

An important facet of the dynamics involved in access to the labour market through international migration is the pre-emigration experience of internal migration in the sending country. In Morocco, the rural exodus was not a product of the attraction of industrial employment (as happened with past European rural–urban migration) but the result of the rejection of rural poverty. Such new urban-directed migration flows may act as a stepping-stone for Moroccan labour migrants to go abroad, perhaps trading on the experience they have accumulated during their time of living in the city –

some educational training or the acquisition of a particular labouring or trading skill. On the other hand, the eventual move abroad may be triggered by an experience of exclusion in the Moroccan urban milieu, bearing in mind the sharp differences in Moroccan urban populations as regards their rural or urban origin, Arab versus Berber ethnicity, educated and non-educated status etc. All these variables will play a considerable role when studying the differentiation patterns among the labour force in the context of international migration.

A second important dimension of change is played out through family strategies, often marking a sexual division of labour inside the family structure. In rural areas of the Philippines, the male labour force makes a living from work in agriculture and fishing, whilst female workers process and market the produce obtained. In sub-Saharan Africa, statistics show that women exhibit the highest activity rates as well as the highest fertility and mortality rates in the world (Adepoju and Oppong 1994). Gambian women possess relative financial autonomy, which is often abandoned when migrating to Spain. In this West African country, tradition marks out very established patterns in the organisation of female labour: older women look after the children while younger women work in the fields, where they suffer many disadvantages compared to their male partners (less access to credit, fewer tools and pack animals, longer distances travelled between the compound and the fields etc.). In the Gambian case, the economic role of migrant women in the destination country often becomes modified – from the position of responsibility in the peasant society to the adopted role of housewife in Catalan society.

Another important aspect, related to the sexual division of the migrant labour force, is the social dynamics of gender at various stages of the migration process. Two migratory patterns are commonly recognised: 'dependent migration', which applies to formal or informal family reunions, usually with the woman joining the man (though the reverse can happen, especially with Filipino migration); and the case of female 'autonomous migration', when women initiate an independent migratory project detached from any relationship they may have with a partner. In reality, both these pathways may not be sufficiently clear-cut to be identified in this way. Although in Spain official statistics usually divide those women who arrived through their husbands' regularisation process from those who did not, individual cases blur the distinction between dependent and independent decision-making. Nevertheless, there is plenty of evidence to support the trend towards a greater quantity of independent female migration towards southern Europe since the 1980s (Campani 1989; Solé 1994; and see also Zontini's contribution to the present volume). But it is also interesting to observe that the counterpoint of those women who migrate by themselves are those who remain in the country of origin by themselves after their male partners have emigrated. This double-edged effect of migration has been observed in the long-established male emigration from the Moroccan Rif to northern Europe (see, for instance, De Mas 1978; Hamdouch *et al.* 1979; Heinemeijer *et al.* 1977). Here, the axiom that the woman stays at home (in the Rif) and the man leaves for Europe (which connotes also the public sphere, the market) is an apt metaphor of the sexual division of space which may, if anything, be reinforced by gendered migrations. Finally, it is worth noting that the emancipatory changes achieved by migrant women are generally examined through the perspective of economic emancipation in the receiving countries (Ramírez 1998). Quite apart from the issue of evaluating true emancipation under the multiple burdens often borne by women who work in the destination setting, there is the diversity of situations deriving from different cultural perceptions relating to paid work for different groups of women.

Reconstructing social organisation

One of the forms of this type of reproduction are ethnically-based organisations, which are numerous in Catalonia given the diversity of ethnic groups and languages in the three countries of origin. In the Philippines, despite the great variety of languages, Tagalog and English appear to be the most dominant. Tagalos seem to enjoy a higher status in the country of origin, and this is reflected in their prominent role in Filipino associationism in Catalonia. In the Gambia, the whole ethnic representation (dominantly Mandinka, followed by Fula, Wollof, Jola, Serahule and Serer) has been reproduced by their geographical concentration in Catalonia. Curiously, for both the Gambia and Morocco, the two groups which are generally considered to be the most traditional by the rest of the sending country's society (the Serahule in the Gambia and the Rifians in Morocco) are also the most numerous amongst Gambian and Moroccan migrants in Catalonia. Both groups are characterised by higher fertility rates, a higher index of polygamous marriage and a stronger adherence to the Muslim religion compared to the norm for migrants from their respective countries.

Another form of social organisation which I observed was the reproduction of family structures, evident in all three national communities studied. In the Gambia the family unit expresses the microcosm of hierarchical social organisation on the criteria of age and gender. The Serahule extended family offers a whole network of economic relations between families which are very influential in creating the support base for any migratory project. However, once in Catalonia, this traditional family structure experiences a breakdown, with the loss of the elders' authority and, in particular, the dilution of the power of the older women.

The Moroccan family too is the core of social organisation; it is the family that feeds the reproduction of cultural and religious Islam. The patriarchal family, seen as the eternal base of Moroccan society, has undergone many changes along with urbanisation, modernisation, industrialisation, secularisation etc. In the so-called traditional society women were subordinated, but it was also the case that they had more guaranteed shelter in the event of divorce or widowhood; nowadays they cannot rely on these family resources in the same way as they did in the past. Nevertheless the family retains many affective connotations, making it still much more than a mere socio-economic unit. Above all it functions as the base for migration networks, connected both to socio-economic aspects (e.g. helping the recruitment of staff for an ethnic business) and with cultural ones, conserving values and a sense of identity. Furthermore, the family is frequently the locus of socio-economic crises which are then reflected in the dynamics of international migration – divorce, lone mothers and migration. Different types of family context in the reception country will open up different forms of integration. In this sense, two main structures can be identified: a changing form, whereby patriarchal influence is weakened because of the absence of the male component in immigrant households; and a 'preserving structure' whereby the solidarity networks of the extended family become migratory chains which act as a form of social control. The latter case thus exerts a dual function, offering protection in a new environment but restricting individuals' freedom.[11]

Examining the various forms of associationism reveals a noteworthy element of social reproduction in each of the three countries of migrant destination. The strong sense of interaction amongst the Filipino community in Barcelona draws on Filipino concepts of *pakikipagkapwa* (human concern and interaction) and *bayanihan* (a common campaign). In my interviews conducted in the Philippines I found the nature of associative life to be greatly affected by the activities of the *barangay* (the smallest Filipino political unit) and by the actions of the Catholic Church, though little through direct participation in political life. In the immigration country too the needs of the migrants are to some extent catered for by 'Catholic-charismatic' fellowship, which reinforces migrants' Catholic faith through their loyalty to *Iglesia ni Kristo*.

Reconstructing identity

Two main settings for cultural reproduction can be mentioned: the school and socio-linguistic divisions. Education and knowledge of certain languages confer advantage in the emigration process. In the Gambia an important division in the population exists between those who have not had access to schooling and those who have and, furthermore, who know the language of the former colonial power, which offers the possibility of upward mobility. On the other hand, literacy in the local language means a reduction in the hegemony of English. In the Upper River Division (the main place of origin of the Gambians in Catalonia), rivalry between languages undermines the whole basis of the education system, opening up the possibility of English-language schools being replaced by Arabic ones. Besides linguistic reproduction as a form of identity for Gambians, we should also add other elements of symbolic reproduction: the role of the Muslim community or *umma* as a community integrator, and the multi-layered identification bonds of the individual – first with the family, secondly with the village, and thirdly with the tribe.

As regards the Gambian population in Catalonia, one cannot understand what identity means for them without first analysing how modernisation has affected Gambian society back home. Like many other countries in West Africa, Gambia is commonly referred to as having undergone a process of Westernisation rather than true development. Gambian modernisation has consisted of a monetarisation of a predominantly rural society and a transition from traditional isolation to a kind of asymmetrical integration into the world economy. This modernisation process made the country almost totally dependent on the production of groundnuts, climatic variation (which impacts much more severely on a specialised export crop economy than it does on a polycultural peasant farming system), and changes in the international economy. Tourism represents another mode of the Gambia's incorporation into the world economy, although this is also achieved via an essentially dependent relationship. Emigration, too, is part of this wider modernisation process. Remittances from Gambians in Catalonia (and elsewhere) enable new residential compounds to be built, mainly in the Greater Banjul area, leading to a chaotic form of urbanisation. Emigration also leads to a growing number of poor, female-headed households, an over-dependence on imported goods and an adoption of supposedly modern lifestyles. If one had to consider how the constantly ambiguous process of modernisation has affected the values of a population like the Gambian one, I would sum it up in the following way: modernisation implies treading a delicate line between what is collective and communal, and what is private and individual. Migration only serves to sharpen these classical opposites. Hence when Gambians try to come to terms with their evolving cultural identity in the countries of destination, this question can only be resolved, if at all, in the ensuing struggle between what is Western and what is the traditional cultural heritage.

The idea of looking for a Moroccan identity amongst the immigrants living in Catalonia is equally intricate. If we bear in mind some of the dimensions of complexity in the society of origin, the basic question about migrant identity shapes further questions: what does it mean to have a Muslim identity? what is an Arab identity? or a Berber one? or indeed a Moroccan identity? These questions are without doubt at the core of many studies carried out not only in Morocco but also in other North African societies. Islam is simultaneously faith (*aquida*), law (*sharia*) and religion (*din*). The *umma* – protected by patrilineal affiliation – gathers under one metaphorical roof all Muslims of the world; it becomes a concept which enables a sense of unity and homogeneity (religious, ethnic, cultural, linguistic) by which the populations of the Maghreb can define themselves in opposition to others – those considered to be *nsara* (Nazarenes, a vaguely derogatory connotation of Christians used extensively for all non-Muslim foreigners) or people who are not from 'The Book'. The parallelism of Islamic culture and religion is a typical feature of Muslim societies but 'cultural Islam' is not always completely opposed to societies which think of themselves as more secular. Further parallels exist when the comparison is extended to Spain and Catalonia. The Catholic Church still plays an influential role in social ideology and everyday life. Within Catalonia there is an insistent Catalanisation process driven by the desire to reinforce the Catalan language and the knowledge of Catalan culture amongst all people living in the region – an aspiration which has frequently been compared to the fight to maintain the Berber cause in the Maghreb. Meanwhile, on the southern shore of the Mediterranean, other types of linguistic instrumentalisation are taking place. Furthermore, like many of its neighbours, Morocco has experienced an arabicisation process which recovers a heritage partially lost under colonialism.

Compared to the other two groups, Filipinos have a more global migratory experience and hence, perhaps, a more readily transplanted identity. In interviews it was stressed that Filipinos easily adapt to other cultures, although it was also emphasised that they managed to hold on to their own customs, religion and national identity. Filipino migrants to Spain are careful savers and tend to assume broadly *nouveau riche* attitudes, especially when they return home. On the whole, migrants consider the Filipino mentality as conservative, built up through a rigid moral system based on traditional Catholic values and a strict sense of discipline. By contrast, foreign countries are perceived as too liberal: migrants can make an accommodation to this freer atmosphere and exploit its potential for accessing greater wealth, but they worry over threats of drugs and moral degradation. In general the Filipino interviewees defended the notion of equal education for girls and boys, but at the same time held a high regard for discipline and traditional values.

Conclusion

The Mediterranean migratory space seems to be the new caravanserai, where the southern European countries represent the spacious court in the middle. Southern Europe collects, holds and then redistributes migrants originating from the other side of the Mediterranean (for example Morocco) and from further afield, both in Africa (for instance, the Gambia) and Asia (e.g. the Philippines). For some of these migrants, southern Europe still represents the traditional role of being a transit route to northern European destinations; for others it is a 'new home', leading to the establishment of more-or-less settled communities; for yet others it functions as one end of a transnational livelihood which sees the migrant shuttle back and forth between southern Europe and the home country. Thus in this chapter I have tried to avoid the simple linear conceptualisation of international migration based on a one-way transfer of location from sending to receiving country; instead I have attempted to depict a more overarching Mediterranean migration system which is, nevertheless, built around the Basin as Europe's 'Río Grande' – a North/South frontier that is the product of particular historical patterns of development and colonialism.

In fact, the Mediterranean is seen here as a paradigmatic instance of North–South imbalances in a globalised world. On the one side, southern Europe represents a new and interesting migratory context when compared to the 'old' immigration countries of north-central Europe. Migration thus acts as a rather sensitive barometer of the various changes that countries in different parts of Europe are going through. On the other hand, the countries on the southern side of the Mediterranean are also changing, and this can be seen in the dynamics of Moroccan emigration flows to Italy and Spain. Overall, I have attempted to demonstrate the complexity in the number and diversity of factors which have to be taken into account when explaining incorporation strategies for trans-Mediterranean migrants, both at an institutional, policy level and in the case of individuals and households.

The organisation of this chapter has been structured around the three factors which interact in the 'contexts of reception' posited by Portes and Rumbaut (1990): the policies of the receiving country, the conditions of the host labour market, and the characteristics of the migrant ethnic communities. I have elaborated on this typology by considering both the receiving and the sending countries, with special reference to Spain (Catalonia) and to Morocco, the Gambia and the Philippines. Regarding the receiving countries, I have underlined the deregulation of policies and the key role of the highly informalised economy; whereas for the sending countries I emphasised the heterogeneity of migrant groups with regard to nationality, sexual division of labour and family strategies of migration. Generally the family – which as a result of migration may be a transnational unit – is seen as the basic socio-economic container wherein changes occur and are to be studied. Therefore, the third factor in the Portes and Rumbaut schema – the ethnic community as the base for the expression of cultural identity and the mediator of different aspects of incorporation into the host society – has been explored through three types of social reproduction studied at the family scale. Given the growing hostility with which migrants are faced in southern Europe in recent years, these family and ethnic group contexts will gain in importance in defending the interests of the 'new immigrants'.

Notes

1   Turkey, of course, is less unequivocally European, a fact borne out by the UNDP data. For a recent exploration of national development indicators for all countries of the Mediterranean Basin see Dunford and King (2001).

2   Buñuel's *Las Hurdes* was censored by the Franco regime which claimed that it projected too starkly an image of a backward Spain – what was called 'La España negra'.

3   J. Goytisolo, ¡ Quién te ha visto y quién te ve ! *El País*, 19 February 1998.

4   The most recent episode occurred in the agricultural town of El Ejido in February 2000 following the murder of a local woman by a mentally unstable migrant worker. Several days of anti-immigrant (more precisely, anti-Maghrebi) violence followed.

5   This last point is clearly evidenced by the chronology of regularisations in each of the southern European countries: Italy (1986, 1990, 1995, 1998, 1999), Spain (1986, 1991, 1996, 2000), Portugal (1992, 1996, 1997), Greece (1998). In addition, Spain has operated small-scale regularisations through the annual quota system since 1993.

6   *Laissez-faire* is perhaps not the most accurate description of Greece's stance on immigration. True, immigrants have been allowed to enter the country in large numbers, but this permissive entry is related partly to an inability to stop the influxes, and there have been periodic episodes of mass deportation, especially of Albanians, as well as recent moves toward regularisation. See Baldwin-Edwards and Fakiolas (1999).

7   According to Portes (1995) the informal economy is defined as 'the sum of all the income-earning activities that are unregulated by legal codes in an environment where similar activities are regulated'. Informal activities are distinguished from criminal ones in that they encompass goods and services that are legal, but whose production and marketing are unregulated. Thus drugs and prostitution are criminal in the United States, while the production of garments in clandestine sweatshops and unlicensed street vending are informal. 'The sociology of immigration has noted a close connection between its subject and the informal economy in the sense that immigrants are overrepresented in those unregulated activities (...). Immigrant overrepresentation in informal activities is closely related to their overrepresentation in small entrepreneurship' (Portes 1995, pp. 29–30).

8   In southern Europe, the rejection of these jobs by young people is heavily related to the increasing number of university degrees, which has formed a new generation that aspires to attain at least middle-class jobs.

9   Global cities are strategic cities in the global economy because of their concentration of command functions and of high-level producer–service firms oriented to world markets; more generally they are cities with high levels of internationalisation in their economies and in their broader social structures. In cities like New York – but also in Madrid, Rome,

Athens etc. – the burgeoning personal service sector plays an important role of demand attraction for migrant women.

10 Interviews were carried out in the Philippines in 1992 (32 interviews, mainly in the island of Luzon), in Morocco in 1993 (22 interviews, mainly in the north, corresponding to the former Spanish protectorate), and in the Gambia in 1994 (participant observation, mainly in the Upper River Division). See Ribas-Mateos (1999a) for a full account of this research. In the present contribution I place more emphasis on the Moroccan case for two simple reasons: Moroccans are the most numerous migrant group in Catalonia, and Catalonia is the main destination for Moroccan migrants in Spain.

11 As an aside, the study of women's associationism in Morocco is interesting because it represents a tool for strengthening democracy (however, Islamists use it as an objective to campaign against). As in other Arab societies, feminist associations have only developed with great difficulty in Morocco and are regularly opposed to the Islamists in the political arena (Mernissi 1991). Hence the feminist movement expresses not just a campaign for greater female participation in civil society but also the core of the political campaign to change the nature of the country (Daoud 1993). As the United Nations Development Programme has stressed in many of its recent Human Development Reports, the study of gender is a good barometer to be used when reading off fundamental social change in a country (for the latest results see UNDP 1999). In Morocco three main strategies of women's mobilisation exist – culturalist, reformist and radical. Interestingly, they find similar parallels and problems in Catalonia where Moroccan women face a multiplicity of cultural references and a problematic gender gap affecting migrant women from different socio-economic positions.

References

Adepoju, A. and Oppong, C. (1994) *Gender, Work and Population in Sub-Saharan Africa.* Geneva: International Labour Office.

Baganha, M. I. (1998) Immigrant involvement in the informal economy: the Portuguese case, *Journal of Ethnic and Migration Studies*, 24(2), pp. 367–85.

Baganha, M. I. (2000) Labour market and immigration: economic opportunities for immigrants in Portugal, in King, R., Lazaridis, G. and Tsardanidis, C. (eds) *Eldorado or Fortress? Migration in Southern Europe.* London: Macmillan, pp. 79–103.

Baldwin-Edwards, M. and Arango, J., eds (1999) *Migrants and the Informal Economy in Southern Europe.* London: Frank Cass.

Baldwin-Edwards, M. and Fakiolas, R. (1999) Greece: the contours of a fragmented policy response, in Baldwin-Edwards, M. and Arango, J. (eds) *Migrants and the Informal Economy in Southern Europe.* London: Frank Cass, pp. 186–204.

Braudel, F. (1972, 1973) *The Mediterranean and the Mediterranean World in the Age of Philip II.* London: Collins, 2 vols.

Campani, G. (1989) Du Tiers-Monde à l'Italie: une nouvelle immigration féminine, *Revue Européenne des Migrations Internationales*, 5(2), pp. 29–41.

Castles, S. and Miller, M. J. (1998) *The Age of Migration.* London: Macmillan.

Daoud, Z. (1993) *Féminisme et Politique au Maghreb, 1930–1992.* Casablanca: EDDIF.

De Mas, P. (1978) *Marges Marocaines.* The Hague: NUFFIC/IMWOO/REMPLOD.

Droukas, E. (1998) Albanians in the Greek informal economy, *Journal of Ethnic and Migration Studies*, 24(2), pp. 347–65.

Dunford, M. and King, R. (2001) Mediterranean economic geography, in King, R., De Mas, P. and Mansvelt Beck, J. (eds) *Geography, Environment and Development in the Mediterranean.* Brighton: Sussex Academic Press, pp. 28–60.

Esping-Anderson, G. (1990) *The Three Worlds of Welfare Capitalism.* Cambridge: Polity.

Ferrera, M. (1995) Los estados del bienestar del sur en la Europa social, in Sarasa, S. and Moreno, L. (eds) *El Estado de Bienestar en la Europa del Sur*. Madrid: Consejo Superior de Investigaciones Científicas, pp. 85–111.

Giner, S. (1995) La modernización de la Europa meridional: una interpretación sociológica, in Sarasa, S. and Moreno, L. (eds) *El Estado de Bienestar en la Europa del Sur*. Madrid: Consejo Superior de Investigaciones Científicas, pp. 9–59.

Hamdouch, B., Berrada, A., Heinemeyer, W. F., De Mas, P. and van der Wusten, H. (1979) *Migration de Développement, Migration de Sous-Développement? Une étude sur l'impact de la migration internationale dans le milieu rural du Maroc*. Rabat: Institut National de Statistique et d'Economie Appliquée.

Heinemeijer, W. F., van Amersfoort, J. M. M., Ettema, W., De Mas, P. and van der Wusten, H. H. (1977) *Partir pour Rester. Incidences de l'émigration ouvrière à la campagne marocaine*. Amsterdam: Université d'Amsterdam, Institut Socio-Géographique, Publication 2.

Horden, P. and Purcell, N. (2000) *The Corrupting Sea. A Study of Mediterranean History*. Oxford: Blackwell.

King, R. (1998) The Mediterranean – Europe's Río Grande, in Anderson, M. and Bort, E. (eds) *The Frontiers of Europe*. London: Pinter, pp. 109–34.

King, R. (2000) Southern Europe in the changing global map of migration, in King, R., Lazaridis, G. and Tsardanidis, C. (eds) *Eldorado or Fortress? Migration in Southern Europe*. London: Macmillan, pp. 1–26.

King, R., Fielding, A. J. and Black, R. (1997) The international migration turnaround in southern Europe, in King, R. and Black, R. (eds) *Southern Europe and the New Immigrations*. Brighton: Sussex Academic Press, pp. 1–25.

Mernissi, F. (1991) *Women and Islam: A Historical and a Theological Enquiry*. Oxford: Blackwell.

Mingione, E. (1995) Labour market segmentation and informal work in Southern Europe, *European Urban and Regional Studies*, 2(2), pp. 121–43.

Mingione, E. and Quassoli, F. (2000) The participation of immigrants in the underground economy in Italy, in King, R., Lazaridis, G. and Tsardanidis, C. (eds) *Eldorado or Fortress? Migration in Southern Europe*. London: Macmillan, pp. 29–56.

Mingione, E., Miguélez, F. and Wening, A. (1990) *Underground Economy and Irregular Forms of Employment (Travail au Noir)*. Luxembourg: Commission of the European Communities.

Pascual de Sans, A., Cardelús, J. and Solana Solana, M. (2000) Recent immigration to Catalonia: economic character and responses, in King, R., Lazaridis, G. and Tsardanidis, C. (eds) *Eldorado or Fortress? Migration in Southern Europe*. London: Macmillan, pp. 104–23.

Piore, M. J. (1979) *Birds of Passage: Migrant Labor and Industrial Societies*. Cambridge: Cambridge University Press.

Portes, A. (1995) Economic sociology and the sociology of immigration: a conceptual overview, in Portes, A. (ed.) *The Economic Sociology of Immigration*. New York: Russell Sage Foundation, pp. 1–41.

Portes, A. and Rumbaut, R. G. (1990) *Immigrant America: A Portrait*. Berkeley and Los Angeles: University of California Press.

Pugliese, E. (1993) Restructuring of the labour market and the role of Third World migrations in Europe, *Society and Space*, 11(4), pp. 513–22.

Pugliese, E. (1995) New international migrations and the 'European Fortress', in Hadjimichalis, C. and Sadler, D. (eds) *Europe at the Margins: New Mosaics of Inequality*. Chichester: Wiley, pp. 51–68.

Ramírez, A. (1998) *Migraciones, Género e Islam*. Madrid: Agencia Española de Cooperación Internacional.

Reyneri, E. (1998) The role of the underground economy in irregular migration to Italy: cause or effect? *Journal of Ethnic and Migration Studies*, 24(2), pp. 313–31.

Ribas-Mateos, N. (1999a) *Las presencias de la inmigración fememina. Un recorrido por Filipinas, Gambia y Marruecos en Cataluña.* Barcelona: Editorial Icaria.

Ribas-Mateos, N. (1999b) Notes on the Southern European model: immigration, family and the welfare state, in Agozino, B. (ed.) *Theoretical and Methodological Issues in Migration Research.* Aldershot: Ashgate Publishers, pp. 107–42.

Ribas-Mateos, N. (2000) Female birds of passage: leaving and settling in Spain, in Anthias, F. and Lazaridis, G. (eds) *Gender and Migration in Southern Europe.* Oxford: Berg, pp. 173–97.

Sainsbury, D., ed. (1994) *Gendering Welfare States.* London: Sage.

Sassen, S. (1995) Immigration and local labour markets, in Portes, A. (ed.) *The Economic Sociology of Immigration.* New York: Russell Sage Foundation, pp. 87–127.

Solé, C. (1994) *La Mujer Inmigrante.* Madrid: Ministerio de Asuntos Sociales, Instituto de la Mujer.

Solé, C., Ribas, N., Bergalli, V. and Parella, N. (1998) Irregular employment amongst migrants in Spanish cities, *Journal of Ethnic and Migration Studies*, 24(2), pp. 333–46.

UNDP (1999) *Human Development Report 1999.* New York: Oxford University Press.

3

Cultural dimensions of African immigrants in Iberian labour markets: a comparative approach

Cristóbal Mendoza

Introduction

With the exception of the social network literature, research on the incorporation of immigrants in labour markets has rarely considered the relevance of cultural factors in explaining immigrant labour outcomes. In fact, cultural factors have been systematically ignored by the two main schools of labour economics. For neo-classical approaches, well-tested in the United States, the performance of immigrants in labour markets improves (in terms of wages) as they 'adapt' to a new country (Chiswick 1978; Long 1980); adaptation is generally measured in terms of investment in human capital after emigration. For segmentation and dual labour market theorists, immigrants are mainly directed into secondary labour markets. Foreign-born workers are consequently seen consistently to fill the most undesirable jobs in destination countries (Piore 1979). Yet, even if incorporation into secondary labour markets is the main labour outcome for immigrants from developing countries in southern Europe (King and Konjhodzic 1995), non-immigrant populations operate there as well (Pugliese 1993). Moreover, segmentation theorists do not explain why immigrants are concentrated in certain 'undesirable' jobs, but not others.

Yet, rather than pure labour market mechanisms arising from supply–demand imbalance, the 'need' for immigrants in Iberia (and southern Europe) must also be related to social considerations. Employment situations have to be seen as socially regulated rather than as simply a market relationship (Granovetter 1985; Portes and Sensenbrenner 1993). Amongst these social considerations that stimulate immigration, existing literature has foregrounded the prominence of 'undesirable' work environments that derive from the dynamism of informal economic activities and small-scale enterprises, and the higher educational levels attained by local young people, which leads to a rejection of socially 'unacceptable' types of work on the part of 'native' workers (Huntoon 1998; King *et al.* 1997).

The aim of this chapter is to explore some social, cultural and policy dimensions of trans-Mediterranean labour migration from Africa to Iberia. Specifically, I examine five non-labour dimensions that have a direct influence on African labour outcomes in Iberia, bearing in mind the likelihood that differences in the character of inflows of African-born workers in Portugal and Spain may provide the comparison on cultural aspects of the incorporation of immigrants into labour markets with contrasting evidence. The first dimension revolves around the role of the state. Here it is argued that both Portuguese and Spanish immigration and naturalisation policies respond to historical and cultural bonds with sending countries, alongside economic considerations. The second dimension concerns employers' attitudes toward immigrant employment. Rejection or acceptance of immigrants for certain jobs are observed through employers' beliefs and perceptions, many of which are based on stereotypes or clichés about immigrants and their work performance, rather than on real knowledge or experience of immigrant workers. Thirdly, the chapter examines female immigrant workers. Contrasting female employment outcomes in the two countries are shown to result partly from different views on paid employment amongst African nationals in Spain and immigrants from the former Portuguese colonies. The fourth dimension focuses on the use of social networks for finding employment. Africans in Portugal are found to rely on conventional channels when searching for work (e.g. newspapers or adverts). Cultural and language affinity, and recent colonial links, are decisive in this strategy, as the contrast with Spain's more culturally distant immigrants shows. Finally, the chapter takes a step further in the analysis of social networks. Through the analysis of two specific groups, immigrant construction workers in Portugal and immigrant farm workers in Spain, the role of social networks and family patterns in shaping internal population mobility is uncovered.

The empirical research on which my analysis in this chapter is based comes from my doctoral fieldwork carried out in Spain and Portugal during 1995–7 (Mendoza 1998).[1] Basing my field research in the province of Girona (Catalonia, Spain) and in the Algarve (southern Portugal) and Setúbal (outskirts of Lisbon), I undertook two interview surveys – of African-born immigrant workers, and of local employers who hired immigrants. In Spain I interviewed 151 immigrants from Morocco, Senegal and the Gambia; in Portugal 69 African immigrants, mainly from Cape Verde and Angola, were interviewed. For the employer survey I interviewed 32 employers in the agriculture, tourism and construction sectors in Girona, and 20 construction and tourism employers in Portugal.[2] Although the main focus of my research was labour market issues, the open-ended nature of the interview schedule allowed interviewees to enlarge on socio-cultural issues, beliefs and perceptions. It is the purpose of the present chapter to focus on these latter issues, various aspects of the labour market analysis having been published elsewhere (Hoggart and Mendoza 1999; Mendoza 1997, 1999a, 1999b, 2001).

Before moving to an examination of the five themes which form the basis of this chapter, it is important to set out a few key points about the nature of immigration in Spain and Portugal which condition the extent to which valid comparisons can be made.

Difficulties of comparing immigration in Portugal and Spain

There is a common recognition that there is a more 'open' attitude toward labour immigration under Portuguese law than is found in most EU countries and that this creates a less hostile labour market for immigrant employment (Marie 1995). Whereas the Portuguese legislative framework puts constraints on entry to new residents (through visa requirements), Spanish immigration laws put constraints on both entry and stay of immigrants. Once visa procedures are overcome, immigrants can move freely in Portuguese labour markets in terms of geographical and occupational mobility. This does not apply for Spain (Mendoza 2001). Moreover, expulsion for unlawful stay in Portugal has been numerically insignificant, despite the growing numbers of illegally-resident immigrants in the country from the 1980s onwards, whereas in Spain expulsion has been systematically enforced since the 1985 Foreigners' Act.

This more 'relaxed' attitude of Portuguese immigration laws may be related to the fact that the bulk of non-EU immigrants came (and still comes) from the ex-Portuguese African colonies. In effect labour immigration from African colonies into Portugal started in the late 1960s. Yet inflows from Portuguese-speaking African countries (PALOP) were at their peak during the refugee crisis which occurred in the aftermath of the independence of the colonies in the period 1974–81 (Esteves 1991; Saint Maurice and Pires 1989). Illustrating the relevance of inflows from Africa during and after the decolonisation process, census data show that more than half a million residents in Portugal in 1981 lived in one of the African ex-colonies in 1973. This constituted 5.1 per cent of the total Portuguese population in 1981. As 60 per cent of these half million people had been born in Portugal, it is reasonable to argue that the bulk of these *retornados* never lost their Portuguese nationality. However, alongside this population of Portuguese origin, substantial (yet less numerous) inflows of Africans with no previous family link with Portugal came into the country (Dubois 1994). This last group, as well as African-born immigrants with no Portuguese ancestry who were already resident in Portugal in 1974, was not automatically granted nationality. In this way, the 1975 Nationality Act created, with retroactive effect, the largest immigrant community in Portugal (Esteves 1991). From the 1980s, with the abandonment of any reference to the *jus soli* principle in the new 1981 Nationality Act, immigration from PALOP countries into Portugal recovered its original labour flavour of the late 1960s and early 1970s (Baganha and Góis 1999; Saint-Maurice and Pires 1989).

These three clearly distinctive periods in Portuguese immigration (before 1974, 1974–81 and after 1981) make it difficult to classify all African-born people in a loose category of immigrants. Certainly African-born whites of Portuguese ancestry would rarely recognise themselves as 'immigrants' in Portugal. Thus, defining 'immigrants' and 'ethnic minorities' becomes unusually problematic in the Portuguese context (Machado 1994). For the purposes of my interview survey of African-born immigrants in Portugal I made no distinction between black Portuguese-Africans (with Portuguese nationality) and PALOP immigrants, since a pilot survey I had carried out in Setúbal showed that all groups of ethnic black Africans shared similar disadvantages with respect to housing and work regardless of year of arrival, nationality or legal/illegal status. And for the survey as a whole, differences in incorporation of African-born workers in the Portuguese labour market were much more sensitively related to levels of education than to years of residence in Portugal or legal status.

By contrast, the history and categorisation of labour migration into Spain are more straightforward. Moroccan immigration into Spain remained low in numbers until the mid–1980s, with inflows in the 1960s being dominated by Jewish migration (Colectivo IOÉ 1994). More than a final destination, Spain was generally considered a transit country to other European nations until the mid–1980s (Colectivo IOÉ 1987; Izquierdo 1992). In this way it is understandable that official statistics only recorded 4,067 legally-resident Moroccans for the whole of Spain in 1980. Nowadays Moroccans are the main immigrant group, numbering 77,189 legal residents in 1996. Unlike Portugal, Spain attracts labour migrants from a wide range of countries, some of them – for instance Senegal, the Gambia, India – with no previous colonial links with the country (King *et al.* 1997). In the case of Morocco, it is relevant to notice previous colonial links with the northern part of the country (Rif) which was under Spanish control until Moroccan independence in 1956. Yet the low scale of

Moroccan immigration in Spain until the mid–1980s (plus the fact that current streams are diversified in their origin and not restricted to the old Spanish protectorate) points to a limited influence of old colonial links on patterns of Moroccan immigration into Spain. In this context, generally speaking, the term 'immigrant' fits for all Moroccans (as well as for other African nationalities) working in Spain.

Cultural aspects of immigration policies

Around the world, immigration and naturalisation laws make different allowances for immigrants, depending on immigrant characteristics – nationality, level of education, skills etc. In the European Union, a clear example of these allowances is the 'privileged' treatment received by EU nationals residing in another EU country. For non-EU nationals, all EU countries nowadays have similarly restrictive immigration laws, with southern European nations being the last to introduce such measures (for instance, the 1985 Spanish Foreigners' Act, the 1986 Italian Law 943 and the 1990 Martelli Law, and the 1993 Portuguese Decree-Law 59). These developments have led some commentators to argue that there are different categories of citizens in the EU, with legally-resident third-country nationals having restricted citizenship rights (Hammar 1990). Despite this general philosophy, efforts toward harmonising immigration regulations for third-country nationals within the EU have so far been limited (Marie 1996). Conditions for working legally, political rights, social security benefits, and access to public housing, public health systems and state education, may apply differently to home nationals, other EU residents, non-EU legal residents and (non-EU) illegal residents. Immigrant rights, either as residents or as workers, tend to vary with the host country's 'sensibility' towards their non-EU population.

In the case of the Iberian countries, Spanish and Portuguese immigration laws adopt a dissimilar approach. As a clear example of this, the names of the bodies these countries have created at the top of the state organisational hierarchy to deal with immigration reveal contrasting philosophies. Thus, whereas the Spanish agency is called the Foreigners' Inter-Ministerial Commission (Comisión Interministerial de Extranjería) and is under the Ministry of Interior, the Portuguese High Commission for Immigration and Ethnic Minorities (Alto Comissionado para a Imigração e as Minorias Étnicas) is attached to the Presidency of the Government (Guibentif 1996). The creation of the Portuguese High Commission was a demand of immigrant associations in return for supporting the Socialist Party, and such organisations are actively involved in Portuguese politics (Machado 1992). For example, before the 1991 Portuguese elections, immigrant associations signed an agreement with the Socialist Party which led to the Party agreeing to change several public policies toward immigrants – these included the legalisation of illegal residents, the right to vote in local elections for legal immigrants, measures to fight poor school performance amongst ethnic minorities, and the rights to job opportunities and public housing for everybody, regardless of their nationality or origin. The position of immigrant groups in Spain is quite different. Here immigrant associations present a more scattered, less organised picture. This is despite the fact that they have introduced many local initiatives and are active in day-to-day dealings with legal problems and other immigration matters. At the state level, probably the most powerful Spanish organisation in terms of political bargaining power on immigrants' rights is the Catholic Caritas. This organisation published the pioneer research of Colectivo IOÉ (1987) on the living and working conditions of immigrants from developing countries in Spain. Indeed, the proposals of Caritas on a new work permit system are almost identical to the rules approved by the Spanish Government in 1996.

All this is to say that immigration policies are not created in a political vacuum. The common political background for both Portugal and Spain is the same overarching EU legislation, with a shared national policy trend toward more restrictive policies. Both countries have certainly implemented progressively more restrictive practices – for instance, Portuguese naturalisation laws have completely abandoned the *jus soli* principle, with children of non-Portuguese nationals born in Portugal being considered foreigners since 1981. However, the two countries have somewhat different political backgrounds, which are reflected in their different approaches to citizens of third nations. The most obvious difference lies in the recent links of Portugal and its ex-colonies (PALOP). As we saw above, it was only in the mid–1970s that the PALOP countries obtained their independence from Portugal. The chaotic process of decolonisation brought half a million new residents to Portugal. Alongside people of Portuguese origin came a substantial inflow of black Africans. That not all these immigrants entered Portugal legally is clear from the 1992–93 legalisation process; one of the two requisites for legalised residence, which applied only to PALOP nationals, was entry into Portugal before 1 June 1986. In this way, the Portuguese government recognised an irregular situation that had been caused partly by decolonisation.

Previous colonial links are also reflected in the numerous economic and commercial interests between Portugal and the PALOP nations (Ferreira 1994). Portuguese collaboration with these African countries is deeply imbued with cultural considerations, notably the common Portuguese language. In fact, the acronym PALOP refers to Portuguese as the official language in these nations. In this regard, it is remarkable to notice that Sampaio, in his first official visit to Cape Verde in 1996 as the new appointed President of Portugal, made it clear that the inclusion of the islands in the group of *lusofonia* (the Association of Portuguese-speaking countries) was beyond question.[3] In this context, an ad-hoc board for accepting diplomas issued by the Portuguese administration in Africa (Quadro Geral de Adidos) was created after the independence of the ex-colonies (Dubois 1994; Pires *et al*. 1987). This eased the 'transference' of qualifications from Africa to Portugal until the mid–1980s, when the Quadro disappeared. Following previous collaboration, university exchanges between PALOP nations and Portugal were in good shape into the 1990s. Through 'co-operation' programmes, Africans can study, and later work, in Portugal. In fact, as the President of the Guinea Bissau Association remarked in an interview, 'the bulk of the Black Africans you see in universities are not second-generation, but students from PALOP countries. Education is a serious problem for second generations.' Either for study or work, countries which have Portuguese as an official language provide the bulk of current legal (and probably illegal) immigration inflows in the country.

By contrast with Portugal, the prime sending country for Spain is Morocco. Despite Spanish colonial links with northern Morocco (plus the Spanish North African enclaves of Ceuta and Melilla), Moroccans have more restrictions on staying in Spain either as residents or as workers than nationals of coutries that are felt to be 'closer' to Spanish culture. For example, less time is required for Latin Americans to obtain nationality or permanent residence (although restrictions on entry still apply). The point to stress here is that the same principle holds for Portugal and Spain, for immigration and naturalisation laws reflect the fact that PALOP Africans and Latin Americans share the same language and supposedly many cultural codes with Portugal and Spain respectively. Spain is often referred to in Latin American countries as *la madre patria*, the motherland. Following this line of analysis, historically-based cultural 'closeness' seems the reason for the more 'relaxed' philosophy underlying Portuguese immigration laws, compared at least with Spanish laws.

Three main differences between Spanish and Portuguese immigration laws can be outlined when comparing their rules (Marie 1996). First, unlike Spain, there is no consideration of sectoral unemployment when deciding on acceptance of a new resident in Portugal (i.e. immigrants can obtain work in sectors of activity or occupations for which there are officially unemployed Portuguese nationals). Second, residence permits allow workers to move freely within Portuguese labour markets, both in geographical and occupational terms, once the first permit is obtained. This is not the case in Spain. Finally, again unlike Spain, there are no distinctions between permits for self-employed activities and for hired work in Portugal. These legal differences directly influence African labour outcomes in Portugal and Spain, with the former defining non-EU citizens as immigrants and the latter as (temporary) migrants who are directed toward unfilled niches in labour markets through a quota system. In fact, non-EU professionals find tight legal restrictions on their entry into Spanish labour markets. By contrast, whether through acceptance of African diplomas or through special programmes, there are openings for African immigrants in professional and clerical jobs in Portugal (Mendoza 2001).

This is not to say that Portuguese law does not discriminate amongst immigrants, as non-PALOP immigrants have more difficulties renewing their legal residence or naturalising than do PALOP nationals (Ministério da Administração Interna 1995). On the other side, the debate on Spanish immigration remains open. A new Foreigners' Law was approved by almost all parliamentary groups in December 1999 (the exception was the ruling Partido Popular, which comprised the minority government), and this Law has been in force since February 2000. The law establishes automatic legalisation for whose who can prove (illegal) residence in Spain for two years. Yet the Partido Popular announced that it would change the law if it were to win the necessary support in Parliament after the March 2000 election (at which this Party secured a working majority). The general point to highlight here is that immigration and naturalisation laws in both Portugal and Spain are imbued with historical and cultural considerations, with the result that measures enacted distinguish between different non-EU immigrants by their countries of origin. Whether these considerations are substituted in the future, perhaps as a consequence of more positive economic circumstances, remains an open question.

Employers' perceptions of immigrant labour

Current Spanish immigration laws link legal residence with hired work (Cornelius 1994; Huntoon 1998). According to segmentation theorists, a primary advantage of immigrants to employers is their vulnerability, deriving from their weak legal position. In this regard, the Comisiones Obreras trade union has estimated that half of those who legalised their status in the Spanish 1991-92 legalisation campaign had not renewed their permit by 1995 (Pérez Oliva 1995). This means that slippage into illegality is a possibility for legal non-EU workers in Spain, if they cannot obtain or renew a work contract. Immigrant vulnerability was clearly perceived by Girona employers whom I interviewed.[4] One said: 'This is not France. Here immigrants are not permanent residents. If they are not good workers, out, out, out [*fora, fora, fora*].'

When selecting employees, employer decisions are influenced by considerations other than an immigrant's legal status. In this regard, opinions amongst Spanish employers from all economic sectors agreed that Africans were 'hard' workers. Capturing a prevailing opinion, a Girona farmer said: 'Africans are good workers, and are used to the hard working conditions of farming. Africans have a good physical endurance, so they put up with hard agricultural tasks.' Yet a large percentage of those engaged in agricultural work learned the appropriate skills (e.g. driving a tractor) whilst in Spain (Hoggart and Mendoza 1999). Furthermore, around one third of the Moroccan farm workers I interviewed had urban backgrounds, the economic crisis in the late 1980s and 1990s having pushed many middle-class members of Moroccan society, especially young students from urban backgrounds, toward emigration (Colectivo IOÉ 1994).

The 'positive' characterisation of Africans as hard workers contrasts with employer images that Andalusians are 'weak' farm workers (Andalusia was the traditional source of the temporary workers needed for Girona harvests). The prevailing opinion amongst farmers was that Andalusians now only want to work long enough to qualify for unemployment payments (on this see García-Ramon and Cruz 1996). Effectively, since 1985, agricultural employees from Andalusia and Extremadura have had the right to claim unemployment benefits after they have worked for 60 days. The tendency amongst Andalusians to seek employment only up to the critical number of days was at first found by employer-farmers to be surprising, as temporary absences from home for work are a long-established income strategy in southern Spain (Mansvelt Beck 1988). Probably other reasons affect the reduction of northward temporary migration from Andalusia, a key factor being the considerable decrease in differences in living standards across Spain (Villaverde Castro 1996). Not only farmers, but other employers as well, agreed that Africans have a good aptitude for work. In this regard, a hotel owner who had hired seven Moroccan workers told me in interview that Spanish workers are unwilling to undertake unskilled tasks such as cleaning.

However, this positive aptitude was also understood by employers as a flexible way of using immigrants interchangeably across jobs, tasks and even sectors. Illustrating this, construction employers explained that, when their companies have jobs on farms, farmers sometimes offer their (African) workforce to assist with the construction work. In a construction employer's words: 'Sometimes agricultural employers or other clients tell us that an African who is working for them will help as an assistant. They save money [as the work can be done in less time, so the work is less costly] and it makes no difference to us.' This is confirmed by African labour trajectories. African farm workers said that they regularly do a variety of tasks on their employer's land or property, apart from the farm tasks that are written into their contract. For instance, one African worker I interviewed had started work in an agricultural town as a temporary agricultural labourer. After two years of working for the same employer (and legalising his residence), he was undertaking minor works on his employer's town properties in the off-peak season (e.g. painting), in order to make these dwellings suitable for renting. This work was undertaken alongside his usual agricultural tasks. A large number of examples build a picture of African labour being 'used' interchangeably between jobs. In local settings, African workers smooth the interaction between employers and businesses by providing an adaptable workforce. Africans take the least desirable jobs and are compelled to accept certain flexible work patterns that would be rejected by their Spanish counterparts. Taking the tourist industry as a further example, fieldwork showed that Africans are likely to be employed in small hotels rather than in large accommodation complexes. In large hotels, trade unions are far more active, so labour standards are more strictly surveyed.

But employers in the accommodation sector made it clear that they were not inclined to hire Africans for skilled or professional jobs. Sometimes they argued that Africans did not have the right skills or experience for a job (even if a third of the Moroccans I interviewed had followed at least secondary education), and sometimes they would not hire Africans for jobs requiring direct dealings with clients (e.g. receptionists or waiters), as they claimed that Africans were insufficiently aware of Western manners or that their firms already had good permanent staff in more skilled jobs. Certainly, in a high Spanish unemployment context, there are plenty of national workers who apply for well-paid jobs in tourism and hospitality industries. However, the reluctance to hire African workers contrasted with the eagerness of employers to take on other EU nationals for certain jobs such as receptionists. Knowledge of foreign languages was argued to be the main reason for this. Yet many young Moroccans I interviewed were fluent in several European languages. Indeed a recent survey by the International Labour Organisation reveals that a third of the legally-resident foreign workers in Spain had been rejected in job selection processes because of their origin (reported in Vázquez and Bayón 2000). According to the same source, this type of labour discrimination is higher in Spain than in many other European countries. Rejection based on racist attitudes is higher in Spanish manufacturing, and hotels and services in general, but less severe in construction and farming.

Not only do employers discriminate against workers by place of origin, but also by sex. For instance, farmers I interviewed in Girona were clear about their preference for male workers. They argued that there is no reason for hiring a woman for agricultural activities. Yet local women regularly picked fruit before immigrants became a feature of the local labour force. In fact, farming in Mediterranean Spain is a family business in which women actively participate in agricultural labour just as men do (García-Ramon *et al.* 1995). Taking the opposite view to farmers, accommodation employers in both Girona and the Algarve made it clear that cleaning was a female job. This preponderance of female immigrants in the tourism industry is also found in other parts of southern Europe. For instance, Leontidou (1994) found that in Greece immigrant women maintain the 'housewife' role in hotel employment (i.e. cooking and cleaning), while men are gardeners and drivers, with waiters and administrative staff being more mixed (with a male majority).

The general conclusion is that Spanish (but less so Portuguese) employers draw on characteristics such as ethnicity, national origin or sex in order to discriminate between potential recruits, as well as using the social status and organisation of immigrant communities as elements of control over performance. Thus immigrants are not simply workers who are endowed with different skills and familiarity with a language, they are used in qualitatively different ways from 'native' employees.

African female work in Iberia

The low participation rate of female immigrants in the Spanish labour market is not related exclusively to employer attitudes. Indeed, employers are more inclined to hire (immigrant) women than men for certain jobs, and structural economic change (e.g. the shift to a service economy or the job losses in certain manufacturing industries) has encouraged the incorporation of immigrant women into labour markets in developed countries. In both Italy and Spain it has been argued that the increase in female activity rates (by 'native' residents) has created jobs in the domestic sector, with these positions seen as suitable occupations for female immigrants (Chell 1997; Solé 1994). In fact, in Iberia the domestic sector is the only economic sector that employs a large number of female immigrants from developing countries (Berges 1993; Machado and Perista 1997; Oso and Catarino 1997).

However, in the late 1990s women only constituted 35 per cent of non-EU legal workers in Spain, with a share of only 16 per cent for Africans.[5] Yet there are significant differences by nationality. Thus, amongst nationals from Cape Verde, Equatorial Guinea, Peru, the Dominican Republic and the Philippines, female workers in Spain were more numerous than their male counterparts in the late 1990s. Even if official data usually underestimate labour participation rates for immigrant women, survey-based research confirms that the majority of Moroccans and Senegambians in Spanish and Catalan labour markets are men (Abril *et al.* 1998; Gozálvez Pérez 1995; Solé and Herrera 1991). My own survey identified only 10 working women out of the 151 African immigrants interviewed in Girona. In the case of Portugal, distribution by sex is more balanced. In 1997 women constituted 46 per cent of non-Portuguese EU nationals and 38 per cent of legal PALOP residents.[6] This is also reflected in my Portuguese survey which has a 40:60 female–to–male distribution.

Differences in the gender (im)balance between immigrants in Portugal and Spain are directly related to the way migration occurs in each country. African women generally follow their husbands to Spain (Oso and Catarino 1997; Solé 1994). Six of the 10 women I interviewed in Girona went to Spain because of their partner (not a single male out of the 141 declared that they moved to Spain because their partner/spouse lived in the country prior to them). As a consequence, female involvement in Spanish labour markets is highly dependent on male work. Since farming is a major employer of African males, most African married women live in agricultural municipalities. This does not help their incorporation in labour markets, as few job openings are offered to African women in this type of locality. According to a social worker whom I interviewed in an agricultural town, none of the eight married Moroccan women or two women from Senegambia who lived in that town had any paid work. It seems that if African women in rural areas want to work, they need to commute to service centres, where there may be jobs available in accommodation establishments or restaurants. As a male Moroccan, who was resident in the agricultural town of Sant Pere Pescador, noted: 'My wife has been offered a job in a pizzeria in Empúria Brava [a neighbouring tourist town], but her working time would be not compatible with mine, so I cannot take her to work. Besides, her Spanish is rather poor and our children are quite young. I'd rather she stayed at home.' In other words, commuting is not an easy option for female married Moroccans or Senegambians in Girona. As Sassen (1995) has pointed out, the locational distribution of female-dominated jobs is different from that for other jobs, as women are more location-sensitive in their journey to work owing to commitments like child-minding and (as the quote above illustrates) patriarchal control. Hence, either for their own beliefs or through marital preferences, family work is viewed as preferential by immigrant women.

Focusing on the 10 working women who were interviewed in Girona, Table 3.1 displays information on current (or last) job in Spain as well as current legal status and year of arrival. Here we see that six out of the 10 did cleaning, either in some kind of establishment or on a personal basis. This is in line with employers' preferences. But also male immigrants agreed on the idea that women are 'better' prepared for cleaning jobs. One Moroccan inerviewee expressed this view with the following words: 'My wife works as a cleaner in a rest home. Women find work quicker than men, cleaning factories, houses, restaurants. There are also old people who need help. They would not hire a man [*No van a contratar a un hombre*].'

Table 3.1   African women in paid work in Girona

Year of arrival	Channel (see notes)	Current legal status	Current labour status	Last or current job in Iberia	Sector of activity
1980	1	Work and Residence permit	Hired employee	Cleaner	Accommodation
1986	1	Residence permit	Non-hired employee	Cleaner	Domestic service
1985	1	Work and Residence permit	Unemployed	Unskilled worker	Manufacturing
1987	1	Residence permit	Non-hired employee	Kitchen assistant	Restaurant
1987	1	Residence permit	Non-hired employee	Cleaner	Domestic service
1985	2	Spanish national	Self-employed	Unofficial guesthouse owner	Accommodation
1987	1	Work and Residence permit	Hired employee	Cleaner	Cleaning firm
1992	2	Work and Residence permit	Hired employee	Kitchen assistant	Restaurant
1992	2	EU family Residence card	Non-hired employee	Cleaner	Domestic service
1991	3	Work and Residence permit	Hired employee	Cleaner	Accommodation

Source: Girona interview survey.
Notes: 1 Family reunion; 2 A girlfriend lived in Girona; 3 An aunt lived in Girona.

The second job for which women are seen to be 'better' prepared is as a kitchen assistant (see Table 3.1). But in this case immigrant women are in competition with men. Amongst male immigrants, there is no rejection of hotel or restaurant tasks as a whole, for 15 out of the 20 interviewees who were involved in these industries were men. Significantly, none of these 15 did a cleaning job, but worked in kitchens or did other jobs such as in security. As made clear in interviews, whereas immigrant men in Girona would not accept a job as a cleaner, they were willing to take a job as a kitchen assistant. This was related to male immigrants' culturally-based perception of jobs, with certain jobs (e.g. cleaning or serving) being considered as unsuitable for men.

By contrast, in Portugal the survey did not find any African-born man in the accommodation and restaurant sector. This appears to be the domain for immigrant women. Amongst the 13 female workers found in these types of employment, the survey identified both cleaners and kitchen assistants. The involvement of female immigrant workers in the Portuguese hotel and restaurant sector is directly related to wages in the industry, which are well below the national average, as well as sharply differentiated between male and female rates, the latter being much lower. Labour shortages in the hospitality sector therefore provide a low-paid niche in which African-born women can find employment.

The broader incorporation of female Africans in Portuguese labour markets (compared with Spain at least) reflects the greater labour market opportunities for African women in Portugal. This in turn relates to dissimilarities in the structure of African populations in each country (we saw earlier the different gender composition of African inflows in Portugal and Spain), as well as to more open approaches to female paid work amongst African communities in Portugal than in Spain. Indeed, unlike Spain, no African-born male in Portugal declared that he would prefer his wife or partner to be at home. Moreover, rather than relying on males, half the interviewed women came to Portugal using their own contacts: in many cases, through female-dominated networks, drawing on girlfriends or aunts. These autonomous female networks reflect a more developed consolidation of social networks between African PALOP nations and Portugal, initiated in the late 1960s with the first black males moving into Portugal. As observed for migration between Mexico and the USA (e.g. Hondagneu-Sotelo 1994), this more 'mature' construction of immigrant networks creates new openings for groups which were not involved in significant ways in early emigration streams (e.g. single women). This is a process that is still incipient amongst Moroccan women in Spain, but widely observed for other national groups such as Dominicans or Peruvians (Solé 1994).

Immigrant networks: help or hindrance to integration?

For immigrants in the so-called developed countries, social networks fostered and channelled immigration in the adverse political context of the 1980s and 1990s (Fawcett 1989; Gurack and Caces 1992). But immigrant groups do not organise themselves all in the same way. For example, the dense social networks that exist between members of the Cuban community in Miami are particular to this setting. Outlining the positive impact of these networks, some researchers have contended that workers in Miami's Cuban community enjoy more returns on past human capital investments, as well as more chances of promotion and skill acquisition, than other immigrant groups in the USA (Portes and Bach 1985; Wilson and Portes 1980). However, social networks make English language learning more difficult, and consequently reduce the chance of immigrants getting a job out of the enclave – as Reimers (1985) found for Mexicans and for Hispanics in general. In sum, then, the literature on immigrant networks sees them as both help (as sources for the acquisition of scarce means) and hindrance (in imposing constraints). A crucial point for the different impacts networks have within labour markets seems to be the nationality or origin of immigrants (or perhaps more accurately their social organisation in reception areas).

With the exception of some research on the Indian community in Lisbon by Malheiros (1997), immigrant networks have not received much attention in Iberia. However, it is clear that networks play an important role in providing information, at least for first employment. A good example of this is the Gambian community in Spain. Data on residence by nationality reveals that almost half of the 5,843 Gambians who were living in Spain in 1997 resided in Girona province. My interviews with Gambians revealed that they came from rural areas, had few years of formal education and had a poor command of Spanish (and English). Clearly, when acquiring a first job, help, advice and support from relatives or friends who are already living in the country are critical to understanding why workers from inland rural Gambia with a poor knowledge of a European language are working in townships in northern Spain.

Table 3.2 confirms the relevance of family-and-friend networks for African migrants. Almost half of the Moroccans, West Africans and workers from ex-Portuguese Africa mentioned relatives or acquaintances as channels through which they found their present job. Note that Table 3.2 excludes self-employed workers, and that all Moroccans, Senegalese and Gambians were interviewed in Spain, and all PALOP migrants in Portugal. Likewise, research by Gabinet d'Estudis Socials (1995) on immigrants from developing countries in Catalonia found that 82 out of the 176 migrants surveyed had obtained jobs through family and friends from their home country. On the other hand I found in my own research that, even if 'friend and family' networks are broadly used in both Portugal and Spain, immigrants in Portugal are more likely to gain access to 'conventional' channels of information gathering on jobs. Here family and friend networks were the second most important way of finding a   job. To be specific, when they secured employment in Portugal, a third of African-born workers relied on conventional channels such as newspapers, adverts on the street, employment agencies or getting registered with a firm as a job-seeker. These channels were barely used by Africans of any nationality in Girona. Indeed, the second most popular job-hunting strategy amongst 'Spanish Africans' is simply going around workplaces asking if job vacancies exist. If employees are needed, the job-seeker starts work as soon as possible. In my survey, a third of African workers in Girona had obtained their current employment in this way (Table 3.2).

Table 3.2 Channel used for African workers to obtain current job in Iberia, by nationality group

	Moroccans	Senegalese and Gambians	PALOP countries	Total
Friends and family	40	30	31	101
'Asking' [1]	30	22	4	56
Employers' initiative [2]	5	4	2	11
Conventional channels [3]	6	3	27	36
No answer	5	3	1	9
Total	86	62	65	213

Source: Author's interview survey.
Notes:
1 Employees go round workplaces checking if job vacancies are available.
2 Employers ask their employed Africans if they know somebody who may be interested in a job. In other cases, employers go round bars or places where Africans gather.
3 Employment agencies, adverts in public places, and registration with firms as job-seekers.

Reasons for divergence in ways of obtaining information and accessing employment are twofold. First of all, it seems that the peculiarities of the Portuguese labour market, with low unemployment rates and low wages in an EU context, make it difficult for employers to get workers for the least desirable jobs (Modesto *et al.* 1992). In this sense, tourist establishments made it clear that it was hard for them to find workers for the peak season.

Set in this context, for the least desirable and worst-paid jobs (such as cleaning), companies have to advertise openings they need to fill. This more active role for employers does occur in Girona for skilled work, where there are specific labour shortages (e.g. metal workers, carpenters). But what is more frequent in the high unemployment context of Spain is that African workers 'do the rounds' of farms or construction sites searching for jobs. This is understood by employers as a sign of the eagerness of Africans to work.

A second reason for the more widespread use of 'official' channels in Portugal seems related to the fact that PALOP immigrants are more 'comfortable' in Portuguese labour markets than their migrant counterparts in Spain. Crucial to this is the capacity of immigrants to use the host country language. In Portugal, African-born workers are generally fluent in Portuguese, even if it is not their first language. Furthermore, because of previous colonisation, many are used to Portuguese work procedures and habits. As an example, it was clear throughout my fieldwork that African immigrants turned readily to the Portuguese Foreigners' and Borders' Service (Serviço de Estrangeiros e Fronteiras). By contrast, Spanish immigrants have more trust in NGOs or lawyers than in the official Foreigners' Office (Oficina de Extranjeros). The general point is that immigrants with language or cultural ties to the destination country find it easier to use mainstream job-hunting methods. From a broader perspective, the historical/cultural/language factor seems to be crucial when explaining current immigrant inflows in Portugal, since this country rarely attracts non-PALOP immigrants (with the exception of those originally from EU countries).

Immigrant networks and labour mobility within Iberia

Social networks not only help channel new immigrants into a host country, but are crucial in determining job mobility once there. For Spain, upward socio-occupational mobility amongst Africans has generally been poor (Colectivo IOÉ 1994; Ramírez Goicoechea 1996). This low occupational progression occurs even if Africans are more likely than Spaniards to move residence in search of jobs. In fact, the greater propensity of African immigrants to change their place of residence constitutes a good comparative advantage for immigrants in the context of the low rates of Spanish internal migration in recent decades (Bentolila 1997). Yet for immigrants the reason for internal migration often stems from their unstable, precarious position in Spanish labour markets, rather than from a search for better working conditions (Mendoza 1998). In fact, the most mobile group of African immigrants in Girona were the unskilled, temporarily-hired farm workers. Working on several harvests during a single year was something that the bulk of immigrants whom I interviewed who were employed in Spanish farming had habitually done in the past. These immigrants tend to transfer into other employment sectors or to more 'permanent' jobs in farming the longer they reside in Spain (Hoggart and Mendoza 1999). However, the need for more workers in the picking season (plus the fact that harvests occur in different months across Spain) stimulates movement in search of work during an 'elongated' harvest time, as well as further immigration. For instance a Moroccan, who was hired as a temporary worker in the apple harvest in Girona at the time of interview, had worked in Barcelona's strawberry picking season, in vegetable collection in Girona, in the peach and apple harvests in Lleida and in cherry picking in Zaragoza. This single example is illustrative of a common trend amongst African immigrant farm workers. Colectivo IOÉ (1994) identified a substantial group of African agricultural workers who move around Spain in search of work (circulating between the strawberry harvest in Huelva, fruit collection in Lleida and Girona, the orange harvest in Valencia and Murcia, and asparagus and potato picking in La Rioja). This 'cyclical' movement has little to do with the skills of the workers, but arises from the needs of sectors that are short of workers in different parts of Spain at different times of the year.

Interviews with Africans in Girona show that most transient farm workers were young, single men. A small number were married, but without their families residing in Spain. Married men with a precarious position in Spanish labour markets maintained that their families were better off in their country of origin, under the 'protection' of relatives. For the mostly Muslim Moroccans and Senegambians, there is a conception of the conjugal family in which separation from spouse or children is only a temporary means of obtaining good wages. However, regardless of immigrants' beliefs on what is best for their families, immigration rules prevent family reunification for those with an unstable position in Spanish labour markets. Only when immigrants can show they have a stable job in Spain and good quality housing (which must be certified by health officials), is family reunification allowed.

The other side of the coin is that good housing is not a top priority for those African immigrants in Spain who see their residence as temporary. As a means of saving costs, they usually share a place of residence with other co-nationals who are often living in similarly precarious conditions. Through friendship networks, these 'unattached' immigrants change residence relatively easily within Spain. In other words, patterns of residential mobility follow job status for non-married men or for those with no partner in Spain. In migration terms, temporary residents are advantaged, as they are less likely to have problems when deciding to move in order to obtain the better wages that are often offered for a limited period of time.

By contrast, for Portugal patterns of internal migration are less dependent on life-cycle or family considerations or on perceptions of length of stay in the country. This point became particularly clear in interviews with Cape Verdean and Angolan construction workers. Analysis of their employment trajectories shows that they had experienced considerable geographical mobility since arriving in Portugal. Construction provides a solid base for immigrant work in Portugal (Baganha 1998; Mendoza 1999b). Immigrant construction workers are geographically mobile not only as a result of casualisation and locational switches in the sector, but also because of a search for better wages. Another main difference is constituted by the demographic profiles of the movers, with Portuguese construction workers being of all ages and having different marital status. Overall, internally mobile immigrants are not characterised as being predominantly young and single (which was the norm in Spain). The general impression that I gained from my interviews in Portugal was that African-born workers have fewer difficulties in spending time out of their families than their counterparts in Spain.

The reasons for the lack of a clear demographic profile for PALOP workers (in contrast to the Spanish case) derive partly from differences in the conception of family between African nationals in Spain and PALOP immigrants in Portugal. Broadly speaking, the organisation of PALOP families is matrifocal, with the mother–child bond being the affective and economic core of the family. Men do not feel an urge to 'protect' their families (or at least not in the same terms as Muslim married men), so they 'enjoy' better chances of moving jobs or places. As a result, solidarity ties in poor neighbourhoods such as the Bairros dos Pescadores in Quarteira (Algarve) compensated for a lack of male support. On the other hand, the crucial position of women in the family restricts job search methods for married females and for those in co-habitation. My findings support the general impression in the literature which points to the divergent role of family ties for women and men when deciding a job change that involves a change of residence – for instance Chant's (1992, p. 197) conclusion that 'even in situations where women are highly mobile ... men seem to be more mobile still. In other words, men are rarely "left behind" by female migrants: it is usually the reverse which applies.' African male workers in Portuguese construction are highly mobile, since family 'obligations' do not restrain their mobility inside the country (or even to other EU nations). For women, this works the other way round, with married females having less chance of changing their homeplace. So rather than labour market mechanisms, differences in patterns of internal mobility for males in Portugal and Spain seem to respond to broader aspects of the structure of families (nuclear family for Spanish Africans versus matrifocal structures for Portuguese PALOP nationals), with internal migration being mainly a choice available to 'unattached' men in Spain.

Conclusion

This chapter has discussed five non-labour culture-related aspects which influence immigrant labour situations in Portugal and Spain, based on fieldwork in three regions. Rather than presenting final conclusions, the aim has been to propose an agenda for future research on cultural aspects of trans-Mediterranean economic migration from North and West Africa to Iberia. The agenda comprises five points.

The first dimension discussed concerns the historically-based cultural factors of immigration and naturalisation policies in Iberia. These are decisive for understanding the uneven treatment of different immigrant groups in Portuguese and Spanish laws. An immigrant-friendly Portuguese policy (at least in comparative EU terms) must be placed in context of the recent process of decolonisation, plus the fact that immigrants are mainly from ex-colonies. Ties of history, culture and language are also evident in Spanish immigration rules. The perceived lack of historical affinity with current sending countries to Spain certainly appears to be a powerful reason for legislators to consider migrants as temporary workers, rather than immigrants. Whether better economic circumstances may help overcome traditional fears of the 'others' in Spain is an open question, particularly as Moroccans are the worst-placed group in this regard (Andrés Orizo and Sánchez Fernández 1991).

The second aspect developed in the chapter revolves around employers' beliefs and opinions. In Spain it is clear that employers use immigrants in a different way from indigenous workers. The use of immigrant labour is based on pre-conceptions or beliefs that, in many cases, are rooted in prejudice and racism. Yet, for others, it is only a rational choice between different sources of labour, with immigrants being perceived and used as a docile, cheap workforce. In this regard employers often characterise African-born workers in Spain with positive tones which contrast with the 'negative' ones used for other workers. This preliminary finding opens up the potential for further research on the perceptions and preferences of employers for different types of immigrant labour.

However, it is not just employers, but also immigrants, who have a particular image of the jobs open to them, although this image is sometimes informed by the prejudice they encounter in local labour markets. The third point of the agenda, therefore, should be focused around immigrants' values and beliefs and how these, in turn, affect paid work. For instance, it became clear during fieldwork that the rejection of cleaning tasks by male immigrants (as well as the rare incidence of married females in Spain) are both related to immigrant conceptions of job suitability. Certainly more research is needed on work-related attitudes amongst immigrants, but also amongst the Iberian population as a whole. For Spain, sample surveys generally reveal that general attitudes toward immigrants are benign and even, in some respects, sympathetic (Cornelius 1994). However the February 2000 events in El Ejido (Almería, southern Spain), when a racist backlash took place after a murder committed by a Moroccan national, are a sad reminder on the necessity of further research on racism, and of the social implications of a rising immigrant population in the country.

The fourth dimension explored here was differences in the use of social networks amongst African-born workers in both countries. Profiency in the host country language (plus knowledge of Portuguese cultural norms due to colonial links) plays a decisive element when analysing the broader use of 'conventional' channels amongst African-born workers in Portugal. Yet, even for this group, friend and family networks still rank first as a job-hunting method. Moreover, leaving aside European immigration, current immigration inflows into Portugal are only understable in the context of dense social networks linking PALOP Africans already living in Portugal with their countries of origin. As for internal mobility, the fifth aspect of this chapter, family is a key element when analysing differences in African labour outcomes in Portugal and Spain. Taking two highly mobile groups (farm employees in Spain and construction workers in Portugal), two contrasting demographic profiles are identified. Behind this description lies a different model of family in both communities: neighbourhood ties in poor housing areas somehow compensate the lack of strong (male) family support for PALOP women.

Notes

1   This research was funded by the 'Human Capital and Mobility' and the 'Training and Mobility of Researchers' Programmes of the Commission of the European Communities (Proposals ERB4001GT931634 and ERB4001GT956581). I am grateful to Prof. Keith Hoggart in the Department of Geography at King's College London for supervising my PhD and for his useful comments on drafts of this paper.

2   A few words about why I chose these places to carry out my fieldwork. Girona was selected because it is the Spanish province with the highest share of African workers in its labour force, such workers being represented in several sectors – agriculture, tourism and construction. In Portugal, the Algarve was chosen because it, too, has the highest proportion of foreign residents, with Africans experiencing particular growth during the 1980s and 1990s. Here, tourism is the main employment sector for immigrant workers,

including construction of tourist facilities. By contrast, industry (and associated construction) is more characteristic of the manufacturing-oriented Setúbal peninsula.

3   See M. Moura, A lusofonia não se negoceia, *O Público*, 15 May 1996. Cape Verdeans speak 'creole' which has been created by different language layers (Portuguese, French and several African languages, Mandinga and Foula mainly). Cape Verdean creole has no official recognition, Portuguese being the only official language of the islands (Carreira 1982).

4   The debate on employers' values and beliefs (and how these affect patterns of African labour outcomes) refers only to Spain. This is because Spanish employers express very clear opinions. By contrast, no clear views on African-born workers were given by Portuguese employers.

5   Data from the annual reports of the Comisión Interministerial de Extranjería, Madrid.

6   Data from the annual demographic reports of the Instituto Nacional de Estatística, Lisbon.

References

Abril, P., Castellet, R., Montenegro, S., Moreno, C. and Salas, I. (1998) *Inmigración Africana y Formación Continua en Cataluña*. Barcelona: Institut per al Desenvolupament de la Formació Ocupacional/Unió General de Treballadors.

Andrés Orizo, F. and Sánchez Fernández, A. (1991) *El Sistema de Valors dels Catalans*. Barcelona: Institut d'Estudis Mediterranis.

Baganha, M. I. (1998) Immigrant involvement in the informal economy: the Portuguese case, *Journal of Ethnic and Migration Studies*, 24(2), pp. 367–85.

Baganha, M. I. and Góis, P. (1999) Migrações internacionais de e para Portugal: o que sabemos e para onde vamos? *Revista Crítica de Ciências Sociais*, 52–53, pp. 229–80.

Bentolila, S. (1997) La inmovilidad del trabajo en las regiones españolas, *Papeles de Economía*, 72, pp. 168–76.

Berges, M. T. (1993) La inmigración filipina, in Giménez Romero, C. (ed.) *Inmigrantes Extranjeros en Madrid: estudios monográficos de colectivos inmigrantes*. Madrid: Comunidad de Madrid, pp. 561–619.

Carreira, A. (1982) *The People of the Cape Verde Islands: Exploitation and Emigration*. London: C. Hurst & Co.

Chant, S. (1992) Conclusion: towards a framework for the analysis of gender-selective migration, in Chant, S. (ed.) *Gender and Migration in Developing Countries*. London: Belhaven Press, pp. 197–206.

Chell, V. (1997) Gender-selective migration: Somalian and Filipina women in Rome, in King, R. and Black, R. (eds) *Southern Europe and the New Immigrations*. Brighton: Sussex Academic Press, pp. 75–92.

Chiswick, B. R. (1978) The effect of Americanization on the earnings of foreign-born men, *Journal of Political Economy*, 86(5), pp. 897–922.

Colectivo IOÉ (1987) *Los Inmigrantes en España*. Madrid: Caritas Española, Documentación Social 66.

Colectivo IOÉ (1994) *Marroquins a Catalunya*. Barcelona: Institut Català d'Estudis Mediterranis.

Cornelius, W. A. (1994) Spain: the uneasy transition from labor exporter to labor importer, in Cornelius, W. A., Martin, P. L. and Hollifield, J. F. (eds) *Controlling Immigration: a Global Perspective*. Stanford: Stanford University Press, pp. 331–69.

Dubois, C. (1994) L'épineux dossier des retornados, in Miège, J.-L. and Dubois, C. (eds) *L'Europe Retrouvée: les migrations de la décolonisation*. Paris: L'Harmattan, pp. 213–46.

Esteves, M. C. (1991) *Portugal, País de Imigração*. Lisbon: Instituto de Estudos para o Desenvolvimento.

Fawcett, J. T. (1989) Networks, linkages and migration systems, *International Migration Review*, 23(3), pp. 671–80.

Ferreira, M. E. (1994) Relações entre Portugal e África de língua portuguesa: comércio, investimento e dívida (1973-1994), *Análise Social*, 29, pp. 107–21.

Gabinet d'Estudis Socials (1995) *Entre el Sud i el Nord: els treballadors estrangers a Catalunya*. Barcelona: Generalitat de Catalunya.

García-Ramon, M.D. and Cruz, J. (1996) Regional welfare policies and women's agricultural labour in southern Spain, in García-Ramon, M.D. and Monk, J. (eds) *Women of the European Union*. London: Routledge, pp. 247–62.

García-Ramon, M. D., Cruz Villalón, J., Salamana Segura, I. and Villarino Pérez, M. (1995) *Mujer y Agricultura en España: género, trabajo y contexto regional*. Barcelona: Oikos-Tau.

Gozálvez Pérez, V. (1995) *Inmigrantes Marroquíes y Senegaleses en la España Mediterránea*. Valencia: Generalitat Valenciana.

Granovetter, M. (1985) Economic action and social structure: the problem of embeddedness, *American Journal of Sociology*, 91(3), pp. 481–510.

Guibentif, P. (1996) Le Portugal face à l'immigration, *Revue Européenne des Migrations Internationales*, 12(2), pp. 121–39.

Gurack, D. T. and Caces, F. (1992) Migration networks and the shaping of migration systems, in Kritz, M. M., Lim, L. L. and Zlotnik, H. (eds) *International Migration Systems: a Global Approach*. Oxford: Clarendon Press, pp. 150–76.

Hammar, T. (1990) *Democracy and the Nation State: Aliens, Denizens and Citizens in a World of International Migration*. Aldershot: Avebury.

Hondagneu-Sotelo, P. (1994) *Gendered Transitions: Mexican Experiences of Immigration*. Berkeley: University of California Press.

Hoggart, K. and Mendoza, C. (1999) African immigrant workers in Spanish agriculture, *Sociologia Ruralis*, 39(4), pp. 538–62.

Huntoon, L. (1998) Immigration to Spain: implications for a unified European Union immigration policy, *International Migration Review*, 32(2), pp. 423–50.

Izquierdo, A. (1992) *La Inmigración en España 1980-1990*. Madrid: Ministerio de Trabajo y Seguridad Social.

King, R. and Konjhodzic, I. (1995) *Labour, Employment and Migration in Southern Europe*. Brighton: University of Sussex, Research Papers in Geography 19.

King, R., Fielding, A. and Black, R. (1997) The international migration turnaround in Southern Europe, in King, R. and Black, R. (eds) *Southern Europe and the New Immigrations*. Brighton: Sussex Academic Press, pp. 1–25.

Leontidou, L. (1994) Gender dimensions of tourism in Greece: employment, subcultures and restructuring, in Kinnaird, V. and Hall, D. (eds) *Tourism: a Gender Analysis*. Chichester: Wiley, pp. 74–105.

Long, J. E. (1980) The effect of Americanization on earnings: some evidence for women, *Journal of Political Economy*, 88(3), pp. 620–9.

Machado, F. L. (1992) Etnicidade em Portugal: contrastes e politização, *Sociologia: Problemas e Práticas*, 12, pp. 123–36.

Machado, F. L. (1994) Luso-africanos em Portugal: nas margens da etnicidade, *Sociologia: Problemas e Práticas*, 16, pp. 111–34.

Machado, F. L. and Perista, H. (1997) Femmes immigrées au Portugal, *Migrations Société*, 52, pp. 91–103.

Malheiros, J. (1997) Indians in Lisbon: ethnic entrepreneurship and the migration process, in King, R. and Black, R. (eds) *Southern Europe and the New Immigrations*. Brighton: Sussex Academic Press, pp. 93–112.

Mansvelt Beck, J. (1988) *The Rise of the Subsidized Periphery in Spain*. Utrecht: Nederlandse Geografische Studies 69.

Marie, C. V. (1995) *The EC Member States and Immigration in 1993: Closed Borders, Stringent Attitudes*. Luxembourg: Office for Official Publications of the European Communities.

Marie, C. V. (1996) L'Union Européenne face aux déplacements de populations: logiques d'état face aux droits des personnes, *Revue Européenne des Migrations Internationales*, 12(1), pp. 169–209.

Mendoza, C. (1997) Foreign labour immigration in high-unemployment Spain: the role of African-born workers in the Girona labour market, in King, R. and Black, R. (eds) *Southern Europe and the New Immigrations*. Brighton, Sussex Academic Press, pp. 51–74.

Mendoza, C. (1998) *New Labour Inflows in Southern Europe: African Employment in Iberian Labour Markets*. London: King's College London, PhD thesis.

Mendoza, C. (1999a) Migración y mercados de trabajo en el sur de Europa: inserción laboral de los trabajadores africanos en España, *Frontera Norte*, 21, pp. 95–116.

Mendoza, C. (1999b) *African Employment in Iberian Agriculture and Construction: A Cross-border Comparative Approach*. London: King's College London, Department of Geography, Occasional Paper 47.

Mendoza, C. (2001) The role of the state in influencing African labour outcomes in Spain and Portugal, *Geoforum*, 32, in press.

Ministério da Administração Interna (1995) *Nacionalidade por Naturalização e Estatuto de Igualdade*. Lisbon: Ministério da Administração Interna.

Modesto, L., Monteiro, M. L. and das Neves, J. C. (1992) Some aspects of the Portuguese labour market, 1977-1988: neutrality, hysteresis and the wage gap, in do Amaral, J. F., Lucena, D. and Mello, A. S. (eds) *The Portuguese Economy towards 1992*. Boston: Kluwer Academic Press, pp. 153–74.

Oso, L. and Catarino, C. (1997) Les effects de la migration sur le statut des femmes: les cas des Dominicaines et des Marocaines à Madrid et des Cap-Verdiennes à Lisbonne, *Migrations Société*, 52, pp. 115–30.

Pérez Oliva, M. (1995) La rueda de la ilegalidad: la mitad de los 105.000 inmigrantes legalizados en 1991 vuelve a estar en situación irregular, *El País*, Catalan edition, 22 October.

Piore, M. J. (1979) *Birds of Passage: Migrant Labor and Industrial Societies*. Cambridge: Cambridge University Press.

Pires, R. P., Maranhão, M. J., Quintela, J. P., Moniz, F. and Pisco, M. (1987) *Os Retornados: um estudo sociográfico*. Lisbon: Instituto de Estudos para o Desenvolvimento.

Portes, A. and Bach, R. (1985) *Latin Journey*. Berkeley: University of California Press.

Portes, A. and Sensenbrenner, J. (1993) Embeddedness and immigration: notes on the social determinants of economic action, *American Journal of Sociology*, 98(6), pp. 1320–50.

Pugliese, E. (1993) Restructuring of the labour market and the role of Third World migrations in Europe, *Society and Space*, 11(3), pp. 513–22.

Ramírez Goicoechea, E. (1996) *Inmigrantes en España: vidas y experiencias*. Madrid: Centro de Investigaciones Sociológicas/Siglo XXI.

Reimers, C. W. (1985) A comparative analysis of the wages of Hispanics, Blacks, and non-Hispanic whites, in Borjas, G. J. and Tienda, M. (eds) *Hispanics in the US Economy*. Orlando: Academic Press, pp. 27–75.

Saint-Maurice, A. and Pires, R. P. (1989) Descolonização e migrações: os imigrantes dos PALOP em Portugal, *Revista Internacional de Estudos Africanos*, 10–11, pp. 203–26.

Sassen, S. (1995) Immigration and local labour markets, in Portes, A. (ed.) *The Economic Sociology of Immigration: Essays on Networks, Ethnicity and Entrepreneurship*. New York: Rusell Sage Foundation, pp. 87–127.

Solé, C. (1994) *La Mujer Inmigrante*. Madrid: Ministerio de Asuntos Sociales, Instituto de la Mujer.

Solé, C. and Herrera, E. (1991) *Trabajadores Extranjeros en Cataluña: ¿integración o racismo?* Madrid: Centro de Investigaciones Sociológicas/Siglo XXI.

Vázquez, L. and Bayón, M. (2000) Un tercio de los inmigrantes legales de España sufre el rechazo xenófobo al buscar trabajo, *El País Digital*, 9 March.

Villaverde Castro, J. (1996) Interprovincial inequalities in Spain 1955–91, *European Urban and Regional Studies*, 3(4), 339–46.

Wilson, T. and Portes, A. (1980) Immigrant enclaves: an analysis of the labor market experiences of Cubans in Miami, *American Journal of Sociology*, 86(2), pp. 295–31.

4

Festes, ferias and hip-hop: images of multiculturalism in Barcelona

Mariagiulia Grassilli

Introduction

Capital of the autonomous region of Catalonia, Barcelona is a vibrant and fascinating city, full of contrast and with its own special balance of tradition and modernity, nature and culture, the new and the old. Although it has always maintained an outward-looking mentality, simultaneously Mediterranean and European, its global image became immeasurably enhanced by its successful hosting of the 1992 Olympic Games.

Barcelona is also a city of migrants. During the early decades of the twentieth century and again during the 1950s and 1960s they came from other parts of Spain, above all from Andalusia. Since the 1980s there has been substantial immigration from various parts of the developing world: Latin America, North and West Africa, the Middle East and Asia. Today, Barcelona projects itself both as the bastion of Catalan nationalism and culture, and as an increasingly multicultural city able to sustain and absorb people from different geographical and cultural origins.

In this chapter I present some results of fieldwork I carried out in Barcelona in 1999.[1] This fieldwork was set within the context of Barcelona as a European city of culture and also as a city of cultural encounters for the various groups of people living there. I was particularly keen to document and interpret instances of organised or semi-organised multiculturalism in which migrants played a key role. Four events which I witnessed (and, to a certain extent, participated in) form the core of my analysis. These are:

- *Festa de la Diversitat* – a three-day festival of art, music, cinema, theatre and cuisine organised by SOS Racisme (5–7 July);

- *Feria d'Abril* – a ten-day festival of flamenco and Andalusian traditions (23 April–2 May);

- *Setmana Intercultural del Casc Antic* – a more informal week of intercultural activity in an old *barrio* of the city (17–23 June);
- *El Raval* – an urban sports and music event in another poor district of the city inhabited by many immigrants groups (26 June).

I devote the largest part of my account to the first of these. As Barcelona's most important showcase for cultural diversity, the *Festa de la Diversitat* was the event where I was able to collect most field data during my stay. I found this festival very thought-provoking and useful as a frame within which to read other events in the city.

The chapter is organised in the following way. First I introduce the city of Barcelona as a setting for new migratory groups, including some data on who the migrants are, where they live, and the city's response in terms of multicultural policy. The main body of the chapter is made up of descriptions and interpretations of the four events, presented in the order listed above. I conclude by deepening the interpretation of multiculturalism in Barcelona by discussing the themes of representation, participation, diversity and identity as they emerge from a comparison of the cultural activities I observed.

Barcelona: city of culture, city of migrants

The city's inhabitants perceive Barcelona as a modern, cosmopolitan and cultural place. They see it as the most European of the Spanish cities but also as very Mediterranean, reflecting its historical role as a port. In defining Barcelona in this way, their accent is on the work ethic and the professionalism and modernity achieved by the city, but also on the many opportunities for entertainment and relaxation. At the *Feria d'Abril* I was made aware that Barcelona is the most Andalusian city outside Andalusia.

Part of Barcelona's vibrancy and internationalism derives from its large student population. There are two large universities, important art schools and design institutes and one of Spain's most prestigious business schools. Barcelona is known throughout the world – and chosen as a place for training and inspiration – for its innovative design and architecture. The modernism of Gaudí and the presence in the past of figures like Dalí, Miró, Buñuel and others have attracted a large artistic community. All this has contributed to an interesting combination of creativity, spontaneity and professionalism in the city's production of culture.

But Barcelona is also the main cultural centre for the celebration of traditions and institutions that reflect the nationalist narrative of the region. In Plaça St Jaume – where both the Ajuntament (town hall) and the Generalitat de Catalunya (regional government) are located – it is common to see traditional Catalan cultural activities. Every weekend in front of the beautiful Gothic cathedral ordinary Catalans join hands to dance the Sardana, the region's national dance. Catalan traditions are also strongly celebrated in the city's various fiestas (St Jordi, St Joan, La Mercé, etc.) and in the *festa major* organised by each *barrio* during the summer. These events are now becoming opportunities for demonstrating the new ethnic composition of the city's neighbourhoods.

Barcelona is therefore simultaneously a centre for the promotion and celebration of Catalan nationalism and traditions, and a progressive and cosmopolitan city which pays particular attention to issues of multiculturalism, social solidarity and immigration. Joan Clos, the current mayor, regards 'cultural diversity' as crucial for the redefinition of Barcelona in its marketing as a 'city of culture'. The next major project for the city is the *Forum Universal de las Culturas*, in 2004. The City Council has launched the 2004 initiative with the support of UNESCO as an opportunity for further urban development and city marketing (the 1992 Olympics having regenerated Montjuïc and the waterfront).

Meanwhile the Ajuntament has started other works of urban regeneration in Ciutat Vella (the old city), in particular in El Raval and Casc Antic. The objective is to restore old buildings as well as create space for modern developments and public areas. The modern area in El Raval where the Museum of Contemporary Art and the Centre for Contemporary Culture are located is the result of recent urban development. As with other instances of urban renewal there is the fear of gentrification – that the newly regenerated areas will attract professionals and force the poorer residents to move out.

Immigration in Barcelona

In-migration has played an important role in the demographic growth of Barcelona. Over the centuries, the city has been fed by various migratory streams with different origins – within Catalonia, from other Spanish regions, and from abroad. At present migration from other countries appears to be the dominant trend, although the quantity of immigration is far below that which originated from the south of Spain during the 1950s and 1960s. In fact the social perception of the importance of immigration from developing countries has constantly exaggerated its extent, as well as glossing over its diversity and complexity. Recently Pascual de Sans *et al.* (2000) have attempted to correct some of these misconceptions, above all with regard to the relative numbers involved and the proportions of the immigrants coming from the developing world and the advanced countries (EU, North America, Japan, etc.).[2]

Table 4.1   Foreign residents registered in Barcelona, 31 December 1996

From developing countries		From developed countries	
Peru	3,973	France	3,299
Morocco	3,838	Italy	2,811
Philippines	2,878	Germany	2,567
Dominican Republic	2,507	UK	2,038
Argentina	1,870	USA	1,216
China	1,301	Japan	930
Pakistan	1,072	Portugal	764
Colombia	937	Netherlands	626
Chile	920		
Brazil	818	All developing countries	27,249
Uruguay	655	All developed countries	15,914
India	653		
Cuba	547	Total	43,214

Source: Permanent Observatory on Immigration in Barcelona (1999, p. 29).
Notes: Only countries with >500 are listed; total includes 51 stateless and unknown.

Table 4.1 sets out some data on legally-registered foreign residents in Barcelona in 1996, for those nationality groups with at least 500 residents. The foreign residents' share of the total population is a surprisingly low 2 per cent. The largest non-European national communities were from several Latin American countries, plus Morocco, the Philippines, China, Pakistan and India; considerable numbers are also present from the United States, Japan and various EU countries, reflecting the city's growing importance as a centre for international business and culture (Pascual de Sans *et al.* 2000). The diversity of immigrant nationalities in Barcelona is rather wide, but this is a characteristic feature of other major southern European cities, as was noted in Chapter 1.

Different immigrant nationalities are concentrated in different parts of the city. The districts with the highest numbers and relative concentrations of immigrants are Ciutat Vella (for migrants from the poorer countries of the world) and Eixample and Sarrià-St Gervasi (for high-status Europeans, etc.).

Table 4.2 sets out this data, based on the City Census for 1986 and 1997 (note that the census gives a lower total than the residence permit data used for Table 4.1). Although the number of foreign residents has increased in almost all districts of the city, this growth has been most rapid in Ciutat Vella where the *barrios* of El Raval and Parc (Casc Antic) host particular concentrations. In these two areas immigrants make up 9.5 and 7.7 per cent of the total residents respectively (Permanent Observatory on Immigration in Barcelona 1999, pp. 42–5), the main nationalities being Moroccans, Filipinos, Indians, Pakistanis, Dominicans and Chinese. Two factors seem to be paramount in helping to explain these immigrant concentrations in Ciutat Vella: the economic factor of the availability of cheap accommodation, and the social network factor of formal and informal community ties.

Table 4.2　Foreign residents in Barcelona by district, 1986–97

District	1986	%	1997	%
Ciutat Vella	2,063	10.6	6,392	21.8
Eixample	4,140	21.3	5,365	18.4
Sants-Montjuïc	1,259	6.4	2,950	10.1
Les Corts	1,809	9.3	1,765	6.1
Sarrià-St Gervasi	4,914	25.3	3,671	12.6
Gràcia	1,693	8.7	2,166	7.4
Horta-Guinardó	1,249	6.4	1,724	5.9
Nou Barris	651	3.3	1,265	4.3
Sant Andreu	705	3.6	1,335	4.6
Sant Martí	978	5.0	2,561	8.8
Total	19,401	100.0	29,165	100.0

Source: City Census, cited in Permanent Observatory on Immigration in Barcelona (1999, p. 42).

The city's response to immigration

From interviews with high-ranking officers of the City Council's Welfare Department I learnt that the authorities are quite prepared to address the issues arising from the city's changing demographic composition. Rather than creating special services for the immigrants, the objective of the City Council is 'to make the normal services suitable for everybody... [hence] to adapt the services ... for everybody inclusive of the needs of everybody.' The document *Un Plan Municipal para la Multiculturalidad*, issued by the City Council in 1999, was aimed at recognising cultural diversity and equality of opportunity. Within the overall objective of making all services equally accessible to all citizens of Barcelona, the Plan sets out the steps that each department needs to take to achieve effective inclusion, and highlights areas where special efforts need to be made – education, employment policy, housing, health and culture.

For instance, in the area of culture, the document acknowledges the widespread ignorance on the part of most inhabitants of Barcelona of the different foreign and ethnic cultures present in the city, beyond the most superficial and folkloristic aspects. The Plan indicates what is needed to foster a better knowledge of the various cultures and to encourage the immigrants themselves to have better access to the cultural life of the city, both as actors and consumers. Among specific lines of action are:

- the planning of a cultural policy which includes full participation of the many cultures present in the city;
- the incorporation of the most important holidays and celebrations of the various ethnic communities within the calendar of celebrations of the city;
- promoting knowledge about the various cultures which have existed in Barcelona over time;
- support for socio-cultural activities of each community by the provision of space and publicity;
- the organisation of cultural activities which are explicitly oriented towards all communities;
- the introduction of awards, grants and competitions to promote the participation of individuals from all communities in the cultural life of the city.

There are some exceptions to the general policy of not creating services *ad hoc* for immigrants. Three may be mentioned. SAIER is a reception facility which gives assistance to new arrivals, helping them to regularise their status and supplying them with social, legal and work information. SAIER also provides special assistance for refugees. The Consejo de Inmigración is a forum via which the immigrants can be consulted in relation to the administration of the city, in some way compensating for their lack of formal voting rights. Each immigrant association elects a representative on the Consejo, which then engages in dialogue with the City Council over various issues.[3] Finally, the Permanent Observatory on Immigration in Barcelona (OPIB) has been created to supply knowledge about the existing situation of immigrants in Barcelona in order to inform City Council policies.

With this background in mind, I now move to my field data, starting with the main public event I observed.

Festa de la Diversitat

Organised every year by SOS Racisme, an NGO working for anti-racism and for the respect of human rights, this three-day festival involves the participation (in 1999) of more than 120 cultural associations – local NGOs and migrant associations – and is supported by Barcelona City Council and several corporate sponsors. The festival, which started in 1992, is an opportunity for reaffirming the city's commitment against racism as well as its wish to 'celebrate' cultural diversity. The motto in 1999 was *'igualtat per viure, diversitat per conviure, gresca per sobreviure'* – that is, 'equality for living, diversity for living together, fun for surviving'. According to Muntañola-Thornberg (1997, pp. 3, 9), 'the inhabitants of Barcelona go to the festival looking for tasty food, brightly coloured crafts, fascinating dance music and shows to feel that they belong to the world and that their city is becoming a multicultural metropolis...the festival is attended by all progressive city dwellers'.

The event started off on Friday evening with a street parade in La Rambla (the main pedestrianised axis of central Barcelona) led by Palo q'sea, a group of Colombian street theatre performers. The Festa lasted all day and all night (until 3 am) on Saturday and Sunday. The immigrant associations offered traditional food and drinks from their countries of origin; the public could sample the cuisine from most of the stands.[4] The aim was for the public to learn, in a relaxed and leisurely atmosphere, of the various cultural activities that the associations organised throughout the year, whilst appreciating a 'taste' of these different cultures. In the evenings concerts, cinema (a short film festival on the theme of diversity), more ethnic cuisine and *discomundi* (a DJ sound-system performed by Mestizo Promo) followed day activities for children and meetings on the topics of racism and immigration. Celebrities introduced the concerts. The immigrant associations also put on children's activities, theatre performances, fashion shows, and ethnic dance workshops. A famous children's celebrity visited the Festa to present a selection of poems and drawings from a competition on 'imagining the ideal world' sponsored by 'Club Super 3' (from the Catalan TV3 channel) and SOS Racisme.

The events were so numerous that it was impossible to observe all of them, so first let me offer some general reflections. The atmosphere was relaxed during the day with an audience composed mainly of families and children. Lunch and dinner were special times, with the public queuing to partake of the 'foods of the world'. Each 'restaurant in camouflage' (to quote a phrase from an interviewee) had a display of food and drink, often accompanied by the music of the place of origin. Towards evening the site filled up with teenagers and young people attracted by the music and exciting atmosphere. Although it was difficult to get detailed interviews with the immigrant associations' members as they were so busy, I was always welcomed with my questions and offered food etc. I drank a lot of mint tea in those three days!

It is important to mention that access to the event was not free: tickets cost 600 pesetas for a day or 1500 for the three days (around £2.30 and £5.75). I found this quite reasonable bearing in mind the professionalism of the organisation of the event and its 'mega-concert' delivery. However, the tickets were expensive enough to exclude many of the people who were being 'celebrated' – the new residents of Barcelona. Many members and representatives of immigrant groups felt the prices were too high. In the words of the leader of a multi-ethnic NGO which works with underprivileged youth in El Raval, 'we can cover the entrances of the kids, but it's expensive ... the kids can't bring their parents ... we have some free entrances, but we need to rotate the kids ... it is not enough'.

Reactions from the Catalan public attending the festival were unequivocally positive. 'I like it ... that's why I come here every year.' 'Different people, cultures, a mix ... I like it, it is important.' 'I think it is a good idea ... it's a way for all people to know the communities who live here in Barcelona ... a way to show friendship.' 'The Festa is an extraordinary meeting place ... it is a necessity, a very positive thing.' 'It helps people open their minds ... in a festival like this people become more aware ... the event is very important for the associations that are invited to work here.'

The festival receives comprehensive media coverage – press, radio, television – at local and national level. The reportage portrays the event as a yearly-awaited appointment where the city celebrates diversity and rediscovers the many cultures that reside there – 'an anti-racist heaven' (*El Periódico*, 5 May 1999). For most newspaper articles the most notable feature is the incredible selection of 'foods of the world' on offer: '*La degustación de especialidades gastronómicas exóticas es uno de los principales atractivos de la fiesta*' (*La Vanguardia*, 5 May 1999). The quality of the evening concerts and gigs is highlighted by the space given to the music in many press reports. If diversity is the key word for food, for the music the key terms are hybridity, fusion, *mezcla*. The Festa is also seen as a useful platform for the launch of new musical groups. Some articles mention the activities of SOS Racisme and the political issues linked to immigration.

A few articles adopt a more critical stance. In one piece the space of the Festa was seen as a kind of artificially constructed ghetto compared to the everyday multi-ethnic spaces of certain *barrios* of the city, and the question of access and expense was raised (*Avui*, 12 May 1999). In *El Mundo* (9 May 1999) a journalist expressed her concerns over certain aspects of 'otherness' projected by the Festa, drawing attention to the myth of the '*bon savage*' and to questions of exoticism and essentialism. The utopia of the celebration of diversity was contrasted with the exclusion of 'ethnic cleansing at the entrances to the city's night-clubs'.

I conclude my interpretation of the *Festa de la Diversitat* by enlarging on four critical points: that the event involves a *ritualisation of ethnicity*, that it represents a *commodification of culture*, that there are issues of *participation and exclusion*, and that the Festa can become *politicised*.

Ritualisation of ethnicity

The Festa has been criticised as a 'ritualisation of ethnicity' (Bissoundath 1994) and for the exoticism behind the event as a 'performance of culture'. Local anthropologist Nora Muntañola-Thornberg describes the reaction of one of her Gambian friends who said to her with a big smile: 'So, Nora, you are here to see me with my authentic dress'. When she was saying this she was wearing jeans and a blouse; a short while later she was 'transformed' into a Madinke from Calamtz, Gambia (Muntañola-Thornberg 1997, p. 4).

Compared to the other events I observed, the *Festa de la Diversitat* seemed to be the place where it was 'expected' that the immigrants would don their traditional costumes. This expectation emerged through interviews with local Catalans attending the festival. All were enthusiastic about being exposed to so many colours, music, aromas and costumes. Traditional clothing was seen as a part of the aesthetic, accepted and welcomed within the context of the Festa. Hence the Festa was the place 'to see how the others are, what they eat, what they look like … it is good to appreciate the flavour of all this different cuisine, to know their customs, their way of dressing'. 'Here it is necessary that they dress up, I mean that they make themselves distinct from us.' But the exceptionality of the situation of the Festa was also made clear: 'in normal life it is important that we all … dress the same and behave the same'. Another interviewee went further: 'It is difficult for barriers to be overcome if the Arabs keep on dressing according to their customs…'

Hence there is a sense in which the Festa offers Barcelona people, once a year, a setting where they can observe diversity. But, Muntañola-Thornberg wonders (1997, p. 10), can diversity only happen in a confined and highly structured place? Delgado (1998a, p. 12) takes this point further: 'In the end, what are the *festes de la diversitat* or the *semanas de la tolerancia* if not a kind of ethnic zoo in which the general public can get close to, even touch, the specimens which shape the human ethnodiversity? Like the lions in the zoo, the members of the ethnic minority communities cannot hide from the public gaze on these occasions; they have to remain visible at all times.'

Delgado's zoo metaphor was reiterated in some of the interviews. In the words of a member of a local NGO, 'it's a bit like a zoo ... oh, look at the Filipinos, ah, the Moroccans ... with their couscous'. According to a Chilean immigrant 'this is the part I don't like, it's a kind of mini-zoo ... also there is a tendency to see the foreigner as something exotic'. Mohammed said 'the gastronomic side – the way in which it is presented – OK, you get to know the food but that doesn't mean you get to know the culture'.

Others, however, challenged the negative connotation of exoticism and defended the ethnic ritualisation. 'Why say it is an exotic festival? Is this exotic? No, everyone has their traditions.' 'Folklore? Why? No, I think food and drink are part of the tradition ... as in Spain we drink wine.' A woman from the Philippines stressed the value of the Festa for allowing the different migrant groups to get to know each other: 'It is very important for us because the other immigrants who live here can get to know our culture, our food, our dances ... this is good for us... In this kind of occasion we can express our feelings and our value as a people.' A Chilean man put it this way: 'My country of origin is my biography ... when I stress my country of origin, I put an accent on my history, my biography ... on what has left a very strong impression on me.'

NGO spokespersons highlighted some of the practical difficulties in guarding against the danger of cultural ritualisation. The Artistic Director of SOS Racisme claimed that 'even if everything in the Festa seems compartmentalised, everybody is there and that creates its own mix which is dynamic'. Another argued that 'in two days you need to give a synthesis ... food is part of the Festa ... a lot of people pass through and need to eat'. Other NGO workers acknowledged the danger of creating stereotypes, but insisted that not all stereotypes were bad. For instance: 'I agree that we need to go beyond stereotypes but at the beginning ... which is the best way to give a flash of knowledge in order to balance the negative stereotypes ... even if the flash produces other stereotypes ... and are stereotypes only bad?' And another interviewee: 'yes, yes, without a doubt, a lot of people say that the Festa is very folkloristic but you cannot deny folklore ... and the good is that each group represents their country as they wish to ... who are we to judge this? It is a way for them to express themselves'.

Let me conclude by referring to two problems which seem to me to have particular weight when considering the folklorisation and ritualisation of ethnic cultures at the Festa. The first is that presenting the Festa as pure entertainment obscures the real lives and problems endured by many immigrants. As a Moroccan student put it to me: 'the people who come here, the Catalans, they see it as a circus. It is good for a day out, to have a good time, instead of going to Maremagnum [the main leisure and clubbing district of Barcelona], but not for the objective of knowing a culture, thinking of the immigrants, the problems they have...'

The second issue concerns what I would term the compulsion to be 'different' or, as Delgado (1998b) has put it, 'the right to be non-different' or even 'indifferent'. Delgado poses the question: what exactly is being proclaimed in the 'multicultural shows' when the gypsies spend their time reading palms and the North Africans are feverishly preparing plates of couscous? The implications are that in (Catalan) society there are *normal* persons and *different* persons, that the *different* ones are always *them*, that the essence of their difference is their 'culture' rather than their position (at the lowest end) in the social structure, and finally that the differences which are being presented are irrevocable. In other words, the Festa places immigrants on a stage to dramatise their difference. It denies the individual migrant the right to be anonymous, to stay reserved, or to express an identity which is theirs alone.

Commodification of culture

Many interviewees lamented the fact that the Festa has become more and more commercialised over the years, in other words that the event is less about migrants' being encouraged to express their own identities through cultural symbols, and more about the supply of a product that is demanded and consumed by the 'market'. Here are some typical reactions: 'Nowadays the Festa is more than anything a business for the associations ... they do food in order to raise money ... they have lost their original goal.' 'It's rather superficial ... you go, you get the food you like and that's it, there's no exchange of ideas.' 'There's too much commercialisation ... everybody's selling things ... it has lost the enchantment of solidarity.'

To these reactions from Catalan 'customers' can be added other views and interpretations from the migrant associations and from the organisers of the Festa. Generally SOS Racisme is critical of associations which only focus on selling food and drink instead of using the Festa to promote the year-round activities they organise. However, many SOS workers stress the importance of the event for migrant groups' fund-raising, pointing out that the Festa is their only commercial activity, without which they could hardly survive. Yet another critical slant is the feeling that some associations appear as if by magic at the time of the festival and are invisible for the rest of the year.

The migrant associations themselves acknowledge the importance of the Festa for income generation but also point to rising costs. A leader of a Gambian association lamented that 'we make very little ... there is money but there are lots of costs'. These costs are above all to do with renting a stand, for which the rate varies between 36,000 and 54,000 pesetas (*circa* £140–£210) according to the size of the stand and provision of cooking facilities. This was the main point of criticism coming from the migrant groups, who tended to suggest that the Festa is big business for SOS Racisme.

This is not the place to go into this issue in detail, not least because of the confidentiality of the information I have access to. Clearly the entrance charge and the perceived high rental for the stands set the context for the commercial viability of the Festa as well as issues of participation. SOS Racisme naturally wishes to guard against going into deficit over the event, also because the Festa supplements all kinds of other activities. It is certain that, if the Festa is to be regarded as a business for SOS Racisme, the profits do not get shared amongst the employees, who are quite poorly paid compared to equivalent NGO workers elsewhere in Europe.

Participation

Although more than 100 associations take part in the Festa, I was not able to put my finger on the precise criteria for selection. A Senegalese interviewee was rather upset at not being allowed to mount a stand: 'This was the first time I went to SOS Racisme to ask ... we wanted to be here to raise funding to send to Senegal ... but they said no ... I don't know why.' In principle groups can participate if they can demonstrate that they can organise a series of activities during the year and have a programme of debates and entertainment during the

Festa. The selection is carried out by CITA, a branch of SOS Racisme responsible for liaison with immigrant groups and societies. Generally groups which had participated successfully in previous years were retained if their relationship with SOS Racisme had been good, or at least unproblematic. I was authoritatively told that some of the groups that were the most critical of SOS in the past were no longer in the programme. One of the volunteers at CITA admitted to me that there was something of a class divide among the associations: the migrant groups which were 'middle-class' and well integrated were more likely to achieve regular participation in the Festa than those which represented more marginalised groups of migrants.

If participation as part of the event is an issue, participation in the ownership and decision-making of the Festa is even more contentious. SOS Racisme was denounced a couple of years ago in a public letter signed by more than 20 associations for not allowing the migrants to have a proper voice in the organisation of the Festa. Here is an abridged and translated version of that document.

> For the attention of SOS Racisme, local, regional and national administrations, the media, public opinion.
>
> **Diversity ... of criteria**
>
> There is a considerable uneasiness among many immigrant associations with regard to the *Festa de la Diversitat* organised by SOS Racisme. Since the first edition of the Festa the feeling has been growing that the organisers do not take into account the immigrants and the other participating groups.
>
> Of course the Festa is made by SOS Racisme and they have the right to organise it as they wish. But we believe that the opinions of the immigrants should be considered more. This should be for the objectives of the Festa – around the theme of cultural diversity – and for the people who contribute the contents – the groups which put up their stands, play music, perform dances, do fashion shows.
>
> They count on us as suppliers of services ... but if this is the role reserved for us ... we feel conditioned by it ... (and we have) the feeling of being used when we are asked 30,000 or 60,000 pesetas to set up a stand for the sale of handicrafts or food. And if they trust us so little that they demand a signature in advance of a formal contract the relationship ceases to be one of mutual trust and collaboration towards a common objective ... and becomes instead a purely commercial relationship, where SOS Racisme acts as a business which makes use of its powerful position.
>
> **The design of the Festa**
>
> Many people wonder why it is necessary to pay for having a stand if the Festa receives sponsorship and donations from the various administrations... We

understand that the organisation of an event of this size costs a lot of money, but it also depends on what is conceived. Opting for mega-concerts with famous stars implies a distribution of funds to the detriment of other aspects. Even if these artists do not demand their normal fees, the money that they receive still contrasts painfully with the fact that many migrant music groups play for nothing, not even covering their costs, in return for the opportunity of 'being known'.

It is not clear if the mega-concerts are of great utility in fighting anti-immigrant stereotypes. The same money could be dedicated to other projects with the same, or bigger, results.

Bullying?

We would like to make it clear that this is not only an economic issue. We also call attention to the attitude of the Permanent Commission of SOS Racisme.

We believe that, faced with the manifest unhappiness of a group of people and immigrant groups, the minimum they could have done would have been to listen to the reasons behind the complaints. Even if they ended by believing that we do not have any reasons, they would have had an interest in clarifying any possible misunderstanding by establishing a face-to-face dialogue, improving relations and exploring possible means to collaborate in the future. But no. We have been met with a very hard and inflexible response – 'the Festa is ours, take it or leave it'.

Above all, it is important to stress that we do not undervalue the importance SOS Racisme has for Catalan society. If we express ourselves publicly in this way it is because our intentions of talking about these things in a calm and respectful way have not made any progress. We think these issues need to be aired so that all the people involved in one way or another can give an opinion.

- We are not killjoys
- We only want SOS Racisme to stop and reflect
- We would like to be consulted
- We would like to open up a dialogue with a clear willingness to achieve an understanding

This document had been circulated a year before I did my fieldwork. I found it quite revealing that nearly all the signatory associations were not part of the 1999 Festa. Nevertheless some of the same views were expressed by members of migrant associations who did participate: 'sure, we accept the conditions...' (Chilean); 'It's SOS that organises everything, we just participate' (Kurd).

There is a meeting before the Festa to which SOS Racisme invites the various immigrant associations.[5] However, many of my informants told me that in reality the meeting is mainly to inform participants of procedures and there is very little consultation. In theory it is a forum where the immigrant groups can voice their opinion and make suggestions, but there is disillusionment about whether their views are listened to. Here is a Gambian view: 'As an association they invite us to a meeting ... but when I get to this meeting I find that the programme has already been sorted out ... so I don't think I can make a contribution... I would like to give ideas, to help organise... I think that we could contribute ... because we have the experience of participating from one year to the next ... (so we know) what works, what are the difficulties ... if they would ask us... I think it would be useful to change a few things...' A Moroccan interviewee gave a very similar interpretation. 'They ask us for opinions ... (but) ... only when they have organised everything do they call us to give us information – you need to pay this, you need to pay that ... this year they sent us a paper to tell us about the arrangements ... what they have changed, what they were going to do ... they have not taken our opinion...'

Another impression I got when I interviewed the associations was that there were some that knew that they had a favoured position and others who were less trusted. For instance, a member of a Filipino association told me: 'Yes, SOS Racisme say that of all the associations that collaborate with them, we are the most loyal, the most punctual in paying...' The Filipinos realise, of course, that participation in the Festa is a good opportunity for fund-raising, contacts, and publicising future activities. Nevertheless it seems that the differential of power between, on the one hand, SOS Racisme as controller of the organisation and funding of the Festa, and on the other the migrant associations as invited and selected participants, makes an equal dialogue difficult to achieve.

Politicisation

Some took the opportunity of the Festa to address political issues. Everywhere there were stickers that expressed solidarity for Kosovo – '*somos todos Kosovaros*'. There was a passionate debating session on the Saharawi situation.[6] Several stands exhibited political statements. Whilst this was clearly a setting for immigrant groups to express their opinions, there was criticism of SOS Racisme for not being fully in control of what was happening. Episodes of racism were reported to me. I heard of a Serbian dissident who left the Festa feeling alienated and threatened by the anti-Serb atmosphere and after having read the slogan 'Death to all Serbs' on a stand. The Jewish organiser of the '*Mostra del Curtmetratge de la Diversitat*' – an exhibition of short films on diversity – was offended by some anti-Jewish writings on the T-shirt of a Lebanese stand-holder, having been made aware of the content of the slogans after they were translated for him by an Arab-speaking friend. Yet he was also sensitive to the difficulties involved: 'SOS as an institution is not guilty for what happens ... but it should be more vigilant ... once you import foreign conflicts within the Festa, it becomes politicised and excludes other groups.' This is exactly the problem: diversity is challenged by the very celebration of diversity.

The Festa was also a high-profile setting for local politics. Many political and public figures visited and spoke at the Festa, using it as an opportunity to voice their opinion not only about the central issue of migration but also about wider political and party themes. Not unnaturally, there were banners throughout the festival site reminding visitors of the various campaigns SOS Racisme was engaged in with regard to immigration and anti-racism. A *patera* (a flimsy boat used for bringing immigrants across the Gibraltar strait) was built and exhibited by SOS volunteers in order to stress the drama and the danger of 'illegal' immigration, and signatures were taken to lobby for migrants' rights to vote and for the closure of the detention centres for illegal migrants.

As a non-native Spanish speaker, one of the things that struck me about the whole experience of the Festa was the use of Catalan as the language for most of the event, including all the public announcements. I found it quite strange that Catalan should be used if one of the key aims of the Festa was to include non-Catalans. Hardly any of the immigrants I met at the Festa could speak fluent Catalan, although many were trying to learn it. As part of my duties as a part-time helper at the Festa I had to contact actors and actresses to introduce the music performances; their involvement was necessary to raise the profile of the event and therefore attract more media attention. Before the meeting with these celebrities I had agreed with my team-mates to lead the talks in Spanish since my fluency in Catalan was at that time quite limited. There was a sudden switch into Catalan when I argued, with little success, for the concert presentation to be done in Spanish so that everyone could understand. In the end it was decided that each speaker should use the language he or she preferred. All those I heard were in Catalan.

Summing-up

Despite the criticisms which I have presented, I believe that the Festa is a very important opportunity for raising awareness across the city of the issue of immigration and multi-ethnicity. Many associations valued the Festa as a way of networking with other groups, getting to know what is being done in the field and starting co-ordinated action for common aims. A Pakistani: 'Yes, it is a very good opportunity ... it's the biggest festival in Catalonia for the immigrants ... we meet, we talk, and then we call each other ... and we do things together.' And a Moroccan: 'The Festa is especially good for uniting all immigrants, for instance between Colombians and Moroccans, and by working with them, we get to know them ... we can keep in contact and solve problems together.' A DJ stressed the importance of the party atmosphere: '... for me it is very important that the Festa exists because it has the character of a party, a popular celebration... I like the Festa in terms of its musical achievements.'

The positive response from local interviewees reveals the strong need for information about how Barcelona is changing although there remains some uncertainty whether this corresponds to a genuinely concerned demand for knowledge about 'the others' or merely a fun 'day out'. Finally the participation of so many volunteers (about 500) in the event and in its four months of preparation creates abundant opportunities for these mostly young people from schools, youth groups and NGOs to discuss and promote issues of multiculturalism, diversity, integration and anti-racism. These experiences extend beyond framework of the Festa itself and help forge networks of solidarity and friendship that are more enduring.

In the remainder of the chapter I contextualise the Festa by comparing it to three other public events I observed during my fieldwork: *Feria d'Abril*, *Setmana Intercultural del Casc Antic* and an urban sport and music event in the *barrio* of El Raval.

Feria d'Abril

Each year the Andalusians in Spain celebrate various religious and leisure events. *Feria d'Abril* is an annual festival of Andalusian traditions, an opportunity for social gathering, dancing, rodeos and culinary feasts. The *Feria d'Abril* in Catalonia is the second largest after the one in Seville. In 1999 attendance across the ten-day festival was estimated at 2 million. This is due to a very high concentration of Andalusian migrants and their descendants in Catalonia, as well as the popularity of Andalusian tradition amongst other people living in Catalonia.[7]

In 1999 the location of the Feria changed from its traditional site in the district of Santa Coloma to a new one within the municipality of Sant Adrià de Besós on the outskirts of Barcelona. The new location has a rather unique setting. The festival boundaries are the old incinerator on one side, the water filter system on the other, and the sea. All around are old tower blocks and construction sites. This is one of the regeneration areas under the Barcelona Forum 2004 project mentioned earlier. The organisers of the Feria, the Federació d'Entitats Culturals Andaluses in Catalunya (FECAC), decided to change the location of the event once the Sant Adrià authorities had given assurance that this could be the permanent site. The Feria is beyond the administrative boundaries of the Barcelona City Council but sufficiently close to attract the residents and support of the city.

Within the Feria site are set up about 60 tents (*casetas*) by various Andalusian cultural groups. Each *caseta* has a stage and a restaurant area, and generates a close sense of 'community'. Andalusian food and drink are sold within the premises and flamenco and *sevillana* music set the musical atmosphere. Traditional dress is worn by many participants. Horses form another integral part of the landscape of the Feria, with men and women exhibiting their skills at rodeos. People of all ages join in the festival and the general atmosphere is of a very friendly social and community event.

For the 1999 Feria, the organisers of the programme promised to take special advantage of the seaside position. According to the local newspaper's special Feria edition, 'The night of 2 May, the closure of the Feria will be on the beach. Together with the usual speeches from various personalities, there will be singing of *habaneras* (traditional Catalan fishermen's songs, with Cuban origins) and everyone will be offered a *cremat de ron*. It will be a most Catalan ending. Fireworks on the beach will follow.'

So much for a summary of the main events and character of the Feria. I now make some comparisons between the *Feria d'Abril* and the *Festa de la Diversitat*; such comparisons are particularly interesting as regards interpretations of essentialism and multiculturalism in Barcelona.

When I asked my Catalan friends and interviewees at the Festa whether they had been to the Feria, there were mixed responses. Some highlighted the political significance of the Feria. '*Feria d'Abril* is the real explosive bomb ... not the few "feathered Indians" or "good blacks" of the *Festa de la Diversitat*... Millions of people go to the Feria ... lots of votes ... all the politicians put in an appearance at the *Feria d'Abril*.... Even the Catalan Nationalist Party has a stand...' Others were put off by the exclusivity of the Feria, which was seen as reproducing and reflecting the migrant Andalusian ghettos in Barcelona in the 1950s and 1960s: 'rather than making the *Feria d'Abril* so big ... it would be good if they could make an exhibition of all the different Spanish communities who live here, not only one ... it becomes a ghetto'.

Then there is the issue of authenticity. One interviewee told me: 'The *Feria d'Abril* I really like is the one in Seville ... that is where it really happens.' According to a SOS spokesperson, 'one cannot pretend that it is authentic ... it is not a product of Andalusia ... more like a reproduction. The industrial conglomerate of Barcelona is the producer ... and the kind of people who go is different [from those who attend the Feria in Seville]'. So, who goes to the *Feria d'Abril*? 'It is the people who have been born here ... it is the young people, they have taken from their parents (first-generation Andalusians) this theme ... some of them have just discovered it ... things that before were rejected and that are now rediscovered'. Is it therefore a question of identity? 'It is a created identity ... there are some people who experience a certain rejection from Catalan society and therefore express themselves through the Feria...'

But how does the expression of identity that is manifest in the Feria differ from that expressed in the *Festa de la Diversitat*? After all, also at the Festa many people dressed up in their traditional costumes, played the music of their countries and displayed and sold their characteristic products. If this 'performance' at the Feria is interpreted as a reaction arising from feelings of rejection by Catalan society, why is it instead celebrated at the Festa? Is the diversity of the Feria somehow more threatening than the diversity of the Festa?

If we read the Feria through the essentialist critique, there was certainly quite an effort geared to 'reproducing' the Andalusian character. Somehow, the *Feria d'Abril* appeared to me as even more essentialist than the *Festa de la Diversitat*. The dresses, the dances (especially flamenco), the food and the drinks were rituals of tradition and performance that suggested that the Feria was very much a stage for a rehearsed demonstration of Andalusian culture.

But exactly how different is the essentialism played out in the Feria from the one enacted by the commemoration of national heritage at the Festa? Where is the boundary between essentialism and the inter-cultural and inter-generational transmission of traditions? The Feria also contains an element of exoticism. The Catalan public visits the Feria because it is a leisure event – a place where one can dance, drink and be entertained by 'diversity' or at least by something 'different'. As one woman told me, 'it gives a whole different experience of Barcelona'. Some of the young workers and volunteers whom I got to know at SOS Racisme went to the Feria for a night of dancing and living the 'flamenco experience'.

In fact, the very recognition of the non-authenticity of the Feria compared to the 'real Andalusian' experience, and the realisation that the Feria itself emerges out of the social reality of life in Barcelona for the Andalusian community, make the event even more interesting to study. In the end, the Feria is a testimony to the shift in the overall 'culture' of

Barcelona which has been produced by the Catalan economy's historic need for particular types of labour. Given the size and geographical position of Spain, the migration of Andalusians to Barcelona can also be seen as another variant of the 'Mediterranean Passage' – from a hot, southern region, almost African in character, to Catalonia, the 'European north' of Spain.

Moreover, the Feria challenges the fixity of Catalan culture. By stating in the press that the event will end in a very Catalan way – by the chanting of *habaneras* and the drinking of *cremant de ron* – FECAC were already representing the hybrid nature of Catalan popular culture, and reinterpreting this syncretism of Andalusia and Catalonia within the Feria. At the same time, by opening up the beach-side site to Catalan traditions FECAC challenges the authentic reproduction of the 'Sevillana' by reaffirming the territoriality of the Barcelona Feria within Catalonia.

Delgado (1998a) has analysed the evolution of Andalusian traditions within Catalonia and how they have been reinterpreted and reinvented within the new context so as to become a specific product of Catalonia, distinct from the 'authentic' Andalusian version. For instance, until very recently, traditional Andalusian religious rites were celebrated in Catalonia without priests. The Catholic Church in Catalonia refused to participate in these Andalusian ceremonial rituals, seeing them as non-Catalan and pagan in origin. Hence the new Andalusian residents celebrated them spontaneously and independently of the Church – but with the support of the Catalan leftist administration who, quite apart from ideological concerns, were keenly aware of the electoral significance of the large Andalusian population in the region. Now, the Church has started to acknowledge and celebrate the Andalusian religious festivals, re-appropriating the 'authenticity' of these rites. The result, according to Delgado, is the development of new hybrid forms of religious ceremony which are quintessential products of the Catalonian context.

But there is another context in which we can interpret the *Feria d'Abril* as both Andalusian and a product of Barcelona/Catalonia: this is the framework of post-Franco Catalan cultural politics of 'normalisation'. Delgado (1998a, p. 50) points out that the cultural events of Andalusian inspiration in Catalonia gather together every year not only hundreds of thousands of citizens of Andalusian origin but also similarly large numbers of Catalans and of participants who originate from other parts of Spain – for instance from Extremadura in the south-west, Galicia in the north-west, and from various of the 'core' Spanish regions of Castille. Delgado suggests that there is an awareness within the Catalan political establishment of the strategic importance of a powerful feeling of ethnic Andalusian ascription.

By facilitating the expression of Andalusian ethnic identity, it has been possible to exorcise the danger of the emergence of a Castillian/Spanish idiomatic base that would have divided the population into two great antagonistic blocs – Catalan and Castillian. The promotion of *andalusianidad* thus suited Catalan politics and linguistic planning by 'avoiding a definitive establishment of a Castillian-Spanish identity amongst the immigrants and their descendants' (Delgado 1998a, p.50).

Could it be that the same strategy is repeated with the newcomers from abroad? Maybe the moral and financial support of the Ajuntament and the Generalitat in favour of cultural diversity is part of the same process of protecting the Catalan identity from the Spanish-Castillian threat. By promoting the expression of diverse identities within Catalonia and by constructing as Catalan 'whoever lives and works in Catalonia' (Pujol 1988, p.17), immigrants are incorporated within Catalonia with their particular cultural identities whilst at the same time they are distanced from an 'unavailable' Castillian-Spanish identity. 'Diversity' as non-Spanish is highlighted whilst the value of recognising cultural heritage is reaffirmed – including the Catalan heritage. Here perhaps originates the strong respect for Catalan identity I found amongst many immigrant interviewees, including their regret and shame at the slow progress they had made toward learning the Catalan language.[8]

Setmana Intercultural del Casc Antic

Compared to the Festa and the Feria, the *Setmana Intercultural* has a low-key character but achieves a lot in terms of participation and intercultural contact. It is a week-long event organised by a collective of neighbours and intercultural associations with the support of the Generalitat and the City Council. The main activities are debates, concerts, dances, theatre, workshops, exhibitions and children's entertainment.

The 1999 *Setmana Intercultural* was the fourth edition of the event, which started in 1996 as a response to a violent incident in the *barrio* – a Moroccan was badly beaten up by the police. People living in the neighbourhood felt that the incident was symbolic of what was happening to this area, an old part of the city centre cut off from the touristic gaze, with widespread poverty and an increasing presence of immigrants. In the words of one of my key informants, a member of the Migra–Media group,

> With the arrival of new residents, many of them without work and documents, there was an increase in criminality and in social conflicts, both amongst the different immigrant communities and with the local people. The episode of violence from the police against the young Moroccan was a further example of how difficult life was getting in this area. On the one hand the *barrio* was controlled by youth gangs, and on the other it was an open battleground for

clashes with the police. The residents of the area felt scared and alienated... Led by the belief that the lack of communication between the new residents and the old-established communities did not help to solve the conflicts, various groups started to liaise with all the communities living in the *barrio*. A large communal dinner was collectively organised by the neighbours and the new residents... The aim was to 'repossess' the *barrio*, to feel at home once again, and to build bridges of communication between the new and the old residents.

A *Plataforma Integral del Casc Antic* was created with the participation of various representatives of cultural associations and immigrant groups to represent the *barrio* in dealing with the City Council, to campaign for regeneration and social support for the area, and to project a different image of the place. The *Setmana Intercultural* developed from the initial work of the *Plataforma* and includes a replica of the first dinner. The event has now become part of the celebration of the *Festa Mayor del Barrio* (in Catalan, *Festa Major del Barri*).[9]

The atmosphere I observed in the 1999 *Setmana Intercultural* was very participative and collaborative. People were working together for a common goal, without the control of a higher institution such as SOS Racisme or FECAC. The location of the event – in one of the main squares of the *barrio* and in an adjacent converted monastery – made it accessible to everybody in the *barrio* and easily reachable by 'outsiders'. The *barrio* is still considered quite a dangerous part of the city; tourists usually avoid walking in the labyrinth of its little streets. The event was an opportunity for people to perceive and use the barrio with a different attitude – one of 'festa' rather than fear. For people living in the *barrio*, it was a chance to demonstrate that by working together the quality of life in the area could be improved.

Moreover, the event was accessible because it was free. Even the unemployed and irregular migrants – who in other settings would be excluded – could freely join in. The crowd was very diverse – multi-ethnic, many generations and classes. The location of the event allowed for the spontaneous involvement of people passing through. Concerts gave an opportunity for local groups to perform. Since participation was free – both for the audience and for the cultural associations and their stands – the event did not have to be 'commercial' and pay off its costs. The cooking was therefore not a buy-and-sell relation but an exchange, a further opportunity for intercultural communication. People were not performing their culture for customers but living it for their own entertainment and for sharing it with others.

Cooking workshops were offered in the mornings. Various groups of women – and a few men – were cooking and explaining to whoever was interested the process of preparation of the food and the recipes. I saw food being prepared by migrants from Honduras, Ecuador, Morocco and the Philippines, and by a local woman giving a workshop on Catalan cuisine. The inclusion of Catalan cooking completely changed the nature of the event, making it no longer an exhibition of the dishes of the 'other' but rather a statement on the different ways food is prepared in the *barrio*.

This mixing of Catalan and immigrant traditions was a recurrent theme throughout the week, including children's activities. One of these was to initiate the children of the *barrio* – many of them of migrant parents – in the very Catalan tradition of *correfoc*. This somewhat bizarre activity sees teams dressed up as devils, appropriately covered and protected, running under fireworks and spinning crackers.

I recall lots of images from the *Setmana Intercultural*: the gender divide reproduced in the Raj dances, the father who started dancing and lost his shopping, the participation of an Arabic-speaking ship's crew, the elderly people watching from the balconies, the kids playing as *diables*, the old Catalan woman who proudly joined in the cooking demonstrations, the Moroccan wedding.

How does the *Setmana Intercultural* differ from the *Festa de la Diversitat*? One could say that this was a mini-*Festa de la Diversitat*. Certainly the accent was on diversity, but this was the living diversity of the *barrio* rather than a chosen or stage-managed diversity as in the Festa. And Catalan traditions were here represented as part of this diversity rather than singled out as the 'norm'. Because the everyday setting of the *barrio* was the centre of the celebration, everybody was included. In fact it was difficult to know who were the organisers and who were the audience: all were having a good time. Everyone was invited to join in and there was no entrance fee; it was not a market relation between those offering a product to match an imagined demand. As a result the attitude of the public was rather different – I would describe it as more humble and appreciative. The people who attended the event were mostly residents of the *barrio* and their friends. When I talked to so-called 'outsiders', the feeling was one of gratitude for being allowed to share the spontaneous 'diversity'. Here traditional dress was not worn as a performance for an audience but because it was part of everyday experience. The gaze of the spectator – allowed in a quasi-private space – was therefore more respectful than in the *Festa de la Diversitat*. By being located in the *barrio*, the event was able to reach all age groups: children, teenagers, adults, families, the elderly. Older people did not need to make an effort to get to the event; the event was brought to them and they could watch and involve themselves from their windows and balconies. Finally the open boundaries and lack of entrance charge meant that *clandestinos* could join in as well. Undocumented immigrants did not have the fear of being recognised or picked up by the police. This was their *barrio* and their festa as well.

I conclude this brief account with an anecdote that in many ways sums up the spontaneous and informal character of the *Setmana Intercultural*. An Arab man who just walked through the square, coming home with bags of shopping for his family, was completely surprised by what was going on. Hearing the sound of traditional Moroccan music, he dropped the bags and started dancing next to me in a kind of happy trance. The bags were in the way of other dancers and so a local woman took them away to a safer place in case they got trodden on. When the man woke up from his dance-trance and was ready to go home he could not find his bags. He started asking everybody 'where is my shopping? It was the food for my children, I cannot lose it... Where is it? I spent 1000 pesetas [about £4] on it.' His despair at not finding the shopping after he had spent what he felt was a lot of money made me feel his poverty. I had seen the woman move the bags and I told him someone had taken them away so they did not get trampled on. Then he got very worried that she had stolen the food. Eventually the woman reappeared and fetched the shopping for him.

This little incident sets the *Setmana Intercultural* apart as a more intimate and spontaneous event compared to the *Festa de la Diversitat*. There, a walkie-talkie call to a security person would have settled the affair, with the poor man being taken away from everybody's eyes. Here the incident became an opportunity for everybody to get involved and a further example of constructive intercultural dialogue within the *barrio*. A few Arab men tried to calm the father down and backed up the woman who had moved, and not wanted to steal, the shopping bags. I was dragged into the whole thing because I had observed the bags being moved, and I asked myself whether I should have reacted differently to the man's questions when he returned to look for his bags. In the end, the whole episode was a learning experience for everybody – me included.

El Raval: hip-hop and skating

In the three events I have described up to now the focus was on traditions – although with varying degrees of essentialism in their representation and translation across space. In El Raval I encountered a manifestation of global youth culture here translated within the specificity of another of Barcelona's inner-city *barrios*.

The gentrification process in the increasingly multi-ethnic El Raval has created an interesting and dynamically evolving social mix in this zone of crumbling houses, restoration and some modern building. Alongside poor native families live newly-arrived immigrants (some of whom are now quite long-established), gypsies, artists and professionals. The modern architecture of the Museum of Contemporary Arts (MACBA) and the Centre for Contemporary Culture (CCCB) contrasts with the faded facades and typical old tapas bars of the surrounding buildings. Kids play and young people meet up in the large square in front of MACBA, including many Filipinos and North Africans. Here is 'everyday multiculturalism', diversity is visible: women in saris pushing prams; African and Asian women wearing the veil, often in combination with modern Western dress; Filipino children swarming out of the local school.

In June 1999, a few days after the *Setmana Intercultural*, a one-day skateboarding and hip-hop competition was organised by a young musician who belongs to the hip-hop group called Macaco which performed in the evening.[10] The event was located next to the aforementioned square, in a playground where youngsters usually gather to play basketball. The three walls that surround the playground are covered in graffiti. The square is a regular venue for skaters, who are attracted by the general ambience and the shape of the pavement. Hence the location of the skating competition built on ongoing social activity and an appropriate physical setting. The event was sponsored by retailers specialising in skating and youth fashion merchandise. Artists and musicians from Mama Latido[11] and *Festa de la Diversitat* were involved, and Mestizo Promo set up the sound system. The audience was mixed, made up of those who usually hang out in the square, others who came especially for the event, and casual passers-by who were attracted by the crowd and the music.

Compared to *Festa de la Diversitat* or the *Setmana Intercultural*, this event was not promoted within the specific framework of 'multiculturalism', diversity or anti-racism. Here 'diversity' was negotiated via global trends and a hybrid manifestation of culture; the hip-hop music and sound-systems carried inflections of Spanish and Latin American sounds. Above all, the style was that of global urban youth culture: baggy pants, large T-shirts, trainers, skates and bandanas with the logos of the best brands, displayed not only by the participants but also on the stands of the sponsors of the event.

This event was not a 'performance of culture' where culture is essentially interpreted in its traditional features. There was, however, here too an unwritten script that organisers and participants followed in order for the event to be successful. The 'script' was that of an urban metropolitan event; the ingredients were graffiti, the attitude of the performers, and sounds – hip-hop music mixed with the screeching of the skateboards and the hiss of spray-cans. Even if it represents a global trend, hip-hop has developed a particular personality from the specific urban context in which it emerges – New York, the French *banlieues*, or the inner city of Barcelona.[12] In El

Raval, the global experience of hip-hop culture was mediated by the local specificity not so much of Barcelona in general but of the mixture of peoples inhabiting this district. Hence globally recognised ingredients of sound-systems, graffiti and break-dancing were here infused with the undeniably Latin features of Macaco and Mestizo Promo.

The strong participation of young people at this event – most of the public were composed of teenagers and people in their 20s – contrasted with the lesser participation of these age-groups in festivals where the accent is on traditional culture. Clearly, the location of the event within the *barrio*, and even more specifically within the space that is frequented by youngsters of immigrant origin, made it much more accessible to them than the two mega-events described earlier. As with *Setmana Intercultural*, the event was free and offered independent of audience participation. In one sense, the feelings of self-sufficiency by the skaters in the square and the hypnotical sequence of break-dance routines set an atmosphere of autonomy so that the event was less participating for the non-*habitué* public. But the participation of the latter was not the main priority for the organisers: uppermost in their minds were the 'urban kids'. Thus, through the event, the identity of El Raval as a special multi-ethnic youth *barrio* was reaffirmed. The event built on the everyday activity of the young people living round the square (skateboarding), while simultaneously amplifying and promoting it. The participation of recognised music groups in their 'playground' conferred status on the skating youth of the *barrio*. Finally the event was a spotlighted opportunity for performing the skills so patiently practised day after day.

Conclusion

The clearest contrast in the four festivals I observed is between the large-scale, centrally-organised events of the *Festa de la Diversitat* and *Feria d'Abril* on the one hand, and the two smaller-scale celebrations I witnessed at El Raval and Casc Antic.

First of all, in the latter two events I found a spontaneous collective atmosphere which was different from that generated by the formalised organisational frameworks of the Festa and the Feria. The location of the smaller events in their respective *barrios* made them more accessible and more or less guaranteed that they had a strong impact at the local level. The Festa, on the other hand, represented a somewhat artificial bringing together of groups which normally would have rather limited encounters with each other in the city, since they lived in different areas and pursued different careers and lifestyles. Both the *Setmana Intercultural* and the skating competition state a specific place identity whilst challenging less diverse representations of Barcelona. Their locations in everyday social contexts made their statements on place identity and 'real' diversity all the more convincing. Their representations of authentic cultural diversity and their hopes for a more friendly cultural encounter were not compartmentalised as a 'special event' but underlined their normality in the everyday life of the city. The 'life of the *barrio*' was celebrated in its various concrete manifestations rather than caricatured in exaggerated and displaced 'ethnic performances'.

Second, the location of the two smaller events within their *barrios* and the lack of boundaries and charges of any kind made them accessible to everybody, beyond any target audience. As a result, it was possible to maximise diversity within the audience to reflect all socio-demographic groups within the city – not just the Catalan middle class, Andalusian families, young adults and students, but also the elderly, the unemployed, undocumented immigrants and otherwise alienated youth.

Third, both events were put on by collective effort between the initiators and the audience. The ownership of these two festivals was not in the hands of a strong institutional actor such as FECAC or SOS Racisme, but shared amongst the many stakeholders who were making the event 'happen'. Certainly the reduced size of the events made them more manageable and less of an economic enterprise. Likewise there were no political parades or posturing in Casc Antic or El Raval. As we have seen, the Festa and the Feria were stages for politicians to be seen and to be heard. I saw only one public figure in Casc Antic (a high-ranking official at the Ajuntament) but he was there in a very unofficial capacity, sitting on his bike chatting to some locals. Had I not known him I would have not recognised him. He was not there to 'parade'.

Compared to the Festa and the Feria, there was no big promotion or media coverage of the events in Casc Antic and El Raval, but the unofficial tam-tam within the *barrios* and the urban artistic community soon made the events well-known amongst those who needed to know. Their low-key character gave them less widespread visibility within and beyond the city but probably suited the objectives of real integration and cross-cultural socialisation much better. As I pointed out above, in the little squares and streets of El Raval and Casc Antic, people do not so much 'celebrate' their diversity as live it on a daily basis. Having said this, I do not want to denigrate the importance of the two big festivals for addressing the broader issues of multiculturalism in Barcelona. After all, there were lots of people at these festivals who were satisfied with what they saw and 'consumed', and maybe this is a valid first step in mass education for diversity. Furthermore, many appreciated the fact that, through these mega-events, Barcelona was declaring itself an 'open city' for diversity and the co-existence of cultural traditions. Politicians and NGOs welcomed the opportunity for networking and lobbying, whilst using the high attendance to support their anti-racist and pro-immigrant campaigns (Muntañola-Thornberg 1997). Undoubtedly the presence in the city of such a strong NGO as SOS Racisme and the organisation of big events like the *Festa de la Diversitat* are important in influencing policy-making and the media's portrayal of migration issues, with indirect effects on integration and combating xenophobia. Similar arguments can be made for the *Feria d'Abril* and its role in cultural and political negotiation with hard-core Catalan nationalists.

Notes

1   I did fieldwork in Barcelona between February and August 1999. This fieldwork forms part of my DPhil at the University of Sussex on immigrants, festivals and cultural policy in Bologna and Barcelona. This research is supported by an ESRC postgraduate studentship. In Barcelona I am very grateful for the help of Lorenzo, the Rodríguez family, the team of SOS Racisme especially Txus, Wagner of Mestizo Promo, Sandro of Macaco, Prof. Nora Muntañola-Thornberg and Prof. Verena Stolke at the Universitat Autonóma de Barcelona, and Prof. Manuel Delgago at the Universitat de Barcelona. At the University of Sussex, I owe special thanks to my supervisors, Prof. Russell King and Dr. Richard Black, and also to Prof. Ralph Grillo.

2   On immigration to Spain, see also Colectivo IOÉ (1999) and Malgesini *et al.* (1994).

3   Interestingly, gypsies are not included in the membership of the Consejo. They are represented instead by the Consejo del Pueblo Gitano. The idea behind the distinction is that the needs of the two groups (immigrants and gypsies) are different: gypsies have Spanish citizenship with no problems of recognition of political rights, however there are issues for them of cultural difference, tradition, stereotypes and discrimination that need to be addressed in a specific forum.

4   There was a sense of exaggerated representation of certain groups as opposed to the real demographic composition of the city. The celebration was very much of the cultures of 'the other' – non-Europeans from poor countries – with a notable absence of gypsy associations.

5   Unfortunately I had to miss this meeting, as I was unwell the day it took place.

6   For some background on the Western Sahara situation, including refugees in Spain, see Malheiros and Black (1997).

7   During my time in Barcelona I came to realise it was quite trendy to go to an authentic Andalusian night in one of the many Andalusian restaurants in town, and join in or watch flamenco dancing. Flamenco dancing classes are a popular post-school activity for children, and not only for *Barcelonins*. At the *Festa de la Diversitat* I was told that the Nigerian woman who helped SOS present the Festa on TV3, Club Super 3 and was in a hurry to get away at the end of filming was late for picking her daughter up from the *Sevillana* dance class.

8   Particularly revealing in this regard was an interview I had with a Syrian immigrant who had joined one of the Catalan Nationalist Parties. For him, 'integration is when you are proud of the culture where you stay... I left my home, my mother-country, and now I have reached a father-country even if I was not born here ... but I love the land where I am... I

am not a fanatic nationalist ... but this is the place I am a citizen of ... this makes me campaign for Catalonia to maintain its personality... I sympathise with this...'

9   In Barcelona, as in the rest of Spain, it is traditional for each *barrio* (or rural village) to celebrate the patron saint with a fiesta. In Casc Antic we see once again how old Catalan traditions are mixed with the customs of the new residents.

10 Macaco is a music group formed by Colombians, Argentineans, Brazilians and Spanish. It also performed at *Festa de la Diversitat*.

11 Mama Latido is a cultural association which was inaugurated in June 1999 with premises in Casc Antic. Its mission is to favour the cultural expression of all groups, offering its premises as a space for meetings for individuals and cultural associations wishing to organise celebrations or regular collaborative activities – 'a different space, available for the encounter of people of all ages and origins'. With its 'salad of cultures and artistic languages', the key-word of Mama Latido is *mestizaje cultural*. Time will tell whether it will really become a meeting-place for the various communities of the *barrio* or a trendy club for underground artists and alternative students.

12 According to Cannon (1997, p.150), hip-hop embraces a wide spread of interconnected street art which originated in the urban projects of New York in the late 1970s. It includes graffiti and dance as well as the specific music form known as 'rap'. Above all, hip-hop is rooted in an urban context. 'The origins of hip-hop from blacks, Puerto Ricans and other new immigrants in the United States make it attractive for other disenfranchised youth. Hip-hop in France is characterised to a great extent by its role as a cultural expression of resistance by young people to the racism, oppression and social marginalisation they experience within France's *banlieues* and its major town and cities' (Cannon 1997, p. 155). For a history of rap and hip-hop, see Toop (2000).

References

Bissoundath, N. (1994) *Selling Illusions: The Cult of Multiculturalism in Canada.* London: Penguin.

Cannon, S. (1997) *Paname City Rapping*: B-Boy in the *banlieues* and beyond, in Hargreaves, A. G. and McKinney, M. (eds) *Post-Colonial Cultures in France.* London: Routledge, pp. 150–66.

Colectivo IOÉ (1999) *Inmigrantes, Trabajadores, Ciudadanos.* Valencia: Universitat de Valencia, Patronat Sud-Nord.

Delgado, M. R. (1997) *Ciutat i Inmigració.* Barcelona: Centre de Cultura Contemporánia de Barcelona.

Delgado, M. R. (1998a) *Diversitat i Integració.* Barcelona: Empúries.

Delgado, M. R. (1998b) El derecho a la indiferencia, *El Pais*, 15 January.

Malgesini, G. *et al.* (1994) *Estranjeros en el Paraíso.* Barcelona: Virus Editorial.

Malheiros, J. and Black, R. (1997) De facto refugees in Portugal and Spain: state policy, informal strategies and the labour market, in King, R. and Black, R. (eds) *Southern Europe and the New Immigrations.* Brighton: Sussex Academic Press, pp. 182–204.

Muntañola-Thornberg, E. (1997) *Portraits of Diversity in a Catalan City.* Paper Presented to AES Meeting, Seattle, 6 March.

Pascual de Sans, A., Cordelús, J. and Solana Solana M. (2000) Recent immigration to Catalonia: economic character and responses, in King, R., Lazaridis, G. and Tsardanidis, C. (eds) *Eldorado or Fortress? Migration in Southern Europe.* London: Macmillan, pp. 104–24.

Permanent Observatory on Immigration in Barcelona (1999) *Foreign Immigration in Barcelona 1994–1997.* Barcelona: CIDOB Edicions.

Pujol, J. (1976) *La Inmigració, Problema i Esperança de Catalunya.* Barcelona: Nova Terra.

Toop, D. (2000) *Rap Attack #3: African Rap to Global Hip Hop.* London: Serpent's Tail.

5

Reinventing cultures: the contribution of the Cape Verdean community to the cultural dynamics of Lisbon

Alina Esteves and Maria José Caldeira

Introduction

For many years migratory movements were mainly seen from a quantitative and economic perspective. Researchers were interested in measuring the numbers of people involved, the productivity of foreign workers, the main sectors in which they worked, the remittances sent home, and the social and economic problems supposedly due to their presence and that of their offspring. This predominantly economic perspective did not take into account the positive, enriching and innovative contributions that migrants, as social and cultural beings, can bring to the host society. The hypothesis presented in this chapter is that appreciation of the important cultural contributions of immigrants to the diversity and social and cultural richness of the host society will lead people to view 'foreigners' not as strangers, but as different citizens. What we propose is that respect and mutual understanding will allow a less contentious acceptance of those who arrive, together with a better incorporation in the receiving society.

Jackson (1986) states that migration is, in itself, an act of change for the migrant with effects on both societies between which he or she moves. In this account we will only observe one of the societies where the changes take place, the side of the Portuguese society. However, one has to acknowledge that 'The Cape Verdean diaspora has an echo in the origin country, reflecting its features not only in the social fabric, which is continually reconstructed, but also in Cape Verdean culture' (Saint-Maurice 1997, pp. 47–8). Furthermore, the acculturation process is dialectic, so that the Cape Verdean immigrants in Portugal, owners of a particular set of cultural and social values, also undergo change. It is extremely difficult to remain immune or indifferent to the social features of the host society. The mass media, the relationship with other citizens (people from the receiving country and other immigrants) and the physical features of the environment do not allow the perpetuation and total reproduction of the habits, traditions and ways of living of the sending country. In the words of Saint-Maurice (1997), immigrants have to rebuild their identities.

In this chapter we will start off by presenting an overview of the history of Cape Verdean emigration, indicating the relative importance of Portugal in the context of the Cape Verdean diaspora. We will also include information on the main housing areas and economic sectors in which Cape Verdeans living in Portugal work. This will be followed by a theoretical consideration of culture as a fundamental variable of the insertion process in the receiving society and as a guarantor of the cohesion and identity of a group. The third part comprises the presentation of several cultural elements of the Cape Verdean community in Portugal, such as language, gastronomy, music and dance, literature, religious rituals and the appropriation of public space. It is the aim of this part of the research to see if the experience of Cape Verdeans living in Portugal has led to changes in their habits and customs brought from Cape Verde and if the abandoning of some traditions has occurred; or, on the contrary, if there has been a reproduction of several cultural expressions in order to reinforce the community cohesion and identity of the group. The main Cape Verdean cultural features incorporated by Portuguese society will be pointed out and the role of immigrants' associations in the diffusion of Cape Verdean culture will also be stressed. Finally, the main initiatives developed by local authorities to promote cultural exchange and the mutual knowledge of Portuguese and Cape Verdean cultures will be presented.[1]

Portugal in the geographical context of the Cape Verdean diaspora

Cape Verde, its history and population are inevitably linked to Portugal. The country is the result of a long-standing historical process that brought together in an archipelago with few resources Portuguese people and African slaves imported from other areas of the continent. With hard natural conditions, long droughts, scarce resources, and a feeble industrialisation process, the people living in these islands soon began to look for better opportunities in other countries. This led to the beginning of a real diaspora based on economic motivations and rapid population growth (Wils 1999). The migratory process of the Cape Verdean people is remarkable due to its dispersion, with important contingents scattered in several countries of three continents – America, Africa and Europe – and also due to the relative weight of the phenomenon (Carreira 1983).

The number of Cape Verdeans living abroad (estimated at 500,000) is higher than the resident population of the country – 400,000 in the mid–1990s.

The Cape Verdeans began their diaspora setting off in the American whalers that called at the archipelago. The permanent flows of emigration to the United States began in the 1870s, mainly involving labour that was going to work in the agriculture and textile sectors. This flow was broken in 1917 with the imposition of restrictive measures on the entrance of foreigners (mainly blacks and people with little schooling). After 1959 emigration to the US was resumed, with less intensity, because the entrance was regulated by quotas and the migrants from Cape Verde, at the time a Portuguese colony, were integrated in the Portuguese share. The North American authorities also gave preference to white people, leaving blacks, mainly from Cape Verde, in second place. Notwithstanding this, emigration to the US was maintained, albeit with smaller numbers of people, with the eventual result of forming the largest Cape Verdean community abroad (250,000 people, including offspring).

From the end of the 1920s until the 1940s, the most popular destinations for migrating Cape Verdeans were neighbouring African countries such as Senegal and the Ivory Coast, as well as Portuguese colonies like Guinea Bissau, São Tomé e Principe, Angola and Brazil, and later on Argentina. In the African countries under Portuguese administration, the Cape Verdeans were used both as labour force for agriculture and (the skilled ones) as civil servants. The option of Cape Verdeans for migrating to Portugal was often used as a platform to migrate to other European countries or even to the United States of America.

However, the real boom in Cape Verdean migration took place in the second half of the twentieth century, with a redirection in the destination choices towards certain European countries. Among these, and in a first phase, were the Netherlands (mainly to the city of Rotterdam where many skilled Cape Verdean men performed tasks related to seafaring), Portugal and Italy (this last destination attracted mainly women who migrated to go into domestic service); whilst France and Luxembourg were added in a second phase.

In the migratory context of Cape Verde, Portugal was often present, although the flows and the profile of the emigrants varied over time (França 1992). The first Cape Verdeans to settle down in Portugal belonged to the higher social strata of the archipelago and were mainly traders, landowners, civil servants and students. Later on, during the period between the mid–1960s and the mid–1970s, the flows intensified and the profile of the immigrating population changed. The migration of Portuguese workers to France and other North European countries, together with a colonial war that mobilised a huge number of men of working age, caused an impoverishment of the Portuguese labour market and the need to attract from the African colonies (overseas provinces as they were then called) a 'replacement' labour force. These workers were needed to carry out a range of public works considered essential to the development of Portugal and also for the private construction sector and industry. Cape Verde had a fundamental role in the supply of workers to build Lisbon's underground, the bridge over the Tagus, and several major roads etc. It was a predominantly male migration but it was difficult to assess the exact figures because Cape Verdeans were citizens of Portuguese nationality who replicated and substituted for the emigration cycle of Portuguese migrant workers in Europe.

After the de-colonisation process, many civil servants from the ex-colonies came to live in Portugal, and in this situation the Cape Verdean contingent was also important because they occupied positions in the public administration of the archipelago and in other Portuguese colonies. The majority had high educational levels and therefore constituted a skilled working force.

During the 1980s and 1990s, the migratory link to Portugal was maintained with family reunion and was based on already existing networks of contacts. After Portugal joined the European Union in 1986, a boom in public works, an increase in the construction of private housing and later the prestigious Expo '98, caused a growing need for an expanded labour force in Portugal (Malheiros 2000). The social networks of Cape Verdeans were then able to come into action, contacting relatives and friends who came to Portugal, some of them without documents.

The Cape Verdeans are today the largest immigrant community living in Portugal. The official figure presented by the Foreigners and Borders Service is 40,093 people on 31 December 1998; however there is an alternative estimate of twice that figure – 83,000 (see Embaixada do Cabo Verde 1999). Cape Verdeans are mainly found in three regions of Portugal. According to the official data, 87 per cent are in the Metropolitan Area of Lisbon (26,894 in Lisbon, 7,896 in Setúbal), with smaller groupings of 2,000–3,000 in Oporto, the second city of Portugal, and the Algarve, the main tourist region. In recent years, emigration flows from Cape Verde to Portugal have slackened off; nevertheless, emigration is still considered as a strong possibility by a substantial proportion of young Cape Verdeans who show a wish to live in Europe, maintaining a migratory chain that has never been interrupted.

It is important to stress the transnational nature of the Cape Verdean diaspora (Embaixada do Cabo Verde 1999, p. 25). The Cape Verdeans keep in touch with their country of origin by going there on holiday, building houses in their communities of origin, sending remittances or simply by receiving news from relatives and friends. They can also keep in touch with other communities scattered all over the world through the circulation of goods, especially food, diffusion of music from several groups living in the countries of the diaspora, telephoning and, for the younger ones who are the children of emigrants, through the internet.

Not only are the Cape Verdeans overwhelmingly concentrated in the Lisbon Metropolitan Area, as noted above, but they are also by far the largest foreign community living in the capital and its region. They are a group with considerable variety, reflected in different forms and degrees of 'integration' in Portuguese society.[2] In this heterogenous community several different groups of individuals can be found (Saint-Maurice 1997, p. 66).

The first and largest consists of people *born in Cape Verde and with Cape Verdean nationality*. The majority of these are of working age and possess few skills. They feel that they have some difficulty in integrating into Portuguese society, above all due to their low ability to master the Portuguese language (they understand Creole better than Portuguese) and their minimal schooling. This situation creates problems for them as regards employment and consequently at the economic level. Their poor incomes and resources are reflected in their housing and in the living standards they can reach. The majority are living in semi-derelict inner-city neighbourhoods or in poor housing districts in the suburbs of Lisbon, where they are an important share of the residents of municipalities like Amadora, Oeiras or Loures (Malheiros 2000).

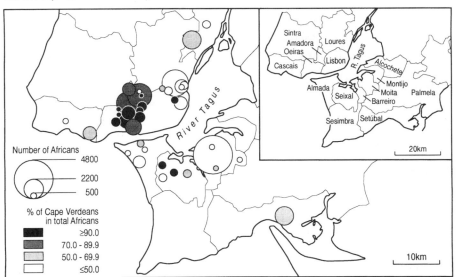

Figure 5.1 Lisbon Metropolitan Area: principal neighbourhoods (>500) with African and Cape Verdean inhabitants, 31 December 1994

Figure 5.1 clearly shows the presence of a spatial pattern of poor neighbourhoods where, at the end of 1994, several African communities lived and in which the Cape Verdeans represented a considerable proportion of the inhabitants. Fonseca and Malheiros (1999, p. 33) describe this pattern as Lisbon's Cape Verdean ring, arching from Amadora and Oeiras municipalities (13,052 and 9,787 Cape Verdeans respectively) across to the borders of Lisbon (4,034) and Loures (2,818) municipalities (figures from Cachada 1995). To the south of the Tagus, the main Cape Verdean concentrations are in Seixal (2,493) and Setúbal (2,151).

One of the most serious problems affecting this first major section of the Cape Verdean community is the lack of access to adequate housing. Having very few economic resources and often lacking documents, the Cape Verdean immigrants turn to their social and solidarity networks to get some form of shelter and a job, resulting in a greater spatial concentration of these poor migrants in socially and geographically marginal neighbourhoods. Their situation in the employment market, despite low unemployment rates, is characterised by extreme precariousness, often aggravated by lack of documents which hinders their access to several fundamental labour rights (a proper work contract, holiday and Christmas subsidies, social security and insurance). They often have to work for longer periods of time than they are actually paid for, and run the risk of being fired without receiving their payment for the work done. It is important to point out that this precariousness is often a short-term choice made by the newly-arrived immigrant because it allows a faster accumulation of capital. The worker does not pay taxes and therefore earns more money in a short period of time. However, in the long term this option has very serious consequences for the worker, who will not be entitled to a retirement pension at the end of the working life (Malheiros 1998). Another feature that must be pointed out about the working situation is the strong concentration of the low-skilled immigrant population in certain jobs. Construction jobs for men, domestic and industrial cleaning or street-peddling (usually selling fish) for women are the jobs they are able to access the most frequently. Nowadays this situation is changing slightly because Cape Verdean women are finding jobs in commerce, mainly as shop assistants, and in low-skilled tertiary sector activities. Nevertheless, for many immigrants in this first group, the lack of documents is also a disadvantage for their families because their access to social protection, education and medical assistance is limited.

The second group includes people who were *born in Cape Verde, but who have Portuguese nationality*. If some of them still have major integration problems (because they are illiterate, for example), others belonging to the Cape Verdean intellectual elite with high schooling levels and/or skills have fewer integration problems in Portuguese society. The third group mainly comprises *the children of Cape Verdean immigrants*, most of whom were born in Portugal. Only a few have been to Cape Verde, and the images they have were given by television. However, they know the Cape Verdean culture and they understand and speak Creole. Finally, the fourth group consists of *young Cape Verdean students* who, with the help of scholarships given by their government and benefiting from co-operation agreements between Portuguese universities and the Cape Verdean Ministry of Education, come to Portugal to study.

Although the situation is from the outset more favourable to them than it was to their parents, the children of African immigrants often feel misplaced because they do not identify themselves with African culture, nor with the Portuguese one (Machado 1994). They adopt 'alternative' cultures developed by African-origin groups from other parts of the world, especially North America. They had no influence over the immigration decision made by their parents and in school they often have learning problems due to their weak command of the Portuguese language (at home they mainly speak Creole) and also due to the lack of suitability of school curricula to their interests. There is a lack of adjustment between the practices and social values at home and those demanded at school. One of the consequences is the premature abandonment of school and consequently increased difficulties in the labour market, conditioning their prospects of social mobility. On the other hand, if these problems can be solved, especially those related to education, this group can potentially have a very important role in Portuguese society resulting from the junction of Cape Verdean and Portuguese cultures.

Culture as a fundamental issue in the 'integration' process

Immigration and culture are tightly linked. Immigrants are the bearers of a specific culture which, with different degrees of intensity, can be altered or preserved, depending partly on the individual, but also on the host society. Various immigrant communities develop different strategies according to their goals and the features of the receiving society. These behaviours can range from a self-closure, so that the integration process is then more difficult, to the development of an outward-oriented strategy promoting their culture.[3] This last approach inevitably brings their culture up-to-date and reformulates it with features picked up from the host society, making the integration process therefore easier. But this is a dialectic process and works both ways, because the host society also goes through a process of cultural change caused by the presence of the immigrants. This is visible by the adoption of new cultural practices in fields such as gastronomy, music, changes in urban areas, etc. Especially in the case of Lisbon and Portugal, this process is continuous and unfinished. So, immigrants are agents of change who bring modifications not only at the economic, but also at the social, political, cultural and spatial levels both in the destination and in the sending countries.

The present is more and more a world where several cultures coexist, relate with each other and receive mutual influences. If there are relationships and changes caused by the presence of other cultures, we can speak of an intercultural society. On the other hand, if the different cultures simply coexist, we have a multicultural society. Independent of the evolution of concepts and arguments, the most important thing is the model of a society where everybody has their place and their value as a person.

Cultural issues nowadays assume a growing importance and are very much part of present debates on inter-ethnic relations. The compatibility of cultures, the ethnicist character of certain groups and the virtues of miscegenation are frequently the targets of research on the nature of post-modern society. This consciousness is also felt by many members of the immigrant communities who are motivated to take a more positive attitude towards their original culture, promoting community initiatives and increasing their visibility in order to reach across to the host society. Culture can therefore act as a means of making integration easier and the interaction can make new cultures. Above all, 'in the current world, ideas of ethno-cultural homogeneity, "natural" or created, do not mirror the actual sociological composition of the population which is made up of diversity' (Martiniello 1997, p. 636).

Cultural features of the Cape Verdean community living in Portugal

'In the host society, [migrants] are particularly visible in the differentiation of the labour market, in the political regulation of migratory flows, in the added value of cultural variability, in the redefinition of spaces of interaction and in the rearrangement of urban areas' (Saint-Maurice 1997, p. 1). Due to the acknowledged importance of immigrants for the cultural diversity of the receiving society, this section will focus on several issues which may be considered as elements of differentiation of Cape Verdean culture when compared to Portuguese society. We discuss in turn language, food, music and dance, literature, religious practices, and territorial symbols and interaction spaces.

Language

Language is one of the issues that bestows greater identity on a community. The official language of Cape Verde is Portuguese whereas the mother tongue is Creole. This dialect is the fusion of archaic Portuguese, taken to the archipelago by the Portuguese colonisers, with African dialects spoken by African peoples brought from continental Africa as slaves. Also present in the mix are infusions from the languages of some European peoples (French, Italian and English). Among the nine inhabited islands composing the archipelago, it is possible to find slight variants of Creole. A process to define and render uniform the linguistic rules of Creole is being carried out so that this dialect, only spoken until now, can be taught in schools. The formal recognition of Cape Verdean bilingualism has only very recently been accepted by the Parliament of Cape Verde (Ferreira 1997, p. 27).

If from the formal point of view all Cape Verdeans speak Portuguese, their real command of this language is extremely variable according to the educational capital of the individual and the frequency with which he or she uses the language to communicate. Creole is the language used within the family in Cape Verde, Portuguese being reserved for official matters and for school classes. According to the important research carried out by Saint-Maurice (1997), when some Cape Verdeans arrive in Portugal they experience major difficulties in communicating with the host society because they do not have a good command of the Portuguese language. The newly-arrived immigrant can go through some frightening and extremely anguishing situations because, besides being a foreigner, he or she does not have the ability to speak fluently the language of the majority group. On the other hand, Portuguese society assumes from the very beginning that all citizens coming from the CPLP (Community of Countries speaking the Portuguese Language) speak Portuguese, and therefore that there is no need to pay any special attention to the newly-arrived immigrants who sometimes speak Portuguese with the typical accent of their countries. Furthermore, Cape Verdeans use Creole to communicate with relatives, neighbours and friends not only because they have a better command of this language, but also to avoid being understood by those who do not share this code. Sharing a code when living in a foreign society gives unity to a group of people and reinforces their group identity. Research on the opinions of Portuguese people about a number of foreign and ethnic communities revealed that 'the way foreigners speak and communicate' is the most important and striking feature of differentiation (see Garcia 2000). However, Luso-Africans (the Portuguese-born children of African immigrants) have been playing a very important role in the diffusion and incorporation of a growing number of Creole words into the Portuguese language. Using songs and music, these youngsters have imported words from several African languages and dialects (e.g. the Angolan *Quimbundo*) which sooner or later become part of the Portuguese urban slang. This slang has been constantly renewed by the addition of new words from African languages or by the invention of new words resulting from specific situations.[4] Therefore, the ethnic diversity associated with the expanding immigration to Portugal has brought new words or expressions, until very recently unknown to the Portuguese, to the daily lives of many people. Some of these new names have to do with the entrepreneurial success of business linked to restaurants. For example, the Brazilian *picanha* (grilled beef seasoned with aromatic herbs) is today a popular food among the Portuguese people, as is the Cape Verdean *cachupa* (a stew made of beans, meat or fish, and cabbage), the Chinese *chop-suey* (from Macao) or the Indian curry (from Goa). Mention of these foods is an *hors d'oeuvre* to the next subsection.

Gastronomy

Cape Verdean cuisine, as with many cultural features of this country, is strongly influenced by Portuguese and African cultures on the one hand, and by the products grown in the archipelago on the other. This last fact is also responsible for the regional variants according to the resources of each island. Although incorporating different ingredients, the basic seasoning is Portuguese (garlic, onion, laurel, paprika, etc). The result, however, is dishes that are typically Cape Verdean in their taste. The diet of the people is based on corn, maize, beans, sweet potato, cassava, fish (mainly mackerel and tuna fish) and several kinds of meat. The most traditional food/dish is *cachupa* and there are several *cachupas* according to the ingredients used to prepare them, the time of day and the purchasing power of the consumer.

Cooking typical dishes from their homeland is a common practice among immigrants. However, the frequency of doing this varies if the basic ingredients can not be easily found in the destination country. This lack of ingredients leads to the invention of a new dish (a deviation from the original recipe) or to the importing of ingredients from the country of origin. With the growth of immigration, and if the demand justifies it, local retailers will import the products to satisfy the market. The immigrants themselves can be retailers dedicated to this kind of business, supplying the community and making ethnic retailing flourish. In Figure 5.2 it is possible to identify restaurants serving African food, exploring not only good business opportunities, but also satisfying a growing demand and interest for this kind of cuisine on the part of the Portuguese. These restaurants are mainly located in the historical centre of Lisbon, near the neighbourhoods where the first Cape Verdean and African immigrants settled. The cluster visible on the south-western side of Lisbon has to do with the closeness to the docklands, the new fashionable location for bars, discos and restaurants following the urban remodelling of this area.

In the recent study on the Cape Verdean community living in Portugal carried out under the auspices of the Cape Verdean Embassy in association with a research team (Embaixada do Cabo Verde 1999), a questionnaire circulated among the Cape Verdean population found that almost all the people interviewed usually had Cape Verdean food for their meals.[5] The frequency of this varied according to their length of schooling: individuals with little schooling had Cape Verdean food more often than those who were more educated. This situation is the result of different income levels and the degree of proximity to the culture of the receiving country. It is, however, important to note that the fidelity of all Cape Verdean groups in Portugal to Cape Verdean food is quite high.

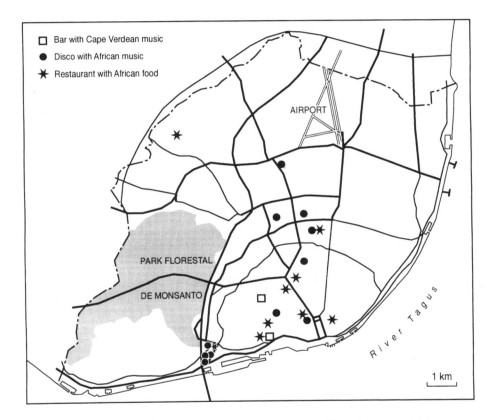

Figure 5.2 Lisbon: bars, discos and restaurants with African and Cape Verdean music and food, 1999

Music and dance

Music and dance are the essence of Cape Verdean culture. Music is not only a strong link among people, but also an expression of the transnationality of the Cape Verdean culture. The music shows a huge richness due to the variety of rhythms, instruments and interpreters. Moreover, authors and singers have a great ability to innovate and invent new rhythms and styles. Music depicts the daily lives of Cape Verdeans and one of the most traditional music styles is the *morna*, recalling the *sodade* (longing, homesickness, nostalgia) of those living in the various countries of the diaspora. By contrast, the *coladeras* and the *funanás* are happy, merry songs inviting people to dance. Besides the stringed instruments, such as the guitar, the violin and a little guitar called *cavaquinho*, the percussion instruments are the most frequently used.

Many Cape Verdean artists live outside the archipelago, being themselves part of the diaspora. In Portugal, both Cape Verdean music and many musicians have already progressed beyond the audience of their community, asserting their positions in the panorama of Portuguese and international music. The singers Tito Paris (living in Lisbon) and Cesária Évora (living in Cape Verde) are popular and well-known musicians. Tito Paris gives concerts that are mainly oriented to the Cape Verdean community living in Europe and in the USA. The itinerary of his recent tour (5 April–12 August 2000) shows a remarkable correlation to the main points in the Cape Verdean diaspora, with seven concerts in the USA in towns with significant Cape Verdean settlement (Boston, Providence, New York, New Orleans etc.), four in the Netherlands (Rotterdam, Amsterdam, Utrecht, Haarlem), four in France, plus Milan and Athens. Cesária Évora, a more internationally oriented ambassadress of Cape Verdean culture, mixes venues within the diaspora with performances in a variety of places like Hammamet (Tunisia), Lund (Sweden), Santiago (Chile) or Vancouver (Canada), according to the routing of her most recent tour (25 March–22 July 2000).

The Cape Verdean Embassy in Portugal indicated to us the presence of more than 30 musicians and composers living in Portugal. Among these one can find people with long and acknowledged careers (Bana, Celina Pereira, Tito Paris, Fernando Queijas, Paulino Vieira) but also new musicians who are now carving out a place in the Portuguese music market (Sara Tavares, Tó Cruz, Olavo Bilac). These young musicians, children of Cape Verdean immigrants and real icons of the present pop music, are perfectly integrated in Portuguese society, preserving however their Cape Verdean culture and identity. They are an example to the younger generations, showing that it is possible to live together in harmony, although having different sources of cultural capital.

The influence of Cape Verdean music is also discernable in the work of Portuguese musicians, especially in the rhythms. Some of the main Portuguese artists, such as Rui Veloso, Ala dos Namorados, Vitorino and Luís Represas, have already incorporated these changes and have been extremely successful in doing so.

Dance is also present, both in the neighbourhoods where immigrants live and also within their associations, for example through the music of traditional drumming groups like *Finka Pé* and *Rinca Finca Pila Torno*. In Lisbon there is a growing number of bars and discos where live Cape Verdean music is a major attraction. This demonstrates not only the musical creativity of the people but also the entrepreneurial capacity of some Cape Verdeans who perceive the increasing interest of Portuguese and Luso-Africans for this artistic expression (Figure 5.2).

Literature

Literature is another way of divulging the culture of a people, and 'Cape Verde is the [non-metropolitan] Portuguese-speaking country where an autochthonous literature, resulting from the work of an elite who defended the need to bring together the land and the people, first flourished' (Ferreira 1997, p. 27). This capacity for generating literary output of major significance, of which the most important came to light around the journal *Claridade*, founded in the island of São Vicente in 1936, reveals the huge literary richness of this country and its ability to overcome the geographical limits of the archipelago.

However, one must take into account the reality that the vast majority of Cape Verdean workers who look to Portugal as a migratory destination has a relatively low level of education and performs poorly-paid tasks in construction, cleaning and domestic services. When there is time and opportunity to read, people prefer daily and sports newspapers and women's magazines, often read on public transport during the long journey to and from work (Embaixada do Cabo Verde 1999). There is an exception to point out and that is the Cape Verdean elite of artists, writers, researchers and professionals living in Portugal. They are people whose high cultural capital allowed an easier and more successful integration in Portuguese society. Their higher incomes and cultural preferences help to promote the more erudite side of the Cape Verdean culture. They are, together with some Portuguese readers, potential consumers of the present and extremely rich literary production of Cape Verde.[6]

The growing interest of the Portuguese intellectual elite for African authors of Portuguese language has led to an increasing number of writers and works marketed by some of the main Portuguese publishers. Authors like Germano de Almeida, João Lopes Filho, Manuel Lopes (Cape Verdeans), Mia Couto, Eduardo White, Suleiman Cassamo (Mozambicans), Carlos Lopes (Guinean), Pepetela, José Luandino Vieira and José Eduardo Agualusa (Angolans), who tell stories of the daily lives of people from their own home countries, are already known among Portuguese readers. Considering the rather limited reading habits of Portuguese people, it is fundamental that publishers engage in a policy of promoting such authors. Certainly, the quality of the works of several CPLP authors has motivated the investment of several Portuguese publishers who have launched collections exclusively dedicated to African authors of Portuguese language. For instance, *Editorial Caminho* publishes the works of African writers in its 'Land without masters' collection.[7] However, the importance of a few authors such as Germano de Almeida and Mia Couto has allowed them to have their works published outside this specialist collection, resulting in substantially higher sales.[8] Other publishing houses like *Vega Editora, Ulmeiro, Plátano, Ática* and *Publicações Europa-América* have also been playing an important role in the marketing of African authors who write in Portuguese.

Religious rituals

Catholicism is the religious confession followed by the vast majority of Cape Verdeans, not only in their homeland, but also in the several countries that make up the diaspora.[9] There are, however, variations resulting from insularity and geographic isolation. In rural areas, people live and practice a form of religion mixed with myths, rites and values associated with animist beliefs, where the supernatural and the weight of Nature's forces are allied to 'conventional' religions (Ferreira 1997, p. 29). Likewise, according to Saint-Maurice, 'the practice of some rites linked to birth and to death is appropriated in different ways in the several islands' (1997, p. 130). For example, the people of Santiago are more African and deeply devoted to traditions, whereas in São Vicente the influences coming from the outside world through the constant traffic of the port have shaped a less traditionalist population.

There are typical Cape Verdean cultural practices linked to the stages of the life cycle, like the celebration of the *guarda-cabeça* and the practice of the mat. The first ritual relates to birth and is essentially a pagan baptism celebrated on the seventh day in the life of the newly-born child (it is also known as 'making-Christian'), whereas the second rite has to do with death. Friends and relatives of the deceased pray for him for seven to eleven days, showing thus their sorrow and loss and keeping his spirit in peace. According to the results of the aforementioned questionnaire research made amongst the Cape Verdean community living in Portugal, 43 per cent of the interviewed people celebrated *guarda-cabeça*, and 44 per cent said they 'put the mat'. These rituals were mainly practised by those individuals with little schooling, because 'these are practices resulting from superstitions usually rejected by those with higher schooling' (Embaixada do Cabo Verde 1999, p. 165).

Territorial symbols and use of space

The urban models from the Chicago School have already analysed the appropriation of space in its several dimensions by different ethnic groups – economic, geographical, social, cultural. The way of utilising and enjoying public and private spaces is extremely different according to the cultural features of each community. What is being discussed above all here is the appropriation of the 'habitat area' – the neighbourhood – where the daily practices of social actors are reproduced (Rodrigues 1989, p. 97). The way Cape Verdeans live and occupy both housing areas and public space shows elements which reflect rural lives that are still quite close. For example, pounding corn at one's door, either in the shared patio of the building or on the pavement, reflects habits brought from the home country. The smallness of the dwellings, the lack of natural light and the dust of the cereal's bran, push this activity, exclusively performed by women, to the airy open spaces where the rhythmic movements of the pestle are easier. Playing traditional table games at the door of cafés, taverns or one's own home is another common practice in the neighbourhoods where Cape Verdean citizens live.[10] The warm climate and the lack of traffic on the streets allows the reproduction of leisure forms identical to those of the native country. Such activities also have the important function of maintaining networks of sociability amongst groups of Cape Verdeans. But the street is not only a place of circulation and sociability. Some professional activities, such as hairdressing, may be carried out there, as Letria and Malheiros (1999) observed in the Alto da Cova da Moura neighbourhood on the outskirts of Lisbon. When the barber does not own a shop, the client has his hair cut at the barber's door, holding a mirror in his hands and a bowl of water on his knees.

The presence of Cape Verdeans and other African nationalities in some neighbourhoods in the metropolitan areas of Lisbon and Oporto is visible in the number of vases, pots or buckets with tropical and subtropical plants at people's doors. These plants are extremely useful for cooking, complementing thus the household economy, and reproducing the features of the homeland. Typical plants are bananas, okra, malaguettas and pumpkins.

Another of the visible territorial symbols of the presence of a group in a neighbourhood or area is the graffiti on the walls. The drawings are made by Luso-African youngsters (the offspring of first-generation immigrants), who face serious integration difficulties in Portuguese society, as well as a huge cultural gap with their parents, and express their rebellion against the 'establishment', often personified by the school and the police, using graffiti. These can be found everywhere in the Portuguese major urban areas and are used to send messages between groups of youngsters living in different neighbourhoods, feeding rivalries based on feelings of belonging to certain areas or groups.

In neighbourhoods of spontaneous (and often illegal) origin, several municipal authorities of the Lisbon Metropolitan Area have been accepting suggestions given by the inhabitants about the names of the streets. Thus, in neighbourhoods now being legalised, and where the presence of African communities is dominant, one can find streets whose names are similar to some Cape Verdean, Angolan or Guinean streets. The special links established between Portuguese towns and towns of CPLP countries (twin towns) may also be one of the reasons justifying this process of name adoption.

When travelling outside and between the neighbourhoods where the Cape Verdean community lives it is possible to observe other signs of the Cape Verdean presence. Public squares like Rossio and Martim Moniz in Lisbon or the Algés roundabout in Oeiras are good examples of this. They have, however, different occupations, uses and goals for those who go there. Rossio, one of the main squares of the historical centre of Lisbon, is not only a social meeting space, to receive news from friends and relatives back in the homeland, but is also used as a small market place to sell typical products brought from tropical and subtropical African countries. The colourful African clothes that some men and many women wear and the many languages and dialects spoken clearly reveal the recent arrival of many immigrants and the variety of their geographical origins. It is also usually possible to find a couple of Cape Verdean or Angolan immigrants who have been living in Portugal for some time and who can move swiftly in the bureaucratic meanders of the legalisation requests. After receiving a certain amount of money these brokers will take care of the 'papers' of those who are undocumented. It is also in Rossio square that Cape Verdean and Guinean subcontractors hire African immigrants – often newly-arrived people without documents – for the construction trade (Rosário 1996, p. 40). This function of a contracting place is similar to that of the Algés roundabout where the Cape Verdean women selling fish on the street try to do their business while escaping from the municipal police. In Martim Moniz the improvements made a few years ago by the local authorities, including the renting of small kiosks and a couple of esplanades, have made this square an important social space for immigrants. There is, however, a division of the space according to ethnic groups: the southern side is mainly occupied by Indians, whereas the northern side is for the Africans. These latter are younger than those found in Rossio square, they dress according to the latest trends of European fashion, and work or documents do not seem to be their main worries.

Ethnic entrepreneurship is another visible form of the presence of foreign communities in Portugal. The number of restaurants, bars and discos of African origin has been increasing every year in the metropolitan areas of Lisbon and Oporto, as we saw in Figure 5.2. This corresponds not only to a greater strength of African and Portuguese entrepreneurs, who explore good business opportunities, but also to an increase in the demand for these kinds of service. If the majority of the clients of African bars and discos are Africans or Luso-Africans, in the restaurants Portuguese people are the most frequent customers. They try to diversify their diet with the exoticism of African ingredients or perhaps they want to recall flavours enjoyed when they lived in the Portuguese African colonies.

Because of their informality, Cape Verdean restaurants and places to eat (not necessarily restaurants!) are difficult to find and locate. There is, however, a group of restaurants where it is possible to enjoy not only Cape Verdean gastronomy but also the cuisine of other African countries such as Angola and Guinea (Figure 5.2). Some immigrant associations, besides the legal support given to their members, also make available a daily restaurant service with live music played several times a week.

Strategies and cultural adaptations developed in Portugal

The foregoing account has attempted to show that the Cape Verdean community is a minority ethnic group with a distinct social and cultural identity of its own. More complexly, it is the relationship between minority and majority, or more precisely its contentiousness, that allows the closure that is necessary to the preservation of the social and cultural identity of the minority group and its existence as a minority (Rodrigues 1989, p. 99). This introversion is, however, never complete and the individuals belonging to the minority group have to develop life strategies and to make decisions about concealing or changing the features of their original culture in order to allow them to interact socially with the majority population. Customs, attitudes and behaviour are changed so that the immigrants can be more deeply integrated into Portuguese society.

The requests for Portuguese nationality handed in to the Foreigners and Borders Service by many Cape Verdean immigrants living in Portugal do not reflect a greatly increased emotional identification with Portugal as much as very practical issues that have to do with an easier circulation in the Schengen space and access to a wider set of rights and social support (Embaixada do Cabo Verde 1999, pp. 139–40). Immigrants renounce Cape Verdean nationality not because they do not love their homeland, but because everything becomes easier and more accessible when they are holders of a Portuguese passport.

When one is living in a foreign country some concessions at the level of the language also have to be made. The majority of Cape Verdeans living in Portugal speak Creole with their children, not only because they speak it better than Portuguese, but also because they want to pass it on to the next generation as an important element of cultural identity. Nevertheless, many Cape Verdeans choose to speak Portuguese with their offspring, recognising the importance of learning the language of the host society in order to ensure a better insertion in the labour market and as regards social life. In a recent questionnaire survey of more than a thousand Cape Verdeans living in Portugal, 39.0 per cent of those questioned said that Creole was the language they used to speak to their children, compared to 29.3 per cent who spoke Portuguese and 31.7 per cent who used both languages (Embaixada do Cabo Verde 1999, p. 147).

The difficulty in acquiring some of the ingredients to cook traditional Cape Verdean dishes is another constraint imposed on the perpetuation of this community's traditions. Despite the growing number of grocers, shops and supermarkets which sell products essential to the preparation of African dishes, it is still difficult and expensive to buy some kinds of fish and vegetables. Thus, abdicating from Cape Verdean cooking, or reducing the number of meals with this food, may be the result of the difficulty in obtaining the right ingredients.

The rules of social behaviour imposed by the dominant group can also restrain some cultural practices of foreign citizens living in Portugal. According to the important study on the Cape Verdean community which we have already quoted many times, the majority of Cape Verdeans (65.1 per cent of those interviewed) said they often listened to music from their country (Embaixada do Cabo Verde 1999, p. 167); many prefer listening to very loud music so that they can share their enjoyment with neighbours. When Cape Verdeans live in neighbourhoods mostly inhabited by African people, this taste for loud music is not a major problem. However, in apartments with low quality standards of construction, bad sound insulation and where the majority of tenants are not African, listening to loud-volume *funaná* or *ferro-e-gaita* may lead to problems with the neighbours and hostile feelings. Therefore, it is necessary to renounce the habit of listening to loud music in order to maintain peaceful neighbourly relations.

The role of associations in the promotion of Cape Verdean culture

One of the most striking features of the Cape Verdean community living in Portugal is the pioneer spirit in the ethnic associative movement (Carita and Rosendo 1993). The first association was established in 1970 but in the 1980s many others appeared whose main goal was to answer the needs of the immigrant population, especially housing problems. Nowadays there are several associations linked to the Cape Verdean community living in Portugal; their aims have altered over time according to the most pressing problems of migrants, as Ricard Morén-Alegret shows in more detail in the next chapter. Some of these associations continued their work of defending the interests of immigrants, mainly from the legal point of view,[11] while others have been concentrating their efforts on the preservation and diffusion of the Cape Verdean cultural heritage. Many combine both goals. There are also some associations which are mainly geared towards cooperation with the home country, especially in the health sector.

The main purpose of the earlier associations that sprung up among the Cape Verdean community was the preservation and reproduction of a Cape Verdean identity, defending the interests of the community and contributing to an integration that respected the culture and the values of the people. Such associations are mainly linked to the more elitist sectors of the Cape Verdean population in Portugal. Then, at a more local level, there are neighbourhood associations related to the concentration of Cape Verdean citizens in several run-down quarters in the major Portuguese urban areas. Their main goals are to solve the housing problems that still affect many people and to support the children. They try to fight for the improvement of living conditions among the immigrant community by developing local projects to solve the very concrete needs of the people they represent. Inside the neighbourhoods there are yet other associations whose aim is to represent and promote the more 'popular' culture of the native country. They organise events involving music and dance ranging from traditional drumming and dance forms to new Rap and Hip-Hop groups, and also try to encourage young people to continue to follow Cape Verdean festivities.

Initiatives developed by the local authorities to promote interculturality

Besides being partners in many initiatives organised by immigrants and their associations, local authorities must also have a dynamic role supporting and defending the right immigrants have to political and civil participation in the life of each municipality. Local authorities' actions in favour of migrant groups have often been concerned with basic needs such as provision of adequate housing, professional training, social support and assistance to children. In these last two issues, non-governmental organisations, notably those under the aegis of the Catholic Church, have been playing a key role.

The municipalities of the Lisbon Metropolitan Area try to solve the many problems resulting from the high concentration of immigrants in their territories. Considering the numerical size of several African communities, some municipalities have felt the need to establish special agencies or departments, often under the responsibility of a deputy mayor, to support these communities, following the example of what has been happening in France and Belgium. This is the case with the municipality of Lisbon which in 1993 established the Municipal Council of Immigrant Communities and Ethnic Minorities with the goal of ensuring the participation of associations representing the migrant groups and ethnic minorities in the planning of projects to improve their living conditions. After solving the most pressing problems, the municipal council has turned its attention to the cultural issues of the various communities. Thus, Lisbon municipality established the Centre of Multicultural Resources, whose main purpose is to be a place of cultural exchange and knowledge for Lisbon inhabitants, whoever they may be – Portuguese, Africans, Indians, Gypsies, etc. It not only organises training courses for young people from the ethnic and immigrant communities living in Lisbon, but also puts on exhibitions about the different cultural features of these communities.

Amadora municipality, just outside the central zone of Lisbon, established in 1994 the Municipal Council of Ethnic Communities and Immigrants. This is a consultative agency with the purpose of ensuring the participation of ethnic minorities and immigrant communities in the definition of policies for equal rights and opportunities and their integration in Portuguese society, whilst also defending the right to be different. In nearby Loures municipality, due to the strong presence of people coming not only from Africa but also from India, a policy supporting the integration of the immigrant communities has been pursued for several years now by the Agency of Religious and Social Affairs. In close cooperation with several associations, the municipality gives financial, logistical and technical support to a large number of cultural and sports initiatives (music and dance festivals, gastronomic gatherings, athletics), revealing the richness and the cultural diversity of Loures. The establishment of a Municipal Council for Immigrants and Ethnic Communities is now under consideration by the Loures local council.

Considering the municipalities that were able to give information about their policies for the ethnic and immigrant communities, it is possible to identify three different ways of working with these groups:

- Municipalities that clearly have a policy supporting immigrant and ethnic communities. Some of them even have specialist consultant agencies bringing together the town councillors and local migrant associations. This is the case for Lisbon, Amadora and Loures municipalities (this last one without a consultant agency).
- Municipalities which have some civil servants working with immigrants in very specific situations, but without a well-defined policy for immigrants and ethnic communities (for example, Seixal municipality).
- Municipalities which have civil servants working in this area, but whose support is mainly an indirect one. The migrant associations are the promoters of initiatives and the local authorities are only partners (e.g. Sintra and Barreiro municipalities).

One of the major problems local authorities have to face when promoting intercultural initiatives has to do with their visibility to attract immigrant and ethnic communities and with the lack of involvement of Portuguese people. Hence social interaction is fostered among the various migrant communities living in the metropolitan areas, but without involving the Portuguese citizens. It is true that there is usually a daily contact between these communities and the Portuguese (mainly through work); nevertheless it is also evident that

Portuguese people know very little about these communities and are not very interested in changing that situation.

Conclusion: inter-ethnic sociability and re-invention of cultures

Despite all the cultural richness and diversity which we have pointed out, a considerable part of Portuguese society does not know or underrates the cultural features of the majority of ethnic communities living in Portugal. For example in the research coordinated by Garcia (2000), a sample of Portuguese people questioned about the cultural relevance of foreign communities for Portuguese society said that none of the ethnic communities living in Portugal made an important or remarkable contribution to the cultural richness of the country.[12] It should be pointed out, of course, that the adaptation to any innovation needs time. There are signs that the Portuguese people are receptive to cultural innovations, especially if it is something fashionable. To establish a less homogenous, richer and more diversified culture is beginning to be seen as something positive and enriching.

The assertion of Cape Verdean culture in Portuguese society is mainly evident in four areas: music, dance, gastronomy and literature. If one observes the municipalities that are part of Lisbon Metropolitan Area, it is possible to note the growing number of activities linked to African culture in general and to Cape Verdean culture in particular. Among such activities can be mentioned restaurants, discos, bars, retailers and bazaars of imported goods from African countries. Indeed, one of the most fashionable cultural issues in the Lisbon region is African culture and African rhythms. It is remarkable the number of nightclubs and discos where it is possible to listen and dance to African music, often played live. Several newspapers and magazines have published features about the importance of African culture, music and night-clubs in Lisbon.[13] The places to visit are many and various: one can start the evening with a Cape Verdean dinner, followed by a concert given by Tito Paris in his bar (*The Enclave*) and end the evening in a disco dancing to *funaná* music. Although the distinction between African and Cape Verdean cultures is not very clear, the relative weight of this community in Portugal, particularly in the Lisbon region, is responsible for the majority of bars and night-clubs of African origin.

When compared to music and dance, the literature with Cape Verdean roots reaches a more restricted audience, but the relevance of some African writers, and Cape Verdeans in particular, justifies the prominence given by Portuguese publishers to these authors. If the number of copies sold of books written by Germano de Almeida, Mia Couto or Pepetela is steadily growing, this means that Portuguese readers are more motivated to partake of a literature that tells about the daily lives, emotions and thoughts of those who have left their homeland in Africa to live and work in Portugal.

The mass media have also been playing an important role in heightening interest in other cultures, and the work of RDP-Africa in the diffusion of news, general information and cultural events of African origin has been especially notable. This radio station began in January 1997 and is one of the major agencies promoting African culture from the PALOP countries in Portugal. The events range from launching books, magazines and records to art exhibitions and music concerts. In its first three and a half years of broadcasting this radio station has already organised the launching of 54 books, four magazines (one of them the Cape Verdean magazine *Kultura*) and 31 records (six of them by Cape Verdean musicians). Every Sunday the radio station broadcasts a magazine programme live from Lisbon's African neighbourhoods.

When organising and promoting intercultural activities, it is important to involve all the communities living in Portugal, including the Portuguese, and not just one or other community organising a specific event, otherwise the activities will not be truly intercultural. In this context, the activities promoted by the immigrant associations and by local authorities should seek the cooperation and participation of other representative groups. In activities and programmes of governmental or municipal initiative it is absolutely essential to avoid having preconceived ideas of what is the culture of a certain community. On the one hand, one may run the risk of reinforcing the idea that ethnic minorities are completely separate entities from one another and from the host society. On the other hand, it is easy to be caught in the trap of stereotyped and folkloric representations of the 'native culture'. It is fundamental to avoid closing people inside the culture the host society thinks is their native culture; instead people should define their own culture. Maybe the preference of Luso-African youngsters for Rap music instead of *mornas* or traditional drumming, or for MacDonald's hamburgers instead of *cachupa* or peanut broth, is a sign that their culture is changing – and yet still significant. The rhythms and the flavours that please their parents are not those of their choice because their life stories in Portuguese society have been very different from those of their parents (Contador 1998).

All institutions dealing with education have a fundamental role in the promotion of mentalities that respect and accept the cultural differences of pupils and students coming from culturally different communities and origins. The youngsters should face the ethno-cultural diversity of the schoolroom as an enriching factor both for the class and for the world outside the classroom. There is nevertheless a set of issues that needs to be guaranteed for a successful insertion in any host society. It is essential that immigrant and ethnic communities have the possibility of political participation, of freely expressing their opinions and feelings about the surrounding social environment, and the right to enjoy a culture defined by them and not one others believe is their culture.

Notes

1 The research on which this chapter is based is part of the Metropolis Project–Portugal. We thank the Luso-American Development Foundation, and especially Charles Buchanan, for supporting the research. Our thanks also to Maria Lucinda Fonseca and Jorge Malheiros of the Centro de Estudos Geográficos at Lisbon University.
2 For the purposes of this analysis, the term 'integration' denotes the various adjustment processes of minorities to the destination society. These adjustment processes are multi-dimensional, and allow the migrants to maintain specific features of their own culture and identity (cf. Malheiros 1996, p. 48).
3 Sometimes, also, foreigners attempt to redefine their identity in order to overcome pejorative stereotypes which may exist in the host society and deprecate their original culture (Domingo i Vals 1996).
4 For example *tempra* means police car in Cape Verdean slang, simply because for many years the Cape Verdean police force drove the Fiat Tempra model.
5 This questionnaire surveyed 1,417 Cape Verdean families living in the Metropolitan Area of Lisbon, in the cities of Oporto and Coimbra, and in the Algarve; in all a total of 5,147 people, representing around 6 per cent of the Cape Verdean citizens in Portugal. The survey was carried out during September–October 1998. For full details see Embaixada do Cabo Verde (1999).
6 In 2000 the PALOP award (for authors from the Portuguese-speaking countries of Africa) was given to the Cape Verdean writer Lúcio de Sousa Mendes for his book *The Thirty Days of the Poorest Man in the World*, written in Portuguese and published in 1999 (*Os trinta dias do homem mais pobre do mundo*). This award is part of a project of bibliographic funding for the Portuguese language financed by the EU.
7 At the 70th Book Fair that took place in Lisbon between 25 May and 13 June 2000, Editorial Caminho dedicated one of its pavilions to its African authors who were present to autograph their books and give press interviews.
8 Just to give an example, a book by the Cape Verdean author Germano de Almeida (*O testamento do senhor Napumoceno da Silva Araújo – The Will of Mr Napumoceno da Silva Araújo*) published by Editorial Caminho since 1989, has sold 7,500 copies in its three editions. His most recent book (*O dia das calças roladas – The Day of the Rolled-Up Trousers*) had a first printing of 5,000 copies.
9 According to Ferreira (1997) approximately 90 per cent of the Cape Verdeans living in the archipelago are Catholics; most of the remainder are members of the Evangelical Church.
10 A typical game is *ouri*, in which two players move 48 seeds around 12 small holes in a rectangular wooden board (Letria and Malheiros 1999, p. 111).
11 It is important to recognise here the role played by several ethnic associations in sensitising undocumented migrants to the benefits of the regularisation programmes of 1992–93 and 1996.

12 To be more precise, the question was framed with reference to the ethnic communities – Cape Verdean, Angolan, Guinean, Indian, Spanish, British and Gypsy – which were the target of Garcia's research.
13 For example in the Portuguese weekly magazine *Visão*, the Portuguese daily newspaper *Público* and the Spanish daily *El País*.

References

Cachada, F. (1995) *Os Números da Imigração Africana*. Lisbon: Cadernos CEPAC, no. 2.

Carita, C. and Rosendo, V. N. (1993) Associativismo cabo-verdiano em Portugal. Estudo de caso da Associação Cabo-verdiana em Lisboa, *Sociologia – Problemas e Práticas*, 13, pp. 135–52.

Carreira, A. (1983) *Migrações nas Ilhas de Cabo Verde*. Praia: Instituto Caboverdeano do Livro.

Contador, A. C. (1998) Consciência de geração e etnicidade: da segunda geração aos novos luso-africanos, *Sociologia – Problemas e Práticas*, 16, pp. 57–83.

Domingo i Vals, A. (1996) Les conditions de vie des immigrés africains et latino-américans à Barcelone, *Revue Européenne des Migrations Internationales*, 12(1), pp. 39–51.

Embaixada do Cabo Verde (1999) *Estudo de Caracterização da Comunidade Caboverdeana Residente em Portugal*. Lisbon: Embaixada do Cabo Verde em Portugal.

Ferreira, L. (1997) *Cabo Verde*. Lisbon: Centro de Estudos para as Migrações e as Relações Interculturais, Universidade Aberta.

Fonseca, M. L. and Malheiros, J. (1999) *Immigrants in Lisbon: Innovation and Spatial Change in a Southern European Context*. Lisbon: Luso-American Development Foundation.

França, L. (ed.) (1992) *A Comunidade Cabo Verdiana em Portugal*. Lisbon: Instituto de Estudos para o Desenvolvimento.

Garcia, J. L. (2000) *Portugal Migrante: emigrados e imigrados. Dois estudos introductórios*. Oeiras: Celta Editora.

Jackson, J. (1986) *Migration*. London: Longman.

Letria, P. and Malheiros, J. (1999) *À Descoberta dos Novos Descobridores*. Lisbon: Comissão Nacional para as Comemorações dos Descobrimentos Portugueses.

Machado, F. L. (1994) Luso-africanos em Portugal: nas margens da etnicidade, *Sociologia – Problemas e Práticas*, 16, pp. 111–34.

Malheiros, J. (1996) *Imigrantes na Região de Lisboa: os anos da mudança*. Lisbon: Edições Colibri.

Malheiros, J. (1998) Immigration, clandestine work and labour market strategies: the construction sector in the Metropolitan Region of Lisbon, *South European Society and Politics*, 3(3), pp. 169–85.

Malheiros, J. (2000) Urban restructuring, immigration and the generation of marginalized spaces in the Lisbon region, in King, R., Lazaridis, G. and Tsardanidis, C. (eds) *Eldorado or Fortress? Migration in Southern Europe*. London: Macmillan, pp. 207–32.

Martiniello, M. (1997) Citizenship, ethnicity and multiclturalism: post-national membership between Utopia and reality, *Ethnic and Racial Studies*, 20(3), pp. 635–41.

Rodrigues, W. (1989) Comunidade caboverdiana: marginalização e identidade, *Sociedade e Território*, 8, pp. 96–103.

Rosário, J. (1996) A preto e branco, *Visão*, 185, pp. 38–42.

Saint-Maurice, A. (1997) *Identidades Reconstruídas. Cabo-verdianos em Portugal*. Oeiras: Celta Editora.

Wils, A. (1999) Emigration and demography in Cape Verde: escaping the Malthusian trap, in King, R. and Connell, J. (eds) *Small Worlds, Global Lives: Islands and Migration*. London: Pinter, pp. 77–94.

6

African immigrants and their organisations in Lisbon: between social and systemic influence

Ricard Morén-Alegret

Introduction

The sub-Saharan African presence in Lisbon is one of the most significant when compared to the origins of immigrants in other southern European cities. This is also in contrast with other Iberian urban areas such as Madrid and Barcelona, where the black African influence is less evident. In this chapter the focus is on how African people have organised themselves in Lisbon, paying special attention to the evolution during recent decades of the associations and groupings created by immigrants from sub-Saharan Africa.[1]

The arrival of African immigrants in Lisbon has to be located within the context of the dramatically changing migration trends in southern European countries from emigration to immigration (King *et al.* 1997). These new immigrations in southern Europe can be related to changes in several aspects of the system and in society. In the analysis which follows, the reinforcement of the systemic processes of institutionalisation, increasing money dependence and bureaucratisation which have characterised the last two or three decades will be related to African migration to Lisbon.[2] At the same time, a key objective of this chapter is to study the foundation and evolution of immigrant associations, communities and groupings as possible sources of social life organised in order to *resist* the system. Social principles based on mutual aid, cooperation, equality, respect or justice are in contrast to systemic logic based on competition, greed, profit, hierarchy or control (Kropotkin 1939).[3] As Jordi Cardelús and Àngels Pascual de Sans (1979) put it in relation to immigrants: social integration is in contrast with solvency – with having access to money.

Social organisations, which are often termed associations, are considered the necessary bridge that may allow social movements to shift from 'short-wave' mobilisations to 'medium-wave' popular movements and, later, to 'long-wave' historical movements (Villasante 1994). A key question is how social organisations relate to capital and the 'state', which can be considered as the two main systemic 'institutions'. Antonio Gramsci (1930-35) considered that the 'state' was the addition of government and civil society, with the latter including associations. But the 'state' is not static; it is the result of dynamic processes. Such processes or relations can become conflictive or integrative, but it has to be taken into account that conflicts can also be (systemically or socially) integrative, and that processes which try to integrate can become so conflictual as to provoke a social break-down.

In these processes, collective actions, social movements or organisations can have a key involvement. Following the sociologist Jesús Ibáñez (1997), their orientation in relation to the dominant system can have four forms:

- *converse* (in the sense of convergent or converted) – when the norms dictated by the dominant system are accepted without any need for change;
- *perverse* – when associations want to change individuals but not structures or basic norms;
- *subversive* – when the collective protest establishes an alternative legitimacy with new norms;
- *reversive* – when the principles of the established system are accepted but then overturned in practice by concrete actions and alternatives.

In order to reach these alternative outcomes, action is necessary. Collective actions, social movements and organisations can also be of several kinds (Sánchez Casas 1997):

- *action groups* are formed by several individuals coming together with a large-scale alternative project in mind to oppose the institutional apparatus (including state and capital) by a strategy of transformation;
- *'ensembles of action'* are composed of individuals who participate in a social movement or organisation with perhaps a longer-term objective and which, at least for the time being, does not question the system;
- *protest groups* include individuals who are involved in actions with the single objective of a concrete protest about a thing or an issue;

To this list, other kinds of action can be added in order to achieve a broader classification (Morén-Alegret 1999):

- *passive groups* unite individuals who do not want to transform anything, but who aim to conserve cultural, social and economic life;

- *safety-valve groups* are composed of individuals who are dedicated to avoiding protest, and who may even be converted into destroyers of alternative projects.

Immigrant associations have been studied in some detail in northern Europe (e.g. Layton-Henry 1990), but much less in southern Europe, which is where my research breaks new ground. After the analysis of the information gathered during my fieldwork, it was possible to see how social organisations often changed positions over time, sometimes being 'action groups', and other times becoming 'safety-valve' institutions. In summary, two main orientations can be found among associations: a systemic one and a social one. The systemic orientation includes converse and perverse logics, while the social orientation includes the subversive and the reversive logics. The state includes governments and institutionalised organisations (i.e. systemic organisations), while autonomous organisations try to foster the self-management of society without mediators. However, the same association can be ruled by different logics in different periods of its history. Thus the state can be understood as the addition of governments plus institutionalised social organisations at a given moment and place. In a sense, following Slater (1997), the state can be identified with 'politics' while 'the political' is the social movement that challenges such ordered and institutionalised 'politics'. Both have strong geographical and spatialisation implications.

Little literature exists on the relationship between capital and social/institutionalised organisations. However, the rule of capital is more than the organisations that openly defend its rule or the business companies; it is a system that can 'colonise' everything, including human beings opposed to it in social organisations (Holloway 1995). In this sense, one of capital's faces is money. Social movements and organisations may be influenced by their relation to money (which may be at the same time a key bond in their relation with governments). Today, under neoliberalism, money is one of the key resources for an organisation; even in the most 'alternative' project, the relationship with 'money' may condition its possible successes and strength (and even when there is opposition to 'money', a relationship to money still exists).

Even so, it is possible to resist in an organised way the system's threat. Such resistance is better understood by bearing space and class in mind. On the one hand, following Steve Pile (1997, p. 27), 'resistance is as much defined through the struggle to define liberation, space and subjectivity as through the élite's attempts to defeat, prevent, and oppress those who threaten their authority. At the heart of questions of resistance lie questions of spatiality – the politics of lived spaces.' On the other hand, in Portugal since the 1980s, the main conflict around 'foreign immigration' has been the legislation passed by central government on the status of 'foreigners', dividing those immigrants from the rest of society. This kind of discrimination may be called institutional racism (Joly 1998). However, such legislation does not equally affect all 'foreign immigrants': the country of origin, relations with the means of production, the amount of money in a bank account, etc. are influences on how differently legislation affects a 'foreign immigrant'. Following Michael Keith (1997), subjectivities of resistance cannot be divorced from the institutions of subjectification, thus government immigration policies have also to be examined.[4]

Furthermore, when 'foreign immigrants' organise themselves into associations or join together with local people in other social organisations, it will be seen that those who struggle for changing or putting an end to legislation on foreigners are, in general, those who are also concerned with conditions at the workplace. This is because there is usually a direct link between denying residence and work permits to foreign workers and a major appropriation by employers of surplus-value from workers (in other words, workers' exploitation is easier if people do not have proper documents). If an employer does not pay social security taxes for workers and keeps them from accessing social benefits, such an employer is probably obtaining more profit from those workers. This situation of minimum labour rights may affect in a similar way a young Portuguese student who works part-time in a pizzeria or a foreign worker who works full-time (often over 12 hours a day) on a building site. However, apart from the obvious distinction in hours, a difference is that the latter can be threatened with expulsion from Portugal at any time, and his/her social situation may be more complex and vulnerable. Both may be considered as 'fresh' labour, as Marx called it, but the struggle to re-appropriate the surplus value may have some differences, due to laws governing foreigners. Thus, the struggle that several social organisations started – in Portugal mainly since the early 1990s – to change foreigners' legislation can be related to a class struggle to avoid over-exploitation of foreign workers, especially those who are undocumented, but also the rest who have to renew residence permits and need a labour contract in order to do so. Bureaucratic procedures certainly militate against foreign workers' rights.

Today, explicitly or implicitly, the main aim for a significant number of organisations is 'partnership', even where the distribution of power may be very uneven: partnership between labour and capital, between capital and government, and between labour and government.

However, there is also another call, a not-always-apparent claim for 'resistance': basically, people's resistance to capital and governments.[5] In the case of foreign immigrants the main resistance may be to legislation, but it is also resistance to Eurocentric cultural imperialism. However, sometimes such resistance may lead to an 'enclosure' and it can be learned from history that closure is not the best way to resist capital oppression, because such enclosed or encapsulated groups can be isolated and consumed as an 'exotic' product ('Chinese food' or 'African music', for example) or attacked for being a supposed threat to society (for instance, islamophobia in Europe and the USA). A way forward may consist in performing as a 'solid' (organisation) just briefly, when it is necessary in order to avoid repression or to fight for their rights, while the rest of the time people can be acting as a 'fluid' (movement) in order to avoid forced and unwanted closures.

African immigrants' social organisations in Lisbon have adopted multiple forms (e.g. based on ethnic background, religion, class, gender, status, etc. and mixtures of these criteria). Even if putting labels on associations is avoided in this text, I do try to make a selection of social organisations according to a few representative factors: age (founded in 1960s–70s, 1980s and 1990s), membership figures (small, medium, large), meeting place (city centre, peripheral neighbourhoods), and the nature of their main objectives (conservation of 'culture', defence of human rights, mutual aid, service provision, religious practices, etc.). Political refugees from East Timor and small associations from Macau, Goa and São Tomé e Principe have not been taken into account to avoid an over-fragmented and unnecessarily detailed account. Instead, the focus of this chapter is on the Cape Verdean Association, the Muslim and Hindu communities, and the Angolan, Guinean and Senegalese groupings. In the conclusion a possible trend will be noted: although the 'Lusofonia' project is getting stronger, it is possible that, after decades of hegemonic sub-Saharan African migration to Lisbon, an increase in North African immigration may take place. In such a case, a 'Maghrebisation' of Lisbon may happen and another door could be open to Mediterranean migrations.

General features of the African presence in Lisbon

Since early times, Lisbon attracted people not only from the whole of Portugal, but also 'foreigners', especially Europeans, Africans and Asians. The Atlantic seaways were the main routes for the Portuguese ships for centuries, and African people arrived in Lisbon in this context. Since the sixteenth century, 'black' people were enslaved to work in Lisbon, as domestic servants in the city or doing the heaviest jobs in the rural areas. According to the historian Tinhorão

(1988, p. 120), in those times the main reason for having domestic African slaves in Lisbon was not ostentation but profit and convenience. In the special conditions of the Portuguese urban economy during the early centuries of oceanic sailing, owning one or more black African slaves at home was big business: if in the countryside they could be considered like human machines together with beasts of burden or draught animals, in cities like Lisbon they were over-exploited to do the heaviest jobs and rented in the streets.

After the official end to slavery, the African presence in Lisbon diminished, although there remained a few people from the colonies in the metropolis as students, etc. In the mid–1960s immigrants from the then Portuguese colony of Cape Verde arrived to work in civil construction and public works, and they became a reserve of cheap workforce. But these immigrant workers were pioneers; in general, it is after the April 1974 Revolution that the inflows from abroad became dominant. In the mid–1970s a change in the characteristics of the migration flows led to the consolidation of several types of migrant (Baganha and Gois 1999; Da Silva *et al.* 1993; Rocha Trindade 1995). Economic restructuring in the North European countries led to the return of the Portuguese emigrants (*emigrados*) who were working abroad, mainly in France. With the decolonisation process in Africa came the return of the Portuguese residents from Angola and Mozambique, the *retornados*. During the 1980s, new migration inflows arrived in Portugal (*imigrantes*); the main origins were the former Portuguese colonies in Africa, East Timor and India (Goa). With the greater economic dynamism reached as a result of joining the European Community in 1986, an increase took place in the numbers of European immigrants, mainly from Britain, Spain, Germany and France. Finally, there was a significant increase in the Brazilian presence on the basis of the long history of relations between Portugal and Brazil.

The number of foreigners with documented residence in the district of Lisbon has risen from 20,737 in 1975 (when the total foreign population in Portugal was 31,983) to 92,441 in 1995 (total foreign population in Portugal 168,316). Thus the concentration of well over half the foreign population resident in Portugal in Lisbon has been a constant characteristic of the last decades. If the focus is on the nationalities, in 1995 there were 18,391 EU residents in Lisbon, compared to 53,175 who had nationality of African countries (Cape Verdeans 25,829, Angolans 10,838, and immigrants from Guinea Bissau 7,895). Brazilians numbered 8,473, North Americans were 4,643 and the population with Asian passports were 4,663.[6] Among Asian immigrants, Indian and Pakistani nationals are increasing in number. Although mostly with Portuguese nationality, in Lisbon there is a significant number of Mozambican-born people with an Indian family origin (see Malheiros 1996).

In the following pages I categorise and interpret several kinds of sub-Saharan African immigrants' self-organisation. As we shall see, there is a wide variety of ways in which, and reasons why, people organise themselves. In the cases studied here, national, cultural or religious solidarity, together with the struggle for social, labour or citizen rights and the provision of services and assistance can be underlined as the main 'organising criteria' which are influential in African immigrants' participation in associations in Lisbon.

The first generation of immigrants' associations: Cape Verdeans under colonial influence

The oldest organisation created by immigrants from Cape Verde which is still running is the Associação Caboverdiana, founded in 1981 on the basis of the Casa de Cabo Verde, which had been created following the idea of a 'regional house' in the 1960s (when Cape Verde was officially considered part of Portugal). Today the Associação Caboverdiana is an association which includes members spread all over Portugal. However, before the 1974–75 revolutionary process most of the members of Casa de Cabo Verde were an elite of skilled men over 40 years old who were based in Lisbon. After the revolution the situation changed, the name shifted to Associação Caboverdiana and the membership composition became much more diverse in socio-economic terms, including unskilled workers, professionals and skilled workers. Most of them are men (80 per cent in 1991, according to an internal report, although its president in 1997 was a woman) and aged between 30 and 50 years old. When asked in an interview in what circumstances the association was created, its president Alcestina Tolentino gave, in a sense, a geographical answer: they were looking for 'a space' to meet people and to affirm their own culture; and they tried to be an association which adapted to the changing situation of the community and of Portugal.

During the last 15 years Cape Verdean associative life has undergone several changes and community associations have mushroomed in the suburbs and shanty-towns where most Cape Verdeans live. Today the tasks are more those of representing Cape Verdean interests in dealings with Portuguese institutions than before, while there are other local associations in the neighbourhoods undertaking grassroots activities. This transformation started in 1991, when a new executive committee was elected, and new members took charge of the association, among them Arnaldo Andrade, then a sociology student and today one of the leaders. After this change of orientation, also in 1991, Associação Caboverdiana became co-founder of a platform of immigrants' associations, religious institutions, trade unions and humanitarian organisations. It first started in an informal way, but later their meetings became a formal committee called Secretariado Coordenador de Associações para a Legalização (SCAL), about which I shall have more to say towards the end of this chapter.

In the early 1990s, the group that won the presidency of the Associação Caboverdiana had five main objectives (regularisation, government integration policy, votes in local elections, education policy, and housing) and a strategy which included taking advantage of certain feelings of imperialist paternalism in some groups of Portuguese society.[7] What have been changing, according to the situation, have been their tactics, which included the creation of SCAL to lobby government and political parties. Thus the Capeverdean Association can be considered as following mainly reversive strategies, because even if accepting the established system it tries to overturn some of its norms by concrete actions. However, as will be noted below, this association also follows a perverse logic, because in some actions it wants to change individuals and not norms or structures.

The executive committee members are all volunteers; there is just a secretary as part-time salaried worker. However, in the headquarters of the Association there is a bar-restaurant that employs five salaried workers. Associação Caboverdiana members are around 500, of whom about one tenth are active members participating regularly. There are members from other nationalities (Portuguese, other Portuguese-speaking African countries, other European countries, etc.), but in the assemblies only people from Cape Verde can vote. The main way of raising money is the membership fee, although there are others like the organisation of cultural and leisure activities in their own bar-restaurant. They have also applied for funding to government and other institutions, such as the Lisbon city government, the Governo Civil, some ministries of the central government, international organisations and the European Social Fund. In this sense, the Cape Verdean Association has seen an increasing monetarisation of its social life, in other words a growing colonisation of the life-world by the system (e.g. money and bureaucracy). This increasing paramountcy of systemic over social modes of operation has paralleled the more general post-1970s shift from fordism to post-fordism under neoliberal ideas which has spread the power of money to spheres previously untouched by it (Holloway 1995).

However, they may also follow a social logic in specific moments. One key instance of the Association's involvement in the defence of

Lisbon's Cape Verdean community was the judiciary case against the extreme-right individuals responsible for the killing of a young Cape Verdean man, Alcino Monteiro, in the Bairro Alto in June 1995. As a response, the Associação Caboverdiana hired a top lawyer for their legal prosecution. A demonstration 'like in the 1970s', in Arnaldo Andrade's words, was organised by immigrants' associations and solidarity organisations to protest over the killing. However, in general, the strategy of immigrants' associations has been to avoid street fighting and instead to work 'within the system', within institutions and governmental bodies (one visible outcome was that there were two African MPs from the Socialist Party in 1998). However, it is also sometimes seen as necessary to have media coverage in order to have 'visible' action.

This visibility may depend, among other things, on gender issues. During my fieldwork, a key difference between Lisbon and Barcelona (where I also did research) was discovered: in Barcelona there are several immigrant women's associations (even if transcontinental immigration is more recent there than in Lisbon), whereas in Lisbon immigrant women's associations are not so clearly defined or well developed. Several reasons can be suggested for this but, as will be shown below, the generally conservative Portuguese social context and certain legal constraints have made women's issues a low priority for immigrant organisations and NGOs. Not that initiatives following the improvement of women migrants' conditions have been entirely lacking in Portugal: special training courses were organised by the Associação Caboverdiana for 20 young women in 'new professions' such as video-making, photography, etc. in order to avoid them working as cleaners or in domestic service (as most Cape Verdean women in Lisbon do). But the problem is that the Association does not have the possibility of organising further training for them or directly placing them in alternative jobs. The only way forward is to give the young women information on other possible places where they could obtain help (just three of them obtained jobs related to the training). Another training course has been for play leaders and cultural entertainers, but this is different because the participants are mainly students and organising activities with kids and youngsters is seen as a secondary issue at that point in their lives. Furthermore, in 1997, the Associação Caboverdiana started a training course on service sector employment techniques for 45 young people, and in 1995 it carried out a training course for 30 youth leaders in the neighbourhoods to supervise children and youngsters.[8]

In relation to coordination with other organisations in Lisbon, the Cape Verdean Association also participated together with the two main trade unions in the elaboration of the recent foreign labour law. There are good relations with SOS Racismo and Frente Anti-Racista in order to tackle discrimination and other conflicts. The relations with some other Lusophone 'foreign immigrant' associations are also good, with regular contact and collaboration. However, there are no relations with European or North American immigrants' associations. In fact, the President of the Cape Verdean Association understands the term 'immigrant' to mean 'unskilled worker'. The Association has occasional links with employers' associations, but only during the regularisation process, in order to ask them to tell their members to implement their role in the process.

There have been several unsuccessful attempts to create a federation of Cape Verdean associations, but differences between them are too significant to allow unity beyond specific actions and objectives. One of the difficulties of creating a federation is 'social class'. There are completely different kinds of associations among the so-called Cape Verdean community: from elitist associations for people with at least secondary or higher education degrees, to neighbourhood associations mainly for unskilled (and sometimes illiterate) workers. Associação Caboverdiana is considered an 'inter-classist' association (i.e. it includes people with different socio-economic status), although its leaders belong mainly to what I would call an educated *petite-bourgeoisie*. In the spring of 1998 a congress of Cape Verdean emigrants from all over the world (America, Africa, Europe and even Asia) took place in Cape Verde in order to discuss these wide-ranging issues and because associations of 'foreign immigrants' may become nodes in transnational human networks. The conference aimed to help to coordinate activities or information exchange at a global scale.

In this regard, the geographer David Harvey (1996) has been suggesting the necessary creation of a global alliance of grassroots social movements to oppose capitalist world-wide exploitation and destruction. In fact, the People's Global Action (PGA) against the World Trade Organisation in 1997 is an instance of what can be done with such an aim in mind (their actions against capitalism in over 40 countries around the globe on 18 June and 30 November 1999, including Seattle, demonstrated its potential and, in a way, follow some of Harvey's ideas). However, the global Cape Verdean congress can not be thought of as a true grassroots event. Firstly, it was designed to be mainly for *quadros caboverdianos na diáspora* (in other words, for educated Cape Verdean emigrants), although later it became a bit wider. Secondly, instead of supporting a horizontal transnational grassroots world-wide social movement (such as PGA), the Cape Verdean congress was reinforcing a nationalist approach to social mobilisation, based on being Cape Verdean. Furthermore, it had a strong institutional ingredient, with the participation of the Cape Verde government, representatives of all Portuguese (and some Italian) political parties, officials from some Dutch local governments, and public personalities from the United States and elsewhere. This institutional side can also be observed in the relationship with political parties. In the case of the Associação Caboverdiana in Lisbon, although there is political diversity among the membership (mainly the Socialist, Communist and, less so, the Social Democratic Parties), preferences in the executive committee are for the *Partido Socialista*, and they have permanent dialogue with several local authorities ruled by this party. However, AlcestinaTolentino points out that only the small far left-wing political parties (PSR, UDP) had been active in the shanty towns before the vote in local elections was granted for Cape Verdeans.

Religious minorities and immigration

Apart from the Cape Verdean Association (mainly composed according to 'national' criteria), another group whose immigrant origins date from the late 1960s is the Islamic community, composed according to religious criteria of three main waves of immigrants: in the 1960s students from the then African colonies; political exiles in the mid–1970s after PALOPs' independence; and since the 1990s 'economic' immigrants from a scatter of countries including Senegal, Morocco and Pakistan.

The process of building the mosque in central Lisbon, the meeting-place of the Islamic community, is a key issue in understanding the history of the Comunidade Islâmica after the problems under the dictatorship. And even before they built the mosque, it is interesting to take into account their religious meeting places to understand the evolution of this community: from a small mosque within the Egyptian Embassy, to an imperial palace 'offered' by the Portuguese government in 1980, to the new building constructed with funding mainly from Saudi Arabia.

According to Yiossuf Mohamed Adamgy, director of the journal *Al-Furqan*, if the Islamic community in Lisbon had received a larger amount of money they would have finished the construction of the mosque earlier. The land is public property but was offered by the Portuguese government to the Islamic community. In order to build the parts that are already completed they obtained funding from several Islamic countries, the biggest contribution coming from Saudi Arabia. All Islamic embassies in Lisbon joined in a commission in order to support the construction of the mosque.

The problem was that there were delays in receiving the money which provoked postponements in the building works and thus increased the costs.

Since the early 1990s more Muslim immigrants have arrived in Portugal, mainly from Pakistan, Senegal, Bangladesh and Morocco. The Imam of Lisbon's mosque, Sheikh Munir, underlines that the reason why there is a new wave of immigrants with a Muslim background is simply economic. Like other members of Lisbon's Islamic community, he is afraid that the level of islamophobia that exists in other European countries may arrive in Portugal, and he makes it clear that there are no shadowy interests in the arrival of Muslims. For Sheikh Munir, there are no major conflicts which specifically affect Muslims; the main conflicts suffered are more generalised and relate to racism. Others, however, like Adamgy, believe there is already islamophobia. In relation to the Muslim headscarf, according to my interviewees there are no problems in Portugal. Imam Munir considers that what happened in France is a cultural and political conflict, not a religious one. Furthermore, it also has to be taken into account that most young Muslim girls in Portugal do not wear the scarf. Adamgy suggested that sometimes when something is banned (as happened in France), people's reaction is to do what has been banned. In any case, their response to both racism and islamophobia is quiet and pacific, trying to explain what they consider the truth is about.

Although there are no official data collected on immigrant numbers by religious affiliation, according to several sources Muslims in Portugal number between 15,000 and 20,000 people, mainly concentrated in the Lisbon Metropolitan Area. Around 3,000 are members of the Comunidade Islâmica (the minimum monthly fee is 100 escudos per person), and among these there is a core of 30–40 active members. In Lisbon's mosque it is possible to find between 12 and 30 people in the daily prayers. According to the Imam, the fact that a significant number of Muslims work in construction (this means long working days) makes it difficult for them to attend daily activities. Those who attend the ceremonies are often the Muslims who arrived during the 1960s and 1970s from Africa, who have Portuguese nationality and a permanent job or their own business. Their age is mainly over 45 or below 18 years.

The Islamic 'community', according to its leaders, is shaped by all those people who share the Muslim religion, and it includes and goes beyond associations of particular nationalities or origins, as for instance the Association of Pakistani Muslims or the Guinea-Bissau Muslim Association. All the work done for the Islamic community is voluntary work, but there is a salaried worker doing secretarial tasks and another one cleaning the building. Its work consists in helping to improve housing conditions, supplying a monthly benefit to over 100 people in need, and a provision of basic food (rice, flour, etc.) once a year. They do not have public funding, only private donations. Although they try to extend their scope, their resources are very limited in comparison to other Portuguese charities.

Comunidade Islâmica has no relations with trade unions or with employers' organisations (strategies like those of French Muslims pushing trade unions to lobby for rooms for praying at the workplace were unknown among the Muslims I interviewed in Portugal). With SOS Racismo and other Portuguese NGOs there is a regular 'cold relation' via postal mail. Although there are some Muslim rank and file members of trade unions and some Muslim small businessmen, as a community they try to avoid any involvement in labour conflicts (including clandestine work in the Expo '98 building site), either because they consider such matters as 'personal' problems or because they are afraid of endangering a source of income.

Cultural and social activities organised by the mosque are open to everybody (for conferences, Arabic language lessons, exhibitions, weddings, etc.), with the exception of religious ceremonies. The main language of communication in the mosque is Portuguese, although there are other languages spoken, including Creole, Urdu, Gujarat and Arabic. Some of the newcomers do not speak Portuguese and this is seen as a major obstacle to integration; they do not trust the Portuguese government to solve these problems due to bureaucracy and because the Muslim community in Portugal is still young.

It is difficult to place the Islamic community in any of the forms suggested by Ibañez (converse, perverse, subversive, reversive), or, probably, it is more correct to note that all of those forms are useful to understand some of the tactics followed by the Islamic community in Lisbon.

The Islamic community has been helping during the regularisation process by providing legal advice to Muslims. They have also been participating in an informal consultation process over the recent Portuguese law on religious freedom, but not in equal conditions with the Catholic Church, which obtained the official recognition of the government (although according to its constitution Portugal is a secular country, in reality the Catholic Church has an impressive influence over state issues).

The Imam of Lisbon's mosque considers political participation important, but recognises that prior to 1998 they were not successful in having officials or MPs in mainstream political parties owing to the recency of the Muslim presence in Portugal in modern times. However in the past, Ali Mamede, the founding member and President of the community until 1995, belonged to the centre-right Social Democratic Party (PSD) and obtained top positions under the previous conservative government (he was president of LUSA, the official Portuguese news agency, and ENATUR, a public body for tourism). Some links have remained after his death; for instance the President of the PSD visited Lisbon's mosque in 1998. Today there are a few members of the Islamic community who belong to the PSD and the PS (centre-left Socialist Party). There are no Muslim members in the PCP (Communist Party) because it is an atheist party, or in the right-wing PP because it is a Catholic party. However, according to Adamgy, the only local government that is funding a Muslim association is the Câmara Municipal de Loures, where the mayor and most of the councillors are members of the Communist Party (PCP). The differences between the PSD and PS government are not significant for some members of the Islamic community.

Relations with the Lisbon local government have been limited to concrete issues, but with a poor record for efficiency: in the late 1980s they applied to have a Muslim cemetery (when Nuno Abecassis was mayor) and it was not until the late 1990s that land was provided in Lumiar cemetery, two mayors later (the property will be municipal, but it will be used by the Muslim community). There are other mosques in the Lisbon Metropolitan Area (Laranjeiro, Almada, Odivelas) and in Oporto there is a room available for prayers. The executive committee of the Islamic community is composed of 10–15 members elected in an annual assembly where both men and women participate. However, today the committee is entirely staffed by men (in the past there was one woman).

The Islamic community in Lisbon does not have an official bulletin or magazine. However, there is an association called Al-Furqan which publishes a journal every two months on Muslim issues (cultural, religious and community information). Around 1,000 copies are distributed. This cultural association was started in Portugal in April 1981, and as time went by it started publishing pamphlets and later books on Islamic topics (in 1998 it had already published 108 items in Portugal). The access of the Islamic community to television is limited to five minutes every three weeks on RTP2, which is seen as insufficient time to explain religious issues. This situation contrasts with the media power of the Obra Católica das Migrações and the Catholic Church as a whole. An alternative medium for the Islamic community is the Internet, where they write articles to explain their points of view.

In Lisbon there is also a Hindu community which grew out of the immigration from Mozambique to Portugal after the independence of this African country. Before 1975 only a few Hindu families were living in Portugal, but they were enough people to function as a bridge between the newcomers and the rest of Lisbon's society and, together with the more recently-arrived, to create an association. Officially the Comunidade Hindu de Lisboa was created in 1982, although informally there had been meetings since the late 1970s. From then on the idea of building a social centre and temple for the community gained force, and has been the main objective of the association until now. The land was bought by the Câmara Municipal de Lisboa, and the location was decided taking into account its proximity to the areas where there is a strong presence of Hindu community members. The temple is still under construction and there is no date for completion because it depends on donations, most of which come from the Portuguese Hindu community itself, although from time to time visitors from Britain have contributed extra money.

So far the Hindu community has been mainly concerned with the building of the temple, but they have also been conducting activities to improve the welfare of the community and, to a certain extent, the rest of Portuguese society. Among the current activities to improve the community social situation are training courses (mainly for professional qualifications and English/Portuguese language training) funded by the Integrar programme of the European Union. Communication has also been a key issue for the community: although for some time they were trying to publish a magazine, finally radio has been the medium chosen. Since 1991 they have rented a commercial Lisbon radio station called Radio Orbital every Sunday, initially just for an hour, and currently from 10 am until 3 pm. The main aim of the programme is to spread Hindu culture and music. They have also taken advantage of the seven minutes and thirty seconds available for them on the public TV channel RTP2 every three weeks (in the programme *A fé dos homens*, Men's faith). Their main language of communication is Gujarati, and on Saturdays they organise Gujarati lessons in their social centre, located in the temple.

Most Hindu people in Portugal are members of the 500 family-strong Hindu Association. They pay a monthly fee of 1,000 escudos per family (plus an initial subscription of 5,000 escudos per family). To become a member it is necessary to be introduced by a person known by the community, and then the proposal is considered by the committee. The only other permanent meeting place apart from their temple (located in the area of Lumiar, Lisbon) is a small place in Oporto available for praying. They consider that today it is easier to practise their religion in Portugal compared to the situation during the early 1980s. Their relations with the central government have been through the Alto Comissário para a Imigração e as Minorias Étnicas (ACIME), and those with the Câmara Municipal de Lisboa have been mainly mediated via Conselho para Imigração e Minorias Étnicas.

However, relations between the Hindu community and NGOs are scarce, and with political parties and trade unions practically nil. Links with other immigrant associations are also very weak, but they have institutional relations with the Rotary Club, reflecting the business orientation of many Hindus in Portugal. Nowadays, there is a gap between old Hindu immigrants from Mozambique (who are in charge of the community and work as traders or professionals) and the new Hindu immigrants from India who work in construction. An example of such distance is that the Hindu community was not involved (as were other immigrant organisations) in the 1996 regularisation process because most of their members already had documents. Thus, in a similar way to the Indian Association in Barcelona, the Lisbon Hindu community is closer, in some aspects, to most immigrants from the rich countries such as Britain or the USA. However, unlike Barcelona's Indian Association, Lisbon's Hindu group is linked to local institutions that deal with ethnic minority issues (like ACIME and the consultative council of Lisbon's local government).

To sum up at this point, there are several differences between the Associação Caboverdiana, Comunidade Islâmica and Comunidade Hindu, but one factor they have in common is that the origin of all three was in a small group of people who arrived as colonial and post-colonial migrants and who had a 'middle-class' background mainly as students and skilled workers from the Portuguese colonies. However, as time went by, more people with a working-class or peasant background have joined these associations, although their involvement, especially as leaders, is limited because of their precarious living conditions. In any case, today their executive committees remain in the hands of those with more experience and time available, typically those who arrived in Portugal during the 1970s or 1980s and who usually work as professionals.

Neighbourhood-oriented associations and the re-orientation of trade unions during the early 1980s

After the aforementioned associations appeared in Lisbon city centre, other kinds of immigrants' organisations were created in the neighbourhoods where most poor 'foreign immigrants' live, the *bairros de lata* on the urban periphery. Among these other organisational forms, Moinho da Juventude ('Youth Mill') stands out because of its activities and involvement in Alto Cova da Moura, a poor neighbourhood in Amadora. Alto Cova da Moura was built during the 1974–75 revolutionary process: some Cape Verdean workers squatted a large piece of land owned by a rich Portuguese landowner who fled to Brazil after the

Portuguese dictatorship came to an end. In this neighbourhood 6,000 people currently live, most of them with a Cape Verdean background, although there are Angolan, Guinean, Senegalese and even Portuguese minorities.

The history of Moinho da Juventude starts when an adult couple (a Portuguese man and a Belgian woman) arrived in the neighbourhood in the mid–1980s, to visit a Cape Verdean comrade of the domestic service trade union who was living in the area. They found a poor area, but with a lot of community life, friendship and mutual help: a sharp contrast with the individualistic situation of the middle-class neighbourhoods in Lisbon impregnated with neoliberal ideology and practices. The couple squatted on some land in the neighbourhood and built their own house. At the starting point of any project with people, there are two main possibilities: to impose a pre-determined vision (leading by example or behaving as a vanguard), or to follow what people want to do (as the *Zapatistas* in the Mexican province of Chiapas learned to do in the early 1990s). In Alto Cova da Moura, they opted for the second way, giving priority to the needs of women and children with their own involvement in the design and development of activities seeking empowerment. At the beginning they found scepticism among people but also interest in discussing common problems and looking for common solutions, as for instance organising literacy courses.

The building of the neighbourhood association was parallel to the building of a place where everyone could meet, organise activities and enjoy social life. Today it has 500 members who sometimes pay a symbolic fee of 600 escudos a year, plus 100 escudos for enrolment, but it is not compulsory. The construction of the social centre was done through voluntary work during weekends and people's spare time.

The sexual and international capitalist division of labour dictates that the jobs available for unskilled women originating from poor countries are mainly limited to domestic service or cleaning. Aware of such constraints, but unable to challenge them in the short term – only a long-term educational project or, more likely, a radical social and politico-economic transformation could do this – Moinho da Juventude started organising short-term training courses for women on domestic service skills, responding to the short-term urgency of obtaining income. These included cooking, using washing machines, sewing and other skills.

Of course it must be recognised that, in this way, the lack of alternatives forced people to reproduce an unfair division of labour. The late 1980s and early 1990s in Portugal were years of neoliberal policies, a sharp decrease in social mobilisation, and increasing monetarisation of virtually all aspects of life. Without feasible alternatives, people reproduce the system continuously, even if they are aware that the system is unfair and that there are individuals who are responsible for injustices. However, despite these general systemic difficulties, for Cape Verdean women in Alto Cova da Moura it was possible to improve their situation in a number of areas through participation in the domestic service trade union (where they could develop a class consciousness and be aware of their rights at work), and through participation in the women's group of Moinho da Juventude (through which they could learn to confront their husbands, who were working in the construction sector in other areas without taking care of the children).

On the first issue – women workers' organisation in trade unions – it is interesting to note the situation of the cleaning services trade union in the late 1970s and early 1980s in the Lisbon Metropolitan Area. As an Angolan female trade union leader indicated to me in interview, it was not easy to be a black foreign worker in those times, even in the cleaning services (one of the economic sectors where it was easiest to get a job), because Portuguese women were suspicious of them. However, there was a turning point in the situation in the 1980s, when Portuguese women started increasingly to reject these kinds of poorly paid jobs and company managers started to be more willing to hire foreign black workers. But in many cases, new immigrants did not know what a trade union was, nor how it worked: it takes some time to see how things work in a new country.

On the second issue – women's self-organisation – after debates on maternity, the family and other issues, these Cape Verdean women became aware their own that situation was not fair and had to be changed. This was not an external imposition, but a process of common reflection on their daily lives. It was not an easy process; at the beginning there were husbands who did not allow women to go to meetings, but after a while and with common effort it was possible to change such 'macho' attitudes. However, it has to be taken into account that patriarchal attitudes are also common among Portuguese men. A general situation characterised by the weakness of the feminist movement in Portugal (an instance is the recent defeat in the referendum on the right to abortion) and conservative attitudes at home (influenced by strong conservative Catholic values) is not conducive to overcoming macho attitudes.

Furthermore, in Moinho da Juventude they also stressed the importance of work with Cape Verdean children and youths, trying to avoid teenagers dropping out of school and offering them alternative activities to drug dealing (professional training, excursions and sport, for example).

Another form of activity consists in giving support, through a group called 'Esperança' (Hope), to young Cape Verdean women who are single parents. Initially, only modest steps can be taken, because of the lack of confidence these young mothers have in themselves. However, in the long term, although there are obvious difficulties, it is seen as necessary to change the political consciousness of young people in order to challenge their problems. In fact, a number of the children who were educated in Moinho da Juventude over a decade ago are today active members of the association. One of the daily problems they had to resolve was to stop police arresting young black boys randomly. They also campaigned to enable young people born in Portugal but with Cape Verdean nationality (the majority) to play football in the Portuguese leagues, and to regularise those without documents. In the 1996 regularisation process almost all in the neighbourhood obtained residence permits, but most of them are still classified as 'foreigners' and need to renew the permit regularly, which is not easy and, consequently, there is a high number of non-renewals due to bureaucracy. In order to carry out some projects they applied for funding to the European Union, which allowed them to contract some psychologists and sociologists to help them in their activities, and to offer youngsters small grants as an alternative to income from drug dealing.

Thus Moinho da Juventude can be seen as a group that follows mostly a reversive logic because they apparently accept some principles of the system and then they try to overturn them in practice by specific actions and alternatives. However, in specific moments this association has followed subversive logic as it has established locally an alternative legitimacy with new norms. This situation is difficult to sustain for a long time in a hostile context.

New immigrants' groups offer services and a common platform appears: SCAL

In 1987, a few years after the creation of Moinho da Juventude, the Associação Guineense de Solidariedade Social was created in Lisbon. However, the roots of the association, according to its leader Fernando Ká, are in the independence of Guinea Bissau, because from then on those who emigrated or were already living abroad (and did not go back to the country) were considered as 'traitors' by their government (and also ignored by the Portuguese government). Thus, the creation of a mutual help association became necessary for the survival of Guineans in Portugal.

The role of immigrant people who had been living in Portugal before the independence of the Portuguese African countries is a key to the success of some associations (as we saw for Cape Verdeans, Muslims and Hindus). As Fernando Ká indicates, his presence in Lisbon since 1969 as a student in a Franciscan seminary was helpful in order to set up the association because he knew the country well and because he had a lot of Portuguese friends, some of them 'influential' people. The genesis of Associação Guineense is closely related to the history of post-colonial Guinea Bissau, as it was the outcome of a political movement (Movimento Bafatá) that decided to have a social affairs branch (Associação Guineense de Solidariedade Social), which finally split from the political 'mother'. Currently this Guinea Bissau association claims 2,420 members and has become probably the largest African association in Portugal, including members from other African countries. They have carried out projects to build social housing for African families with the support of the European Union and local government in the Lisbon Metropolitan Area.[10] They have also developed professional training projects for the integration of young people in the car industry; they have organised courses for the training of cultural entertainers; they give food to 100 families (500 people) every month with the support of the Banco Alimentar Contra a Fome; they give legal advice on regularisation, police harassment and labour rights issues; they give support to people who suffer illness; and, furthermore, if they can not resolve problems, they direct people to other sources of information.

The Guinea Bissau Association has better relations with the Câmara Municipal de Lisboa than with the central government, although with the Alto Comissário para a Imigração e as Minorías Étnicas (ACIME) relations are also good. On the other hand, the Guinean Association is an active member of SCAL (which they see as a positive instrument for social organisations), but relations with trade unions are few, and there are no relations with the main Lisbon mosque (although there are several Muslim members). At the international level, Fernando Ká has friends among black members of the British Labour party, and he regards their role as a model for the Portuguese black community (in fact, he has invited them to meetings with African communities in Lisbon a couple of times).

The headquarters of the Association are located in the working-class estate of Chelas.[11] The office is open eight hours a day, except at weekends. It is designed as an association of services with three permanent salaried workers (the president and two female secretaries: one from Angola and the other a Portuguese local) and five permanent volunteers (one Guinean and four Portuguese).

Among the members there are immigrants from other African lusophone and francophone countries, but no Asians. On the other hand, young people in the Association have gained autonomy, and a recently-created African young people's association called GENOVA (Geração Nova) meets at the same place, organising their own activities. The current location of the Association was decided by chance, as it was offered by the Câmara Municipal de Lisboa in 1992 when they outgrew their previous premises (near Praça Espanha, in Lisbon city centre). However, currently Fernando Ká considers it useful to be located in a working-class neighbourhood.

Although Fernando Ká was trained to be a priest, the Guinean Association has no formal links with the Catholic Church beyond its participation in SCAL. The branch of the mainstream church in Portugal which deals with migrants and social policy is Obra Católica das Migrações (OCM). Its leader, Padre Manuel Soares, together with relevant members of the Brazilian community and people from various African groups, trade unions, etc. created the Secretariado Coordenador de Associações para a Legalização (SCAL) in December 1992. SCAL is the aforementioned platform of organisations campaigning for the documentation of 'foreign immigrants' living in Portugal. The organisation of the first SCAL general assembly was carried out by immigrants' associations such as the Cape Verdean Association and the Guinean Association, but they needed a person to chair the platform, and thus the director of OCM was elected to hold this post. In fact, informal meetings had already started in 1991. There have been several other general assemblies of SCAL since 1992. In one of them the organisations participating elected a representative to a government body in charge of the analysis of the regularisation process, the Comissão Nacional para a Regularização Extraordinária (CNRE). The person elected was António Tavares, member of SOS Angola. Other organisations which are members of SCAL include CGTP, UGT, Oikos, Casa do Brasil, and Associação de Coordinação de Imigrantes Angolanos (ACIMA); this organisational membership has remained fixed since the beginning. However, by 1998 they were already thinking of enlarging the group and becoming more formal (they were just an informal platform) in order to become partners with the government on immigration issues, as trade unions are on labour issues. This 'statist' approach is shared by other community leaders, for example the President of the Casa do Brasil de Lisboa, and is in tune with the conceptualisation of the state in today's capitalist system inspired by Gramsci, namely the combination of government plus institutionalised civil society. In fact, in interview Carlos Viana, President of the Casa do Brasil, went further in his analysis of the relations between the state, government and society; in his view the state, understood as government, should be an instrument of society, although he recognises that this does not happen because society is divided into classes.

After the regularisation process ended in December 1996, the Portuguese government thanked the social organisations that were involved in SCAL and gave 20 million escudos to the platform. The money has been used to fund social projects presented by secular organisations and churches with a cost of up to 500,000 escudos. In this way, processes of institutionalisation, monetarisation and bureaucratisation go forward together but ever more intertwined. Thus SCAL can be seen as a safety-valve institution, because it is dedicated to reaching agreements with the government with the minimum public conflict.

SCAL has seen a change in governmental policies on immigration issues since the PS has been in power, and it is very critical of the European pressures to have more control over immigrants. According to a widespread view among the associations I interviewed, there are more comments on the EU's repressive policies than on its social funding. Furthermore, SCAL is not recognised as an institution by the EU, and therefore some projects submitted for funding have been rejected (an information guide for immigrants, for example).

Another immigrants' association which appeared in Lisbon in the early 1990s is the Associação de Solidariedade Angolana (ASA), created in 1992 by a handful of Angolan immigrants and students resident in Portugal in order to support needy Angolan children living in the Lisbon area. This initiative happened in a context where the Angolan government was not concerned about emigrants abroad, and where Angolan associations that already existed in Lisbon were considered elitist. ASA participated in the regularisation process by providing information to Angolan immigrants, but their main work is in helping children who are living in a precarious situation in the shanty-towns of the Lisbon Metropolitan Area (and also in Braga, Coimbra and the Algarve). ASA is a small association of volunteers, without headquarters, and without economic support from city councils or the central government, although they acknowledge that they have never applied for public funding. The reason why ASA has not sought government help is because they only have 25 members and they are waiting to become larger before applying. Most of the members are young people and women, although there are also some older members up to 60 years old. In 1998 they were trying to create an NGO in order to support street children in Angola. According to my interviewee, Josefina Belo, ASA work with Angolan immigrants is very limited owing to the lack of agreements between the Angolan and Portuguese governments on immigrants in the latter country (their legal status is much more precarious than the Cape Verdean immigrants).

The last generation of immigrants' groups in the 1990s

In the mid–1990s a 'new wave' of immigration arrived in Portugal. To be more precise, people from countries previously not included in the statistics issued by the Serviço de Estrangeiros e Fronteiras (SEF) started to migrate and settle in Portugal. Even if the Portuguese government's policies and laws are not helpful for their 'settlement', the need of fresh labour for public works (prior to, during and after Expo '98) has been reason enough to allow them to stay for some years. These people came to Portugal from Eastern Europe (Romania, Russia, etc.), the Indian subcontinent (Pakistan, India, Bangladesh), West Africa (Senegal, Mali, etc.), and North Africa (Morocco, Algeria, Tunisia).

Associational life among them is just starting. Some Pakistani and Senegalese immigrants have been able to organise themselves thanks to the mosque, which is a meeting place and a source of help and advice. On the other hand, in the cases of 'communities' like Romanian people (but also Senegalese), some members of Olho Vivo have been helping them to organise their fellow-country people. Olho Vivo is a secular NGO, based in Queluz (near Lisbon), with several kind of activities, including protection of historical heritage sites, environmental struggles, and defence of human rights. It was in its premises that a Senegalese man and a Romanian man started participating in social organisations in their new country of residence. Both had previous experience of participating in associations in their countries of origin and once they had the chance (enough leisure time available and enough knowledge of the Portuguese language) and they knew about Olho Vivo, they joined the organisation. That occurred in late 1997 and early 1998, and in a few months Olho Vivo membership grew because workers from Romania and Senegal started to join this NGO. However, they also realised the possibility of organising a Romanian association and a Senegalese association, as an addition to their participation in Olho Vivo. They were supported by Olho Vivo in this enterprise and started talking to people and contacting authorities in order to do so. In May 1998, when the 'Universal Exposition' started, the process was still in its initial stages; a year later the organisational process was more advanced and the involvement in Olho Vivo even greater. One process was reinforcing the other.

A Senegalese immigrant, Seck Mohammed, has been the bridge between Olho Vivo and Senegalese people in Portugal. Around 100 Senegalese immigrants joined this NGO after he became a member. Seck Mohammed's reasons for doing so are based on the struggle to make human rights respected everywhere, also for 'foreign immigrants'. Beyond the already existing Muslim Senegalese Association linked to the mosque, Seck Mohammed wanted to create a secular Senegalese association. However, his priority was the work with Olho Vivo, because he considers himself a universalist and it is a 'universalist' NGO, beyond religion and nationalities. This universalism is also reflected in national demonstrations. Each 25 April (the anniversary of the 'Carnations Revolution') there is a big demonstration in Lisbon with the participation of several thousands of people to celebrate the dictatorship's collapse. In 1998 a contingent of 'foreign immigrants', mainly from non-lusophone countries, joined the demonstration to stand up for their rights.

With regard to people with a North African background, the public works that took place in Lisbon in association with Expo '98, together with the 1996 regularisation process, attracted workers from Morocco, Algeria and Tunisia. Some of them came from other European countries to find a job and documents (e.g. from Spain, France, Belgium, Italy and the Netherlands) and others came straight from North Africa. Even if a significant number of them applied for residence and work permits, according to some NGOs and trade unions, they were discriminated against by the Portuguese government, which favoured lusophone immigrants. Thus most of them do not appear in official statistics. Their arrival may be just an occasional flow or could become a new trend in trans-Mediterranean migrations.

Conclusions

In these post-fordist neoliberal times, some organisations participate as part of the state, getting involved in providing services or implementing policies. Many NGOs and some trade unions can thus be found to be part of the state without being government. In compensation these organisations receive money and other benefits from the government, and hence become part of the systemic logic discussed in the introduction to this chapter. However, at the same time, small groups of people and associations (coordinated or isolated) struggle to organise (parts of) society against the state's colonisation of the system. They try to preserve their autonomy from the state and capital.

In this chapter I have refrained from a categorisation of associations according to external labels; instead there has been an attempt to uncover the several logics that affect migrant social organisations in Lisbon. The type of influence may vary from time to time, e.g. an association may be boosting social relations with a mutual aid workshop in the morning while it provides a top-down service during the afternoon. This mixture of logics followed also applies to groups if attention is paid to reversive and subversive logics on the one hand, and perverse and converse logics on the other. However, from the fieldwork it can be seen that there are some organisations that maintain a steady hegemonic systemic trend during a long period while others follow mostly a social path for a long time.

These interlinked (or linked) processes of institutionalisation, bureaucratisation, monetarisation, etc. that have been impregnating Lisbon's social organisations during recent decades were originated in northern European countries and expanded all around the world during a century or more of capitalist colonialism. Countries like Portugal were the bridge that made possible the expansion of such processes to countries like Angola, Mozambique, Cape Verde, etc. At the same time, Portugal is southern Europe, but it is the only southern European country that has no Mediterranean coast. Furthermore, it has been more influenced by sub-Saharan African countries than by North African ones. Portugal has been also a bridge – or perhaps a side-door – bringing people from some parts of Africa to northern and Mediterranean Europe.

Lisbon, being part of the Atlantic South, has particular ways of life that make it different from the northern European Atlantic cities and closer to the Mediterranean. This is Lisbon's uniqueness: it is part-Atlantic and part-Mediterranean. But more than any other southern European city, it has historically functioned as an outward-looking city of a vast colonial empire. Thus, whilst Lisbon shares common features with other cities discussed in this book (similar physical structures of an old city centre, poor peripheral neighbourhoods, institutional involvement of the Church and a few NGOs etc.), there are also important differences with regard to the ethnic, cultural and national make-up of its immigrant populations, which are overwhelmingly from sub-Saharan Africa. However, a final question can be posed. In the long term, do the new inflows from Northern Africa imply a shift in such composition? So far the Portuguese state is implementing policies to avoid it, as the 1996 regularisation process showed.

Notes

1   This chapter is based on the author's PhD thesis entitled *Integration(s) and Resistance. Governments, Capital, Social Organisations and Movements, and the Arrival of Foreign Immigrants in Barcelona and Lisbon*, awarded at the Centre for Ethnic Relations, Warwick University in 1999 (Morén-Alegret 1999). Fieldwork comprised tape-recorded interviews with key members of social organisations and institutions, participant observation, document analysis, triangulation and statistical work. In this chapter just some data from my Lisbon fieldwork are analysed, although a few comparisons with Barcelona are made to enrich the text. This chapter has been improved by helpful comments from Àngels Pascual de Sans and Abel Albet (Universitat Autònoma de Barcelona), Zig Layton-Henry (Warwick University) and Russell King (University of Sussex). Furthermore, I am grateful to all the interviewees and people who shared time with me in Lisbon. I dedicate the chapter to my 'original family' from Barcelona and to my 'social family' in Vale de Amoreira and Baixa da Banheira (Lisbon), together with my friends there and elsewhere.

2   In Lisbon's streets and academy, to call somebody 'African' is to make automatic reference to 'sub-Saharan Africans'; North Africans are not usually included in this category. However, there is an important debate on how to name those people whose geographical background is sub-Saharan Africa. All categorisations and labels are

problematic, especially in Portugal where there is such a wide diversity of people with African links.

3   It is also important to distinguish between the neoliberal propaganda on the need to foster a 'virtual cooperation' among salaried employees at the workplace (without removing hierarchies) and, on the other hand, the cooperation among equal people (who try to be free of systemic relations) based on mutual aid inspired by friendship, fellowship, solidarity or affinity.

4   However, in this chapter there is no room for an analysis of government policies, so just a few brief references are made. For more information on this, see Morén-Alegret (1999).

5   Production is not a main concern for European social movements. This contrasts with the Brazilian landless movement's (MST) motto *'ocupar, resistir e producir'* (to squat, to resist, and to produce), and their network of small cooperative companies. In southern Europe, except to a certain extent in Italy, even the squatter movement is mostly just concerned with squatting in a place and resisting.

6   These data are from *Estatísticas Demográficas 1995*, Lisbon: Instituto Nacional de Estatística.

7   In Lisbon, in January 1998, a conservative Portuguese language teacher told her casual pupils (I was among them) a story according to which the Portuguese ex-colonies in Africa are seen by some Portuguese people as children who, later, when they became teenagers, wanted to be emancipated (independence in the 1970s) and to have nothing to do with their parents (Portugal); however, some years later (in the 1990s), when they were more mature, they (the former colonies) wanted to have good relations with their parents (Portugal). This is a Christian comparison based on the Prodigal Son tale. It demonstrates an imperialist paternalism which is common among a significant number of Portuguese people.

8   Associação Caboverdiana also carried out information campaigns for the registration of voters for the Portuguese local elections in 1997 (together with the Casa do Brasil), for the documentation of immigrants in 1992–93 and 1996, for improvement in health conditions, young mothers' education, and adult literacy during the 1980s. Some years ago they published a bulletin called *Montanha*, but it is not distributed any more because of lack of funding. Among their activities there has also been a campaign to improve housing conditions, cooperating with local authorities and central government. The Cape Verdean Association also has cultural activities and celebrations such as Independence Day (5 July). However, there are no formal programmes of cooperation with Cape Verde beyond a few isolated and *ad hoc* actions.

9   For a geographical reflection on the *Zapatista* movement see Slater (1997).

10 At the time of my fieldwork, in 1998, they were managing a project with 30 flats with the Câmara Municipal de Lisboa. They claimed to be the only African association in Portugal engaged in social housing projects.

11 Chelas is an example of a neighbourhood built to host immigrants and other poor Portuguese people who were living in shanty-towns. The hip-hop singer General D (1997) has mentioned Chelas in a song as a case of 're-ghettoisation', of re-creating ghettos with concrete.

References

Baganha, M. and Gois, P. (1999) Migrações internacionais de e para Portugal: o que sabemos e para onde vamos? *Revista Crítica de Ciencias Sociais*, 52/53, pp. 229–80.

Cardelús, J. and Pascual de Sans, À. (1979) *Movimientos Migratorios y Organización Social.* Barcelona: Península.

Da Silva, M. B. N., Baganha, M. I., Marenhão, M. J. and Pereira, M. H. (eds) (1993) *Emigração/Imigração em Portugal.* Algés: Fragmentos.

Gramsci, A. (1930-35) State and civil society, in Hoare, Q. and Smith, G. N. (eds) *Selections from the Prison Notebooks of Antonio Gramsci.* London: Lawrence & Wishart, 1971, pp. 206–76.

Harvey, D. (1996) *Justice, Nature and the Geography of Difference.* Oxford: Blackwell.

Holloway, J. (1995) Global capital and the national state, in Bonefeld, W. and Holloway, J. (eds) *Global Capital, National State and the Politics of Money.* London: Macmillan, pp. 116–40.

Ibáñez, J. (1997) *A Controcorriente.* Madrid: Fundamentos.

Joly, D. (1998) Introduction, in Joly, D. (ed.) *Scapegoats and Social Actors. The Exclusion and Integration of Minorities in Western Europe.* London: Macmillan, pp. 1–12.

Keith, M. (1997) Conclusion. A changing space and a time for change, in Pile, S. and Keith, M. (eds) *Geographies of Resistance.* London: Routledge, pp. 277–86.

King, R., Fielding, A. and Black, R. (1997) The international migration turnaround in Southern Europe, in King, R. and Black, R. (eds) *Southern Europe and the New Immigrations,* Brighton: Sussex Academic Press, pp. 1–25.

Kropotkin, P. (1939) *Mutual Aid. A Factor of Evolution.* Harmondsworth: Penguin (originally published 1902).

Layton-Henry, Z. (1990) Immigrant associations, in Layton-Henry, Z. (ed.) *The Political Rights of Migrant Workers in Western Europe.* London: Sage, pp. 94–112.

Malheiros, J. M. (1996) *Imigrantes na Região de Lisboa. Os Anos da Mudança. Imigração e Processo de Integração das Comunidades de Origem Indiana.* Lisbon: Colibrí.

Morén-Alegret, R. (1999) *Integration(s) and Resistance. Governments, Capital, Social Organisations and Movements, and the Arrival of 'Foreign Immigrants' in Barcelona and Lisbon.* Warwick: University of Warwick, Centre for Research in Ethnic Relations, PhD thesis.

Pile, S. (1997) Introduction. Opposition, political identities and spaces of resistance, in Pile, S. and Keith, M. (eds) *Geographies of Resistance.* London: Routledge, pp. 1–32.

Rocha Trindade, M. B. (1995) *Sociologia das Migrações.* Lisbon: Universidade Aberta.

Sánchez Casas, C. (1997) Movimientos sociales y integración, *Papeles de la Fundación de Investigaciones Marxistas,* 8, pp. 161–8.

Slater, D. (1997) Spatial politics/social movements. Questions of (b)orders and resistance in global times, in Pile, S. and Keith, M. (eds) *Geographies of Resistance.* London and New York: Routledge, pp. 258–76.

Tinhorão, J. R. (1988) *Os Negros em Portugal.* Lisbon: Caminho.

Villasante, T. R. (1994) *Los Retos del Asociacionismo,* Madrid: Caritas Documentación Social, 94.

7

Immigration and national literature: Italian voices from Africa and the diaspora

Alessandra Di Maio

An introductory anecdote

In September 1996, a young, beautiful black woman, a naturalised Italian citizen born in the Dominican Republic, was awarded the title of Miss Italia by the unanimous decision of a group of beauty pageant judges and nine million Italian tele-voters. Although Denny Mendez's victory was the result of what amounted to a popular plebiscite, her coronation as beauty queen of Italy sparked heated controversy throughout the country and raised curiosity abroad (see, for example, Gennari 1996; Pinkus 1998). To some extent, the magnitude of the attention that this event garnered may be compared to that which followed Vanessa Williams' winning of the title of Miss America in 1984. If the fact that an African-American woman being chosen to represent her country's beauty throughout the world was regarded as an extraordinary event in the United States of America, which prides itself on being one of the world's largest multi-ethnic societies, one can imagine what a debate a black Miss Italy stirred among Italians, many of whom regard themselves as a monochrome, if not mono-ethnic, species.[1] A certain Donna Elvira wrote to *Panorama*, one of Italy's most popular political magazines,

> In this country, they are making us swallow anything, even a black Miss Italy. This beautiful young woman will represent us all over the world for an entire year, and people who do not know geography very well will believe that our girls are the colour of chocolate.[2]

Donna Elvira's remarks show that the recent rhetoric of a multicultural community proposed by one of Italy's best-known clothing companies – the world-famous 'United Colors of Benetton' motto and visuals – is based on a false premise: the colours of Italy are not quite united yet.

With this anecdote, I certainly do not intend to assess the validity of such events as beauty pageants, but I mean to illustrate how Italy envisions itself, and is envisioned, at the turn of the century and millennium. In fact, the debate over the true nature of contemporary Italian beauty reflects a new, more general concern with the redefinition of the Italian cultural identity which, in the last few years, appears to have undergone dramatic transformation.

Italian national identity and immigration

Since Unification in 1861, Italy has struggled to define its own national identity in a way that takes into account what Verdicchio (1997, p. 156) concisely calls its 'indigenous cultural diversity'. Italy resulted from the political union of a number of relatively small, contiguous states which, although connected by the semi-isolation of the geographic territory, similar histories, frequent inter-marriages and the power of the Papacy, had developed their own cultural identities throughout the centuries. Their unification was rather problematic, and gave rise to a wide range of issues, the aftermath of which the modern Italian nation is still facing. Umberto Bossi's *Lega Nord* (Northern League), for instance, is only one of the most recent aspects of the still unresolved Southern Question, which Antonio Gramsci, amóng many others, recognised as being one of the new nation's central concerns. However, the richness of Italian culture – the 'Italianness' recognised throughout the world in the country's arts, fashion, food and so forth – derives from this unique century-long, dynamic, often problematic, but extremely fertile syncretism.

During the last few years a further variegated layer has been added to Italy's already multi-layered society. Traditionally a source of emigrants, the country has recently become a hub for immigration. The Second National Conference on Emigration, held in Rome in 1988, reported that for the first time since Unification, the number of people entering the country exceeded that of those leaving. People have been arriving from various parts of the world: from the Maghreb, especially from Morocco and Tunisia; from sub-Saharan African countries such as Ghana, Senegal, Nigeria and Kenya; from the Middle East; from Eastern Europe, in particular from Poland, Rumania, Albania and the former Yugoslavia; and from a variety of countries geographically, if not culturally, as far away as the Philippines, China, Sri Lanka, Cape Verde, Argentina, Peru and Brazil.

Initially considered transitory by both the newcomers and the host country, immigration to Italy soon tended to assume a permanent status. The immigrant question was immediately regarded by Italy as a European question, not only because some newcomers were arriving from neighbouring countries, but especially because the immigration inscribed itself within the broader context of a migratory trend that concerned the European Union as a whole. The increasing presence of immigrants from the four corners of the world imposed a reconsideration of the transnational European community discourse, and raised issues of borders, nationality, ethnicity, race and civil tolerance.[3] Umberto Eco (1990) observed that this massive, diversified immigration toward Western Europe was a far more significant phenomenon for the formation of a new European identity than the crisis of communism in the former Eastern block.

Italy was caught totally unprepared to receive such a plethora of people, whose augmenting presence called for prompt regulation. Social controversy, within both the national and the European borders, quickly arose. Concurrent with an attempt to promote a culture of acceptance and solidarity was a relapse of nationalism, racism or, in the best case, bewilderment – all sentiments which are conflated in Donna Elvira's letter to *Panorama*.

The birth of an immigrant literature

Although often forced to the margins by the 'welcoming' Italian society, the manifold heritage of the newcomers has increasingly interacted with, and added to, the complex social, political, economic, religious, intellectual, artistic and, as is clear in the example of Denny Mendez's election as Miss Italy, even aesthetic Italian texture. As a result, the Italian landscape is changing, even literally in some cases: besides St. Peter's and the imponent synagogue on the opposite bank of the Tiber, Rome now boasts Europe's largest mosque (see Richards 1994, pp. 233–56).

The immigrants' presence has become increasingly apparent in big urban centres as well as in the countryside, in schools as much as in factories, in the media as much as in sports, and in politics as much as in the arts. One of the major fields in which their presence has become progressively more visible is literature. In 1990, the publication of Pap Khouma's *Io, venditore di elefanti* (I, the elephant seller), Salah Methnani's *Immigrato* (Immigrant), and Mohamed Bouchane's *Chiamatemi Alì* (Call me Alì) marked the beginning of what one can refer to as the new Italian literature of immigration, which has been flourishing ever since. Several denominations have been suggested to refer to this emerging literary corpus – Italophone literature and *meticcio* writing, among others.[4] At this point in history, I prefer the first-mentioned nomenclature above, because it highlights the experience of immigration to Italy, which all these authors share and address in their works, regardless of their original cultural background. In fact, if on the one hand each of these pieces reflects a personal experience and incorporates the author's original tradition, on the other hand they all originate from within the circumstances of Italian society, at the same time addressing it as an audience.

It is interesting to notice that the first three extended immigrant narratives are all written by Africans, and recount, through the prism of fiction, their personal experiences as migrants. Recently the African diaspora has spread northwards, not only towards the former colonial nations, but in general towards the lure of the so-called 'first world'. Italy, perhaps mostly because of its crucial geographic position, has been a prime destination, especially for North Africans. Khouma, Methnani and Bouchane are among those African diasporic writers who have contributed to telling the story – and the history – of their people's recent migrations to the North of the world (on this see the recent collection edited by Bellucci and Matteo 1999). Methnani's novel narrates the experience of a young Tunisian man who travels Italy, the country of his dreams, from South to North, only to meet with disappointment. Khouma tells the story of a Senegalese street-vendor who, after briefly residing in France, tries to make a life in Italy. Bouchane's novel is about a young Moroccan who, after joining a group of migrant labourers, decides to change his name (Abdullah) to Alì, so that Italians will be able to pronounce it properly, while allowing him to retain his Muslim identity.

The fact that these narratives were first published in 1990 is not an accident. In February of the same year, the controversial Martelli Law, the first to systematically address the question of immigration in Italy, granted *in situ* immigrants – those who had entered the country prior to December 1989 – a right to citizenship. This law was called, in Italian legal jargon, a *sanatoria* – an amnesty, aiming to regularise the position of the considerable number of clandestine immigrants and to prevent further illegal entry into the country (although it eventually failed in this last intent). The word *sanatoria* derives from the verb *sanare*, which means 'to heal', to restore somebody's health. Graziella Parati notes the misleading connotations of this metaphor in the age of Aids. She remarks that this terminology, borrowed from the rhetoric of sickness, seems to assume that becoming a nation of immigration involves a contamination of the body of the country, which in this legal text is narrated as diseased (Parati 1997a, p. 119). This malady, according to the legislation, should be cured, and further contagion prevented. Yet, Parati suggests, '[In] narrating the multiracial nation through the legal text, Italy has attempted, and failed, to "practice safe text"' (1997a, p. 119).

Only a few months after the promulgation of the Martelli Law, Methnani, Bouchane and Khouma offered their interpretation of the aching Italian socio-political, legal and narrative body in their works, opening the path to what would soon become a copious and diverse literature of immigration. Claiming for themselves the right to speak with their own voices, to tell their stories from their own standpoints, and to write the history to which they were contributing participants, these writers re-manipulated and revolted against the narratives created on and about them. With the force of their own creative imagination, they portrayed their own experience as immigrants, therefore appropriating the reins of the nation's discourse on immigration. From narrative objects, they made themselves narrative subjects. Asked what he intended to demonstrate with his book, Khouma answered,

> I did not start writing because I wanted to demonstrate something. What I wanted to do was to take the floor. Because Italians were talking about us, but they were asking questions and answering them all by themselves. That's why we took the floor: to interrupt this monologue and establish a dialogue. This was the goal of my book.[5]

The genre develops: autobiography, collaboration, encounter, dialogue

The example set by Khouma, Bouchane and Methnani was soon followed by a number of other writers. Among these, in 1991, Saidou Moussa Ba wrote *La promessa di Hamadi* (Hamadi's promise), which tells about the life of two Senegalese brothers in Italy (he eventually wrote a screenplay based on the book, which was made into a film entitled *Waalofendo*). In 1992, Tunisian-born Mohsen Melliti published the novel *Pantanella. Canto lungo la strada* (Pantanella. A song along the road), about an abandoned pasta factory in Rome, in which a heterogenous group of immigrants settles, but is eventually forced by police to leave.[6] In 1993, Nassera Chohra, a first-generation French woman of Algerian parents who only later in life moved to Italy, wrote *Volevo diventare bianca* (I wanted to become white), one of the first extended narratives by an immigrant woman, which recounts the various stages of her life-long journey. In 1994, Fernanda Farias de Albuquerque wrote *Princesa* (Princess), the story of a Brazilian transvestite who works the streets in Italy (on which the late Fabrizio De Andrè, one of Italy's most famous singer-songwriters, based his song of the same title). In 1995, times were ripe for the creation of the first literary prize exclusively dedicated to the literature of immigration – the Eks&Tra Prize – which in 2000 reaches its sixth year.

It is notable that many of the narratives mentioned so far contain an autobiographical reference in the title and often propose a first-person narrator/protagonist – I, the elephant seller; I wanted to become white. The autobiographical element has been crucial to the development of the Italian literature of immigration. Yet, although most of these narratives – especially, but not exclusively, the earliest works – are usually written in the first person, they are the product of collaboration between the immigrant authors and native Italian writers – journalists, authors, editors, transcribers, interviewers. Methnani wrote the story of *immigrato* Salah with Italian writer Mario Fortunato. Khouma's novel was transcribed and edited by journalist Oreste Pivetta. Bouchane's was edited by Carla De Girolamo and Daniele Miccione. *Princesa* was written by Fernanda Farias with her/his jail-mate, former Red Brigade terrorist and intellectual Maurizio Jannelli. Even an exceptional immigrant writer, well-known Moroccan-born Tahar Ben Jelloun, had an 'accomplice', as he himself said (1991, back cover), in Egi Volterrani when he published his collection of Italian stories *Dove lo stato non c'è* (Where the State is not present).

The literary collaboration between an immigrant and a native Italian writer fictionalises and symbolises the actual encounter between the host society and the newcomers. Much like the social ones, these artistic encounters have been extremely positive at times, laying the bases for professional relationships and personal friendships; but at other times they have proven to be problematic and conflictual. For instance, Nassera Chohra lamented that Alessandra Atti Di Sarro, who edited her book *Volevo diventare bianca*, pressed her to re-forge her narrative materials; whereas Saidou Moussa Ba, who wrote both *La promessa di Hamadi* and *La memoria di A.* (A.'s memory) with the collaboration of Alessandro Micheletti, remarked, 'Our books assume political meaning, because the immigrant and the native worked together, tried together. Therefore, these are books of encounter, dialogue, and culture.' (quoted in Colace 1995, p. 87B).

Interpreting and valuing Italian immigrant literature

This collaborative aspect, the autobiographical theme, the hot socio-political subject, the direct style and the often explicit language shared by these books determined that many readers – literary critics and writers likewise – regarded these narratives as 'pre-literary experiences with mere sociological value'.[7] I believe that in order to appreciate the importance of these recent works by immigrants to Italy, one has to read them as conscious, individual pieces of literature, without thereby denying their valuable social testimony (cf. King *et al.* 1995, pp. x–xi). In fact, if one really wants to understand in full their profound anthropological, sociological and historical value, one has to regard them in the first place as literary, artistic pieces produced by, and within, a society – the Italian, first of all, but also the European – in a process of rapid transformation. In 1905, one of Europe's first modern, controversial migrant writers, Joseph Conrad, stated: 'Fiction is history, human history, or it is nothing.' But, he added, it is also more than that, because 'it stands on firmer ground, being based on the reality of forms and the observation of social phenomena' (Conrad 1949, p. 17). Re-considering Conrad's comment nearly one hundred years later, one could argue that being deaf to the immigrants' fictional voices would mean being unwilling to hear how history is evolving, how society is changing, and how literary traditions are being transformed. Volterrani, in the introduction to Ben Jelloun's *Dove lo stato non c'è* (1991, p. vi), claims, 'In this book, we recognised the fundamental status and essential function of literature, which is to create fiction with the materials of reality.' Far from being an element of disruption, or of dishonour for the composite Italian literary tradition, the immigrants' works add to it, and offer alternative models and modes to its canon.

The Italian immigrants' literature is the result of individual and social 'acts of mediation' (Parati 1997b, p. 174) through various cultural, national and linguistic planes. These acts of mediation, which ultimately are acts of translation[8] from one culture into another, imply inclusion and connection among people and across spaces, which migrant writers enrich, expand and help redefine. From this perspective, I consider the often-proposed collocation of the Italian immigrant literature – or of any other literature resulting from acts of mediation – in a hybrid or in-between space as limiting. Even when employed with the intent to avoid the subordination of these emerging voices to one or more dominant discourses, I believe that this critical language, borrowed from the (dominant) postcolonial discourse, rather than eliciting connection, evokes incongruity and infertility – both connotations of the word hybridity. By doing so, it powerfully contributes to squeezing this new literature into a marginal, interstitial, possibly sterile space; a 'third space' as Homi Bhabha calls it which, ultimately, appears to be the by-product of two or more dominant canons (see Bhabha 1992; 1994, pp. 207–21). On the contrary, the immigrants' literary texts stretch across a plurality of spaces which they open and connect, as the authors stress, in an effort to establish a dialogue.

My hesitation in adopting *in toto* the language of postcolonial criticism for discussing the Italian literature of immigration derives from a double consideration. First of all, we are dealing with a new literature, resulting from a social phenomenon – that of immigration – which does not necessarily derive from that of colonialism, although in many ways it often intersects with it. Also, many immigrants come to Italy from former European colonies, but only a few come from the former Italian colonies in Africa – Somalia, Ethiopia, Eritrea and Libya. In brief, differently from England and France for instance, Italy is not in a pervasive 'Empire Writes Back' situation. Moreover, many of the so-called postcolonial writers themselves have a problem with the rhetoric of the postcolonial discourse, especially those from the youngest generations whose roots and routes often stretch across several nations and even continents. Caribbean-born and English-bred writer Caryl Phillips once recounted that, after having read a book on migrants and minorities in Britain entitled *Between Two Cultures* (Watson 1977), he distressfully thought, 'Hell, that's it, isn't it? I *am* between two cultures.'[9] Only eventually did he realise how false and disturbing the assumption proposed by that title was; because, he explained, 'people are never in-between two cultures; they *inhabit* two cultures, or even more'. Similarly, Senegalese–Italian writer Moussa Ba, on being asked whether he felt that he occupied a space in-between cultures and literatures, replied: 'First of all, I consider myself a man who has had the chance to transmit something. Then, I want to struggle to conquer *one* space in this world. But there are still obstacles to overcome, walls, which impede the dialogue among subjects of different cultures. The common goal is speaking with one another without frontiers.'[10]

Writing the 'Mediterranean Passage', writing plurality

The risk of marginalising literary production deriving from the contact of two or more worlds is not new. Alessandro Portelli has advanced an interesting comparison between the beginnings of a literature of the 'Mediterranean Passage' and those of African–American literature, hoping that Italians might prove less myopic than Americans were in accepting their so-called ethnic literature.[11] In an analysis of some African–Italian narratives, Portelli remarks that, although the experience of slavery is obviously altogether different from that of immigration, 'twoness' – a concept which he borrows from W. E. B. Du Bois – constitutes the central organising textual principle in both literary traditions. Twoness, Du Bois declared in 1903, is 'double consciousness, this sense of always looking at one's self through the eyes of others, of measuring one's soul by the tape of a world that looks on in amused contempt and pity'. The history of the African–American people, Du Bois explains, is based on this strife (Du Bois 1994, p. 5).

My argument is that the metaphor of twoness, masterfully used by Du Bois at the dawn of the twentieth century to describe a very specific historical context, can be amplified and succeeded by one of plurality at the onset of the millennium, when words such as multiculturalism, migrancy, transnationalism and globalisation have become so pivotal not only to the literary but also to the historic and economic discourses of many traditions. Plurality constitutes the organising textual principle of the diverse Italian literature of immigration, whether it is written by authors coming from Africa, the diaspora, or other regions of the globe. In fact, frequently the Italian immigrant writers' routes run across several countries while their roots plunge simultaneously into different soils. Chohra, for example, was born in France of Algerian parents, and only later in her life moved to Italy; Khouma came to Italy via France; Farias de Albuquerque via Spain; and Palestinian-born Salwa Salem, author of the novel *Con il vento nei capelli* (The wind through my hair), spent many years in Austria before settling in Italy (Salem 1993).

Each in his/her own way, the Italian immigrant artists – writers, as well as musicians, actors, directors and so forth – are exploring new ways of expressing their experience of plurality, by inverting, revising, revaluing and especially expanding not only cultural binary oppositions, but also the ideologies that propose them. Khouma says, '[In my book], I could have introduced the immigrant in a negative light, or vice versa; I could have said nice things about Italians, or I could have said nasty things about them. What I did, instead, was gather actual facts and let the readers judge for themselves.'12

In order to illustrate how this concept of plurality can become an organising textual principle, I would like to refer to part of a poem by the Cameroonian–Italian poet Ndjock Ngana, also known by the Italian name of Teodoro. This poem is included in the collection *ÑindôNero* (1994), where it appears, as all the other pieces in the book, *en-face* in Baasa and Italian (significantly, the title is made up of the two words that mean 'black' in each language). Here, beside the Italian, I want to propose a third version of part of the poem – my English translation – confident that I will remain faithful to its spirit.

Vivere una sola vita,
  in una sola città,
  in un solo paese,
  in un solo universo,
  vivere in un solo mondo
  è prigione.

[...]

Conoscere una sola lingua,
  un solo lavoro,
  un solo costume,
  una sola civiltà,
  conoscere una sola logica
  è prigione.

Living only one life,
  in one town only,
  one country only,
  one universe only,
Living only in one world
  is prison.

[...]

Knowing only one language,
  one craft only,
  one custom only,
  one civilisation only,
Knowing only one logic
  is prison.

One-ness, in Ngana/Teodoro's poem, is prison. Only plurality – of voices, places, bodies, thoughts – is freedom. Thus the migrant – at once immigrant and emigrant, *ñindô* and *nero* – represents the free person *par excellence*, because s/he is the one who can freely move across names, spaces, languages and traditions. Indeed, in the era of multiculturalism and globalisation, the migrant becomes the ultimate metaphor for man/woman. As Salman Rushdie, one of the most eminent contemporary migrant writers, suggests:

> The migrant is, perhaps, the central or defining figure of the twentieth century. ... Migration also offers us one of the richest metaphors of our age. The very word *metaphor*, with its roots in the Greek word for *bearing across*, describes a sort of migration, the migration of ideas into images. Migrants – borne-across humans – are metaphorical beings in their very essence; and migration, seen as a metaphor, is everywhere around us. We all cross frontiers; in that sense, we are all migrant peoples (Rushdie 1991, pp. 277–8; author's italics).

Thus one could argue that the migrant writer is, in many ways, the crucial figure of late twentieth-century (and later) literature (King *et al.* 1995, pp. xii–xiii). By celebrating multiplicity, in his poem-manifesto, Teodoro/Ngana claims for himself and his peer immigrant artists a broad, unrestricted artistic space, which includes and yet transcends the conventional boundaries imposed by national and cultural constructions.

Multiplicity is not only the artistic principle of composition but also the central theme of Fernanda Farias de Albuquerque's autobiographical novel *Princesa*, published in 1994. In my opinion one of the most intense and superb stories of the new Italian literature of immigration, *Princesa* is a trans-story altogether. It is the account of how Fernandinho, born in the Brazilian Nordeste – one of the main destinations during the slave trade – becomes first Fernanda, a prostitute transvestite, and then Princesa, not quite a transexual but not exactly a man any longer. Young Princesa undertakes a transatlantic journey to Europe. After spending a short time in Spain, she reaches Italy, where she works the street with the other *viados* – Brazilian transvestite and transexual street-walkers – and develops an addiction to heroin, experiencing some of the most violent aspects of illegal immigration. Princesa is finally arrested and imprisoned in Rebibbia, Rome's all men's jail, where she finds out that she has contracted Aids.

In *Princesa*, names, sexual identitites, bodies, nationalities and even languages are multiple. While in prison, Farias de Albuquerque – who was later deported to Brazil where she died in 2000, and who used her female identity as an author – told her story in a peculiar mixture of Portugese and Italian to Giovanni, a Sardinian shepherd jailed for life. Giovanni, whose first language was Sardinian, translated, transcribed and then passed the story on to Maurizio Jannelli, a renowned former terrorist, who ultimately wrote its final draft in Italian – an Italian which, as he states in his introduction to the novel, resulted from the chemistry of the three inmates' native tongues. This plurality of authorial voices, in Jannelli's words, 'opened a space for an encounter, and for mutual knowledge' which 'proved crucial to resist the devastating act of seclusion'.[13] Yet, if the narration was made possible by a multiple act of translation, the protagonist experiences multiplicity – of bodies, genders, love affairs, streets, homes etc. – as fragmentation, alienation, suffering, isolation and, eventually, imprisonment. While providing textual organisation, multiplicity appears as both a condemnation and an act of liberation in *Princesa*. If one reads this novel versus Teodoro/Ngana's poetry, one can discern two opposite faces of the same theme – that of migration: while the poem is an optimistic plea for inclusion and celebrates unity within plurality, *Princesa* denounces the unreconcilable yearning of a fragmented human being and of the pain of becoming.

Plurality is also at the centre of Tahar Ben Jelloun's short story *Pietro il matto, Pietro il saggio*, (Peter the madman, Peter the wise man), included in his Italian collection *Dove lo stato non c'è* (1991, pp. 177–89). The protagonist is a Sicilian *cantastorie* (literally, a story-singer) with a peculiar disability: every time somebody interrupts him while he is speaking, he begins to stutter. Pietro travels through the squares of Italy to tell people 'the truth'. Because, he suggests, 'Truth is not what you see. Truth is not what it is; truth is what you tell. I tell my stories without interruption, so that the truth can come out.' Yet he recommends, 'If the truth is stuttering in my mouth, be ready to catch it, and hold on to it; put its pieces together.' (Ben Jelloun 1994, p. 183). Only the act of narration, which implies the active collaboration of both authors and audiences, can turn fragments into significant plurality.

Plurality is also brotherhood in Ben Jelloun's story. Pietro has two brothers: Cicciu, his Sicilian *maestro*, who 'proclaims the truth while singing' (Ben Jelloun 1994, p. 185), and Moha, his Moroccan double, a ventriloquist storyteller who can clearly hear, understand and repeat without hesitation the stories of all those people – women, children, young militants – whose voices history has tried to silence. Sometimes, Pietro imagines that his Moroccan brother – already identifiable as the protagonist of Ben Jelloun's (1978) celebrated novel *Moha le Fou, Moha le Sage* (which opens a plurality of resonances and establishes a further dialogue among literary traditions) – now lives in Italy; in Sicily, specifically, which geographically and historically is the region of Italy closest to Africa:

> Often, I think I may meet [Moha] in Sicily. I can't find him, but I imagine him. Once I even believed that I saw him in Mazara del Vallo's *Casbah*, in a café full of Tunisian fishermen.[14] They were all there, around him, listening to the latest stories from their country. The Tunisians were watching and listening to him. They were sturdy young men, who had long left their villages, and had recreated their original place in Mazara; but they still lived in sadness. (Ben Jelloun 1994, pp. 184–5).

In Pietro, Moha and Cicciu, migrant, wise and mad storytellers of the Mediterranean, one can recognise a glimpse of their ventriloquist creator, and his burning desire – as well as the Italian immigrant writers' desire – to break the transnational walls of silence by telling the truth in an unedulcorated, yet highly lyrical, fashion. Moha's, Pietro's, Cicciu's and Tahar's voices are angry, painful, lyric, cathartic and, above all, sincere, when they amplify those of the silenced, wretched creatures of the earth.

Some have advanced the view that Ben Jelloun should not be considered an Italian immigrant author, by virtue of the fact that he was an established francophone writer well before his Italian book was published. I believe this is a moot point. First of all, quite a few immigrant authors had already written in one or more languages before they even learned Italian; some of them indeed were established writers before migrating to Italy, such as Albanian poet Gezim Hajdari. Moreover, by choosing to set *Dove lo stato non c'è* in Southern Italy ('Italian Stories' is the explicative subtitle of the book) and to write it directly in Italian, with the assistance of Egi Volterrani, his Italian translator who appears as a co-author, Ben Jelloun meant to make a precise statement: he wanted to offer his own vision of Italy, one of the countries in which he works and resides. But the Italy he describes in his stories is not flattering at all. It is a divided nation, corrupt and indeed diseased. His unflattering portrait may be one of the main reasons why *Dove lo stato non c'è* has been received with such negative criticism. Perhaps many Italian readers refuse to recognise themselves in Ben Jelloun's portrait, in which he argues that the perennial negligence of the state, and certainly not the relatively recent presence of immigrants, has been the main cause of the socio-economic and political problems of the South. He makes this point particularly clear in *Villa Literno*, which tells the story, based on a real event, of the murder of South African immigrant Jerry Masslo in an agricultural town south of Rome in 1989.

Exploring the experience of the immigrant woman

By writing his 'Italian Stories', francophone Moroccan writer Ben Jelloun has established new connections among literary traditions, further expanding and making ever more visible the 'open' space of the immigrants' literature. During her opening speech to the 1996 Eks&Tra Prize, Brazilian-born author Christiana de Caldas Brito remarked: 'Even if I was not forced to come here, to Italy, by reasons of poverty or by the necessity of finding a job, I feel I am an immigrant in every way. For me, immigrants are those who leave behind their traditions, habits, language, and their way of living and thinking, in order to immerse themselves in a new country, with all the fascination and risk that such a situation involves.' (de Caldas Brito 1997, p. 11).

De Caldas Brito is the author of a brief, powerful monologue, rich in pathos and irony, *Ana de Jesus*, in which the protagonist/narrator imagines a conversation with the *signora* for whom she works as a domestic helper (de Caldas Brito 1995). The first person narrator, in this piece, is not autobiographical any longer. Yet, it still expresses the necessity of telling an immigrant's story from an immigrant's point of view and with an immigrant's 'inflected' voice. De Caldas Brito (whose Italian is practically perfect), appropriates and manipulates the very idiolect through which native Italians discriminate against the immigrants, inventing what Parati (1996, p. 20) defines as a 'transgressive grammar ... of emigration and silence', in which Brazilian–Portuguese and Italian intertwine, becoming indistinguishable.

Madam, I don't feel good in Italy. I go back.

No, not like this. Better little by little.

Madam, don't mind? I want talk. I have little problem and I want solve with you.

Yes, when you wake, is good.

Good morning madam. You sleeped well? I? Not sleep well.

But she never ask how I sleep. I talk during the lunch, so. I feel sick, madam, I can't serve the table. I not know why.

But if I know, why say I not know?

Madam ... I like you and the doctor but ... I remember my country ... and ... I think all night and ... day too.

No, no time.

I want go back to my town because there I sing always. I feel sick here. I want go away. Understand, madam?

This way she understand nothing. So, slow. I tell the life in my town.

Madam, here sad and cold. I know, you gived me the beautiful coat, but in my country I not need the coat. Last night, madam, rained strong, no? And I took rain on my body, on my hair. All wet. I laughed, happy. All people look how I was crazy. In my country, I always take rain, no pneumonia. Italy rich, all people covered, they not feel pleasure in take rain on the body. [...] No heat in my country too. In Italy people is so rich that I am shamed. I wanted bring my daughter here, but why show my daughter so rich people? If the foots are without the shoes and the fingers are happy because they walk on the ground, you tell me, madam, why my daughter need use shoes? I know, you talk of disease, but the soul is more free if the foots feel free. Italy, big thin boot. What number, the shoe? [...]

I know. You have no time for hear me. You say: we speak after. You do always this.

And I continue speak to me.15

In *Ana de Jesus*, de Caldas Brito explores another complex aspect present in the immigrants' literature: that of the role of the immigrant woman. In her caustic monologue, the author emphasises how immigrant women occupy the margins of the margins of Italian society, even when they decide to speak (like Ana) or to write (like de Caldas Brito herself). In the so-called welcoming Italian society, immigrant women are often the subject of bodily invasions (prostitution, the sex industry, legal and illegal domestic labour are among their primary occupations), toward which the law seems to be willing to turn a blind eye.

Although too often easily dismissed, the female's presence is central to both the experience of immigration and its literature, as much as to the language that narrates and constructs the body of the nation – suffice it to think about metaphors such as *terra madre*, *madre patria* (motherland), and *lingua madre* (mother tongue). Somalian-born Shirin Ramzanali Fazel, author of *Lontano da Mogadiscio* (Far from Mogadisciu), when asked how she would explain the fact that the number of immigrant men writers greatly exceeds that of women, replied, 'I believe that many immigrant women will start to write soon. But right now they have the problem of looking for a job, a house, etc. Once they solve these immediate problems, it will be easier for them to talk.'[16]

In her novel, Fazel writes, 'The entire world is heading toward a multiracial, cross-cultural society, and people must accept that this mechanism cannot be halted.' (Ramzanali Fazel 1994, p. 63). Denny Mendez's election as Miss Italy makes ever more visible the irreversibility of such a mechanism, which the literature of the Italian immigration explores from different perspectives and with a variety of voices, while re-telling – or rather re-writing – the national literary identity.

Notes

1 In *I Razzismi Possibili* Laura Balbo and Luigi Manconi write, 'Italian society should be described as a monocultural and monochrome system. We are, more or less, white.' (1990, p. 29). This translation, as with the others in this chapter, is mine unless stated otherwise.

2 *Panorama*, 3 October 1996, p. 52.

3 During the past few years, many studies have been conducted on the causes, effects and dynamics of immigration both in Italy and in the rest of Europe. The following have been particularly relevant to the development of my discourse: Bolaffi (1996); Bonifazi (1998); Calavita (1994); Montanari and Cortese (1993); Papademetriou (1996); Papademetriou and Hamilton (1996).

4 See Colace (1995); Parati (1995). Armando Gnisci prefers to speak of an 'Italian literature of migration' (Gnisci 1998).

5 See Pap Khouma, interview by Graziella Parati, in Parati (1995, pp. 115–20).

6 For an interesting analysis of the Italian media's treatment of the Pantanella episode see ter Wal (1996).

7 Mario Fortunato, L'immigrato racconta in italiano (interview by Adriana Polveroni), *L'Unità*, 27 April 1995.

8 It is interesting to note that the verbs 'to transfer' and 'to translate' both stem from two different tenses of the compound Latin verb *trans-fero, fers, tuli, latum, ferre*, meaning 'to carry over'.

9 Caryl Phillips. Interview by Pico Iyer, *Lannan Literary Videos*, 44, 1995.

10 Saidou Moussa Ba. Interview by Parati (1995, pp. 104–7).

11 Alessandro Portelli, Mediterranean Passage. The Beginnings of an African Italian Literature and the African American Example, unpublished lecture delivered at Smith College, 22 September 1997.

12 Pap Khouma. Interview by Parati (1995, p. 115).

13 Maurizio Jannelli. Introduction to Fernanda Farias de Albuquerque, *Princesa* (1994, p. 7).

14 Mazara del Vallo is a fishing port in Sicily; facing the north coast of Africa, it hosts one of the largest Tunisian communities in Italy.

15 Cristiana de Caldas Brito, *Ana de Jesus*, translation by R. A. Franconi and G. Parati, in Parati (1999, pp. 162–3).

16 Shirin Ramzanali Fazel. Interview by Parati (1995, pp. 108–14).

References

Balbo, L. and Manconi, L. (1990) *I Razzismi Possibili*. Milan: Feltrinelli.

Bellucci, S. and Matteo, S. (eds) (1999) *Africa Italia: Due continenti si avvicinare.* Santarcangelo di Romagna: Fara.

Ben Jelloun, T. (1978) *Moha le Fou, Moha le Sage.* Paris: Editions du Seuil.

Ben Jelloun, T. (ed. and with a Preface by Volterrani, E.) (1994) *Dove lo Stato non c'è. Racconti italiani.* Turin: Einaudi.

Bhabha, H. (1992) Postcolonial authority and postmodern guilt, in Grossberg, L., Nelson, C. and Treichler, P. (eds) *Cultural Studies.* New York: Routledge, pp. 56–66.

Bhabha, H. (1994) *The Location of Culture.* London: Routledge.

Bolaffi, G. (1996) *Una Politica per gli Immigrati.* Bologna: Il Mulino.

Bonifazi, C. (1998) *L'Immigrazione Straniera in Italia.* Bologna: Il Mulino.

Bouchane, M. (ed. by De Girolamo, C. and Miccione, D.) (1990) *Chiamatemi Alì.* Milan: Leonardo.

Calavita, K. (1994) Italy and the new immigration, in Cornelius, W. A., Martin, P. L. and Hollifield, J. F. (eds) *Controlling Immigration. A Global Perspective.* Stanford CA: Stanford University Press, pp. 303–29.

Chohra, N. (ed. by Atti Di Sarro, A.) (1993) *Volevo Diventare Bianca.* Rome: E/O.

Colace, G. (1995) Nascita di una scrittura meticcia. Gli immigrati africani in Italia, *Linea d'Ombra*, 13(106), pp. 87–9.

Conrad, J. (1949) *Henry James. An Appreciation (1905)* in his *Notes on Life and Letters.* London: J. M. Dent.

de Caldas Brito, C. (1995) Ana de Jesus, in *Le Voci dell'Arcobaleno.* Santarcangelo di Romagna: Fara, pp. 59–61.

de Caldas Brito, C. (1997) Lo zaino della saudade, in *Memorie in Valigia.* Santarcangelo di Romagna: Fara, pp. 11–14.

Du Bois, W. E. B. (1994) *The Souls of Black Folk.* New York: Gramercy (originally published 1903).

Eco, U. (1990) L'Africa e l'Est: migrazione e liberazione, *L'Espresso*, 15 April.

Farias de Albuquerque, F. with Jannelli, M. (1994) *Princesa.* Rome: Sensibili alle Foglie.

Gennari, J. (1996) Passing for Italian, *Transition*, 72, pp. 36–48.

Gnisci, A. (1998) *La Letteratura Italiana della Migrazione.* Rome: Lilith.

Khouma, P. (ed. by Pivetta, O.) (1990) *Io, Venditore di Elefanti.* Milan: Garzanti.

King, R., Connell, J. and White, P. (eds) (1995) *Writing Across Worlds: Literature and Migration.* London: Routledge.

Melliti, M. (transl. by Ruocco, M.) (1992) *Pantanella. Canto Lungo la Strada.* Rome: Edizioni Lavoro.

Methnani, S. with Fortunato, M. (1990) *Immigrato.* Rome–Naples: Theoria.

Montanari, A. and Cortese, A. (1993) Third World immigrants in Italy, in King, R. (ed.) *Mass Migrations in Europe: The Legacy and the Future.* London: Belhaven, pp. 275–92.

Moussa Ba, S. (1995) *La Memoria di A.* Novara: De Agostini.

Moussa Ba, S. with Micheletti, A. (1991) *La Promessa di Hamadi.* Novara: De Agostini.

Ngana, N. (Teodoro) (1994) *ÑindôNero.* Rome: Anterem Edizioni Ricerca.

Papademetriou, D. G. (1996) *Coming Together or Pulling Apart? The European Union's Struggle with Immigration and Asylum.* Washington DC: Carnegie Endowment for International Peace.

Papademetriou, D. G. and Hamilton, K. A. (1996) *Converging Paths to Restriction: French, Italian and British Responses to Immigration.* Washington DC: Carnegie Endowment for International Peace.

Parati, G. (ed.) (1995) Margins at the Centre: African Italian Voices, special issue of *Studi d'Africanistica nell'Africa Australe/Italian Studies in Southern Africa*, 8(2).

Parati, G. (1996) Ospitalità italiana e letteratura immigrata, in *Mosaici d'Inchiostro*, Santarcangelo di Romagna: Fara, pp. 15–25.

Parati, G. (1997a) Looking through non-Western eyes: immigrant women's narratives in Italian, in Brinker-Gabler, G. and Smith, S. (eds) *Writing New Identities. Gender, Nation and Immigration in Contemporary Europe.* Minneapolis and London: University of Minnesota Press, pp. 118–42.

Parati, G. (1997b) Strangers in Paradise: foreigners and shadows in Italian literature, in Allen, B. and Russo, M. (eds) *Revisioning Italy. National Identity and Global Culture.* Minneapolis and London: University of Minnesota Press, pp. 169–90.

Parati, G. (ed.) (1999) *Mediterranean Crossroads. Migration Literature in Italy.* Madison: Fairleigh Dickinson University Press.

Pinkus, K. (1998) Miss (Black) Italy, *Black Renaissance/Renaissance Noire,* 2(1), pp. 80–93.

Ramzanali Fazel, S. (1994) *Lontano da Mogadiscio.* Rome: Data News.

Richards, C. (1994) *The New Italians.* London: Michael Joseph.

Rushdie, S. (1991) *Imaginary Homelands.* London: Granta and Penguin.

Salem, S. (with Maritano, L.) (1993) *Con il Vento nei Capelli. Vita di una donna palestinese.* Florence: Giunti.

ter Wal, J. (1996) The social representation of immigrants: the *Pantanella* issue in the pages of *La Repubblica, New Community,* 22(1), pp. 39–66.

Verdicchio, P. (1997) *Bound by Distance. Rethinking Nationalism through the Italian Diaspora.* Cranbury NJ: Associated University Press.

Watson, J. L. (ed.) (1977) *Between Two Cultures: Migrants and Minorities in Britain.* Oxford: Blackwell.

8

Inclusionary rhetoric/exclusionary practice: an ethnographic critique of the Italian Left in the context of migration

Davide Però

Introduction

This chapter explores some important political aspects of the question of new cultural encounters in southern Europe. This is done by examining the relationship between the mainstream Italian political Left and the 'new immigrants', who for the most part come from the southern and eastern shores of the Mediterranean. Examining this relationship is of crucial importance in assessing the transformation that Italian Left-wing political culture has undergone as a result of this encounter. Such an analysis is crucial for appraising the extent to which this political culture has responded to the new immigrants' presence by redefining its own political identity in terms of 'transformational multiculturalism' (Martin 1998). The examination is done by following an 'anthropology of policy' approach (Shore and Wright 1997; Wright and Shore 1995), and is located in Bologna, the traditional 'showcase' city of the Italian Left. In particular, the ethnographic research presented in this chapter draws attention to the sharp discrepancies existing between the (inclusionary) rhetoric and the (rather exclusionary) policy practices of the mainstream Left with regard to the new immigrant population of the country. In doing so I will show how important it is to distinguish between the 'rhetorical/ideological' level and the 'practical' one when considering immigrant-related policies and politics in Italy, especially with regard to the mainstream Left.[1]

The chapter is structured as follows. It begins by presenting material on the rhetorical aspects of the Left in the context of migration both nationally and locally in Bologna. Extracts from various documents and policy statements are discussed; all translations from Italian are mine. Then I provide an account of the immigrants' views on the attitudes and policy practices of the Left. This account will be followed by two ethnographic cases of policy practice, the first concerning Moroccan workers in a housing centre and the second looking at Rom in a refugee camp. The insights gained from these two cases will then be compared and contrasted with the Left's claims as well as with the immigrants' perspectives on the mainstream Left. As will become evident later on in the essay, these findings not only appear at odds with the positive attitudes the Left claims to have in relation to the well-being of the immigrants, but they also diverge from some rosy academic representations of the Left in the Bologna region. Finally, inferences will be drawn with regard to the nature of the encounter between the Italian mainstream political Left and the new immigrants, especially with regard to how the former has been capable of taking the presence of the latter as an opportunity to 'update' and pluralise its political vision, concern and practices.

The rhetoric

This section initiates the discussion of contemporary Left-wing politics in the context of new immigrations by examining ideological aspects.

The official ideology of the PDS

Among the various reasons which led to the demise of the PCI (Italian Communist Party) and the birth (from its ashes) of the PDS (*Partito Democratico della Sinistra*, Democratic Party of the Left), was an attempt to regain touch with society which the former seemed to some extent to have lost. At an ideological level this meant changing the party's privileged referent, moving from *la classe* ('class') of the old PCI to *il cittadino* ('the citizen'). In the words of Piero Ignazi (1992, p. 69), 'Out the centrality of the working-class; out Marxist ideology, and its interpreters, even the Italian ones; out the respect for the Party organisation and its theory (democratic centralism)... Their place is taken by the concept of citizenship [*cittadinanza*], i.e. of the individual as carrier of rights as such, and not as member of a class.' This transformation was apparently considered essential to enable the Party to tune in with the emerging 'post-materialist' needs of Italians and in particular with those of the progressive parts of 'civil society' and the 'new social movements' (Ignazi 1992, p. 56). Writing at the time of the transition from PCI to PDS, David Kertzer (1990, p. 280) commented: 'According to Occhetto [the party leader who took the decision to move from the PCI into what was to become the PDS], the larger "thing" that he seeks to create will join together Communists (soon to become ex-

Communists) with a variety of other dispersed forces of the Left. He listed progressive Catholics, environmentalists, women's liberationists, pacifists, and human rights activists.'

Here is a selection from the constitutional principles of the PDS which open its *statuto* – the Party Charter.

> The Democratic Party of the Left is a party of women and men who profess shared fundamental values: the values of freedom, equality, solidarity, peace, and the defence of nature. Of women and men who recognise themselves in a project and a political programme: the project of democracy, road to socialism; a political programme of reforms for the profound transformation of human society.
>
> ... The Democratic Party of the Left is founded by the Italian Communists, together with those who see the historical need for a new beginning for the entire Left in Italy. Different political cultures, ideal inspirations and historical experiences interact and come together in constructing the common heritage of the values and political programmes of the Party which is coming into being.
>
> A Party of women and men. This is because the renewal of culture, politics and social relationships originated by the women's movement is considered essential. The construction of a society which responds to the needs of both genders becomes a goal of the Party, because it recognises the political productivity of the gender conflict, and the political autonomy of women.
>
> A Party of freedom. This is because: the Party struggles in the name of right [*il diritto*] and for the rights [*i diritti*], for the self-affirmation of individuals, for the appreciation of autonomies and differences; it recognises the value and the autonomy of the religious dimension; it promotes the liberation from forms of oppression and dominance which derive from the current capitalist social relationships.
>
> A Party of equality/egalitarianism. This is because it opposes injustice, and aims at humanising and liberating work/labour, as well as representing it according to its new articulations and modern characteristics, while fighting its exploitation; it develops men and women's control over their own work as well as over the accumulation and distribution of social wealth; it is for offering to all citizens equal opportunities at a civil and social level; it is for attributing social value to the plurality of jobs and activities specific to the reproductive sphere, within the perspective of overcoming sexual divisions of and within labour; it is for rendering all workers protagonists of that deep transformation which society is facing at this turn of the century.
>
> A Party of solidarity. This is because *it struggles for the overcoming of the terrible contradictions between rich and poor, between the North and the South of the world, between development and environment, between those who have power, science and information and those who are excluded from these.* The Party supports a reform of the welfare state moving towards a society where the right to work and to social security is guaranteed for everybody, a society in which the civil value of voluntary service, of individual and group engagement with the management of the structures of service and in the promotion of widespread networks of solidarity is

appreciated. *This is also because it repudiates racism, xenophobia, chauvinism, anti-Semitism, intolerance and fanaticism.*
    A party of peace...
    A party for the defence of nature...
    The project of the Democratic Party of the Left is Democracy, the road to Socialism, at a national and international level. Democracy is not only the historical instrument of the process of human emancipation and liberation: Democracy is its permanent expression... The goal of the Democratic Party of the Left is to overcome the existing social, cultural, and economic obstacles to the full development of democracy and to achieve the progressive democratisation of politics, economy and civil society. (Partito Democratico della Sinistra 1991, pp. 9–12; my translation and emphasis).

Thus, with the birth of the PDS, the process of formal ideological re-examination which the PCI had begun in the late 1980s is accomplished. The citizen, individual rights and civil society have officially replaced the working class as the 'core' reference for the Party (Ignazi 1992, p. 132). Differences, identities and pluralism become celebrated.

'The citizen': linking the official ideology of the PDS with the 'new immigrants'

It is necessary at this point to clarify the connection between the PDS concept of citizenship and the immigrants. This is of particular importance, given that there are no explicit references to the immigrant population in the *statuto* of the Party.[2] The first step is then to establish whether at an ideological level 'the citizen' which the PDS claims to represent includes the immigrant, or not. In other words, it is important to see whether immigrants are, at least in principle, part of those 'new social subjects' that the Party makes claims to represent.

With regard to immigrants, Enrico Pugliese (1996, p. 106) highlights two very different concepts of citizenship: 'When talking about immigration in a given country, the citizenship issue can be addressed either in strictly legal terms (as a set of conditions and constraints for the acquisition or the maintenance of the right to be a citizen of a state) or in social terms as the possibility of enjoying all the rights, social and economic, envisaged in citizenship.'

Although the PDS *statutory principles* (translated above) make no explicit reference to immigrants, it seems quite plausible to assume that a 'social' definition of citizenship would apply to the PDS ideology. This appears to be the case because of all the explicit claims made in relation to equality, solidarity, pluralism, freedom, and the repudiation of racism, xenophobia, intolerance, as well as exploitation and oppression (to mention but a few). Furthermore, if this were not the case, then questions about the party's ideological consistency and indeed its 'progressive' or 'reactionary-racist' nature would be inevitable. Hence, it is assumed that the PDS is a party which, at least in principle, is concerned also with the 'new social subject' represented by the 'new immigrants' and does care about the specificities of these citizens' conditions and status, along with the other parts of the population.

As highlighted by Pugliese, the main problem for immigrants in Italy is not legal citizenship (still the concern of only a few) but that of social and economic citizenship:

> These rights consist of access to the benefits of the social policies concerning health, education, housing and, above all, social security. They were originally obtained by the national working classes and have been generally extended to immigrant workers... The most relevant question now is therefore the access to these rights by people who are *de facto* resident, and to a more limited extent, also *de jure* resident... The access to the social rights of citizenship for these people cannot be conditioned by the access to legal citizenship. On the other hand, some of these rights (for example health and education for minors) are universally recognised by principles enacted by the UN. In the specific case of Italy there is a contradiction between a tendency to recognise such rights in principle and difficulties of access to them (Pugliese 1996, pp. 119–20).

This persistent discrepancy between the formal definition of the rights of the immigrants and their actual implementation has also been highlighted by Melotti (1997, p. 91). Thus, the question to ask with regard to the political Left in this context is: to what extent is it facilitating immigrants' fuller access to 'social citizenship'?

Ideological aspects of the mainstream Left at the local level

This section provides an account of what the Bolognese Left claims to be doing about immigrants (especially with regard to the improvement of their conditions in Bologna and the promotion of a more socially just multicultural society) by considering its ideology as expressed in sources ranging from web pages to more conventional forms of political communication (e.g. brochures). The basic idea which the Left offers of itself in these sources is one of champion of egalitarian multiculturalism.

I would like to begin this overview of the ideology of the Left in Bologna by reporting one of the institutional goals of the Bolognese administration, as formulated in the Council Statute (also available from the web). 'The Council promotes the solidarity of the local community particularly towards the most disadvantaged strata of the population, also through the articulation of services. It appreciates the diverse cultures which coexist in the city' (Comune di Bologna 1997, Title I, Article 2).

Surfing the web sites of the Municipality of Bologna during the 1990s one could easily find many web pages dedicated to migration and related issues. In order to give an idea of the official discourse, I here reproduce some of the many explicit statements on multiculturalism and migration that I came across, a few of which were also available in English. The first of such statements (this one in English) is by 'The staff of the Institution for Immigration Services of the Municipality of Bologna', which is the section of the Council dealing with immigration-related questions.

> Welcome to *La città multietnica* (the multi-ethnic city), the WWW Information Service on immigration and minorities in Italy run by the Immigration Service of the Municipality of Bologna. ...We do believe that *differences* (individual, social, cultural, ethnical [sic]) are great values and resources to society and that humankind becomes enriched rather than threatened by them (Comune di Bologna 1998).

The Council, through its Institution for Immigration Services, seeks to 'facilitate the full social, cultural and economical integration of *extracomunitari* immigrants present in the area. The activities of the Institution are among those aiming at removing directly or indirectly the conditions of social insufficiency affecting *extracomunitari* immigrants' (Comune di Bologna 1997, p. 4). The Council has created the *Istituzione* 'with the intent of ensuring the co-ordinated and participatory management of the activities and policies concerning immigration in its broad sense... The *Istituzione* recognises cultural difference as a positive value for the collectivity' (Comune di Bologna 1997, pp. 4, 7). Furthermore, 'Taking as the basis of its own action the recognition of cultural difference as a value, the *Istituzione* operates in order to make this resource an effective element in the enrichment of services and actions of the public administration and citizens' (Comune di Bologna 1997, p. 5).

However, these formal claims in favour of the integration of immigrants and multiculturalism made by the city's administration are not a recent phenomenon. They seem to date back to before the creation of the Institution and the set-up of the web site. In an old report of the city councillor for social policy dated 1989 we read:

> We believe that for civic and political reasons it is necessary to operate so that those people who arrive among us – women, men and increasingly children – find in the social fabric of our city and surrounding towns a real reception and shelter so as to determine a cultural and social integration at all levels which is respectful of their histories, cultural characteristics and differences (Bartolini 1989, p. 1).

And from the same document we also discover that the commitment of the Bologna council towards immigrants was not new even at that time:

> ...our Council decided several years ago to deeply commit itself to the problem of *extracomunitari*... The role of the municipal administration of Bologna has therefore been that of both drawing attention towards the problem, broadening solidarity towards *extracomunitari* citizens who live in particular conditions of discomfort, and promoting within the city these new citizens' cultures and traditions... This effort constitutes clear evidence of how the problem of immigration is for us today a real priority. It is a priority first of all because we feel, as council administrators, that we must be the first to support and protect citizens' rights, especially those of the new citizens... (Bartolini 1989, pp. 4–5).

On a more explicitly party-political front (which in Bologna until very recently was broadly coincident with the municipal administration), we find similar claims. In a recent brochure of the PDS we read that 'dignified hospitality and citizenship rights must be given to the immigrants who work and produce for the benefit of the city'. In a PDS mayor's electoral manifesto we learn that:

> ...the key to realising the goals of a city in which people with different origins and cultures live together as citizens avoiding conflicts ... is the full involvement of the immigrant communities in the administrative decisions and in the progressive affirmation of the social, civil and political rights of the new citizens (Vitali 1995, p. 20).

Finally, in another party-political publication (by the Bologna PDS Federation) we read:

> Bologna is an open community which has been capable of welcoming new citizens over the years and of offering opportunities for social contact, access to work, housing and services: Bologna is an open and solidaristic community (PDS Federazione di Bologna 1995, p. 27).

Moreover, the PDS Federation appears anxious to convey the idea that the contents of its manifestos are to be taken seriously.

> Constitutional rights, and above all substantial rights – those concerning the material life of the people in Bologna – have not been and are not just 'words', but they become translated into operative guarantees of opportunities of civil participation and of accessibility to a wide network of services (PDS Federazione di Bologna 1995, p. 30).

To sum up, the extracts reported above show a mainstream Left seeking to promote an image of itself which is one of serious engagement with the improvement of the conditions of immigrants on a whole range of issues – cultural, social, economic and political. This image is broadcast through well-mastered, new and powerful technological media.

In order to assess the extent to which the claims of the Left about the promotion of immigrants' rights, appreciation of cultural diversity and the participatory management of migration are well-founded, I will now present the immigrants' views of the Left, as they emerge from printed texts. This will be followed by two ethnographic cases of Left-wing policy practices in the context of migration: that of the 'centres of first shelter' and that of the 'refugee camps'.

Dissonant views: a survey of the immigrants' own 'texts'

This section presents some 'voices' coming from immigrants themselves which make explicit reference to the Left and its policy practices in Bologna. I deliberately limit my discussion to those immigrants' views which appear in the form of 'texts' (usually books and reports); I will use my ethnography to assess their 'accuracy'. As Alessandra Di Maio pointed out in the previous chapter in this volume, it is still quite rare to find such voices in the form of texts, not least because immigrants do not seem to enjoy much access to communication channels. However, from the little material authored by immigrants which is publicly available, the image of the mainstream Left which tends to emerge is not quite as positive as that projected by the Left-wing's own sources.

Hamid Bichri is one of Bologna's immigrant leaders and author of the only book written by an immigrant on these issues in the city. Here are some extracts from his book (Bichri 1995, pp. 35, 42, 47):

> In Italian institutions the needs, aspirations and dissatisfaction of immigrants are never discussed, because this would lead to political conflicts. For this reason alternative solutions away from official institutions are sought. These things considered, it is easy to react by appearing to want everything or nothing ... exclusion from the receiving society becomes increasingly unbearable ... thronged in overcrowded huts and dormitories. The Moroccan immigrant in Bologna is forced to live in a parallel city to the one which surrounds him/her.

> Immigrants are considered intruders. In order not to see them around in the city centre they are put into prefabricated huts and school dormitories in peripheral districts. And even in order to gain access to such ghettos, the immigrants must submit to the examination of the municipal bureaucracy. Besides only single men can enter them (single here but married in their own countries).

The opportunity of expression and self-realisation is denied to the immigrants, who in this way are prevented – also through the use of paternalistic discourses on human rights – from improving their conditions, with their rights only existing in posters and conferences. Immigrants' rights are dealt with in a patronising and ambiguous way in which it is difficult to distinguish the positive aspect from the repressive one.

More explicitly on the mainstream Left, Bichri (1995, p. 61) states:

...we have a Left that, while talking in favour of immigrants' rights, in practice vigorously opposes the immigrants' presence in the name of the 'good of the city'. Immigrants are held responsible for delaying the move of the majority of public opinion to the Left, and actually steering it to the Right.[4]

Further criticism is contained in the following statement by Bichri (1995, p. 60):

...even among the ranks of the Left there have been those *responsabili* who pretended to be dealing with the question of immigration, but in practice relegated it to the status of assistance and 'emergency'.

Although Bichri's text is the only existing book about politics and the condition of immigrants in Bologna, a few other immigrants' views appear in local conference proceedings (although the space made available is very limited indeed). During the proceedings of a public meeting organised by the local Council, Fariba Khmesei pointed out the lack of consistency, clarity and determination in the municipal policies of Bologna: 'It is not tolerable that in Bologna, every time that an *assessore* changes, the policy and the structural decisions change too' (Comune di Bologna 1991, p. 167). This is especially the case, I would like to add, when the ruling party remains the same. At another meeting, organised by the local Catholic organisation, Caritas, and before being silenced by one of the 'experts' on the panel, Abdullai pointed out from the floor that 'our relationship with political parties in Bologna has been only a history of controls and neglects of our culture' (Caritas di Bologna 1995, p. 41). A longer critique of the Left-wing municipality was presented by Ahmed Zaka Shakil, of which I report an edited and shortened version:

When we arrived in Bologna, the only accommodation that we found was a ruined homestead (without doors, windows, lights, water or gas) in Castelmaggiore. We ended up there because in Bologna houses cannot be found. The few that are available are not given to foreigners... With the arrival of winter the situation became unbearable, and we were pushed to occupy the school in Via Rimesse as we did not have other alternatives. Even in here we failed to obtain an answer from the Council and therefore we will do another demonstration... This is our condition, and we are tired of living in such precarious and irregular conditions, despite having the permit to stay [*permesso di soggiorno*]... We waited five months in Castelmaggiore and six months in Via Rimesse for a reply from the Council, but we obtained nothing (Comune di Bologna 1991, pp. 130–1).

Although I would not claim that such 'voices' encapsulate the view of the entire range of immigrants present, they do signal very clearly the presence of 'discontent' and disappointment among immigrants.

So, from all this, the image of the mainstream Left and its everyday politics in the context of migration does not emerge as outstandingly supportive of immigrants as its self-portrait tends to suggest. Is the situation really as described by Bichri: 'For the immigrant there are two kinds of politics available: that which is forbidden to him and that which exploits him' (1995, p. 59)? The following ethnographic examination of two policy practices will also be relevant to an assessment of the extent to which the above critical views from the immigrants are well-founded.

Policy practices, case 1: centres of first shelter

The examination of the 'centres of first shelter' or CPAs (*centri di prima accoglienza*) offers one key to an understanding of the nature of the politics of the Left which is grounded in policy practices and not merely based on rhetoric and declarations of good intent. CPAs were a kind of emergency solution to the accommodation crisis faced by newly-arrived immigrants in Italy, a crisis which was particularly severe in Bologna. Because of the very high prices (worsened by 'racial' prejudices), housing quickly became the major problem that immigrants had to confront in Bologna (Bernadotti and Mottura 1999; Però 1997). By the late 1980s this housing problem had worsened to the extent of becoming commonly addressed as *emergenza* (emergency). Immigrants were having to sleep in fields, cars, abandoned houses, old caravans, or to take up 'exploitative' types of accommodation which were illegal, unhealthy and unsafe. However, it was only with the immigrants' occupations of empty public buildings that the housing question reached public opinion, thereby forcing the indifferent (if not reluctant) municipal institutions to intervene.

In the meantime, the Italian parliament had finally approved the famous Martelli immigration law (Law 39 of 1990). One of the merits of this controversial law was that it contributed to addressing, albeit partially, the issue of immigrant housing by funding the municipal authorities (via the regional governments) to create CPAs. At the beginning of the 1990s Bologna had about 1,000 'first shelter beds', distributed in eight CPAs, in which the immigrants were housed, distributed according to their nationality/ethnicity. As specified by the above-mentioned law, the CPAs were meant to offer *accoglienza* ('shelter/reception') to immigrants for 60 days, after which they were supposed to have access to 'proper' housing. However, since after such a short period the situation generally remained unchanged, the municipal authorities simply extended the 'first shelter period' to six months and after that for another two years, instead of developing policies aimed at promoting immigrants' access to 'proper' housing. In other words the CPA structures, which originally came into being with the intent of providing a very temporary service, had become officially acknowledged as virtually permanent (cf. Del Mugnaio 1993). This semi-permanency also implied a *de facto* policy of keeping the immigrants concentrated and organised according to ethnic criteria in conditions like those described below. In this way 'cultural diversity' became coupled with extremely poor and marginalising housing provision as well as chaotic management.

An example

Let us now look at one of the CPAs in the city to gain a more detailed impression of these residential schemes. The CPA which I studied was opened in early 1991 and is located on the outskirts of town bounded by a major highway, a factory, a parking lot and uncultivated fields.[5]

The CPA consists of 18 prefabricated light metal bungalows plus two other buildings (a mosque and an office) made of a similar material. Internally each of the 18 bungalows is subdivided into two double rooms of about 2x3 metres separated by a small bathroom. The bungalows are organised in squares of six so as to form three internal courtyards, from which the six bungalows can be accessed.

The CPA residents were all Moroccan men and numbered 72. They were 'legal' immigrants and registered residents of Bologna. They all had a regular job (mainly working as unskilled labour in the industrial and building sectors), although occasionally a few were temporarily unemployed. Although the municipal authorities portrayed and addressed them as a 'community', this was far from being the case because of sharp differences in educational level, age, place of origin, migratory project and marital status.

The lifestyle in the CPA

Most of the daily non-work activities of the CPA residents took place in their metal bungalows, and in particular inside the double room which each of them shared with another fellow resident.[6] This little room contained two beds, a few small pieces of furniture for the storage of clothes and food, a small table (used for the preparation of food), a refrigerator, suitcases, a stereo and a television (often connected to a satellite dish installed on the roof of the bungalow). A small electric cooker was often located in the tiny corridor by the bungalow entrance.

In winter, when the average temperature in Bologna is close to 0° Celsius, all the everyday activities such cooking, eating, washing and ironing take place indoors. In Spring, the warmer weather enables some of these activities to take place outdoors. In summer, cooking, eating and sometimes sleeping outdoors become a necessity, given the unbearably high temperatures reached inside the metal bungalows.

Despite the residents' cleaning efforts, the CPA is quite unhealthy and unhygienic. Cockroaches and blackbeetles are everywhere, and one can also note the presence of rats. Thus, it was not a surprise to learn that there have been at least two cases of TB and that several residents apparently suffered from other ailments, including periodic nose-bleeds. Perhaps more surprising is that the normal compulsory health and safety regulations do not apply in the CPA.

The CPA and the 'outside'

The isolation of the CPA from the surrounding area is reflected in the conversations I had with people who lived nearby. The Italian residents of the district would normally know that 'in there' lived *extracomunitari*; but this was the only accurate information that most of them appeared to have about the CPA and its inhabitants. False allegations were made about the ethnicity of the residents ('Tunisians', 'gypsies' etc.), about their living conditions ('good', 'too good') and about their working lives ('they all work in the black economy').

With the exception of working hours, the CPA residents had little social contact with the Italian population, and in particular with Italian women. With the exception of one Caritas volunteer, the CPA had no contacts with the civil and political society of the district – for instance with the local party branches (still a significant phenomenon in Bologna), civic associations or other organisations. The residents' relationships with the outside during leisure time were predominantly with fellow-immigrant friends and relatives.

Finally, the CPA was disadvantaged from the point of view of communications: the mail was often undelivered or went missing (to the extent that some immigrants had to hire post-office boxes), and for a long time there was not even a payphone in the whole complex.

Management policies, danger and discontent in the CPA

From the above findings on the immigrants' living conditions and their relationship with 'outside', I now move to an overview of the range of management policies adopted for the CPA by the Left-wing administration over the years. These management policies moved from an initially paternalistic and authoritarian stance to one of *autogestione* or self-management. This latter policy was supported by a local NGO-funded project of 'participatory action research' in which I was myself involved.[7]

Right at the outset of my relationship with the CPA residents, it became clear how hard and dangerous it was to live in the centre, especially since the implementation of the self-management policy. Since this policy had been introduced, the control of the centre had increasingly been taken over by a group of squatters together with some gypsies (who were camping at the edges of the CPA) and their visitors. The residential complex had been turned into a centre for selling and buying stolen goods and drugs (which were also consumed there). This situation meant that even the most basic function of the CPA – that of a dormitory – was being negatively affected. The lifestyle of many of the unauthorised persons, in fact, strongly clashed with that of the legitimate residents, which was characterised by hard physical labour, self-imposed economic restrictions and savings.

The immigrants largely attributed the cause of such a degraded environment to the policy of *autogestione* recently imposed by the municipal administration. Such a policy was commonly interpreted by the residents as a deliberate act of abandonment on the part of the council authorities. Under such circumstances of neglect, nobody was therefore minded to try and implement such a policy. Moreover, self-management would have been extremely difficult (and even dangerous) for the immigrants to implement in such a situation of precariousness, with lack of adequate support from the municipal and police authorities. Thus, the residents of the CPA not only found themselves unable to satisfy the council's (top-down) policy prescriptions of *autogestione*, but they actually found this request quite irritating and even dangerous.

However, the situation described above was not the only argument used in the residents' critique of the council and its policy. References to the living conditions in the centre under previous management policies were also often brought out. In particular, it was highlighted how the council had always been incapable of guaranteeing good management – and that, as a result of this, residents had always experienced an oppressive life in the centre. A situation of harassment was reported to have characterised the previous period of centralised authority; then the harassment had come from those who were supposed to keep order (i.e. the armed guards of the security team, rather than from the squatters). The previous management in fact was rightly described by the authorities as *gestione forte* (strong management). The immigrants' complaints concerning the armed surveillance of the previous management regime described some of the guards' attitudes and behaviour as racist and harassing. The immigrants also pointed out the absolute lack of continuity between one management policy and the next. The inconsistency of moving from an unwanted situation of strong authoritarian management to another of unwanted *autogestione* (which in practice meant chaos) was perceived as a lack of genuine concern towards immigrants on the part of the Left-wing administration.

Immigrants' distrust of the municipal administration came also from the clear perception (grounded in prolonged direct experience) of occupying the bottom level of a politico-administrative system which, despite its official claims (of efficiency, transparency, democracy and equality – some of which have been reported above), actually seemed to oppress and exclude the immigrants in many ways. Hierarchically made up of different centres of interest (co-ops, NGOs, associations, consultants...) which too often seemed to pursue goals of their own (rather than providing the good and integrated service to the immigrants that they were meant to), and with some of them placed in direct and horizontal competition with each other (over resources, contracts and appointments), the system ended up providing a poor service.

From the descriptions given above, it is clear that the immigrants were very upset, disappointed and disillusioned with the policy practices of the local institutions which they held responsible for the very oppressive living conditions in the centre.

Conclusions on the politics of the centres of first shelter

This case-study has addressed the politics of the centres of first shelter by examining significant aspects of one of the immigrant housing schemes set up by the Left-wing Council of Bologna. The case presented has shown how this residential scheme contributed to the geographical, social and political marginalisation of its residents. The analysis reveals how the Council policy during the 1990s has tolerated, if not encouraged, permanent 'emergency' housing conditions for the immigrants (i.e. the CPA schemes, which are parallel arrangements of 'ethnic' public housing for which ordinary regulations about health, safety and security do not apply), rather than facilitating migrants' incorporation into 'ordinary' residential patterns. Indeed, the project of creating 'centres of community' in the CPAs rather than showing sensitivity to ethnic diversity on the part of the Left (as its rhetoric claims), reveals an attitude of 'cultural imperialism' (cf. Young 1990), that is to say an attitude in which the dominant group seeks to impose its own 'ethnocentric' discourse on the immigrants through its powerful institutions. This attitude seems to be informed by an essentialist understanding of 'culture', 'community' and 'ethnic identity' and to be operationalised by seeking to order a considerable part of the immigrant population into (supposedly) homogeneous communities located in geographically segregated areas, in conditions of precariousness, and managed through a pseudo-democratic and pseudo-participatory style of management.

In conclusion, the material presented in this section enables us to see that the housing policy of the Left concerning legal immigrant workers throughout the 1990s in Bologna was informed by an ethnic discourse coupled with an astonishing inertia. The result has been a combination of neglect and marginalising and disempowering practices. Moreover, the housing policy practices to which the immigrants have been subjected seem to disclose a differentialist attitude which largely avoids addressing the structural processes of exclusion which affect the immigrants. Although the experience presented in this case-study is perhaps not representative of the entire immigrant population of Bologna,[8] it is definitely revealing of the general attitude which the Left seems to have towards the immigrants, as the following ethnographic case-study also shows.

Policy practices, case 2: refugee camps

This section continues the ethnographic examination of the administrative policies of the Left initiated in the previous one by focusing on the policy practices adopted in relation to a group of Rom refugees from ex-Yugoslavia. My attention was immediately drawn to the Rom when, in the Spring of 1995, the city mayor decided to locate the refugees in a velodrome in the district where I was already conducting fieldwork. The story unfolds around their 'regularisation' process as they were successively shifted from the quagmire of the river bank to a velodrome in the city and then to a 'proper' refugee camp on the periphery of Bologna. The refugees – who numbered 70 (25 families) – had fled to Italy in search of shelter at the onset of the war in Yugoslavia from the area of Sabac (Serbia) in which they had apparently settled several decades earlier. Because of legal and social obstacles, their time in Italy before their relocation to the velodrome had been characterised by extreme marginality, powerlessness and exclusion.

The refugees were admitted to Italy in the early 1990s but were never officially recognised as such. Without the 'permit to stay' the refugees were thus lacking the only title which would have legitimised their presence in Italy and given them entitlement to some basic rights. This forced the refugees to live in conditions of 'enormous precariousness and instability, as they could in principle be expelled at any time and could acquire neither a right to stay, nor to health assistance, nor any of the rights normally linked to the entitlements of a permit to stay' (Zorzella 1996, p. 110). This absence of any legal status exposed the refugees to the whims and abuses of the various state authorities they encountered; given the widespread and atavistic prejudice against gypsies, their treatment was particularly insidious.

Before their transfer to the velodrome, the refugees had been living in the most appalling conditions for some two years, while the relevant authorities, the *Prefettura* (the local organ of the state authority) and the *Comune* (the municipal authority) apparently 'bounced the ball' to each other. Their 'unlawful' status technically precluded them from having access to work and forced them to beg and resort to minor illegal activities in order to survive. For two years they had been squatting on a river bank on the periphery of the city, living in old caravans and self-built cardboard and wooden huts. In this rat-infested muddy site, without any source of clean water, it is not surprising that they suffered from a range of afflictions and illnesses, including TB, scabies and lice.

Only after a two-year delay did the relevant authorities develop a sufficient degree of concern to slowly begin tackling this situation. The starting point was the regularisation of the refugees' legal status so that they could at least qualify for some welfare provision. In the relevant city councillor's own words 'the *operation velodrome* [as this intervention was referred to] must be seen within the broader context of the improvement of the quality of life of non-Bolognese in Bologna: moving from emergency to normality'.

In the temporary refugee camp

The transfer from the muddy river bank to the velodrome took place during one rainy day of August 1995 under the supervision of the municipal authorities.[9] The velodrome was bounded by a wall and its new inhabitants were subjected to a 24-hour regime of surveillance, discipline and management by the specialised personnel of a cooperative appointed by the Council. During their stay in the velodrome the refugees were 'legalised', given the official status of *sfollato di guerra* – a legally recognised status similar to that of refugee.

What I found interesting about the 'operation velodrome' was the generally 'de-humanising' set of discourses and practices through which the Council dealt with the refugees. Excluded from the decision-making processes concerning their life and freedom, the refugees were 'objectified', disciplined and controlled through the 'technologies of power' of the host society: in this case the refugee camp. Drawing on Foucault, Liisa Malkki has provided an effective illustration of the technology of power in this context:

> It was toward the end of the World War II that the refugee camp became emplaced as a standardized, generalisable technology of power ... in the management of mass displacement. The refugee camp was a vital device of power: the spatial concentrations and ordering of people that it enabled, as well as the administrative and bureaucratic process it facilitated within its

boundaries, had far-reaching consequences. The segregation of nationalities; the orderly organisation of repatriation or third-country resettlement; medical and hygienic programs and quarantining; 'perpetual screening' and the accumulation of documentation on the inhabitants of the camps; the control of movement and black-marketing; law enforcement and public discipline; and schooling and rehabilitation were some of the operations that the spatial concentration and ordering of people enabled or facilitated. Through these processes, the modern, postwar refugee emerged as a knowable, nameable figure and as an object of social-scientific knowledge (Malkki 1995, p. 498).

In return for stripping the refugees of their human qualities via the above-mentioned technology of power, the Rom refugees were granted some much-needed basic material assistance: they became entitled to a personal allowance which was administered on their behalf by officials and social workers to pay for medical tickets, education, food and travel expenses. This allowance enabled the refugees to receive a weekly *buono spesa* (shopping coupon), from which alcohol and cigarettes were specifically excluded.

I will now provide a sense of the paternalistic and patronising institutional discourse which informed the policy practices of the Left in relation to the refugees by reporting three episodes I witnessed. The first is about the language used by the council official in charge of the 'operation velodrome' to describe the operation to a delegation of the 'pro-refugees' committee.[10] Here are some examples. With regard to the general rationale of the intervention she explained:

> The period in the velodrome is needed in order to carry out a series of tasks and checks. First of all, controls on the refugees' health and hygienic conditions; secondly, the regularisation with the *Questura* [police office] for the *permesso di soggiorno* [permit to stay]; thirdly, the regularisation with the Council for the residence permit.

As for the refugees, she portrayed them as follows:

> they all speak Italian, and if they don't speak they understand... On the whole the women are better workers than the men, accustomed as they are to being *oggetti* [objects]. The men are very susceptible and individualistic and smoke like Turks[11] ... we are really faced with another culture here!

Finally, on the health check-ups on the refugees that she was responsible for carrying out:

> as soon as they arrive in the velodrome, we take them, we make them undress, we throw away their clothes and, dressed as nature created them, we make them take a shower and then we make them dress with clean clothes.

All these explanations were given as if they were quite normal; no doubt they must have appeared as such to the municipal official.

The second episode concerns the visit of the mayor of Bologna to the velodrome camp a few weeks after the arrival of the refugees, to see with his own eyes how the 'operation velodrome' was progressing. During his visit the refugees were never really given the chance to talk to him, nor did he appear to be interested in their perspectives. The mayor's visit also featured a press conference, which was hosted in the courtyard around which the refugees' caravans were positioned. In spite of the subject being discussed (themselves) and the proximity of the event to their 'homes' just a few metres away, no refugee considered it appropriate, or was confident enough, to go within hearing distance (let alone participate in the event). This revealed that not only the decisions, but also the talking, about the refugees' lives and immediate future was a 'private business' of the host society and its institutions. This dispossession of the refugees' own voice and freedom became even clearer after the press conference when a journalist and I tried to talk to the refugees directly. As soon as the camp supervisor realised what was going on he rushed over – visibly annoyed – to silence the refugees, who quickly stopped talking to us. To one of my interlocutors the supervisor said 'don't try to be clever ... you know that I have got eyes everywhere!!!' It thus became evident that, from the point of view of the authorities, an unsupervised conversation with 'outsiders', journalists or otherwise, was not welcomed. However, those few minutes spent alone with the refugees were sufficient to discover that they lacked electricity (and therefore had no light in the evening and night), they shared one fridge among 70, and that the pocket money they received (in addition to the *buono spesa*) was not enough to buy cigarettes, and that a family of four had to struggle to live on the weekly allowance.

The third episode is an example of the camp supervisor talking to a meeting of the pro-refugees committee. Evidently he was keen to illustrate to the local civil society the fine level of discipline and surveillance to which he was subjecting the refugees both inside and outside the camp. During the meeting, he proudly presented some of his management strategies and practices. Here is a sample of them. Defending his 'prohibitionist' policy, he explained:

> I am checking the receipts from the supermarket since alcohol has been forbidden, and I don't want them turning up with trolleys loaded with beer.

With regard to the refugees' begging in the streets – an activity which, since the transfer into the velodrome, had become absolutely forbidden – he informed us that he and his team were also patrolling the nearby traffic lights:

> we take good care to go searching for them by the traffic lights and chase them *home* [sic]. I'm not happy that they receive alms, they must learn to count and manage their budget now.

Implementing a policy like that of the 'management' of refugees is certainly not easy. Although the officials involved did not seem like 'nasty' persons, but rather benevolent professionals (who to an extent acted in 'good faith', probably convinced that they were doing their job well and helping the refugees), this does not alter the overall oppressive character of their discourses and practices. The refugees' stay at the velodrome camp served to subject them to the gamut of bureaucratic interventions deemed necessary to confer on them the new official status of refugees. Once the requirements, controls and check-ups prescribed by the dominant sedentaristic society had been fulfilled (such as registration with the police, the council and health authorities), the refugees were considered ready to be 'integrated' into society.

In the properly equipped refugee camp

After the three-month period spent at the velodrome, the refugees were moved to a specially designed *campo profughi attrezzato* (properly equipped refugee camp). This new residential scheme was located in the middle of the countryside, far from public transport, and around half an hour by car from Bologna.[12]

When I visited the camp, my attention was immediately attracted by the light-metal portacabin buildings. 'That looks like a CPA!' I commented to the contact person who had taken me there, and in fact it soon came out that the refugee camp had been set up by recycling the bungalows of a recently dismantled CPA (of the kind described in the previous section). According to the refugees, the 'second-hand' bungalows that they had 'inherited' were in such a filthy state that before they could be re-used they required professional disinfecting. What was different from the CPAs I was familiar with was the dislocation of the buildings, and the fact that these had been allocated to families rather than to four men. However, what impressed me most about the 'properly equipped refugee camp' was that it had been sited right next to the *canile municipale* (the municipal dog pound). On the peculiar appearance of their housing scheme, the refugees (in the absence of camp operators) pointed out that on several occasions people had entered their camp by mistake, convinced that it was the *canile* next door. This extraordinary location of the refugee camp is quite emblematic of the social status imposed on the refugees. On the question of the siting of the refugee camp it is interesting to highlight how 'thin' was the gap separating 'progressive' Bologna from less progressive cities in this respect. In Bologna, the refugee camp is next to the municipal dog pound, in Verona it is next to the rubbish tip (Maher 1996, p. 171), while in Turin it is positioned in between the tip and the pound (Boursier 1999). This is revealing of how what has been called *'l'urbanistica del disprezzo'* (the urban planning of contempt) is at work even in areas which are considered socially advanced (Marcetti and Solimano 1996).

My initial 'reading' of the municipal policy practices toward the refugees as 'oppressive' found confirmation in an article which had in the meantime been produced by the Council. In this article one of the camp co-ordinators described the effectiveness of the rules introduced in shaping and disciplining the daily life in the camp:

> Friday afternoon is a special day: it is when the distribution of the shopping coupons takes place. Before distributing the coupons, however, the operators do an inspection survey of the camp. Subsequently the general cleaning of the camp begins: all the sixty-four guests, children included, are provided with a rubbish bag and rubber gloves. Only when the work is completed, are the coupons distributed and the journey by van to the supermarket can begin (Lodi 1996, p. 167).

Further confirmation of the oppressive nature of the policy practices came from the refugees' own views, which I was able to listen to when I visited the camp in the company of a trusted contact. Perceiving the conditions as 'safe' (the absence of 'surveillance', my being introduced by a person they obviously trusted, the informal and spontaneous character of the conversation), the refugees recounted the institutional practices they had experienced. Their criticisms showed a common consensus. Their narratives of several unpleasant episodes further revealed the authoritarian, paternalistic and patronising character of the institutional practices towards them and re-stated the profound powerlessness of their conditions. In this context, it was not surprising for me to learn that one of the organisations which the Council had appointed to run the camp had degenerated into illegal dealings involving misappropriation of funds.

Some conclusions on the treatment of the refugees

This section has provided an analytical description of the policy discourses and practices deployed by the Left-wing administration of the municipality of Bologna in relation to a group of Rom refugees from the former Yugoslavia. In all, this examination has shown how these people have been geographically ghettoised, patronised and infantilised. Apart from providing for their most pressing material needs, the council policy has achieved little in terms of a more thorough incorporation, especially in the spheres of housing and work (for a discussion of this latter question see Però 1999a and 1999b). This poor policy achievement is, once again, quite disappointing especially in consideration of the 'democratic' claims being made.

First, the policy practices through which the politics of the Left were articulated have been revealed to be highly marginalising in many respects. Initially, there was absolute neglect for a period of two years. The concern subsequently coincided with the refugees' entering into a relationship of dependency upon the authorities for shelter, food and assistance, which were supplied through rather authoritarian, patronising, paternalistic, infantilising, arbitrary and ghettoising practices. Second, the persistent exclusion of the refugees from those decision-making processes significantly affecting the conditions of their life suggests a rather disempowering attitude on the part of the Left-wing council. The material presented indicates clearly that the interpretations, models and narratives that prevailed in the process of emplacement of the refugees were overwhelmingly those of the municipality. Third, given all the rhetorical emphasis and self-proclaimed sensitivity of the Left-wing authorities to the question of cultural identity and difference, one would at least have expected avoidance of cultural imperialism. This expectation was also frustrated because of the notion of 'the camp' as the central policy technology. In fact,

> The 'nomads camp' is a habitat which is extraneous to the history of the Rom, to their social and family structure. It is a contemporary invention. It is an example of how space can become an element of violence against the identity of a people. Indeed, the very concept of camp ... upsets the fundamental element of Rom culture, which is based on the flexibility of relations and structures. Besides, the camp is not thought of as the Rom's own living space in which they can independently manage their own lives, but as a 'municipal' space, in which the Rom are guests and, as such, subject to rules... (Marcetti and Solimano 1996, p. 66).

In other words, in resorting to the camp as the operational technology, the municipal policy does not seem to have attributed much importance to the refugees' distinctive values, norms and social organisation. So, despite its self-proclaimed sensitivity to, and defence of, cultural diversity, the Left appears to be involved in oppressive and culturally imperialist processes of top-down, external, essentialist, stereotyped and prejudice-driven definition and attribution of difference and identity.

Conclusions

Through an ethnographic examination of the politics of the Left in relation to the 'new immigrants' in Bologna, this chapter has argued that in the context of migration the mainstream Italian Left appears to be characterised by a profound 'mis-match' between its rhetoric and its policy practices. The inclusionary language spoken in its rhetoric is shown to be rather inconsistent with the exclusionary practices of the centres of first shelter and refugee camps through which much of its everyday politics has been operationalised at a local administrative level. In fact, the language of equality, solidarity, participation, empowerment, appreciation of cultural difference and ethnic diversity which characterises the rhetoric of the Left is quite contradicted by the mix of neglect, inertia, inconsistency, paternalism, authoritarianism, marginalisation, essentialism and cultural imperialism which has been shown to inform its policy practices in relation to both immigrants and refugees in Bologna. Thus, the Left emerges as inadequately responding to the challenges posed by the new immigrant residents, such as their call for recognition, representation and participation.

Besides being consistent with the views expressed in immigrants' texts, these findings reappraise the more positive image of the mainstream Left in the context of migration in Bologna and Emilia-Romagna that has been put forward both by the Left itself and by some recent studies (see Delle Donne 1995; Orsini-Jones and Gattullo 1996 and 2000). Of course, the criticism contained in this essay is not to deny the differences that undoubtedly still exist between the inertia and inconsistency of the mainstream Left and the xenophobia and racism of the Italian Right. Rather, my aim has been to draw attention to the fact that even the so-called 'progressive' forces are currently operating within an exclusionary logic and reproducing exclusionary mechanisms.

Besides making the general theoretical point about the crucial importance of considering policy practices when studying political formations and cultures in the context of migration, the material presented in this chapter suggests that if the mainstream Left in Italy intends to adequately represent the interests of its immigrant residents – as its rhetoric claims – it has to engage in a process of rethinking its policy practices. Such a process of rethinking would seem to include a shift from an essentially 'national' vision of egalitarianism to a more 'transnational' perspective capable of fully 'including' the interests of the new immigrant groups among its top concerns. Thus far, the new cultural encounters have represented a missed opportunity for the mainstream Left to seriously 'modernise' its egalitarian vision, scope and practices.

Notes

1 This chapter draws on and develops material from my doctoral thesis at the University of Sussex (Però 1999a); the thesis was supported by an ESRC studentship which I gratefully acknowledge.

2 The lack of such references constitutes an extraordinary silence (and an omen of the research findings presented in the following sections) if we consider that in 1990 (the year before the approval of the PDS statute and the year in which the statute was being drafted) the question of immigration was possibly the most important theme in the Italian public and political debate.

As observed by Cole, 'in 1990 immigration made the front page on a regular basis' (1997, p. 103).

3 PDS Gruppo Due Torri, Comune di Bologna. *Lavoriamo in Comune*. Bologna, 1997, p. 6.

4 Partly for this reason the mainstream Left would very much prefer immigrants not to undertake any initiative or course of action attracting (political) attention (such as the occupation of empty buildings), but to wait patiently for the relevant Left-wing authorities, institutions and organisations to deal with the issues on their behalf, as they supposedly know better what the 'right thing' to be done is.

5 For a fuller description of this CPA, including a map, see Però (1997). I did 'participatory action research' in this CPA in 1995, plus occasional subsequent visits.

6 It is worth noting that certain activities like sex or studying are quite simply prevented by the CPA structure.

7 Participatory action research (PAR) is a radical 'action-research' methodology which seeks to empower a disadvantaged group by involving them directly in the process of enquiry. On the principles of PAR see Hussein and Però (1998) and Però (1996). For a critical ethnography of PAR in the CPA see Però (1997).

8 In fact the immigrants living in the CPAs are a minority of the overall immigrant population in Bologna, even though a very significant minority. Besides, the immigrants I considered were males living as single people, whereas the overall immigrant population is made up of a large and growing number of women, families and immigrants' children born in Italy; see Elisabetta Zontini's chapter in this volume. Finally, even though Moroccans are by far the largest immigrant group in Bologna, they are not the majority of the overall immigrant population.

9 For an extended discussion of the policy practices and socio-political impact of the operation velodrome see Però (1999a and 1999b).

10 This committee had been set up in the local neighbourhood in order to facilitate the Council's decision to relocate the refugees: for details see Però (1999b, pp. 214–15 and p. 224, note 28).

11 To 'smoke like a Turk' is the literal translation of the Italian expression '*fumare come un turco*' commonly used to indicate heavy smokers.

12 See Però (1999b) for a fuller account of the camp, including a map.

References

Bartolini, S. (1989) *Progetto Immigrazione. Relazione dell'Assessore*. Bologna: Comune di Bologna.

Bernardotti, M. A. and Mottura, G. (1999) *Il Gioco delle Tre Case. Immigrazione e politiche abitative a Bologna dal 1990 al 1999*. Turin: L'Harmattan Italia.

Bichri, H. (1995) *I Soldi della Miseria*. Bologna: Extra Edizioni.

Boursier, G. (1999) Un luogo per i Rom di Torino, non un canile, non una discarica, *Il Manifesto*, 17 October.

Caritas di Bologna (1995) *La Porta*. Bologna: Caritas di Bologna.

Cole, J. (1997) *The New Racism in Europe: A Sicilian Ethnography*. Cambridge: Cambridge University Press.

Comune di Bologna (1991) *L'Immigrazione a Bologna: Le politiche comunali per il 1991. Incontro di Studio* (Bologna, 24 Maggio 1991). Bologna: Comune di Bologna.

Comune di Bologna (1997) *Statuto*. Bologna.

Comune di Bologna (1998) *La Città Multietnica*. http://www2.comune.Bologna. it/bologna/immigra/intreng.htm.

Delle Donne, M. (1995) Difficulties of refugees towards integration: the Italian case, in Delle Donne, M. (ed.) *Avenues to Integration. Refugees in Contemporary Europe*. Naples and Los Angeles: Ipermedium, pp. 110–44.

Del Mugnaio, A. (1993) *Documento Programmatico della Giunta Comunale sulle Politiche per l'Immigrazione. Relazione dell'Assessore*. Bologna: Comune di Bologna.

Hussein, K. and Però, D. (1998) *Linking Participatory Methodologies with People's Realities: Towards a Common Agenda*. Brighton: Institute of Development Studies.

Ignazi, P. (1992) *Dal PCI al PDS*. Bologna: Il Mulino.

Kertzer, D. I. (1990) *Comrades and Christians*. Prospect Heights: Waveland Press, revised edition.

Lodi, V. (1996) La realtà del campo profughi del Trebbo di Reno, in Comune di Bologna/Osservatorio Metropolitano delle Immigrazioni, *La Società Multietnica*, no. 2, pp. 164–70.

Maher, V. (1996) Immigration and social identities, in Lumley, D. and Forgacs, D. (eds) *Italian Cultural Studies*. Oxford: Oxford University Press, pp. 160–77.

Malkki, L. H. (1995) Refugees and exile: from 'refugee studies' to the national order of things, *Annual Review of Anthropology*, 24, pp. 495–523.

Marcetti, C. and Solimano, N. (1996) Allontanate le vostre tende, avvicinate i vostri cuori, in Brunello, P. (ed.) *L'Urbanistica del Disprezzo*. Rome: Manifestolibri, pp. 63–75.

Martin, B. (1998) Multiculturalism: consumerist or transformational? in Willett, C. (ed.) *Theorizing Multiculturalism*. Oxford: Blackwell, pp. 121–50.

Melotti, U. (1997) International migration in Europe: social projects and political cultures, in Modood, T. and Werbner, P. (eds) *The Politics of Multiculturalism in the New Europe*. London and New York: Zed Books, pp. 73–92.

Orsini-Jones, M. and Gattullo, F. (1996) Visibility at a price? Black women in red Bologna', *Tuttitalia*, 14, pp. 24–38.

Orsini-Jones, M. and Gattullo, F. (2000) Migrant women in Italy: national trends and local perspectives, in Anthias, F. and Lazaridis, G. (eds) *Gender and Migration in Southern Europe*. Oxford: Berg, pp. 125–44.

Partito Democratico della Sinistra (1991) *Statuto*. Rome: Partito Democratico della Sinistra.

PDS Federazione di Bologna (1995) *Bologna Sono Persone*. Bologna.

Però, D. (1996) Political anthropology of Italy in action, *Anthropology in Action*, 3(3), pp. 36–8.

Però, D. (1997) Immigrants and politics in Left-wing Bologna. Results from Participatory Action Research, in King, R. and Black, R. (eds) *Southern Europe and the New Immigrations*. Brighton: Sussex Academic Press, pp. 158–81.

Però, D. (1999a) *The Politics of Identity in Left-wing Bologna. An Ethnographic Study of the Discourses and Practices of the Italian Left in the Context of Migration*. Brighton: University of Sussex, unpublished DPhil thesis.

Però, D. (1999b) Next to the dog pound: institutional discourses and practices about Rom refugees in Left-wing Bologna, *Modern Italy*, 4(2), pp. 207–24.

Pugliese, E. (1996) Italy between emigration and immigration and the problem of citizenship, in Cesarani, D. and Fulbrook, M. (eds) *Citizenship, Nationality and Migration in Europe*. London and New York: Routledge, pp. 106–21.

Shore, C. and Wright, S. (1997) Policy: a new field of anthropology, in Shore, C. and Wright S. (eds) *Anthropology of Policy. Critical Perspectives on Governance and Power*. London and New York: Routledge, pp. 1–39.

Vitali, W. (1995) *Per Bologna. Appunti per un programma di governo*. Bologna.

Wright, S. and Shore, C. (1995) Towards an anthropology of policy: morality, power and the art of government, *Anthropology in Action*, 2(2), pp. 27–31.

Young, I. M. (1990) *Justice and the Politics of Difference*. Princeton: Princeton University Press.

Zorzella, N. (1996) La normativa in materia di profughi della ex Jugoslavia. Aspetti di tutela delle minoranze etniche, in Osservatorio Metropolitano delle Immigrazioni, *La Società Multienica*. Bologna: Provincia and Comune di Bologna, pp. 107–12.

9

The double passage: Tunisian migration to the South and North of Italy

Faïçal Daly

Introduction

The purpose of this chapter is to explore the migration of Tunisian workers to Italy. In doing so I conceptualise their migration as a double passage: initially from Tunisia to Sicily and the South of Italy, and then an onward journey to the North of Italy. This staged migration is examined both as a physical movement and as a socio-economic and cultural transition. The migrants' passage must also be set against the background of the evolution of the countries of origin and destination. Hence, in the case of Tunisia, I frame the emigration in the context of the socio-economic and political changes which have shaped Tunisian society over recent decades. Likewise the reception context is examined with reference to the changing economic profile of Italy and its various immigration laws and amnesties. These legislative measures have permitted a kind of free movement of migrant workers across the country and enabled many of them to improve their working conditions but not, or only to a lesser extent, their socio-cultural integration into the host environment.

The chapter is in four main parts. The first highlights the changing course of Italy's experience with international migration since the early 1970s, when Italy's traditional role as a 'reserve army of labour' for the more prosperous North European economies came to an end. Since then, Italy has completed its transition (which started in the 1950s in the northern half of the country) from a peripheral and less-developed European economy to a fully-fledged capitalist society. Now, for Italy too, significant immigration of mainly low-status workers seems imperative for the efficient functioning of the national economy. The second part of the chapter concentrates on the historical relationship, geographical proximity and economic links which have evolved between Tunisia and Italy since the 1980s; these have shaped the main causes of Tunisian migration to Italy during the last two decades. In the third part of the chapter I focus on the settlement and locational distribution of Tunisian migrant workers in Italy, tracing their movement from the southern Italian regions of arrival to the better economic opportunities available to them in Italy's central and northern regions. I argue that the temporary and emergency nature of Italian immigration policy measures implemented during the 1980s and 1990s have increased migrants' insecurity and instability and delayed their permanent settlement and integration. Some of these issues are then exemplified in more detail in the fourth part of the chapter which relates some of the experiences of Tunisian migrant workers I interviewed in Modena, a prosperous industrial town near Bologna, in 1997.[1] Particular attention will be given to the mobility strategies of the migrants and to their experiences of work and social exclusion in Italy. The conclusion stresses the dynamic relationship between the incorporation of Tunisian workers into the Italian economy and their struggle to establish themselves within Italian society.

The changing course of migration in Italy

Emigration has shaped the modern history of Italy since its unification as a nation-state in 1861. This fact should not be ignored when we examine the changing course of external migration in Italy over the past 30 years. Until the early 1970s millions of Italians played the protagonists' role in Italy's international mass migration; they emigrated and settled in just about every corner of the globe (Gabaccia 2000). Between 1945 and the late 1960s, Italian migrant workers contributed a vital element in the reconstruction and industrial development of the European economy. Italy's membership of the European Community permitted Italian migrants to obtain equal employment rights to those of indigenous workers in the traditional countries of immigration – France, Germany and the Benelux countries. To some extent, this constituted an incentive for many employers in these countries to replace Italian migrants with cheap labour from other Mediterranean countries (Castles and Kosack 1985, p. 38). For instance, Germany signed bilateral labour recruitment agreements with Turkey in 1961 and 1964, Morocco in 1963 and Tunisia in 1965.

Meanwhile, strong Italian economic development, the so-called 'economic miracle' of the 1950s and 1960s, reduced the gap in per capita gross domestic product between Italy and the northern European countries. The living standards of Italians substantially improved; consequently the economic motives for Italian emigration diminished. In 1973 Italy ceased to be a net 'exporter' of migrants, bringing to an end the country's traditional role of supplier of migrant workers for other more powerful European economies. This 'migration turnaround' of the late 1960s and early 1970s also coincided with the onset of a vertiginous decline in the country's birth-rate which, by the 1990s, was seen as threatening the very long-term viability of the Italian population (King 1993; King and Rybaczuk 1993).

Conversely, to the south, the income and demographic differentials between Italy and the countries of the southern Mediterranean shore dramatically widened; for these latter countries emigration became a compelling necessity in order to combat unemployment and poverty. Per capita income statistics quoted by Venturini (1988, pp. 132, 135) show how, at current prices, the Italian figures ($620 in 1960, $6,907 in 1980) jumped massively ahead of those for countries such as Tunisia ($194 and $1,370) and Egypt ($160 and $887).

Italy's rapid evolution from a peripheral economy of Europe to an advanced and prosperous economy of the European core meant that, in turn, it too became a country of immigration, as was demonstrated in Chapter 1. Apart from the Chinese community, which had been established in a small number of major cities before the Second World War, the earliest migrant groups to settle, in the 1960s, were the Tunisians in western Sicily and Yugoslavians in the north-eastern regions of Italy. Around this time Italy also allowed the inflow of some people from its former African colonies of Eritrea and Somalia. However, as we shall see later, it was only in the 1980s and 1990s that the bulk of the Tunisian migratory flow to Italy occurred. Ministry of Interior data on the total numbers of immigrants legally present in Italy (i.e. those holding *permessi di soggiorno*) show a rapid growth from less than 150,000 in 1970 to 450,000 in 1986, 781,000 in 1990 and more than 1.2 million in 1997.[2] Although a fundamental characteristic of the immigrant population in Italy is its heterogeneity, a significant fraction – around 18 per cent in 1997 – is made up of migrants from the geographically close countries of North Africa – Morocco, Algeria, Egypt and Tunisia.

The development of Tunisian migration to Italy

The origins of Tunisian migration to Italy can be traced through centuries of commercial links and conflict over trade and power in the Mediterranean Sea. Movements of population between the two countries have always existed. In fact, in the aftermath of Tunisian independence in 1956, nearly a tenth of the country's population of 3.8 million were foreigners. Before the agrarian reforms of the 1960s, there were 180,000 French and 67,000 Italian settlers, mainly occupying the best land. However, the failure of these land reforms and of the cooperative system led to the impoverishment of rural areas and the creation of a large mass of proletarian workers ready to move anywhere in search of a job.

The first wave of migration was to the capital. The 1966 Tunisian census showed that the majority of the 36 per cent of migrants who lived in Tunis came from rural areas, and more than two-fifths of these internal migrants came from the North-West region (Hertelli 1994, pp. 23–4). This massive displacement of people not only constituted a large reserve of labour that the industries of the capital could no longer absorb, but also accelerated migration abroad. As Bel Hadj Amor has noted (1992, p. 2), since the earliest economic development plans the Tunisian authorities have relied on emigration to provide work for all or part of the excess of labour that domestic economic growth was unable to absorb. Hence, unemployment and poverty in post-independence Tunisia and the contemporaneous shortage of labour in most European industrial countries were the structural economic conditions that made a strong Tunisian migration flow to Europe practically inevitable.

A series of bilateral agreements between Tunisia and various European countries (France in 1963, Germany in 1965, Belgium in 1969, Austria in 1970 and Switzerland and Norway in 1971) orchestrated much of the Tunisian migration to Europe. Although considerable, reaching an annual maximum of 50,000 in 1969, Tunisian emigration never reached the massive proportions attained by the Italian 'mass exodus' during the early years of the twentieth century or even in the 1960s. Nor did Tunisian emigration, almost entirely aimed at Europe, have the wide global distribution which characterised Italian emigration (Hertelli 1994).

The role of Italy in the Tunisian migration field developed in a particular way, partly conditioned by the historical links between the two countries mentioned earlier, and partly by the fact that, before the European 'halt' on immigration in 1973, Italy had been used as a bridge by Tunisian migrants moving to France, Germany and other European countries. After 1973, Italy offered one of the few easily accessible routes to Europe for Tunisian (and other North African) migrants. Weiner (1995, p. 59) described Italy as the 'soft underbelly' of Fortress Europe: a popular entry point, transit route and, eventually, destination for many North African migrants looking for a back-door entrance to the European Union. Over time, the Tunisian migrant flow to Italy has come to be characterised by a high level of circulation and mobility not only between Italy and Tunisia but also with other EU countries such as France and Germany as well as within Italy itself.

Other factors have also contributed to the consolidation of the Tunisian migratory link with Italy. Since the change of political leadership in 1987, the Tunisian regime has sought to forge closer economic and political links with Italy as a strategy of reducing the significance of the old colonial relationship with France. Geographical proximity, inexpensive sea and air transport links and mass media (such as the reception of Italian television in much of Tunisia) have also played key roles in making Italy the second most important destination for Tunisian migrants after France. Chain migration fostered by networks of relatives and friends has also had an important influence on the fast growth of the Tunisian community in Italy. This was especially the case at the time of the major migrant amnesties of 1986 and 1990 which enabled many Tunisians to mobilise themselves (in a literal sense) and to regularise their status. According to the 'permit to stay' data, the number of Tunisians legally present in Italy grew rapidly after 1986 to reach a plateau of around 50,000 in the early 1990s, since when the number has oscillated within the range 40,000 to 50,000 (Caritas di Roma 1998, p. 79). So-called 'illegals' are, of course, excluded from these figures.

Four main stages can be recognised in the development of Tunisian migration to Italy. These phases reflect not only the dynamics of the migration process but also the changing socio-economic situation in Tunisia and the continuous evolution of Tunisian settlement in Italy, including migrants' perceptions of various opportunities in different parts of the country and the role of Italy's periodic regularisation schemes.

The first wave of migration took place in the 1960s and early 1970s and was quite distinct from those which followed. This wave was composed of skilled workers and unemployed former agricultural labourers, the 'victims' of the failed agrarian reforms. The skilled workers came from Tunis and the adjacent urbanised coastal areas. First-wave migrants were mainly single males who came to work in the fishing and agricultural sectors in Sicily and other parts of southern Italy. Particular points of concentration were Mazara del Vallo in western Sicily, Naples and other parts of the Campania region (Carchedi 1992; Vaccina 1983; Vizzini 1983).

The second wave was articulated around the first Italian immigration laws of 1981 and 1986 and their associated regularisation programmes. The amnesties were designed to stabilise the numbers of immigrants in Italy but they produced, if anything, the opposite effect and the numbers of immigrants, of many nationalities, continued to increase. Montanari and Cortese (1993, p. 280) estimated that regularisations only succeeded in legalising 20–25 per cent of 'hidden' migration during the 1980s. The number of Tunisians registered as being in possession of residence permits grew quite rapidly in the 1980s, as was noted earlier, but the implication is that many others were present in Italy in an 'irregular' situation.

The third wave started in 1990 following the large-scale amnesty associated with the Martelli Law on migration. By this time the northern Italian regions were becoming an increasingly important destination for Tunisians, particularly for those who had legalised their position. As we shall see in more detail presently, new arrivals tended to turn southern Italy into a transit region during the early phase of their migration project, acquiring knowledge of living in Italy before then moving north. Southern regions of Italy came to be regarded as a safe haven for illegal migrants, who often succeeded in finding employment in the black economy, helped by their friends and other contacts. The leniency and corruption of many local police officers and the increasing involvement of organised gangs, including the Mafia, created a boom in the migrant smuggling business into the South of Italy.

The fourth phase is characterised by a consolidation of the northward migration of Tunisians within Italy, following new regularisations in the 1990s. At the same time, there has been a further increase in illegal migration, reflecting the migration pressure emanating from Tunisia and other source countries and the huge profits available to traffickers. Several Tunisian ports have become important transit points for migrants coming not only from Tunisia but also from other North African and sub-Saharan countries. Smuggling of illegal immigrants from Tunisia – *El Harkhan* as it is called in Tunisian dialect – has become big business due to the involvement of the Mafia, the complicity of corrupt police and customs officers, and the participation of Tunisian and Sicilian fishing-boat owners.

My interviewees told me about the details and various stages of the smuggling of migrants from Tunisia to Italy. First, an intermediary establishes contact with potential immigrants, most of whom are from Tunisia, Morocco and Algeria. An initial meeting is set up between the migrants and the boat-owner. The vessels can accommodate around 20–50 passengers at a time. A price for the journey is agreed, usually around 400–600 dinars (£200–300); this corresponds to about three or four months wages for an average Tunisian worker. Prior to the trip, the migrants will be hosted in a rented house and 'prepared' for the passage, which takes place by night to the south coast of Sicily or the little Sicilian island of Lampedusa. The main areas used as bases for the smuggling are the fishing villages of Shabba, Louza, Ouled Hassan El Awabed and Salgtha; all are located along the coast near Sfax, an industrial city in central Tunisia. The crisis in the fishing industry has encouraged the development of smuggling as an alternative and more lucrative activity. According to my informants, it is relatively easy for a Tunisian to find a passage to Italy, especially if he or she lives in or within easy access of one of the coastal towns.

It is crucial to understand that the pressure for migration from Tunisia will continue because the unemployment rate is still high and the economic gradient dividing Italy and Tunisia remains very sharp. Despite a major economic restructuring programme and some encouraging performance indicators over the past 10–20 years, Tunisia is still unable to create enough jobs for its burgeoning labour force. Therefore the incentives to migrate will remain strong in the short term; indeed the migration pressure is quite likely to increase because more migrants can afford the migration costs.

Inter-regional movement of Tunisians in Italy

In the late 1960s and early 1970s, during the first wave of migration, Tunisians mainly settled in Sicily and Campania in the South, and Lombardy in the North. By 1981 they were present in every region of Italy (Di Comite 1986) and by 1990 half of the Tunisians in Italy had migrated within the country from one region to another at least once (Labib 1996). Hence high levels of internal mobility and spatial redistribution have characterised Tunisian migrants in Italy. Four main factors have contributed to this high level of mobility within Italy:

- various amnesties which made Tunisians free to move without the fear of being 'picked up' and deported;
- opportunity of legal and better-paid jobs in the Centre-North of Italy, especially in small and medium-sized industries;
- better social and welfare provisions in the North compared to the South;
- possibility of seasonal jobs in tourism and agriculture, which naturally encourage a pattern of geographical mobility from one part of the country to another.

The main characteristics and motivations of Tunisian migrants' 'second passage' can therefore be readily identified: benefiting from the legalisation measures of 1981, 1986 and 1990, they have moved from southern to northern Italy to improve their economic situations and to try to achieve a better integration into Italian society; in doing so they have responded to the employment opportunities created by the demand for low-paid (by Italian standards), unskilled and semi-skilled labour in the dynamic small firms of the northern half of the country.

Several authors have pointed out the different economic and social roles that immigrants perform in the different macro-regions of Italy. Iosifides and King (1996, p. 73) highlight the contrast between the 'Mediterranean' South and the 'European' North with the result that immigrants figure differently in each. Venturini (1994, p. 327) states that 'this north–south division finds a parallel in Italy's migration patterns: the northern one, with mainly steady and formal employment of migrants in industry and the service sector; and the southern one, with migrants filling mainly irregular jobs in agriculture and services'. Pugliese argues that there are several 'migrant Italies' and a diversity of regional models, not only with respect to the position of migrants in the labour market but also with regard to the availability and efficiency of infrastructure and services for immigrants, such as voluntary associations, community centres, housing and health (Pugliese 1996, p. 116). Tunisians are one of the migrant groups which fulfil different roles in different Italian regions whereas some other immigrant nationalities, such as the Filipinos, Peruvians, Senegalese or Bangladeshis, are more sectorally and regionally concentrated. In the South of Italy, Tunisians are mostly employed in the primary sector (fishing, farming) and in the flourishing informal economy. In central regions, above all Rome, migrants work in low-skill jobs in the service sector such as cleaning, restaurant and hotel work. In the North Tunisians are employed mainly in factories, foundries, quarries and the construction industry.

Let us look at some of these sectors in a little more detail, paying particular attention to Sicily and Emilia-Romagna, respectively the most important regions for Tunisians' arrival and onward migration in Italy.[3] Tunisians' initial migration to the coastal towns of western Sicily in the late 1960s was obviously dictated by geographical proximity and maritime linkages but also acted as a 'replacement migration' for the local Sicilian workers who since the 1950s had been abandoning their traditional jobs in the fishing and agricultural sectors and migrating to the 'industrial triangle' of northern Italy where their labour was much in demand. Tunisians rapidly took up the available jobs in the fishing industry in Mazara del Vallo, Marsala and Trapani, and worked in the vineyards which are spread over this fertile part of western Sicily. They also took up other general labouring jobs, especially in construction.

The experience of Tunisian migrant workers in northern Italy clearly confirms the north–south regional model noted above: from fishing and labouring in the vineyards of western Sicily they have moved to become engineering, steel and building industry workers in Emilia-Romagna and other regions of the North. The mechanisms of migration for this land-based onward passage are also different. Unlike their migration to Sicily, which was mainly individual in its decision-making process, most of the movement of Tunisian migrants to Emilia-Romagna has developed as a result of chain migration. Employers in desperate need of flexible and cheap labour encouraged their Tunisian employees to bring their relatives and friends from the South, or in some cases direct from Tunisia. Individual case-histories of this process will be presented in the next section.

Emilia-Romagna can be regarded as the epitome of the success-story of the so-called 'Third Italy' – that part of the country which has benefited economically from the restructuring processes of the post-Fordist period which impacted negatively both on the South with its artificially-implanted industries and legacy of corruption, and on the North where most of the obsolete heavy industry was located. The regional economy of Emilia-Romagna is based on a healthy mix of small and medium enterprises, many of them highly specialised and keenly market-oriented, together with a range of efficient public and private services, tourism and intensive agriculture. The region's myriad small and medium firms depend for their survival and growth on the supply of a cheap and easy-to-hire-and-fire labour force. Moreover the globalisation of the Italian economy and the increased need for competitiveness have further enhanced the need for a low-waged, non-unionised and flexible work force which accepts long and unsociable working hours and is ready to adapt to a wide range of circumstances or organisational needs.

Flexibility is indeed the keynote. By this is meant both a flexible use of the job according to the day-to-day needs of the firm (flexible working hours, willingness to do any kind of work etc.) and flexibility in relation to the local labour market – workers taken on and laid off quickly and easily, short-term contracts (or no contracts at all), geographical and occupational mobility etc. (Frey and Livraghi 1996, p. 11). Furthermore, most of the family-run businesses which predominate in Emilia-Romagna continue to be managed in an old paternalistic fashion. Employers expect their workers to work long hours, accept low wages or be paid cash-in-hand for some hours and be available at any time to do any kind of job.

Subcontractors and franchising firms constitute another important feature of the economic system of Emilia-Romagna. Many of them supply large companies with a semi-finished product or a component for a finished product. These firms, because of the dependency relationship and the increasing market sensitivity of the large companies, tend to commit themselves to maximum forms of flexibility and elasticity, and hence become reliant on migrant workers. Meanwhile technological progress, whilst considerable in some industrial sectors in the region, has not been able to fully compensate for the shortage of indigenous labour by machines and robots. Some sectors, such as the textile and building industries, remain heavily dependent on high labour intensity. Building trades enjoy some protection from international competitiveness and have made only slow technological progress; this sector offers many opportunities to migrant workers and many Tunisians have found work there, accepting types of work, wages and working conditions which are shunned by the local labour force. Even in firms where there have been high levels of technical advance, marginal jobs in cleaning and maintenance remain to be done. A survey conducted in Bologna found that technological innovation does not constitute an alternative option to the recruitment of migrant workers. Many firms which had introduced such innovations were if anything more keen to employ migrants because they offer the flexibility and lower production costs which are an integral part of the implementation of such changes (Bruni *et al.* 1993, p. 77).

Socio-demographic reasons also lie behind Tunisians' rapid and successful insertion into the Emilia-Romagna labour force. The indigenous working class is heavily unionised and militant, reflecting the long-standing communist tradition in this part of Italy. The bargaining power of trade unions and factory councils has been very effective in the management of any major changes in production processes. Now, the availability of cheap and plentiful labour, from Tunisia and elsewhere, has allowed employers to recover some control over wage rates and working practices and hence challenge trade union intervention and ease labour regulations. Meanwhile the improvement of educational standards, professional qualifications and living conditions on the part of local young people had elevated their life and career expectations. Family businesses are no longer attractive to them, particularly when the work involved is heavy, dirty manual labour. They prefer to acquire white-collar jobs, to work fewer hours in more congenial surroundings, and to be well-paid. In these situations, the use of immigrant workers becomes vital to compensate the lack of local labour supply. But there is also, of course, a less noble objective for the employers: to accrue bigger profits through the exploitation of labour that is flexible because it is vulnerable (Barsotti and Lecchini 1995).

Finally there is the demographic context. Fertility decline and a growing older population are the most threatening factors for the survival of small and medium enterprises over the longer term. Italy has now reached zero population growth with a total fertility rate (number of children per woman) of below 1.3, one of the lowest ever recorded anywhere in the world (King 1993). Kazim (1991) and King (1993) attribute the causes of this decline to the increasing selfishness and materialism of Italians' lifestyles, where the acquisition of consumer goods and second homes becomes more important than family life and having children. For Emilia-Romagna, where the birth-rate is one of the lowest in Italy, Bruni *et al.* (1993, p. 84) have estimated the net requirement for an 'external' labour force (i.e. provided by in-migration) over a ten-year period to be around 100,000 units. Although there may be some scope for internal migration, especially from the South of Italy, the expectation is that the developing countries will provide the bulk of this workforce.

Tunisian migrants in Modena

In this final main section of the chapter I narrow the focus to the city and province of Modena, and draw on some of the findings from my fieldwork there. I carried out a major questionnaire survey (300 distributed; 165 valid responses) with Tunisian migrants in Modena; this was supplemented by 50 interviews with migrants, employers and other key informants as well as archival work on migrant statistics in the province (for full details see Daly 1999a). Modena is one of eight provinces of the Emilia-Romagna region. It is located in the centre of the region, immediately adjacent to the province of Bologna, the regional capital.

After the mid–1980s, the intensity of immigration into Modena increased considerably. The number of *permessi di soggiorno* released by the *Questura* (the local police authority) virtually quadrupled from 3,995 in 1989 to 14,346 in 1994 (Caritas di Roma 1995, p. 98). The most recent data, for 31 December 1998, show further growth to 17,483 (Caritas di Roma 1999, p. 124). This shows that Modena is the second most important city for immigrants in Emilia-Romagna after Bologna, and the fifteenth most populated by immigrants at national level (out of more than 90 provinces). Even so, officially registered immigrants make up scarcely 2 per cent of the province's total population.[4] The main concentrations of migrants are in Modena city and adjacent communes such as Campogalliano, Nonantola, Bomporto and Spilamberto. Nearly 60 per cent of the migrants are from Africa, and the vast majority of these are made up of the three major immigrant communities in Modena – Moroccans, Tunisians and Ghanaians.

One of the most striking aspects of Tunisian migration to Modena is the imbalance between males (90 per cent) and females. This imbalance is greater than for any other group (cf. Moroccans 73 per cent); in fact most of the other migrant groups – those from the Philippines, Latin America, Eastern Europe, Ethiopia and Somalia – have a female majority of around 70–80 per cent. Half of the Tunisians resident in Modena are under 30 years of age; 55 per cent are single and most of those who are married have left their spouses in Tunisia. The Tunisians' employment rate – 86 per cent – is very high, and second only to the Filipinos' rate of 87 per cent. The main working activities of Tunisians are similar to those of other male migrants from developing countries: 58.8 per cent of Tunisians work in the engineering, metallurgical or food-processing industries, 27.5 per cent are in the building sector, and the remaining 13.7 per cent work in low-tech service occupations such as cleaners, waiters, drivers etc, or in agriculture. Only a tiny percentage – about 1 per cent – have jobs which could be classified as professional, administrative or highly skilled.[5]

The survey and interviews provided useful data on the timing of Tunisians' migration to Modena, their movements within Italy and their places of origin in Tunisia. More than two-thirds of the interviewees had come to Italy between 1986 and 1990; the rest were equally divided between those who arrived before 1986 and after 1990. The two main periods when respondents arrived and settled in Modena coincided with the two main regularisations of 1986 and 1990. The opportunity presented by the 1990 legislation campaign was crucial in Houcine's decision to stay longer in Italy:

> When I left Tunisia in 1990, my intention was not to stay in Italy. I just wanted to make some money during the agricultural season in Sicily and then go back to Tunisia. I entered with a tourist visa. At the time I arrived, a legalisation campaign started and I decided to apply for a residence permit. I stayed and worked in Sicily for three months and then I decided to join some friends in Modena. My friend found me a job in a small building firm and I've been working there since 1991.

Survey responses on place of origin in Tunisia and area of arrival and prior residence in Italy are set out in Table 9.1. For the purposes of this analysis, both Tunisia and Italy are divided into three regions, North, Centre and South. Two-thirds of respondents originated from central Tunisia, and two-thirds of these (43 per cent overall) came from the city of Kairouan, 150 km south of Tunis. Of the 165 respondents to the questionnaire, half had come to Modena from the South of Italy, mostly from western Sicily (Trapani, Mazara del Vallo, Marsala, Palermo) and Naples. If we remove the 28 respondents whose routing to Modena is unknown or unrecorded, the percentage who had been first in the South of Italy rises to 60. Less than a quarter had moved direct from Tunisia to Modena. The pattern of movement in Table 9.1 highlights the role of southern Italy, and Sicily in particular, as a temporary and almost compulsory phase of their migration process.

Table 9.1 Geographical composition of Tunisian migrants in Modena

Geographical region in Tunisia and Italy	Tunisia		Italy	
	no.	%	no.	%
North	47	28.5	38	23.0
Centre	109	66.1	17	10.3
South	5	3.0	82	49.7
Unknown	4	2.4	28	17.0
Total	165	100.0	165	100.0

Source: Author's survey

Four families from Kairouan have dominated the chain migration system from this town to Modena via Sicily. Between them they have brought hundreds of people to Modena and Emilia-Romagna. Most initially settled and worked in farming or in casual jobs in the underground economy in the South. Then they were attracted by the possibility of more stable and better-paid jobs in Emilia-Romagna, and encouraged to move by a relative or friend who would provide support in terms of fixing a job and temporary accommodation.[6] Many onward migrants from the Italian South also moved in order to escape the exploitation, intimidation and inhuman conditions imposed on them by the regime of casual agricultural employment in Sicily.[7]

During the 1990s, much of the Tunisian migration to Modena was based on a detailed knowledge of conditions in Italy. Dense networks of information among groups of kin and friends led back to Kairouan. One interviewee told me:

> I was working as a builder in Kairouan when I was told about job opportunities in the building industry in Modena by a friend. I decided to emigrate first to the South of Italy because I was told that I could enter easily, find illegal work and sort out my documents. I went to Trapani where I applied for a residence permit. Then I moved to Modena in 1990 where I found a job in a small building firm.

The existence of social and family network contacts in Modena has increased the confidence of some older migrants to undertake the journey from Kairouan. Abdallah related that:

> I had emigrated to France in the 1970s and Libya in the 1980s where I worked as a builder. I had never thought to emigrate to Italy until a friend of mine from Kairouan who works in Modena informed me that there were a lot of job opportunities in the building sector... I first travelled to Trapani and then to Bari where I applied for a resident permit, and then I joined my friends in Modena.

Karim, on the other hand, had his first contact with Italy when he was much younger:

> I came to Italy for the first time in the mid–1980s during the school holidays. I stayed for twenty days ... I liked Italy. The following year, during the summer vacation, I went back to Italy and decided to stay there for ever. I left school and my family lost contact with me for five years. I worked for some time in the South... I was not paid for some of the jobs I carried out and I was threatened on several occasions. In 1988 I decided to move to Modena. I immediately found a job in a small firm, where I have been working ever since.

As well as the networks of friends and relatives facilitating the longer-term settlement of Tunisian migrant workers in Modena, the diffusion of accurate information and better transport links have also increased the frequency and amount of temporary mobility between the two countries. For instance many Tunisian peasant farmers spend three or four months in Italy during the harvest period and then go back to Tunisia to work their own land. Those who do not have land and who work in the construction industry in Italy tend to make many return visits, fitted in around their short-term building work. Over 70 per cent of my sample of respondents returned home at least twice a year, and 79 per cent believe their migration to Italy to be temporary.

Other questions from the questionnaire survey confirmed the essential economic character of this migration. Four-fifths of the respondents declared that the main reason for their emigration to Italy was to improve their economic situation, and all of the interviewees who were 'onward migrants' had a clear expectation of improving their living standards by relocating to Modena from the South of Italy. However, none of the interviewees expected that they would be able to earn better wages than Italians or other EU citizens working in Italy. This demonstrates a double dualism in the labour market: not only between Tunisians and Italians, but also between migrant workers from Tunisia (and other poor countries) and those from the developed world of Europe and North America.

Campani (1993) has analysed the wage discrimination and racialisation of the divisions within the labour market in Italy. The majority of migrants from developed countries are employed as professionals, teachers, translators, business representatives etc. By contrast, most migrants from poor countries occupy a subordinate position in the labour market, confined to low-status, marginal and precarious jobs, despite some tendency to self-improvement through their growing access to somewhat more secure (but still low-status) industrial employment in the North of Italy. Drawing on my interviewees' experiences of employment in Modena, typical sectors of employment included agriculture, food processing, the tobacco industry, engineering and foundry work, the construction trades, factories making products such as rubber, plastics, resins, paper, ceramics and textiles, street-peddling and menial jobs in the service sector such as cleaning and domestic service. This stratification of the labour market is found not only in Modena but throughout Italy wherever there are migrant workers (King and Andall 1999; Mingione and Quassoli 2000; Reyneri 1999).

My field research uncovered a lot of evidence of racism and discrimination against Tunisian migrants in Modena. Despite the widespread system of exploitation and abuse of foreign labour in the South (see for instance Karim's interview above), most of my interviewees contrasted the more relaxed and friendly social environment in the South with the widespread climate of racism in Modena.[8] I was told of countless instances of racism experienced by Tunisians in the workplace and in the streets and bars of the city, whilst the local press, especially the right-wing newspaper *Il Resto del Carlino*, fomented an anti-immigrant climate of public opinion. These themes have been the subject of a separate paper (Daly 1999b), so here I will give just a short summary of two types of social exclusion experienced by Tunisian workers in Modena.

First there is discrimination in the workplace. Whilst employers in Modena were grateful for the availability of Tunisian and other immigrant labour – indeed many of them stressed how they now depended on it because of the rejection of manual jobs by the local labour force – many interviewees complained of unfair and patronising treatment at the hands of their bosses and Italian co-workers. Some felt that they were being spied on by Italian fellow-workers and then unfairly criticised. One interviewee recounted a more serious incident. Whilst carrying a 50 kilo bag of cement he had stumbled and badly damaged his leg (the doctor diagnosed a fracture); since his supervisor claimed that there were no witnesses to the incident, the employer refused to acknowledge that he had been injured during the course of his work and therefore he received no sick pay. Other interviewees reported how their employers treated them almost as children, giving them Italian names or calling them all 'Ali' (Daly 1999b; pp. 180–1).

A second setting for overt racism against immigrants is the public space of Italian bars. The bar is a micro-spatial setting where processes of differentiation, exclusion and control between 'insiders' and 'outsiders' can be observed almost as in a laboratory. Many instances were reported to me (and I witnessed some myself) of bar-owners trying to exclude Tunisian and other African immigrants from their premises (for more details see Daly 1999b, pp. 176–8). Some bar-owners display signs and posters which explicitly ban immigrants from buying drinks. In other instances, differential treatment keeps racialised migrant groups at the peripheral spaces in bars, standing rather than sitting down, under pressure to stay only a short time, and served with plastic beakers rather than glasses or cups and saucers. A not untypical incident is related by Karim who had been working for a construction firm in Modena for many years. The quote contrasts the relatively 'normal' routine of his working life, like that of many Italians, and the highly discriminatory treatment he received in a bar:

> When I drive the truck which transports building materials to the company, I usually stop at a bar ... on the outskirts of Modena... One day I stopped as usual and as I hadn't had any breakfast, I asked for a cappuccino, an espresso and a cake. The bar owner served a cappuccino and an espresso in two plastic cups. I thought someone must have ordered drinks to take away, but the barman said they were for me. I turned around and saw that everyone else was drinking from normal cups, and that I was the only one served with plastic cups. I said 'What's this – why have you served me in plastic cups?' He said 'That's the law.' I was furious and left the bar without drinking or paying for anything.

Conclusion

The case of Tunisian migrant workers in Italy clearly shows the dissonance between the Italian economy's need for labour power and the unwillingness of the Italian state to promote a proper and effective integration policy. This contradiction (or is it?) between economic inclusion and social exclusion is central to an understanding of the distribution and geographical movement of Tunisian migrant workers in Italy. Whilst some aspects of Italian migration policy, such as the periodic regularisations of clandestine migrants, are clearly 'pro-immigrant', at least on the surface, other policy initiatives are more repressive, such as the more rigorous measures for the expulsion of migrants and the increasingly onerous criteria for non-EU migrants to obtain Italian citizenship.

I would argue that Italian immigration policy is consistent with the objective of building up a reservoir of illegal as well as legal migrant workers, who provide the economy with a cheap and flexible labour force. The examination of Tunisians' experience of employment in Italy shows that they have been allowed access to certain very restrictive types of undesirable work: farming and fishing in the South, construction and heavy factory work in the North. But their continued marginalisation and denigration (a common media discourse is to associate Tunisians with drugs) prevents their proper settlement and integration into Italian society and blocks their access to better kinds of employment. Other stigmatised groups such as Moroccans and Albanians are similarly subjected to multiple social exclusion.

Tunisian migration to Sicily and other parts of Italy offers an interesting historical parallel, separated only by a few years, to Sicilian migration to northern Europe. This consciousness of a shared history of migration, and the memory of racial prejudice that Sicilians themselves have suffered, makes the islanders nowadays generally more sympathetic than north Italians to immigrants from North Africa. In the North, racist attitudes persist and develop, despite the likelihood that international migration will need to play a central role in sustaining the population and labour force. In Emilia-Romagna it seems that the recruitment of migrant labour has become essential for the survival of the local economy, since the entire labour market system depends on an elastic supply of labour which local workers, with their disdain for low wages and unregulated conditions, cannot provide (Bruni *et al.* 1993).

Push factors from the Tunisian side also imply the inevitability of at least some migration for the next several years. As the Tunisian economy modernises and levels of education rise, so too will aspirations to travel and work abroad; and as the nearest rich European country, Italy is the obvious first target. Any restrictive immigration policy implemented by Italy or any other EU country which does not appreciate the main causes, as well as the changing context, of North African migration is unlikely to have much impact (Sciortino 1991).

From a migrant's perspective, the lax attitude to migration control in the South of Italy has its advantages. Despite their exploitation, intimidation and lack of legal protection, Tunisian migrants, especially those who arrive 'illegally', find a source of safe refuge and a gateway to northern Italy and northern Europe. So, although the South plays a crucial role in the lucrative trafficking of migrants from North Africa and beyond, many migrants gain access to work, learn some Italian, familiarise themselves with Italian culture (or the southern variety of that culture), regularise their status, and eventually move north for a better economic future. Stable settlement in Italy is still in its early stages, however, and Tunisians' mobility patterns are characterised by their frequency of movement, both within Italy and back to the country of origin.

Finally, a few words on the wider context of Tunisian migration to Italy. Since the mid–1990s, the Euro–Mediterranean partnership seeks to promote trade and development within the Mediterranean Basin in order to depress the forces of migration from North Africa and bring political stability to countries whose regimes pose what is perceived to be a threat to Europe. Put crudely, European investment aid and the achievement of a liberalised trading regime (in order to allow Mediterranean products free access to the massive European market) are offered as the price to 'buy' security from mass migration and political upheaval (Pierros *et al.* 1999). Within the framework of the partnership, bilateral agreements such as the one between Tunisia and Italy have a key role, although in practice these seem only to sharpen the focus on migration control. The Italian–Tunisian agreement concluded in 1998 sought not to recruit migrants in an orderly fashion for the Italian economy but instead put the onus on the Tunisian government to curtail the migratory flow to Italy.[9]

The effects of the partnership's aid and development programmes may in the long term alleviate the need for migration but in the short term they are likely to increase the number of potential migrants and the propensity to migrate. In fact the pressure for migration from Morocco and Tunisia (the first countries to sign the agreement) might increase because of the economic pressures inherent in the creating of a Free Trade Area between North Africa and Europe by 2010. Many businesses in Tunisia will have to undertake severe restructuring measures in order to be competitive in this free market. Recent closure of some firms in Tunisia has inevitably led to an increase in unemployed people who are likely to migrate, and there is evidence in the last couple of years that this is beginning to happen.

The Euro–Mediterranean partnership should not be used to further fortify Fortress Europe but as an opportunity to create sustainable development conditions on the southern Mediterranean shore. Free trade and a freer movement of people are essential ingredients for any future cross-Mediterranean cooperation, but they are positively linked rather than substitutable one for the other. As Garson has argued, 'it will be difficult ... for the Mediterranean region to regain its economic and commercial vitality if persons cannot move about as freely as goods and capital (1992, p. 92).

Notes

1 This fieldwork was for my PhD in Sociology at the University of Bristol: see Daly (1999a). I acknowledge the financial help of a University of Bristol research studentship and the invaluable support of my supervisors, Dr Rohit Barot and Prof. Theo Nichols. I am also grateful to Dr David Walters for his helpful and constructive comments on an early draft of this chapter, and to Professor Russell King for his editorial guidance.

2 The 'permits to stay' statistics released by the Ministry of the Interior constitute the main means of data collection on immigrants in Italy but they have many deficiencies, including their unreliable and even contradictory nature. This source attempts to measure the stable and regular part of the migrant population, but there is no systematic review or cancellation of the permits of migrants who return to their countries of origin and, of course, clandestine migrants are automatically excluded from the figures. For a thorough review of the permit data, and other sources of statistics on migrants in Italy, see Bonifazi (1998, pp. 105–33).

3 In 1997, the year I carried out my fieldwork, there were 47,272 Tunisians in possession of a permit to stay, 4.2 per cent of all immigrants in Italy. By far the largest regional concentration was in Sicily (15,317 Tunisians), followed by Lombardy (6,649), Emilia-Romagna (6,349), Latium (4,198) and Campania (3,229). In terms of *relative* concentration, however, the picture is somewhat different. Sicily is the only Italian region where Tunisians are the most important migrant nationality (they account for 21.2 per cent of the total legal immigrant population in Sicily). Emilia-Romagna, where Tunisians are second after the Moroccans, has the next biggest relative concentration, 6.9 per cent. Tunisians are relatively less important in Campania (5.0 per cent), Lombardy (2.8 per cent) and Latium (1.9 per cent) because of the very large numbers of other migrants in these regions, above all in their respective major cities of Naples, Milan and Rome. These figures are taken from Caritas di Roma (1997, pp. 335–41).

4 Once again, the caveats noted above (see note 2) about the statistics on immigrants in Italy have to be borne in mind.

5 The figures in this paragraph are based on Tunisians officially registered as resident in Modena in 1995. This data-set is more restrictive than those based on *permessi di soggiorno* collected by the *Questura*. In order to become *residente* a migrant has to be in possession of a *permesso di soggiorno* and living in accommodation that fulfils the requirements of hygiene and housing regulations. Because of a shortage of housing in Modena, migrants who live in dormitories and other emergency accommodation may be allowed to register as *residenti*, but only exceptionally. Otherwise, those who are unable to find proper accommodation are excluded although they may be traced through police statistics or employment office records.

6 Cifiello (1991, p. 300) has likewise stressed the role of networks of friends and family members in the development of Tunisian migration to Emilia-Romagna.

7 Unscrupulous agricultural employers and the Mafia collaborate in the notorious *caporalato* system. A *caporalato* is a middleman who acts as an intermediary in the procurement of labour power, above all of migrant workers. Migrants are recruited, transported to the place of work and supplied with a drink and a sandwich, for which they have to pay an obligatory 5–10 per cent of their daily earnings.

8 This north–south contrast in racism in Italy has been analysed in detail by Jeffrey Cole (1997); see also Booth and Cole (1999). Cole (1997, pp. 100–29) draws the contrast between the Italian North where immigration is politicised through the discourses of the right-wing parties (Lega Nord, Alleanza Nazionale) and immigrants subjected to the organised violence of extreme-right thugs (the so-called 'nazi-skins')

and other organised vigilante groups (he cites evidence from Florence, Rome, Milan, Verona and other cities), and Sicily where tolerance towards immigrants seems to derive from a shared historical experience of emigration and racism in earlier decades when Sicilians themselves migrated in large numbers to northern Europe and the North of Italy. Cole also suggests that Sicilians are strongly conscious of their island's Mediterranean character deriving from its pposition at the geographical and historical crossroads of the Mediterranean Basin, midway between Europe and Africa. It is worth mentioning that the field research carried out by Cole and Booth in Palermo and other parts of Sicily included many interviews with Tunisians.

9   The main points of the agreement consist of financial support (Italy promises to invest $50 million per year in Tunisia to create jobs to discourage migration), Italian commitment to buy more Tunisian olive oil, and cooperation between coastguards and security forces to police the maritime borders and identify individuals for expulsion and repatriation. However, all the signs are that the agreements are proving ineffective in stopping the movement of Tunisians to Italy. In fact the tragic death of five Tunisian stowaways on 27 July 1998 during a fire on board the Italian cargo ship *Linda Rosa* in the port of Genoa prompted an hysterical campaign against Tunisia which was accused of failing to comply with the agreement and its international obligations. See *La Repubblica*, 11 August 1998, p. 3 and Agence Tunis Afrique Press, Death of five Tunisians aboard an Italian cargo boat, Internet edition, http://www.tunisiaonline.com/news/290798–2.html.

References

Barsotti, O. and Lecchini, L. (1995) Social and economic aspects of foreign immigration to Italy, in Fassmann, H. and Münz, R. (eds) *European Migration in the Late Twentieth Century: Historical Patterns, Actual Trends, and Social Implications.* Cheltenham: Edward Elgar, pp. 81–92.

Bel Hadj Amor, M. (1992) *International Aid to Reduce the Need for Emigration: the Tunisian Case.* Geneva: International Labour Office, World Employment Programme, Migration for Employment Working Paper 66E.

Bonifazi, C. (1998) *L'Immigrazione Staniera in Italia.* Bologna: Il Mulino.

Booth, S. S. and Cole, J. E. (1999) An unsettling integration: immigrant lives and work in Palermo, *Modern Italy*, 4(2), pp. 191–206.

Bruni, M., Lugli, L., Pinto, P., Sciortino, G. and Tugnoli, S. (1993) La presenza extracomunitaria nelle aziende bolognesi: imprenditori e lavoratori tra carenza di offerta, pregiudizio e solidarietà, *Economia e Lavoro*, 27(2), pp. 69–99.

Campani, G. (1993) Immigration and racism in Southern Europe: the Italian case, *Ethnic and Racial Studies*, 16(3), pp. 507–35.

Carchedi, F. (1992) I tunisini, in Mottura, G. (ed.) *L'Arcipelago Immigrazione: Caratteristiche e Modelli Migratori dei Lavoratori Stranieri in Italia.* Rome: Ediesse, pp. 127–42.

Caritas di Roma (1995) *Immigrazione Dossier Statistico '95.* Rome: Anterem.

Caritas di Roma (1997) *Immigrazione Dossier Statistico '97.* Rome: Anterem.

Caritas di Roma (1998) *Immigrazione Dossier Statistico '98.* Rome: Anterem.

Caritas di Roma (1999) *Immigrazione Dossier Statistico '99.* Rome: Anterem.

Castles, S. and Kosack, G. (1985) *Immigrant Workers and Class Structure in Western Europe.* Oxford: Oxford University Press.

Cifiello, S. (1991) Per una ricerca sociologica sui lavoratori extracomunitari in Emilia-Romagna: alcune note metodologiche, in Minardi, E. and Cifiello, S. (eds) *Economie Locali e Immigrati Extracomunitari in Emilia-Romagna.* Milan: Franco Angeli, pp. 31–98.

Cole, J. E. (1997) *The New Racism in Europe : A Sicilian Ethnography.* Cambridge: Cambridge University Press.

Daly, F. (1999a) *The Working Conditions of Tunisian Migrant Workers in Modena, Italy.* Bristol: University of Bristol, Department of Sociology, unpublished PhD thesis.

Daly, F. (1999b) Tunisian migrants and their experience of racism in Modena, *Modern Italy*, 4(2), pp. 173–90.

Di Comite, L. (1986) L'immigration tunisienne en Italie: quelques données censitaires, *Studi Emigrazione*, 82–83, pp. 217–27.

Frey, L. and Livraghi, R. (1996) Jobs refused by nationals, with special reference to Italy, in *The Jobs and Effects of Migrant Workers in Italy.* Geneva: International Labour Office, pp. 3–22.

Gabaccia, D. (2000) *Italy's Many Diasporas.* London: UCL Press.

Garson, J. P. (1992) Migration and interdependence: the migration system between France and Africa, in Kritz, M. M., Lim, L. L. and Zlotnik, H. (eds) *International Migration Systems: A Global Approach.* Oxford: Clarendon Press, pp. 80–93.

Hertelli, H. (1994) Emigration et immigration des Tunisiens en Europe, *Migrations Société*, 6(36), pp. 19–32.

Iosifides, T. and King, R. (1996) Recent immigration to Southern Europe: the socio-economic and labour market contexts, *Journal of Area Studies*, 9, pp. 70–94.

Kazim, P. (1991) Italy: two perspectives. Racism is no paradise! *Race and Class*, 32(3), pp. 84–9.

King, R. (1993) Italy reaches zero population growth, *Geography*, 78(1), pp. 63–9.

King, R. and Andall, J. (1999) The geography and sociology of recent immigration to Italy, *Modern Italy*, 4(2), pp. 135–58.

King, R. and Rybaczuk, K. (1993) Southern Europe and the international division of labour: from emigration to immigration, in King, R. (ed.) *The New Geography of European Migrations.* London: Belhaven Press, pp. 175–206.

Labib, A. (1996) L'immigration maghrébine en Italie: du transit à l'installation, *Hommes et Migrations*, 1194, pp. 26–32.

Montanari, A. and Cortese, A. (1993) Third World immigrants in Italy, in King, R. (ed.) *Mass Migrations in Europe: the Legacy and the Future.* London: Belhaven Press, pp. 275–92.

Mingione, E. and Quassoli, F. (2000) The participation of immigrants in the underground economy in Italy, in King, R., Lazaridis, G. and Tsardanidis, C. (eds) *Eldorado or Fortress? Migration in Southern Europe.* London: Macmillan, pp. 27–56.

Pierros, F., Meunier, J. and Abrams, S. (1999) *Bridges and Barriers: The European Union's Mediterranean Policy, 1961–1998.* Aldershot: Ashgate.

Pugliese, E. (1996) Italy between emigration and immigration: the problem of citizenship, in Cesarani, D. and Fulbrook, M. (eds) *Citizenship, Nationality and Migration in Europe.* London: Routledge, pp. 106–21.

Reyneri, E. (1999) The role of the underground economy in irregular migration to Italy: cause or effect? *Journal of Ethnic and Migration Studies*, 24(2), pp. 313–31.

Sciortino, G. (1991) Immigration into Europe and public policy: do stops really work? *New Community*, 18(1), pp. 89–99.

Vaccina, F. (1983) Alcuni aspetti dell'immigrazione tunisina a Mazara del Vallo, *Studi Emigrazione*, 71, pp. 319–26.

Venturini, A. (1988) An interpretation of Mediterranean migration, *Labour*, 2(2), pp. 125–54.

Venturini, A. (1994) The dualism of Italian immigration, in Cornelius, W. A., Martin, P. L. and Hollifield, J. F. (eds) *Controlling Immigration: A Global Perspective.* Stanford: Stanford University Press, pp. 327–9.

Vizzini, S. (1983) Su talunni aspetti demografici ed economici dell'immigrazione araba a Mazara del Vallo, *Studi Emigrazione*, 71, pp. 362–6.

Weiner, M. (1995) *The Global Migration Crisis : Challenges to States and to Human Rights.* New York: Harper Collins.

10

San Salvario, Turin: the creation of a dangerous place, 1990–99

John Foot

Introduction

For much of the late 1990s, the small, central, grid-like Turinese neighbourhood known as San Salvario became the symbol of Italian urban conflict over immigration. San Salvario developed into the most famous example of a zone 'at risk', of a 'hot' area, of urban 'degrado' and the immigrant 'emergency'. Zones like San Salvario, it was argued, were 'under siege' from immigrants with whom the phenomena of danger, fear and *microcriminalità* were associated. This chapter will look to analyse the sedimentation of this process of identification in a series of ways.[1] First, what were/are the conditions through which a neighbourhood becomes viewed as 'dangerous'? Why San Salvario and not somewhere else? Second, how is this 'dangerousness' related to the social and cultural realities of San Salvario? Third, which specific events or moments can be associated with this 'dangerousness'? Finally, how are the conflicts over urban space in Turin related to those in other Italian and European cities and to urban transformations in post-industrial societies?[2]

San Salvario was originally constructed in 1852–54; 73 per cent of the housing stock standing today was built before 1919. In 1995 San Salvario contained some 6,600 houses and flats, of which 1,055 were unoccupied. The zone consists of a series of interlocking streets (the so-called '*quadrilatero*') bordered on one side by the central station (Porta Nuova) and on the other by the park and the Po river. In reality, the area known as 'San Salvario' in the 1990s is smaller than this, running from the station to the park and omitting the more well-to-do streets of the city centre.

The zone has always been extremely mixed socially and economically, with residents ranging from the well-off elements towards the Po to the more run-down systems of exchange linked to the station area. The area around the station platforms and goods yards formed, for years, a kind of frontier docks where legal and illegal economic networks and trade survived side by side. In addition, San Salvario has an extraordinary collection of religious, political and cultural organisations. There are two Valdesian churches, the main Turinese synagogue (and Jewish school), a number of Catholic churches and parishes and, now, two mosques (one in Via Berthollet in a garage and another in an ex-warehouse in Via Baretti). All these buildings lie within sight of the others (apart from the more anonymous mosques). San Salvario was also host to the first Fiat factory, the offices of the newspaper *La Stampa*, various universities and other cultural organisations.

San Salvario has always been a zone of immigration, like most big-city areas close to central train stations (Corso Buenos Aires, Milan; San Lorenzo, Rome). The first wave of immigrants came from the Piedmontese countryside, as Turin became the 'Petrograd of Italy' in the early twentieth century. Immigration continued throughout the fascist period and then peaked again with the mass internal migrations, from the Italian South and elsewhere, during the postwar boom. Finally, the most recent immigrations have, for the first time, been predominantly non-Italian and from outside the European Community. San Salvario became the first port of call for many of these new immigrants, due to the availability of cheap housing, the *milieu* of the zone and its location close to the station, markets and other key sites of exchange and commerce.

By 1995, there were 724 non-Italian immigrants recorded as living in San Salvario. The total population was 11,000, with a density of 290 persons per hectare (the average for Turin was only 74). The official number of resident foreigners was hence only 6.6 per cent of the total, but the 'real' number was estimated at around 2,000. Moreover, many others *used* the area for various activities – from commerce to information exchange to semi-illicit trading. These immigrant *city-users* were often the focus of 'local' protests during the 1990s. By 1997 the official number of foreigners in the statistical zone which includes San Salvario was 2,879, coming from at least 25 different countries.[3] These numbers give some idea of the immigration into the area, but are more or less useless as a real indicator of the phenomenon, given the problems in documenting immigrant numbers and the highly bureaucratic nature of residence regulations.

What do we mean by dangerousness?

According to Jane Jacobs (1961, p. 30), 'the bedrock attribute of a successful city district is that a person must feel personally safe and secure amongst all these strangers ... a city district that fails in this respect also does badly in other ways and lays up for itself, and for its city at large, mountain on mountain of trouble'. Jacobs argued that 'communities' and populated streets produced safety, or at least a feeling of safety (for an alternative argument see Sennett 1977).

The experiences of danger and fear cannot be measured objectively. Statistics can identify areas with high crime rates or pockets of poverty but the experience of fear is closely related to different subjective conditions – to *mental maps* or virtual *labels* attached to various micro-zones and experiences. Your fear of a place depends on who you are, your past and your daily experiences. Young children are often quite unaware of the very concept of fear. Fear is related to gender, to ethnic origin, to the representations of the city in the media and urban myths. Thus, a young Moroccan immigrant in Turin may be quite unafraid of San Salvario *as San Salvario*, but wary of the possible arrival of the police at any minute. Alternatively, 'local' residents express their fear of even leaving their houses at certain times. *The mere presence of groups of immigrants is frightening to them*, and leads them often to call the police and ask for 'action' (see Palidda 1999; 2000). Fear is also linked to light, time and season. Immigrants may be *less* afraid at night, locals more so.[4] The difficult relationship between insiders and outsiders is central to the understanding of these complicated patterns of fear, danger and security.

Objectively, San Salvario is no more 'dangerous' than many neighbourhoods in Turin and much less 'dangerous' than many other Italian urban areas. Even the numbers of arrests in the zone (exaggerated by the massive police presence at various times) are no greater than that for other neighbourhoods in Turin.[5] When we talk about 'dangerousness' in this context, therefore, we are describing a series of subjective states of fear *and* a representation of the neighbourhood in the press and other media. This dangerousness should not be seen as confined to one social or ethnic group alone (the so-called locals) but as a pattern of dangers, fears and securities which vary from person to person and group to group. Politically, the demand for security has tended to be translated as a demand for the 'liberation' of the city from outsiders. 'Security' for one group has often meant harassment and surveillance for another. In the sections that follow I attempt to trace the evolution of the 'dangerousness' of San Salvario through a series of conditions which create a dangerous place.

Conditions of dangerousness: how is a dangerous place created?

Visibility

For a place to become 'dangerous' it helps for it to be visible. This visibility operates at a number of levels. First (but not necessarily in terms of importance), there is *literal visibility*. Millions of people see San Salvario every year, as they pass through the central station, or drive through the centre of Turin, or visit the banks of the Po, or simply as they shop in central markets and stores. This visibility both created and fed off the notoriety of San Salvario in the 1990s, as increasing visibility led to increased 'watching', voyeurism and identification of where San Salvario is. Dangerousness is attractive to many and part of the pleasure of living or using urban space derives from the *frisson* of getting lost, of the dark, of the contemporary presence of numerous cultures, institutions, peoples and places and modes of entertainment. The very centrality of San Salvario is important. Its dangerousness seems to make the whole city 'dangerous', whereas the far more run-down and abandoned peripheral zones of the city (Falchera, Le Vallette) are too isolated and 'outer' to be even part of Turin, let alone a dangerous, 'infected' component of the city centre.

A second type of visibility relates to the immigrants themselves, and is far harder to pin down. It is often assumed that immigrants, by the mere fact of being such, are more visible. In one sense, this is just a banality. Immigrants are visible because they are different; they look, talk, act, eat and live in different ways. But this obvious point helps us very little in the analysis of the complicated processes surrounding visibility. The really important and interesting questions relate to the subjectivity of visibility – visible to whom? visible as what? In fact, the visibility assumed to be possessed by immigrants as immigrants is also a form of *invisibility* – of a loss of individual identity, of the reduction of people to crude stereotypes.[6] To view all immigrant women as potential prostitutes, or all young Moroccan men as drug dealers is to be *blind* to the reality of immigration in Italy, in Turin and in San Salvario. It is to *fail* to see the variety and economic mosaic of contemporary male and female immigration into Italy over the last 25 years.

This point leads on to one of the key features linking visibility and dangerousness in San Salvario. Most contemporary accounts, in the press and in academic studies, concentrate their analysis of 'problems' relating to immigration on the conflicts between so-called locals and a series of public criminal activities linked to the zone. Above all, this concerns prostitution and the drugs trade. Prostitution on the streets is, by its very nature, a highly visible profession. Turin 'specialised' in Nigerian female prostitution throughout the 1980s and 1990s. Much of the conflict and stereotyping of San Salvario and female immigration in general has derived from an exaggeration (and exploitation) of the so-called problem of immigrant prostitution. Once again, the realities of immigration and economic integration in the city were ignored in favour of a discussion over some 300–400 prostitutes. The drugs trade is less obviously visible than prostitution, but requires public space (usually street corners) to operate. It is also strongly associated with young immigrant men.[7] The widespread call to clean up San Salvario is often reduced to a call for the simple removal of these groups from the streets (which, in practice, simply shifts them to other micro-areas of the city). Alternatively, the desire is to rid the neighbourhood completely of *the public presence of foreign immigrants*, which is seen as threatening in itself. Interviews carried out in San Salvario by researchers found no direct evidence of violence against 'locals', but 'feelings of insecurity, bother, unpleasantness' (Cicene 1996, p. 29).   The majority of police calls regarding immigrants are not related to any specific crime or event but to the simple existence of individuals or groups of non-Italian immigrants (Palidda 1999, 2000). Hence the idea, common to 'local' discourse concerning the zone of San Salvario, that their problems are obvious and 'visible'. The feeling is that if only politicians would actually come and *look* at the area, they would immediately realise what real problems there are (De Corato 1996).

A final level of visibility relates to the representations of San Salvario in the local and national press and mass media. In this realm, San Salvario has proved to be a highly visible space. Continually at the centre of both local and national reports, San Salvario began to dominate the immigrant debates after 1995. A simple analysis of the headlines dedicated to the neighbourhood in *La Stampa* or *Corriere della Sera* shows this trend. San Salvario became a *cause célèbre*, a symbol of the failure and explosive nature of the modern Italian city. Every city has its own San Salvario, with specific historical and cultural features. The local press, particularly the 'Turin' pages of *La Stampa*, was crucial to this transformation and fame relating to San Salvario, but the national press played its part and a series of sensationalist pieces linked to the events of 1995 were also instrumental. Finally, local and national television has used San Salvario as a symbol (a visible symbol) and camera teams have often visited the zone to collect examples of '*degrado*', 'uncontrolled immigration' and 'criminal activity'. The media did not just report events, but selected and highlighted them over a considerable period of time. In this way media do much more than simply reflecting social reality, they define it in a particular way, and this defining role becomes particularly crucial at moments of crisis and rapid change, as we shall see presently. As Muncie and Fitzgerald (1981, pp. 422–3) point out, 'in times of rapid social change when traditional values are shaken up and disturbed, the ensuing public disquiet is resolved by the media by identifying certain social groups as scapegoats or folk devils. They become the visual symbols of what is wrong with society, while the more intractable and structural problems to do with restricted opportunities are simultaneously overlooked or passed by.'

Key actors: the local politician, the priest and the avenger

For 'dangerousness' to take off as an identifier of a zone, the role of the local politician is central. Once the problems of one particular area became linked to national debates and political struggles over more general questions (immigration, crime, racism), then the visibility and notoriety of San Salvario became a fixed motif. In the case of San Salvario, this role has been played by Mario Borghezio. A rotund, bespectacled 53-year-old lawyer, Borghezio joined the *Lega Nord* (the right-wing northern separatist party) in the early 1990s and was elected in the Piedmont area throughout that decade. He began to organise around the immigrant question in the early part of the decade. Throughout the 1990s, Borghezio made the immigrant issue his central campaigning weapon. He appeared frequently on local television and became the Lega's official expert on immigration and related policy.

Borghezio became one of the most prominent political entrepreneurs dealing in racism and fear (and he was even a junior minister for a short time in 1994). He was both a manager of fear, and a creator of conflict. He both rode the wave of the anti-immigrant protests as well as organising and igniting tensions in the zone. Often, his language was crude, racist and inflammatory. His solutions to the 'dangerousness' of San Salvario were simple – expulsion of illegal immigrants, a massive police presence, closure of immigrant businesses. In 1995 Borghezio tabled a parliamentary question listing a number of addresses in Turin as drug-dealing dens, and calling for their clearance. He also complained about the presence of Nigerian prostitutes on trains between Turin and Milan. 'These women', he said, 'disturbed the commuters.'[8]

Borghezio was also a man of action, a highly visible politician in the city and its 'dangerous zones'. His office was close to San Salvario and he attended all the important demonstrations and *fiaccolate* (torch-light marches) in Turin throughout the 1990s. Borghezio intervened frequently in local council debates and in parliament and made constant statements to the press concerning Turin, immigration and San Salvario. Borghezio had no qualms about using racism openly and his plans for future immigration policy included the ethnic selection of potential immigrants.[9]

In November 1995 Borghezio proposed that the police and *carabinieri* be armed with rubber bullets in order to confront the 'emergency' linked to the immigrant presence and to act more effectively against the *clandestini*. This idea was rejected by both the Prefect and the Mayor but came at a time of further arguments after police squads were involved in a clash with immigrants at Ponte Mosca. There were also rumours of collusion between Borghezio and the police, and of his presence at raids on various immigrant-run shops.[10] Borghezio also called for *i clandestini* to be rounded up and taken to 'work camps'.[11] During the same month Borghezio took part in (and spoke at) an anti-gypsy demonstration in the centre of Turin which culminated in the dumping of rubbish outside of the Palace of the Prefect.[12] As debates began over what was to become the Turco-Napolitano immigration law, Borghezio used the example of San Salvario as a weapon. The law, he argued,

> overlooks too many problems. It doesn't take account of concrete issues like the security and peace of mind of citizens. Just one example: the district of San Salvario in Turin. A situation which could repeat itself in any part of Italy. We will campaign fiercely against the law through a series of amendments. If the law must pass there will be a referendum to repeal it.[13]

By 1997, Borghezio was again an official candidate in the local elections (held in April), but the Lega put forward the much more moderate Comino as its mayoral candidate. With no chance of overall victory, Borghezio (like Costa, the centre-right candidate; see below) ran a campaign almost entirely focused on the immigrant question. In mid-April he organised a '*ronde*' (vigilante groups patrolling the streets) in the Porta Palazzo zone. This consisted of 20 or so Lega militants, in green uniforms, 'armed with mobile phones to inform the police of episodes of criminality'. The *ronde* ended in farce when the militants were stopped by police and forced to put away their flags and banners. Yet the very idea of these virtual *ronde* – which rarely materialised on the streets themselves – was a potent threat used by Borghezio and others to force the state into visible action – i.e. the deployment of more police on the streets. The politician often claimed he was merely *reflecting* the opinions of local people, and he also could alter his propaganda to meet particular situations. Borghezio continued to organise anti-immigrant demonstrations and *ronde* throughout 1998, but San Salvario itself began to lose the national mobilising power around this issue. The Lega politician began to be seen to be as much part of the problem as part of the solution.

In general, Lega propaganda did not limit itself to complaints about the alleged activities of 'clandestine' immigrants. Lega policy was in opposition to *all* immigration and to the notion of a 'multi-racial society' and called for institutionalised racism against immigrants (for example over access to public housing) and the expulsion of both legal and illegal foreigners. The Lega dealt in apocalyptic and violent language, talking of the 'destruction of our people' and the disappearance of traditional customs and ways-of-life.[14] 'Increases in crime' were blamed almost entirely on immigrants. The Lega made a priority of the anti-immigrant struggle and organised the collection of 700,000 signatures (with the help in some areas of the neo-nazi *Forze Nuove* grouping) for a referendum to abolish the 1998 Turco-Napolitano immigration law (using the slogan 'one more signature, one less clandestine immigrant'). This referendum was rejected by the Constitutional Court in early 2000. Lega propaganda was crude and unashamedly racist, and complained about the (mild) anti-racist clauses in the 1998 law. Lega solutions to these 'problems', apart from mass expulsions, closed frontiers and new laws, included the formation of citizens' defence committees. Borghezio shifted his political activity to Bergamo at the end of the 1990s, a move which saw a decline in the national attention paid to San Salvario.

Over time, other political groups have also tried to take advantage of the explosive situation in San Salvario. *Alleanza Nazionale* (AN) opened offices in the area in 1995: 'we are here because this is an important neighbourhood. We have nothing against immigrants who are integrated. But we are against clandestine immigrants and delinquents.' The neo-fascist off-shoot of AN, the MSI-Fiamma, also has offices within San Salvario. Leading politicians began to make regular visits to the zone and refer to it in their speeches. San Salvario became part of the political itinerary of Turin (and Italy).

Another key local figure linked to San Salvario is the parish priest Don Piero Gallo. Don Gallo played the key role of 'spokesman' for the 'people of San Salvario' throughout the 1990s. In 1995 he depicted the local population as on the edge of violence, sick and tired of the daily indignities to which they were being subjected. He pointed to 'the arrogance of the *extracomunitari* with their pockets full of dirty money' and added 'if nothing is done at the earliest possible moment, there will be civil war.'[15]

Don Gallo gave frequent interviews to the press and appeared on a series of television programmes in the mid–1990s. He represented the respectable face of intolerance. If such a moderate figure painted a picture of imminent violence and an emergency situation, then surely this was a reflection of a dramatic 'reality'. Don Gallo also played an important organising role in some of the key demonstrations which blazoned San Salvario across the national press, particularly the *fiaccolata* of 1995.

A third key figure in the *quartiere* was Giordano Cavallo, the acknowledged leader of the aborted *ronde* in Borgo Dora in September 1995. Cavallo, 'hero of the neighbourhood', explained that the attempted violence had been a case of self-defence. 'The first to start were them: those damned Moroccans. For months they have been tormenting us. They take our girls, beat up our brothers...'

The press and television: how to manufacture a 'crisis'

For the local and national press, the situation in San Salvario was simplified and made 'spectacular' through a dramatisation of the problems of the zone. Each small protest by 'locals' was reported. Immigration and crime were linked in an uncomplicated and common-sense fashion.[16]   The zone was analysed in a straightforward pressure-cooker way. That is, a picture was painted of the 'locals' as patient, hard-working and honest people exasperated by the decline of their neighbourhood caused by the arrival of criminal and immoral immigrants. It was natural for this patience to run out at some point. Violence *against* immigrants was therefore blamed on the supposed bad behaviour of the immigrants themselves, or on the weakness of the authorities. Even racism was blamed on the victims of racism, or on the state, but never on the racists.[17] Immigrant deaths were often dismissed in the press (usually without much evidence) as 'the settling of accounts' and rarely investigated with any enthusiasm by the police.[18]   Therefore, the argument ran, something had to be done: the state had to react and intervene in order to prevent further outbreaks of vigilante violence.

Key moments

Fiaccolata, ronde and protest: the demonstrations of 1994–95

According to Alessandro Dal Lago (1998), the so-called 'immigration emergency' of 1995 was played out at three levels in Italian society – at the local, communal level; at the political level; and via the communication and media system.

In 1994, protests began to emerge from within the Italian communities in San Salvario and elsewhere. Most of these protests were linked to the supposed 'invasion' of the city by criminal–foreign elements. In January 1994 a banner appeared near Porta Palazzo bearing the words '*è ora di finirla, siamo stufi! Gli extracomunitari qui spacciano droga. Le autorità cosa fanno?!*' ('It's time to end it, we're fed up! Here the immigrants are drug-pushers. And what do the authorities do?!'). The police removed the banner but the press described the situation as one of a 'state of siege'. At the end of the same month local Italians organised another protest in which traffic was blocked on a Sunday. Borghezio spoke to the protesters, who complained that their zone had become 'a drugs bazaar'. Protests continued throughout February 1994.[19]

In 1995, San Salvario developed into *the* national symbol of problems related to immigration. The neighbourhood became the most famous *quartiere a rischio* in Italy, yet this fame was linked to very minor episodes of violence and tiny demonstrations. The effect of and space given to these events went far beyond their actual content. San Salvario became a political battleground within the context of the debates over immigration legislation and the need for the Left to cement its (short-lived and politically expedient) alliance with the regionalist Northern Leagues. In this particular situation, a small aborted *ronde* and a march (*fiaccolata*) of no more than 300 people took on national significance.

The *fiaccolata* of 9 October 1995 was also important for the participation of the official Left and important local figures such as Gianni Vattimo. Vattimo went public in *La Stampa* two days after the aborted violence (discussed below) in the zone. Vattimo admitted his suspicion of some of the racist and intolerant attitudes of the demonstrators, but claimed that as the march continued he became more and more convinced of the 'civil content' of the protest. Vattimo separated the *fiaccolata* from the *ronde*. Why had such a peaceful march led to violence so quickly? Why was there so much support for the *ronde* in the zone? The violence grew from deep and widespread unease. According to Vattimo, this was not linked necessarily to the presence of immigrants but to a generalised decline in the area, intensified 'to an enormous extent' by the 'arrival of clandestine immigrants'. There was a generalised distrust of the institutions which were supposed to maintain legality.[20] The threat of violence against immigrants was a constant feature of this period. Don Ellena, a priest working near Porta Palazzo, called for the state to act, and quickly. For *La Stampa*, 'in the quarter of San Salvario alone there live 4,000 immigrants, most of them clandestine, always on the brink of a "brawl with iron bars" (in the words of the local priest) with the 13,000 Italian residents'.[21]

On the night of 11 October 1995, this brawl seemed imminent: 58 people ('all Italians living in the quarter' and aged between 15 and 35 years old) were stopped by police near Borgo Dora at 10pm. They were armed with (one) baseball bat, iron bars, sticks, knives and 'karate weapons' and, it seems, were on their way to 'hunt the black criminals who are besieging Borgo Dora' and who 'for some time have been threatening the area'. Eight police cars arrived after phone calls and headed off the group. The explanation given by *La Stampa* for these events was simple – 'violence is born out of fear'. Locals echoed this analysis: 'We are afraid. The immigrants must go away from here. Immediately. Or we will make a revolt.'[22]

Some of the details about the group of young men contradicted their image as brave and honest defenders of their neighbourhood. Eleven members of the group had previous convictions for drug-related offences and theft and many were well-known to the police. The police hinted at political inspiration for the *ronde*, others at a war between drug dealers. Locals expressed pride that something had been done to draw attention to their zone. 'We are fed up with the Moroccans and this is only the beginning.' 'The real victims are us.' For the father of one of *ronde* members 'the state has abandoned us, we are in the hands of criminality'. Even the local priest defended the group, 'they reacted as any young man who occasionally loses his patience would react. But I say categorically, there was not the intention to be racist.' The '58' wrote a letter to *La Stampa* denying that they were racists and describing themselves as victims: 'we are absolutely not racists, but we are fed up with all these injustices'.[23]

The reaction of the authorities to the attempted *ronde* was one of near-panic, as the story became national news.[24] The Mayor made an appeal, strangely, directed at 'immigrants'. An emergency meeting was called at the Turin Prefecture of the 'Committee for Public Order and Safety' (a body consisting of the police chief, the Mayor, the head of the *carabinieri*, the head of the urban traffic police, the assessor for shopkeepers, and the 'expert on San Salvario', Vincenzo Manna). The agenda was made up of 'the problems linked to the presence of *extracomunitari*'. After an hour-long debate, the Prefect announced, 'we will extend police controls to all the "hot zones" of the city'. On 17 October, 20 dawn arrests (of *clandestini*) were made in a house in Via Cecchi, centre of the protests at Borgo Dora, and 15 'Moroccans' were arrested at two addresses in Corso Taranto.

Mayor Castellani went walkabout in the neighbourhood, the 'hell' of Via Cecchi. He concluded that the problems of the zone were real ones and the responsibility of the state. The visible police presence in these so-called hot zones was stepped up considerably. Two weeks of 'blanket controls' followed in San Salvario. A free phone number was used 335 times in two weeks, leading (it was claimed) to 63 arrests and 82 charges. The police authorities acknowledged that their presence was more or less a cosmetic propaganda exercise, designed to placate 'public opinion'. Police Chief Giuseppe Grassi likened the police action to 'an aspirin, which at best will make the fever abate'.[25]

At the national level, the response was extremely significant. The Dini decree on immigration contained far more severe measures than had ever been seen in Italian immigrant legislation. A new amendment was prepared in the wake of the events in Turin which allowed for the immediate expulsion of immigrants caught in the act of committing crimes (within three days), the construction of detention centres for those awaiting expulsion and the restriction of appeals against expulsion orders. According to *La Stampa*, the inspiration for this change of policy from the centre-left government came from Piedmont. Centre-left politician Magda Negri spoke of 'sending out a strong signal ... the hardship of the citizens has reached the limits of tolerance'. The turning-point consisted of the events in San Salvario and Borgo Dora. The task of the Left was to 'guarantee legality'. Piero Fassino, a leading member of the centre-left government, used arguments directly related to the fears of residents. 'If the pensioner is afraid to leave his or her home, if girls are afraid to go out in the evening ... the consequence will be the criminalisation of all the immigrants.' The decree was the object of heavy criticism from within the Left coalition and there were doubts about its compatibility with both the Italian constitution and European legislation.[26]

San Salvario became the subject of documentaries and television chat-shows. At the height of this crisis, presenter Michele Santoro dedicated a whole evening to the debates over immigration in his RAI 2 programme *Tempo Reale*. In front of audiences which touched 10 million, Borghezio, Maurizio Gasparri of *Alleanza Nazionale*, Don Gallo, Claudio Martelli (author of the 1990 immigration law) and Luigi Manconi (Green Senator and immigration expert) discussed various aspects of the new decree against a background of angry residents and sensationalist instant documentary reportage. With the new Albanian crisis, immigration had become the talking-point throughout the country; locally, debates were rooted in the neighbourhood of San Salvario.

The Dini legislation was issued in November at the height of the national panic over immigration. Notably in its Article 7, the decree accepts the arguments put forward by the protesters in Turin and the police. Immigrants were 'dangerous' *per se – by the fact of their presence in Italy* (especially if without documents, even if these had just run out). The decree used the term 'socially dangerous' to portray immigrants. The solution to this 'problem' was expulsion, the removal of the subject from Italian soil. As one part of Article 7 reads 'The foreigner who is found within the territory of the state in an irregular condition must be expelled'. In many cases, no trial was needed, just the 'catching in the act' of the immigrant – which usually boiled down to the word of the immigrant against a policeman or 'local resident'. Article 7 grew directly out of the *fiaccolate* and aborted *ronde* of San Salvario and Borgo Dora. The demands of the demonstrators had been met within a month of their protests. Only the political demand (from Borghezio and others) to make clandestine immigration a crime had been resisted.[27]

A new *fiaccolata* was organised in San Salvario on 17 November 1995: 350 people marched 'with anger' under banners which included 'pushers go home' and 'S. Salvario Banana's Republic' [*sic*].[28] The march was called by the *Comitato spontaneo del quadrilatero* and excluded all official institutions and parties. Individual members of various right-wing parties did attend, including a deputy from Berlusconi's *Forza Italia*. The *fiaccolata* began at Don Gallo's church and used torches borrowed from the priest.

Some marchers made a distinction between 'delinquent' and good immigrants, whilst others went further and condemned all immigrants and 'blacks' in a torrent of racial abuse.[29]

The murder of Abdellah Doumi

On the night of 19 July 1997 a 21-year old Moroccan man, Abdellah Doumi, drowned in the Po river in Turin's city centre. The man had been chased by at least ten young Italians (some of whom wore motor-bike helmets) who, whilst he was in the water, not only had not come to his aid, but had thrown bottles, rocks, wooden boxes and even a vacuum-cleaner at him. One of the gang had then shouted to Doumi to 'Go, go, and now swim, get out on the other side.' Those responsible were arrested almost immediately – 24 year-old Piero Iavarone and three of his friends.[30] The week after, three hundred immigrants demonstrated near the point where Doumi died, calling for justice for the drowned man. At their first trial Iavarone and the other three were convicted of murder and sentenced to 22 years in prison. After a long campaign in their favour, this sentence was reduced on appeal in December 1999, and the protagonists of the murder were released under house arrest. The reaction of Borghezio to the murder was to call for more police patrols in the area.

The whole issue of violence in the Murazzi zone (where the drowning occurred) exploded again on the eve of the first round of the mayoral elections in April 1997. More than 50 young men, armed with iron bars, stones, bottles and toy guns, and dressed in bomber jackets and balaclavas, went on the rampage. Foreign immigrants were forced to flee and one man was beaten around the head. The gang, many of whom were linked to far-right groups active amongst the football fans of Torino, then continued their violence in the city centre, smashing a number of cars. The explanations for this event were manifold (Fumagalli 1997). Some saw the violence as a political act, others as the natural consequence of 'high' immigration, others argued that there was a battle between rival criminal groups for control of the Murazzi zone. The reaction of the authorities, beyond the arrest of three of the gang, was, as usual, the patrol of the zone with police cars and vans.

The mayoral election campaign of 1997

Questioner: 'But do you understand the people who protest because the Africans urinate in their doorways, inject themselves or push drugs or have sex a few metres from their children? Do you understand those who say that there are too many immigrants and that their numbers must be controlled?'
Castellani: 'I understand what the people are saying' (Castellani 1996, p. 144).

Soon after the 'immigrant emergency' of 1995–96, Turin's mayor, Valentino Castellani, came up for re-election. His opponent this time came not from the Left (as in the 1993 campaign), but from the Right in the shape of ex-minister and Liberal Raffaele Costa. Castellani had always resisted calls from the Right to 'get tough' with immigrants (Castellani 1997), but during the campaign he was under pressure. Typical of such pressure is the following statement by Lelio Lantella, supporter of Costa: 'If we dwell so much on this problem, it is because entire quarters – think of San Salvario, or Murazzi or Pellerina – suffer from the most serious problems created by illegal immigration: prostitution, drugs…'[31]

Castellani managed to resist pressure for a tougher policy on immigration in the city and his official programme separated out crime, immigration and inner-city decline.   The programme applauded the measures in the planned Turco-Napolitano law including those relating to expulsion and police powers. In addition, the programme promised a series of measures to aid the insertion of immigrants, including projects related to specific areas and funding for a series of support groups and schemes. Nonetheless, the tone and the agenda of the whole campaign were set by Costa, and the immigration question dominated the debates and press coverage of the elections. Castellani lamented that 'my political opponents have pursued a strategy of fear, a barbarous electoral campaign which insists on the risks and dangers of immigration, portraying immigrants as delinquents'.[32] Castellani was often forced into a harder public position under pressure from Costa and the Lega. The campaign itself, despite Castellani's very narrow victory (he won by 4,000 votes, polling 50.4 per cent to Costa's 49.6), shifted the hegemony of 'common sense' further towards positions on the Right and anti-immigrant ideas in general.

Geography, space and conflict

The conflicts we have seen emerge in San Salvario have also been about the control, use and shape of public, urban places and space (Tosi 1998). Some locals resent the ways in which new immigrants use streets, bars, corners, hotels and markets for their own economic and social ends. Certain complaints concern the specific use of these spaces – with regard to noise, customs, violence or semi-criminal activities. Others involve the mere presence of immigrants in general, without any real relationship with their actual behaviour. The scale moves from a kind of invisible unease with the immigrant presence right up to specific complaints involving specific places and their use. The geography of these social and cultural conflicts can be traced over time and space through the use of maps and photographs – such as the positive photographic record of San Salvario compiled by D'Ottavio (1997) – as well as reports of incidents, demonstrations and protest.

These micro-conflicts often involve a simple request: that the 'problem' be moved elsewhere, perhaps just a few hundred metres away. These are conflicts over corners, borders and parking spaces, but they are no less violent and deep-rooted for all that. The lack of possible mediation or communication between the various ethnic and social groups involved often leads to the build-up of tensions which in previous periods were defused through communication or compromise (Fiasco 1996). The securitisation of homes and buildings creates places of conflict in public spaces visible to all – the street.

After an 'anti-prostitute' demonstration in the zone of Borgata Parella (on the edge of San Salvario, towards the park) during the crucial month of October 1995, one demonstrator argued that 'the pavements have become pavements again; this hasn't been the case for a couple of years'.[33] The immigrants, it was frequently claimed, had taken control of certain zones of the city. Certain bars became ethnically identified, such as the 'Tunisian bar' in San Salvario. In June 1996, 300 Italian residents laid siege to an immigrant bar-restaurant in Via Saluzzo and forced it to close.[34] Other spaces became notorious for certain, often short, periods of time, such as the 'evil corner' where Via Principe Tommaso and Via Bernardino Galliari meet (Neirotti 1997).

One of the paradoxes here is that the campaign against immigrant use of public space *as* public space (in a whole series of ways) has led to the closure of these (rare) spaces. Administrators have built fences and gates, removed benches, put huge flower pots on steps – all to prevent immigrants using these spaces collectively. Meeting places are placed out-of-bounds in these physical ways, or else immigrant groups, whether they be prostitutes or families cooking Sunday lunch, are also moved on and effectively banned through police controls and other forms of micro-hostility. Some of these processes (architectural and others) mirror those analysed by Mike Davis in his classic work on Los Angeles, *City of Quartz* (Davis 1990). New barriers were needed because so many, it seemed, no longer existed. The Other was not just close by, but actually 'inside'. Cohen links the demands for a 'safer city' to the 'dreadful realization that while the medieval fortress town has been a place of safe retreat against the external enemy, the enemy was now within the gates' (Cohen 1985, p. 211).

At a macro-level, these micro-conflicts are also the outcome of the broad social and economic changes which have transformed modern cities. As a result, in the words of Manuel Castells (1997, p. 59), 'Ethnicity becomes the foundation for defensive trenches, then territorialized in local communities, or even gangs, defending their turf.' Despite falls in resident population (that of Turin has been in decline throughout the 1980s), the globalised post-industrial city has seen an increase in the *use* of urban space by various groups. These *city-users* are extremely mobile and flexible in their relationship with urban space and are also less likely to use that space in a responsible manner. These uses often enter into conflict with the classic desire of residents for control of 'their' space and other values such as noise/silence and cleanliness/dirt. In addition, the traumatic shift to a post-industrial society (which has been particularly dramatic in Turin, once the industrial city *par excellence*) has generated a crisis of identity amongst many urban dwellers. According to Revelli (1999, p. 47) the factory in Turin has been practically the only medium of social composition and of shared public discourse; the decrease in the number of factory workers has had inevitable consequences on the city's social fabric. The loss of identity through industrial work and the factory has led (in some cases) to an increase in identification with the neighbourhood and the home. In addition, the crisis of the welfare state model means fewer resources are available for distribution and the creation of social safety-nets in moments of crisis. The conflicts with immigrants are therefore also linked to a presumed loss of identity or change in identity in a period of epochal social and economic change. Organisationally, this territorial identity politics has been expressed through various citizens' committees, neighbourhood committees and commercial and shopkeeper bodies. For Castells (on a world scale) where once urban movements were radical, proactive and often anti-capitalist, since the 1980s they have often become inspired by 'a defensive identity, an identity of retrenchment of the known against the unpredictability of the unknown and the uncontrollable' (Castells 1997, p. 61).

The Lega, as Biorcio (1998) has noted, has been particularly adept in mobilising and capturing this crisis of identity, attempting to transform 'social conflict into identity conflict'. Local identities have been exalted through the use of folklore and propaganda, but above all through the creation of a series of enemies against whom this identity is to be constructed. These enemies have ranged, over time, from 'southerners', to 'The South', to 'The State', to 'Rome' and have concentrated, in recent times, on foreign immigrants. Lega propaganda is simple, powerful and crude: 'Immigration equals criminality.' 'The immigrants must be expelled.' 'Stop them all.' 'Millions are arriving.' The complicated problems of urban change and economic transformation are reduced to the forced removal of a few hundred drug dealers, car window-cleaners and prostitutes, the most 'visible' members of the immigrant community. Of course, this propaganda cannot withstand even the most superficial of analyses (for example, the notion that the labour shortages in the North of Italy be filled by immigrant labour) but the power of identity politics in northern Italy should not be underestimated.

Anthropologies of daily life: fear on the streets and moral panic

Societies appear to be subject, every now and then, to periods of moral panic. A condition, episode, person or group of persons emerges to become defined as a threat to societal values and interests; its nature is presented in a stylised and stereotypical fashion by the mass media; the moral barricades are manned by editors, bishops, politicians and other right-thinking people; socially accredited experts pronounce their diagnosis and solutions; ways of coping are evolved or (more often) resorted to; the condition then disappears, submerges or deteriorates and becomes more visible (Cohen 1972, p. 28).

Much of the debate over the 'dangerousness' of San Salvario concentrates on the 'fear' experienced by local long-term residents. What is the content of this 'fear'? In the first place, the fear is linked to certain places, moments and groups. Fear tends to increase with night time, on particular street corners and with regard to groups of immigrant men. A picture is painted of continual acts of violence amongst immigrants and threats by immigrants towards 'locals'. *This fear can be removed by the removal of the public presence of immigrants* (whether or not they are committing any crime) and by the visible presence of the 'forces of law and order' (Maneri 1998, p. 255).

But how realistic is this fear? For whom is San Salvario actually dangerous? Looking at the figures and reports concerning San Salvario, it is clear that the neighbourhood (and Turin in general) is a far more dangerous and fearful place for the immigrants than it is for the locals. Immigrants are continually worried about being stopped by the police. If they forget their documents, or do not possess the right documents, they can be arrested, imprisoned in the new detention centres and eventually expelled. Immigrant women working as prostitutes are in constant danger from violent clients or their minders and pimps, as well as the fear of disease. Violence *against* immigrants is far greater than any violence committed by them. Immigrants are far more likely to be imprisoned and attacked than non-immigrants.[35]

Yet these fears and dangers are dismissed in the public and political debates over immigration and the city. All that matters, the only fear that counts, is that of the 'locals'. These fears are prioritised (of course, these people also have votes), and if these 'scared' locals club together and commit acts of violence, then this is merely the logical consequence of the fear they have lived with for years.

Alongside fear lies common mistrust and *disgust* regarding foreign immigrants. The disgust is commonly directed towards prostitutes in the zone. Locals express their fears that children will be shocked or corrupted by seeing prostitutes on the streets, and similar complaints are directed towards drug addicts who inject themselves in public. Here, historical comparisons are made between the prostitutes of the past and those of the present. The 'good', local and healthy prostitution of the past is contrasted with the 'bad', foreign and unhealthy prostitution of the present (Bagozzi 1995). Similar distinctions are made between 'good' (Italian) homeless people – usually described as *clochard* or *barboni* (tramps) – and 'bad' foreign immigrants without housing.

The symptoms of these local fears are, it is claimed, twofold. First, the local residents simply avoid the dangerous parts of the zone or the street and public space altogether. They 'do not go out any more'. They barricade themselves in their homes behind a forest of large doors or gates (locked at night), doorkeepers, iron bars, intercoms (with videos), alarms and weapons. The public city is to be avoided at all costs; it has been usurped by a foreign army. Another presumed symptom of this fear, and of the dangerousness of San Salvario in general, is economic. Shopkeepers complain about a decline in business as the zone became notorious, and the sharp fall in local house prices has begun to worry local residents.

The events of 1995 (and the following years) bear all the hallmarks of a series of moral panics over crime and immigration. As Cohen (1972) concluded after his work on 'mods' and 'rockers' in the 1960s,

> when policy-makers, judiciary, politicians and editors similarly perceive the 'threat' in stereotypical and overactive terms, then a moral panic may be created which could have serious and long-term repercussions not only in changing legal and social policy, but also in affecting the way in which society conceives itself.

The folk-devils in this case are immigrants of various types, who have invaded the spaces previously occupied or controlled by Italian 'locals'.

The reaction of the authorities to the events of 1995 did little to defuse the image of San Salvario as a dangerous place. For a number of weeks the police presence in the area was massive and highly visible (as it was meant to be). Immigrants were stopped on numerous occasions and asked to show their documents. In some cases, the 'entrance' and 'exits' to the neighbourhood were blocked and those entering (in practice, foreign immigrants) were all stopped and searched. These tactics were designed to satisfy local public opinion for 'order' and a 'visible presence' of the police and *carabinieri* on the streets of San Salvario. By 1997, the police chief of the city had ordered three permanent 'flying squads' in the zone. One was stationed in the centre of the zone and two others were always on the move.

Good and bad immigrants

One of the mechanisms whereby the new immigration to Italy has been classified as 'dangerous' and 'criminal' has been in comparison with the good stereotype of the Italian immigration (internally) of the 1950s and 1960s. We can pick out this stereotype in many of the interviews with local residents (often ex-immigrants themselves) concerning the behaviour of southern immigrants in the city during the years of the boom. The mythical re-working of the past contrasts strongly with the hostility towards southern immigrants during the economic miracle in Turin and the strong links made (at the time) between crime, southerners and their supposed 'passionate nature'. Here is one view:

> At the beginning we all thought that the situation concerning foreign immigration was the same as thirty years ago, when the special trains from the South (of Italy) used to arrive, full of southern workers for Fiat. The point is that they had a job; the blacks who are here now go around with wads of 100,000 lire notes.[36]

But there are also 'good' and 'bad' immigrants *within* the new immigrant groups. Reference is made continually to the contrast between the 'honest' immigrants who work and pay taxes and those involved in criminal activity. Often, these stereotypes are classified ethnically. Thus, Nigerian women are viewed exclusively as potential or actual prostitutes, and young Moroccan men as linked to the drugs trade, whilst Egyptians are often classified as 'honest' and 'hard-working'.[37] This can be characterised as a kind of not-in-my-backyard syndrome. We all see the need for rubbish dumps, incinerators and, in this case, immigrant labour. But when these are to be found close to our 'backyards', people demonstrate, protest, block traffic and occupy space. Not here (but somewhere close by) seems to be the simple demand of these micro-conflicts over territory and urban space. One (southern Italian) Porta Palazzo bar-owner summed up these contradictions in a 1995 interview: those immigrants whom he employed in his bar were described as 'good people'. A Sicilian building constructor described his immigrant employees as *bravissimi*. But these entrepreneurs also complained bitterly about the other immigrants: the 'bad ones', the 'drug-dealers'.[38]

These are classic cases of the 'needed but not welcome' syndrome. Immigrant labour meets a number of needs at the dirty end of the service economies – cleaners, cooks, waiters, new domestic servants – but their presence in society and in public is often rejected (Zolberg 1997). They express, as I have written elsewhere, the contradiction between the profitability of their function as economic actors and the undesirability of their presence as members of Italian society (Foot 1995).

Comparisons: Turin and Milan

Why did San Salvario become (albeit briefly) the national symbol of urban conflict over immigration, and not somewhere else? The obvious comparison here is with Milan, but other comparisons can and should be made with much poorer cities in the South such as Naples and Bari.[39] Milan was, for a time, the national centre of 'immigration conflict', especially in the early 1990s. For a time, as the Lega campaigned on the issue, the historic immigration zone around Corso Buenos Aires, again close to the central railway station, attracted the attention of politicians, protest committees, priests and the mass media. Yet, despite the fact that the Lega actually ran Milan for four years (1993–97) and certain key moments before and since – such as the violence in Via Meda and the arguments over crime in 1998 (Foot 1999) – the focus has undoubtedly shifted to Turin throughout the 1990s.

Three broad explanations can be advanced. First, economically, the shift to a post-industrial city and society in Milan has been far quicker and more successful than it has been in Turin. The growth of enormous service and other post-industrial activities to fill the gaps left by traditional industry and the continuing (and increasing) importance of Milan as a centre for all kinds of trade and exchange activity have created large spaces for the economic incorporation of immigrants at the cheap labour end (but not only) of the economy. Turin has not been able to transform itself in this way. It is still Fiat-dependent, but with a much smaller Fiat. Turin is no Detroit, but it is no Milan, and the poverty and unemployment levels in the city are far higher than those for Milan. Immigrant 'economic' space is not as available as it is in Milan. Turin is also not able to exploit the regional advantages allowed to Milan as a nodal economic and transport link centre.

Geographically, the 'problems' in Turin have been far more visible than in Milan. Milan expelled most of its working-class residents from anywhere near the historic centre of the city years ago, and any residual groups were forced out by the property prices of the 1980s and 1990s. Turin has maintained a popular feel and central population to this day, and these areas, with their cheap rents and run-down housing, have attracted new immigrants to them. In addition, the importance of the vast market zone of Porta Palazzo should not be understimated. This massive public space, with its tradition of informal economies and flexible labour employment, has remained a powerful magnet for immigrants either as residents or as city-users (or both). Milan's markets are far more ephemeral (spatially) and less frequently open. The permanence of Porta Palazzo is another important factor in the visibility and centrality of the 'immigrant question' in Turin as opposed to Milan.

Finally, in the cultural sphere, my explanations are merely hypotheses. Milan is certainly a more cosmpolitan city than Turin, with a richer history of immigration from outside Italy. Yet Turin was host to vast movements of Italians throughout the 1950s, 1960s and 1970s. Many of those in the 'front line' of the 'war' against foreign immigrants are precisely those southern immigrants who arrived during and after the boom. These groups seem to feel directly threatened by the presence of foreign immigrants, and by the economic loss implied by the *degrado* of their neighbourhoods. The status of being an immigrant or even a recent ex-immigrant has never been a guarantee against hostility to even newer arrivals. In this case, this status may form part of the explanation of the problem, but any 'ethnic' considerations of this kind should remain tentative and open to question.

Conclusion

The 'dangerousness' of San Salvario has implications far beyond Turin and local politics. San Salvario has become the most important symbol of a new paradigm of post-industrial Italian politics. At a macro-level, the concentration on issues of crime and immigration is an outcome of irreversible and traumatic social and economic change. Industrial society, so powerful in the 1960s and 1970s, has disappeared. Urban society is in the throes of a deep and organic crisis. The virtuous communities and movements created out of earlier waves of immigration and class conflict have turned defensive and often xenophobic. This new paradigm resembles that of the UK in the 1970s. There, the response to the crisis of late capitalism concentrated around 'race', 'order' and 'policing'. For the discourses on 'mugging' analysed by Stuart Hall *et al.* (1978) we can compare the debates over *microcriminalità* in Italy today. Crime has begun to dominate everyday life, and political life. The particular conjuncture of immigration movements and urban crisis has accentuated this centrality. The response of the authorities has been, in the main, both weak and repressive: weak in combating the stereotypes branding immigrants as criminals, repressive in responding to local 'fears' by mass arrests and the creation of detention centres. In the UK, this process led to the birth of a new hegemonic project – Thatcherism – which was to transform British society in every sphere. In Italy the outcome may well be different, but the prerequisites for Thatcherism Italian-style (at least in the spheres of law and order and policing) are all in place.

Notes

1   This chapter is based on research carried out under the auspices of the City and Identity Research Project based at University College London and financed by the Arts and

Humanities Research Board. I would like to thank Sandro Dal Lago, Penny Green, Russell King, Robert Lumley and Sandra Wallman for their advice at various points during the preparation of this piece.

2   The issues of crime, immigration and the city go to the heart of sociology, anthropology and criminology, from the Chicago School onwards. See for example Wirth (1956), Whyte (1943), Morris (1957) and, for an Italian view, Pollini and Scidà (1998).

3   Ufficio di Statistica della Città di Torino, *Cittadini stranieri residenti a Torino suddivisi per circoscrizioni (estrazione delle prime 25 nazionalità)*, data for 31 December 1997. In addition San Salvario hosted 1,112 businesses in 1995, including 406 shops, of which 34 were directly managed by foreign immigrants. For the entire city there were 9,000 documented foreigners in 1985, rising to 32,000 in 1995 (of whom 27,000 were so-called *extracomunitari*). See Morbello (1996).

4   'Here, so to speak, we are fifteen mothers, but none of us dares to go out after seven in the evening ... we live barricaded in our homes' (Giuseppina Di Gregorio, interviewed in *La Stampa*, 10 October 1995).

5   The discussion of immigrant crime rates in Italy is a highly controversial one, veering between Lombrosian ideas of the 'social dangerousness' of immigrants to more sophisticated studies such as that of Barbagli (1998). The social questions relating to crime and marginality of many new urban immigrants are often forgotten in favour of a concentration on the *ethnicity* of the criminals used *as an explanation*. It is worth pointing out that these debates are hardly new. Of course, the criminal and legal systems are not neutral towards new immigrants. Many crimes, such as those relating to immigrant laws, can only be committed by immigrants, who have limited access to the legal and financial (and political) resources used by Italians to avoid or by-pass (or negotiate their way through) the legal system.

6   Often, immigrants are treated as if they simply did not exist, as 'non-persons', as completely invisible, as in the claim of one local shopkeeper interviewed in *La Stampa* (10 October 1995): 'And if the area wasn't guarded by the police? There'd be nobody out and about.' That is, no 'locals' would be out and about (*in giro*), only immigrants. See also the reflections of Roberto Escobar, who illustrates the process whereby immigrants 'are something monstrous, belonging to a savage non-place which has no boundaries' (Escobar 1997, p. 156).

7   Another key 'visible' group are the *lavavetri*, a small and mobile group of semi-beggars who wash car windscreens at road junctions and traffic lights and who have been used as representatives of a threat to the local population. In *La Stampa* (8 November 1995) *lavavetri* were described as 'a plague widespread throughout the city against whom the traffic wardens do not intervene'.

8   See reports in *Corriere della Sera*, 15 June 1995 and 15 November 1995.

9   'We will favour all those (non-EU) immigrants who have characteristics most like our own, with a mentality which matches best with that of the *padani* (inhabitants of the Po Plain, the Lega's "homeland"). In other words, the East Europeans... The others will have greater difficulty in entering. Then there's the problem of those who are already here in Padania. As a first measure we will make clandestine entry an offence. Then we will make a careful and rigorous examination of all the regularisations already granted by the Italian state. Because they have been issued too leniently.' *Corriere della Sera*, 14 September 1996.

10 *La Stampa*, 11 November 1995.

11 *Corriere della Sera*, 12 January 1997.

12 For an analysis of anti-gypsy protests in the city see the biting and angry account by Marco Revelli (1999).

13 *Corriere della Sera*, 11 February 1997.

14 For a typical interview with Lega leader Bossi see *L'Espresso*, 25 March 1999.
15 *Corriere della Sera*, 16 September 1995.
16 Unfortunately, many academic studies tend to reproduce these simplistic stereotypes. Davico and Mela (1999, p. 38), for example, in an otherwise useful study, claim that 'it is not so much the absolute number of immigrants in these quarters [San Salvario and Porta Palazzo] which gives rise to a problematic situation, as much as the concentration of specific groups of foreigners in a few specific places... The concentration in a restricted area ... tends to increase their social visibility ... for instance, groups whose activities take place mainly on the streets are much more visible.' And again, 'in these quarters one can verify the most dramatic examples of social conflict ... illegal activities proliferate which, in various ways, *can be connected to the presence of specific groups of immigrants or, on the other hand, to a certain part of public opinion that perceives the link to such an immigrant presence*' (Davico and Mela 1999, p. 57; my emphasis). Other authors take a different line, delighting in contrasting the opinions of the Left or the Catholic Church on immigration with the 'reality' which one can see 'just by looking around'. For example, Umberto Melotti, an acknowledged expert on immigration, was able to write this in the early 1990s: 'Our urban areas are full of degradation and in not a few cases this urban decline is directly or indirectly linked to the new migrations. Historic squares in many of our finest cities are being transformed into squalid *souks* where the immigrants sell their pseudo-exotic junk or their fake and contraband goods... Peripheral districts are suffering from the impact of illegal settlements, dirty and unhygenic.' Melotti called for the immediate expulsion of, amongst others, car windscreen cleaners and prostitutes. See Melotti (1993, pp. 193, 221–5).
17 See, for instance, the comments of the ex-Communist and now Forza Italia militant Saverio Vertone in *Corriere della Sera*, 20 November 1997.
18 See, for example, the case of a North African immigrant found dead in Turin in November 1995 – *La Stampa*, 15 November 1995.
19 See the coverage in *La Stampa*: for instance 'Via gli extracomunitari, spacciano' (20 January 1994); 'È il bazaar della droga' (31 January 1994); 'Via Cottolengo, il nostro suk' (1 February 1994).
20 Gianni Vattimo, in *La Stampa*, 13 October 1995; see also the debate between Vattimo and Manconi in *La Stampa*, 19 October 1995.
21 *La Stampa*, 10 October 1995, p. 11.
22 Quotations from *La Stampa*, 12 and 14 October 1995. The origins of the (non-)battle were over access to public space, notably the small park used both by Italian youths and immigrants. By 14 October this was being called 'the garden of the iron bars'.
23 See *La Stampa*, 13 October 1995. Don Carlo Vallero (the local priest) was cited in the article 'Un chilometro di disperazione' in the same issue. Don Gallo, the priest mentioned earlier in the chapter, was more critical, contrasting the peaceful and effective march with the attempted violence of the '58'. See Don Piero Gallo, 'Ma la violenza non è soluzione', also in the same edition of *La Stampa*.
24 In the words of *La Stampa*'s headline, 'Task force in tutta la città', 14 October 1995.
25 *La Stampa*, 14 October 1995.
26 Luigi Manconi of the Green Party called the Dini decree an example of a 'racial law' which punished foreigners because of their foreignness. See *La Stampa*, 17 October 1995, from which all quotes in this paragraph are taken.
27 In all probability, this was for practical reasons, since the need for trials etc. would slow down the whole expulsion process. This remains true after the Turco-Napolitano Law of 1998, which set up detention centres for those awaiting expulsion. These centres were at the centre of vigorous protests throughout 1999.

28 See *La Stampa*, 18 November 1995. The importance and visibility of these new demonstrations were linked strongly to their night-time timing and their claim (as with the feminist demonstrations of the 1970s and 1980s) to 'reclaim the night' from the control of 'other groups'.

29 See, for example, the interview with local resident Silvana Mollica in *La Stampa*, 18 November 1995.

30 Piero's brother Paolo, a far-right activist and member of the 'Granata Corps' group linked to the Torino football team, had originally been accused of the murder. The brothers were sons of Neopolitan immigrants. The family dog was called Adolf. For these details, and for the reactions of the police and some politicians who denied that the murder had been racist, see *Corriere della Sera*, 20 July 1997, 30 July 1997, 7 August 1997 and 7 October 1997.

31 Quoted in *Corriere della Sera*, 28 April 1997.

32 *Corriere della Sera*, 12 May 1997.

33 *La Stampa*, 14 October 1995.

34 *Corriere della Sera*, 10 June 1996.

35 A few statistics to exemplify this statement. During the period January to October 1995, 181 people were arrested in San Salvario: 90 per cent of them were foreigners. Of the arrests, 89 related to drug dealing, 25 were for theft, 23 for violent assault, 13 for insulting behaviour and 11 for extorsion. In Piedmont, foreigners are approximately 20 times more likely to be arrested than Italians. During 1997, 24,202 foreigners were arrested in Italy and 90,356 Italians; hence foreigners made up 21 per cent of the total. They also contribute 21 per cent of the national prison population. These, and other data, from Caritas di Roma (1997); ISMU (1999).

36 Giancarlo Clara, President of the Associazione Commerciale l'Oasi San Salvario, quoted in *narcomafie*, November 1995, p. 4.

37 For a series of crude racist stereotypes see the letters published in *La Stampa*, 13, 20 and 27 November 1995.

38 Interviews in *La Stampa*, 13 October 1995.

39 Revelli (1999, p. 46) argues that southern Italian cities can absorb more immigrants due to their long tradition of ethnic and cultural mixing and their integration into a more typically 'Mediterranean' culture. Other accounts (e.g. Cole 1997) highlight the informal opportunities available within the economies of these southern cities – see also Faïçal Daly's chapter in the present volume.

References

Bagozzi, F. (1995) Tutti gli spigoli del quadrilatero, *narcomafie*, November, p. 3.

Barbagli, M. (1998) *Immigrazione e Criminalità in Italia*. Bologna: Il Mulino.

Bertoluzzo, M. (1995) I 'sassi' del terzo millenio, *narcomafie*, November, p. 6.

Biorcio, R. (1998) Agitazione politica, *Gomorra*, 3, p. 125.

Bovone, L. (ed.) (1999) *Un Quartiere alla Moda. Immagine e racconti del Ticinese a Milano*. Milan: Franco Angeli.

Caritas di Roma (1997) *Immigrazione Dossier Statistico '97*. Rome: Anterem.

Castellani, V. (1996) *Il Mestiere del Sindaco. Ricominciate dalle città*. Milan: Cantiere Italia.

Castellani, V. (1997) La sinistra ha rifutato la cultura della legalità, *Corriere della Sera*, 27 August.

Castells, M. (1997) *The Information Age: Economy, Society and Culture. The Power of Identity*. Oxford: Blackwell.

Cicene (1996) *'Quartier Latin'. San Salvario – Torino*. Turin: Cicene.

Cohen, S. (1972) *Folk Devils and Moral Panic*. London: MacGibbon.

Cohen, S. (1985) *Visions of Social Control*. Cambridge: Polity.

Cole, J. (1997) *The New Racism in Europe: A Sicilian Ethnography*. Cambridge: Cambridge University Press.

D'Ottavio, M. (1997) *7° a est di Greenwich. Nuovi volti di un luogo chiamato Torino*. Turin: Lindau.

Dal Lago, A. (1998) Come si costruisce l'emergenza immigrazione, *Gomorra*, 3, p. 115.

Davico, L. and Mela, A. (1999) Aspetti spaziali dei nuovi fenomeni migratori in Piemonte, *Sociologia Urbana e Rurale*, 21(59), pp. 33–76.

Davis, M. (1990) *City of Quartz. Excavating the Future of Los Angeles*. London: Verso.

De Corato, R. (1996) Gli immigrati dividono il centrosinistra, *Corriere della Sera*, 14 July.

Escobar, R. (1997) *Metamorfosi della Paura*. Bologna: Il Mulino.

Fiasco, M. (1996) Se 'città' non significa più 'società', *narcomafie*, January, pp. 6–7.

Foot, J. (1995) The logic of contradiction: migration control in Italy and France, in Miles, R. and Thränhardt, D. (eds) *Migration and European Integration: The Dynamics of Inclusion and Exclusion*. London: Pinter, pp. 132–58.

Foot, J. (1999) Immigration and the city: Milan and mass immigration, 1958–98, *Modern Italy*, 4(2), pp. 159–72.

Fumagalli, M. (1997) Notte di terrore nel quartiere dello spaccio, *Corriere della Sera*, 19 April.

Hall, S., Critcher, C., Jefferson, A., Clarke, J. and Roberts, B. (1978) *Policing the Crisis. Mugging, the State, and Law and Order*. London: Macmillan.

ISMU (1999) *Quarto Rapporto sulle Migrazioni 1998*. Milan: Franco Angeli.

Jacobs, J. (1961) *The Death and Life of Great American Cities*. New York: Vintage House.

Maneri, M. (1998) Lo straniero consensuale. La devianza degli immigrati come circolarità di pratiche e discorsi, in Dal Lago, A. (ed.) *Lo Straniero e il Nemico*. Milan: Costa e Nolan, pp. 236–72.

Melotti, U. (1993) Migrazioni internazionali, povertà e degrado urbano: il caso italiano e le esperienze europee, in Guidicini, P. and Pieretti, G. (eds) *La Residualità come Valore. Povertà urbane e dignità umane*. Milan: Franco Angeli, pp. 193–225.

Morbello, G. (1996) Che fine ha fatto San Salvario? *narcomafie*, April, p. 14.

Morris, T. P. (1957) *The Criminal Area: A Study in Social Ecology*. London: Routledge.

Muncie, J. and Fitzgerald, M. (1981) Humanising the deviant, in Fitzgerald, M., McLennan, G. and Pawson, J. (eds) *Crime and Society. Readings in History and Theory*. London: Routledge, pp. 403–28.

Neirotti, M. (1997) Quartiere San Salvario ai confini di Torino, *Lo Specchio della Stampa*, 99, 13 December.

Palidda, S. (1999) Polizia e immigrati: un'analisi etnografica, *Rassegna Italiana di Sociologia*, 40(1), pp. 77–114.

Palidda, S. (2000) *La Polizia Postmoderna: etnografia del controllo sociale*. Milan : Feltrinelli.

Pollini, G. and Scidà, G. (1998) *Sociologia delle Migrazioni*. Milan: Franco Angeli.

Revelli, M. (1999) *Fuori Luogo. Cronaca da un campo rom*. Turin: Bollati Boringhieri.

Sennett, R. (1977) *The Fall of Public Man*. Cambridge: Cambridge University Press.

Tosi, A. (1998) Lo spazio urbano dell'immigrazione, *Urbanistica*, 111, pp. 7–19.

Whyte, W. F. (1943) *Street-Corner Society: The Social Structure of an Italian Slum*. Chicago: University of Chicago Press.

Wirth, L. (1956) *The Ghetto*. Chicago: University of Chicago Press (first published 1928).

Zolberg, A. (1997) Richiesti, ma non benvenuti, *Rassegna Italiana di Sociologia*, 38(1), pp. 19–40.

11

Family formation in gendered migrations: Moroccan and Filipino women in Bologna

Elisabetta Zontini

Introduction

Recent literature on female immigration to southern Europe has drawn attention to the importance of immigrant women's economic function, moving beyond earlier conceptualisations of migrant women as dependent followers of males in migrations of family reunion. A number of studies in Italy and Spain have started to analyse the role of immigrant women particularly in the domestic sector (Andall 1998; Chell 1997; Escrivà 1997; Ribas-Mateos 2000; Vicarelli 1994). What emerges from these studies is how domestic work seems to be almost the only type of work available to immigrant women both in Italy and in Spain (and for that matter in Greece and Portugal) and how the demand for this type of work has continued to increase from the 1960s up to the present. The reasons given for this growing demand are related to rapid socio-economic changes undergone by southern European countries in the last twenty to thirty years. Such changes include the poor quality or absence of services available from a declining or never fully developed welfare state and also the persistence of traditional and fixed gender roles, whereby the care of the house and the children is almost exclusively a woman's responsibility. The increased difficulty for local women to cope with both productive and reproductive roles, the increased affluence of southern European societies, the reluctance of local working-class women to work as domestics and the breakdown of the traditional extended family are all explanations offered to account for the current demand for foreign domestic labour. These arguments are important for they stress the role played by pull factors in favouring immigration, i.e. they show how the presence of female immigrants (and to some extent this is also true for males) is linked to local conditions, both social and economic, and cannot be explained solely in relation to poverty and deprivation in the 'Third World'.

Some authors have also pointed out that immigrant women's work in support of local families has a profound impact on their private lives and on the possibility of enjoying a family life of their own. The Cape Verdean women interviewed by Jacqueline Andall in Rome, for instance, were often single-parent working mothers with young children, a condition uncommon in Italy and for which few public structures are in place (Andall 1998; cf. also Maher 1996). This imposes tough choices on immigrant women: either postponing procreation, placing their children in residential homes, or sending them back to be raised by relatives in the country of origin. Similar difficulties were noted by Victoria Chell (1997) with reference to the situation of Filipina and Somali women in Rome. She too noted how migration was having an (often negative) impact on the family relationships of the migrants. In many cases migration results in long-term separation from the family in the home country determined by a series of impediments – physical, financial, legal and political – that the migrant cannot control. The implications of this are that marriages may be delayed, fertility is reduced and family structures are altered (Maffioli 1994).

In the literature on migration new attention has been given to the role of the household and the family in shaping and influencing migration. The household is now seen as an important unit of analysis in mediating between the individual migrant and the broader structural context within which transnational migration occurs (Boyd 1989). The household is described both as a motivator and financier of migration, and as a recipient and spender of remittances. But migration functions are not limited to the economic role of the household. Moreover, households are not homogeneous entities; they are divided by gender and generational hierarchies that shape the way in which decisions – such as that of migrating or of marriage and reproduction – are taken (Bjerén 1997). Other aspects related to how transnational families are formed and maintained need, in my view, to be studied in more detail, with reference also to the role of the country of immigration in shaping these processes and to the role of gender. The research I am currently conducting – on which this essay is based – aims at addressing these issues.[1]

In my research I adopt a feminist perspective, focusing my analysis primarily (although not exclusively) on the experiences of women. This is because immigrant women represent one of the weakest and most vulnerable groups in society; this is as true of southern Europe (Anthias and Lazaridis 2000) as it is in other migration contexts, for instance in northern Europe or in the developing world (Buijs 1993; Phizacklea 1983). They are subjected to a double burden: as immigrants they are often excluded and marginalised by society at large, and as women they have to fight against patriarchal forces present both within and outside their 'communities'. I have chosen to analyse the experiences of two different groups of women – Moroccans and Filipinas – because I believe that it is important to show the different forms that their marginalisation can take. However, I also think that – in spite of the differences – immigrant women do share a number of common experiences, some of which are a direct result of their precarious position within the context of the 'host' country, most notably their position in gendered niches at the bottom level of the labour market. The setting for my research is the Italian city of Bologna, capital of the prosperous Emilia-Romagna region.

Another important factor in the choice of the two groups is that they are both unbalanced in terms of sex distribution: Moroccans are a predominantly male group and Filipinos a predominantly female one, although in recent years both groups are acquiring a more balanced gender distribution. Both groups are well inserted in the local labour market, male Moroccans being mainly employed in the small and medium-sized industries of the city and Filipinas working as domestic helpers in the numerous wealthy families of Bologna or as carers for the growing elderly population of the city. By choosing these groups – one predominantly male and one predominantly female – I want to take into account the role of gender in processes of family formation.

Family formation is a broad concept that has a variety of meanings. It includes the reunion of already married people (with or without children); marriage that happens abroad; birth of children abroad; transnational splitting of a family formed abroad; different forms of cohabitation; and a lot more. At this stage I just want to highlight the heterogeneity of the concept of 'family formation' and point out the need to understand it more fully through ethnographic analysis rather than through *a priori* definitions. This chapter aims at providing some examples of immigrant women's biographies as they have been gathered by me in the city of Bologna. In my analysis I took up Victoria Goddard's recommendations and contextualised the individual biographies within the strategies pursued by their family of origin and the particular division of labour that these strategies entail (Goddard

1996, p. 163). As in her study about outworkers in Naples, it will emerge clearly from my own work how 'women's agency is constrained by the practical and ideological conditions governing family life' (Goddard 1996: 180). My case-study will further show how migration adds another dimension to this analysis. As far as practical constraints are concerned, in the context of migration they are not only a product of women's position in the local labour market but also of the local policies concerning immigration (e.g. in terms of housing, welfare, etc.). As far as ideological constraints are concerned, they derive both from the ethnic group of origin (both at home and abroad) and from the dominant values of the host society. Because of this added dimension – as we will see in the following pages – I believe that migration offers women both further constraints and new possibilities, which in many respects are shared by women with very different cultural origins.

The account will be organised around the biographies of six immigrant women at different stages of the developmental cycle of their household. In each of the three sections the story of a Filipina woman will be followed by that of a Moroccan woman, so as to show more clearly the influence of different cultural constraints. The three sections represent three possible stages in family formation. The biographies presented here have been chosen to be broadly representative of the much larger numbers of immigrant women I interviewed. They are by no means the only ones possible. Several other possibilities emerged from my fieldwork, but for reasons of space in this chapter I will limit my case-studies to these. Thus, the topics addressed by the three sections are: women in relationships without children; single-parent working mothers; married women with children. All names are pseudonyms.

Women without children

The first pair of stories are about two women who have partners from their country of origin and do not have children yet. They are both at the initial stage of the developmental cycle of their household.

Maria

Maria is 28, she is Filipina, a qualified nurse and works as a live-in maid in Bologna. She arrived in Italy in 1991 as a clandestine immigrant. She has four brothers; two are in the Philippines, one lives in Florence and another is in Canada. It was her father who told her to leave because she had to support her youngest brother who was in Canada studying to become a doctor. She did what she felt was her duty as daughter and sister and sent money regularly to Canada. With a slight sense of resentment she told me that her brother did not become a doctor in the end but only a medical technician. The positive thing is that now he is working so she has stopped sending him money and can now spend more on herself. The brother who is in Italy works like her as a live-in home help. He is married and has a daughter of four. His wife works with him for the same family and their daughter lives in the Philippines with her maternal grandparents. Maria told me that if she had a baby she would prefer to keep him/her with her rather than sending the child back to be raised in the Philippines. Besides, she could not count on her mother to help since she is already too busy with the children of her two brothers who are still in the Philippines. One of them is a teacher yet, according to Maria, his wage is really low. The other is currently unemployed. He has paid an agency twice to get a visa to emigrate but on both occasions the agent has disappeared, stealing all the money. Her family comes from a provincial town two hours from Manila. Her father drives a jeepney (a kind of taxi) and her mother is a housewife.

Maria is now working as a live-in maid for an elderly woman who is 84 and suffers from Alzheimers. She found this job through a contact that a friend gave to her. Her friend told Maria that in Bologna it was easy to find work with elderly people. Before arriving in Bologna Maria was working in Florence but was fed up with the job she was doing there. She could not cope any longer working for a family of four members because the workload was too heavy. She wanted to work with an elderly person because she knew that this would be less trying.

Her current work consists of cleaning the house of this elderly woman, cooking for her and making sure that she eats, washing her, dressing her and looking after her during the day and, if anything happens, also at night. Although Maria can never leave her alone she says that the job is fine. Looking after one person is less demanding than having to be responsible for four members of the family, particularly if there are small children. At the time of the interview the old lady was quietly sitting in front of the television, only stopping from time to time to ask who I was. Maria says that she does not complain about the job but she would like to earn more. She is currently earning L 1,400,000 (£460) per month. As a live-in maid she does not have to pay rent and food, so she can save a substantial part of her salary. She has total control of the house and the daughter of the elderly woman has complete trust in Maria and only comes to check things out once a week. During the rest of the time Maria is in charge of the house and of the elderly woman whom she considers as a member of her family; she actually calls her '*nonna*' (grandma).

As a live-in maid Maria is entitled to one day and a half free per week. She uses this free time to shop, look after her interests (for instance, I met her for the first time on a Wednesday when she was queuing at the trade union to get some advice about her holiday payments) and to go to Bible Studies. This is a charismatic Catholic group very popular with Filipinos (their priest is a Filipino). Bible studies and the church choir are not only occasions for worship but they are also, and above all, a space for socialisation and gathering. It was here that Maria met her fiancé, Jimmy. He is also Filipino and they were planning to get married in December 1999 during their visit to the Philippines.

At the time of the interview (October 1999), Maria was saving hard for the wedding. She said that traditionally it is the man who pays for the entire wedding but now things are changing; since she was working she was going to pay for half of all expenses. She was really looking forward to the wedding and quite relieved that it was finally going to take place. She confessed to me that in the last few months she had stopped going to Bible classes because she was embarrassed about her current situation. Her fiancé was living with her in the house of the elderly woman. He had his own job in a cleaning company but was staying with Maria and was paying L 200,000 towards rent. She did not feel at ease about living with her boyfriend before being married. She will join the Bible group again after she has been to the Philippines and got married. Pressure and fear of losing her reputation with fellow Filipinas seemed very important for Maria. She told me that 10 months before the interview she fell pregnant but, although she claims that she wants a baby, she had an abortion; her view was that she preferred to get married first and then have children.

In order to be able to go to the Philippines Maria has already found a replacement for her job. One of her cousins would come directly from the Philippines to fill this two-months gap. After the wedding Maria and Jimmy will come back because, as they told me, 'the work is here'. They will continue with the same arrangements living with the elderly woman since finding a flat at an affordable price is very difficult for immigrants in Bologna (see Zontini 2000). Maria's employer does not mind this because she is effectively paying Maria only L 1,200,000 since L 200,000 are paid back to her through Jimmy's rent. Besides, the fact that he is around (he goes to work at 6.00 a.m. and is back at noon) means that he can keep an eye on the old lady when Maria has to go out, for instance, to do the shopping.

Maria says that she has no plans for the future apart from getting married and eventually having babies, ideally two. All her energies and savings were dedicated to the wedding that was going to take place in the Philippines and would be the occasion to gather together all her numerous relatives and those of the groom, including several who are living abroad.

Fatima

Fatima is 29, married and has just arrived in Italy. She came legally under the legislation that permits family reunion, joining her husband, Said. She comes from Casablanca. Her father was an employee in an insurance company but he is now dead. She has six brothers and sisters. One of her sisters, who is divorced and has a daughter, is living in Genoa, Italy; one of her brothers lives in Kuwait; the other brothers and sisters are all living in Morocco. Two of her brothers are still living with her mother, one of them is unemployed and the other is a train driver. All her brothers have studied and she too has been to university, where she attended the faculty of chemistry and physics for two years. She then had to stop when her father died. She switched to a shorter course which trained her to make models for clothes and which allowed her to find employment in various factories in Casablanca. During the period between the death of her father and her marriage she had to sacrifice her studies and to help her family. She not only contributed economically through her work in the factory but also – because her mother had fallen ill – by carrying out most of the domestic chores.

She had arrived in Italy two months before I met her for the first time. I met her at a charity where immigrant women go to find employment. The volunteers there told Fatima that they could not give her any work unless she learned some Italian. She said she was very keen to learn the language but she did not know where to go to find classes. At that time I had already started giving classes to three other Moroccan women so I invited Fatima to join our group. Our interview conversations were initially mainly in French; later we used some Italian and benefited from the help of her close friend, Aisha, who helped us with interpretation.

Fatima lives in a small flat 90 km from Bologna. This is the only place that her husband managed to find at a reasonable price in order to start the procedure for family reunion. The flat is not only far from Bologna, but is also in a mountainous area, which means that on a couple of occasions Fatima and Said got stranded there because of the snow. It is also very cold and damp. Said has to commute from there to Bologna every day and this is costing him a lot in terms of petrol. Also there is no public transport reaching that area which means that he has to rely entirely on his car. If the cars breaks down – as has happened on two occasions – it means that he has to miss a day at work. Fatima told me that he had promised her that he would try to look for another place but she thinks he is not doing enough.

Her husband is now working as a specialised worker in a factory that produces machines for making ice-cream. He had found a job for Fatima in the same factory but she told me that she did not want the job for two reasons. The first one is that she does not want to work in the same place as her husband. This is because he is very jealous and she prefers to avoid the arguments that would arise if he thought she did not behave properly, i.e. if he were to see her talking or laughing with male workers. The second reason is that the job in the factory is full-time and so she would not have time to do anything else. She prefers to look for jobs such as a domestic, cleaner or carer because she thinks that these can allow her more flexibility and freedom.

As she is not yet working Fatima has a lot of free time. Her husband brings her to Bologna in the morning when he goes to work and leaves her with Aisha, the wife of one of his Moroccan friends. Fatima chats with Aisha, helps her with some household chores and with her children and goes around with her when she goes out to buy things or to run errands. She also follows Aisha when, twice a week, she goes to do the cleaning at an old lady's house. Fatima told me that by watching her friend she is learning how to do the job and she can also practice her Italian by chatting with the old woman while Aisha works. Sometimes the two women go to see another friend who is Egyptian and is also – like Fatima – a practising Muslim. Fatima enjoys her company because she likes discussing religious matters with somebody who is educated. She complains about the fact that with the other Moroccan women whom she has met so far in Italy one cannot have any serious conversation. According to Fatima, 'Moroccan women in Bologna only think about work, about getting free clothes from the Church, and about staying at home with their children. Their minds are empty.'[2]

Fatima is very happy about being in Italy and she is full of enthusiasm about the things she might do in Bologna. She wants to get a job, find a better flat to live in, carry on learning Italian, and she is also thinking of organising a group of women to talk about religion and other issues that concern their everyday lives. She is particularly relieved now that she has managed to join her husband and escape the control of her mother-in-law. Fatima married Said three years ago but it was only now that she managed to convince him to take her to Italy with him. She explained to me that it was a long time since Said started to ask to his mother to find him a wife. She never found anybody suitable and Fatima says that it was because the mother wanted her son to remain single. In this way he would continue to send large remittances and presents to his family of origin. Even when he did get engaged to Fatima (thanks to an uncle) and then married her, his mother did everything she could to prevent Fatima from joining him. Once his wife was going to be in Italy with him he would stop sending money back to Morocco. Fatima says that, now she is far away from her mother-in-law, she is happier and her relationship with her husband has improved now that nobody is interfering.

In the near future she would like to have children, ideally two, but she is scared that she will not get pregnant because the place where she is living is too cold and unhealthy. If she can get a job and can therefore contribute to the family income she would like to help her husband to build a house in Morocco. This does not mean that they want to go back to Morocco; on the contrary, they intend to settle down in Italy permanently. They want to have their own base when they go back to Morocco for the annual holiday that most Moroccans take during August.

Similarities and differences

Maria and Fatima are two examples of the women involved in the gendered migrations that I introduced and discussed at the beginning of this chapter. As we have seen, Maria came on her own from the Philippines to work as a domestic, whereas Fatima arrived in Bologna to reunite with her husband, a Moroccan factory worker. Their stories present both similarities and differences. They are similar insofar as both women had to sacrifice their careers (as nurse and university student) and postpone family formation in order to carry out what they perceived were their duties towards their families back home. This duty-bound role in her household of origin was at the root of Maria's migration, whereas for Fatima, migration was a difficult goal to achieve since for a while it was prevented by her role as a new member of her husband's household.

Once in Italy, both want to work. For Maria it is a necessity since she will continue to be expected to send remittances to contribute to her Filipino household and also, since she has a better job than her future husband, she will probably remain the main earner of her newly-formed household. Fatima is not expected to send money home; now she should take care of and help her husband. She has decided that part of this help will consist also in going out to earn money for realising some plans of her newly-formed family, such as that of buying a house in Morocco and moving to a better flat in or near Bologna.

Both Fatima and Maria, partly because they do not have children yet, have some free time. Both of them like occupying part of it with religious activities which have both spiritual importance and also a social dimension, since prayer groups are an occasion on which to meet like-minded people to discuss topics that go beyond religion and involve other aspects of daily life. Finally, both Maria and Fatima plan to have children and for both of them the ideal number would be two, despite the fact that they themselves come from much larger families.

Single-parent working mothers

The two life stories that follow are about two single-parent working mothers. Rita, who is Filipina, arrived in Italy several years ago but only now has started her own family, having worked as a full-time domestic and contributed financially to her household of origin for a long time. Saida had a husband in Morocco but she bravely left him and came to Italy, where she raised her two children on her own.

Rita

Rita is 33, she is a qualified midwife and works as a full-time maid in Bologna. She arrived in Italy in 1987, as a *clandestina*. She already had a job in Pisa that her sister had kept for her. She comes from a large family of ten brothers and sisters. Her father left her mother for a period of ten years when many of the children were still young. The family survived through their work on the farm and the remittances of the eldest daughter who had come to Italy to work as a maid; she had replied to an advertisment that she saw in a paper while in Manila looking for jobs. It was this sister, Rosalynn, who called to Italy two other sisters and then Rita by paying the agency that would arrange for their clandestine arrival in Italy. At the time of the interview two of Rita's sisters were still living in Italy, both of them married and living in Bologna. Rosalynn has now stopped working and, after fulfilling her duties as the eldest daughter by helping her sisters, is now reunited with her American husband and lives in Hawaii. Rita's father has died. She is now supporting (together with her sisters) her widowed mother and the four brothers who are younger than her.

At present Rita is working as a full-time maid for a wealthy Italian couple. The husband is a businessman and the wife works in the stock market. She has been working for them since 1993. At first she was working there only in the mornings (she was then still living and working for another employer) but subsequently also took up the afternoon job, which consists of ironing and doing the 'thorough' cleaning (*pulizia a fondo*), which involves, for instance, cleaning the silver. Rita complains that her employer is very strict but she does not want to change because she says that she does not want to 'learn the character and the habits of another employer'. Another reason is that after many years she has reached a good level of pay. She now earns L 2,000,000 (£650), which is slightly above the monthly average for this kind of employment.

At the time of the interview Rita was sharing a three-bedroom flat with her eight-month-old baby girl (Claudine), a Filipino man and his daughter (his wife stayed there only once a week since she was working as a live-in maid), and an Italian student. I visited Rita twice on a Sunday, the only day in the week when she is at home and has a bit of time. Before I arrived at 10.00 a.m. she had already done her part in the weekly cleaning of the flat and while we were talking she was also doing her laundry and cooking the daily meal. We were also playing with the baby and later on Rita was breast-feeding her.

Claudine's father does not live with them any more. Rita and he broke up when she was still pregnant. He was a Nigerian whom she had met through a friend. Apparently he told the common friend that he was looking for a Filipina. Rita explained to me that this was because everybody knows that 'Filipinas are patient with men ... you know ... they are a bit martyrs'. They stayed together six years but the relationship did not work out:

> That was a mistake in my life... I always make mistakes with men, my sister told me that all men are the same... Filipinos are always drunk and then you have to do all the work on your own, everything ... then I said – what do you have to get then? Some of the Italians are also bad, then you take the blacks, but with them also it doesn't work, what shall I do then? Then in the end do you know what I do? I have a baby and that's it!

Rita's reasons for leaving him were the following:

> I was tired ... you know ... to always look after a man, you have to do everything for them, they are never happy, they are never satisfied, you have to shop, cook for them, you have to wash, iron... I was fed up.

An important reason for leaving him that Rita did not mention in the interview was that in 1999 she found out that her boyfriend was already married in Nigeria and had children there. He had no intention of marrying Rita, although she had hoped that with the arrival of their baby he would. I know this and other parts of her story through an Italian woman for whom she was occasionally working and who was the person who had introduced Rita to me.

At the time of the interview Rita was a single-parent working mother who also had familial responsibilities back in the Philippines. She was still economically responsible for a number of relatives back home. Her daily life in Bologna was hard and required a lot of juggling skills.

> I get up at 6.20 am, I wash myself, I get ready, I have breakfast and when I'm done I wake her (the baby) up around 6.40 am, at 6.45 I dress her...because you have to allow a bit of time for her...so when we are ready at 7.10 we go out and we walk to the crèche, it takes 15 minutes, so we get there at 7.25 and then we wait until 7.30 when the teacher comes, at 7.30 I leave her with the teacher and I run to catch the bus, at 7.37. If I miss that bus the next comes at 7.45 and this would be a little late for me because my *signora* counts every minute.

Rita has to start working at 7.45 so as to be allowed to leave at 4.45 and be at the crèche at 5.00 before they close. If she arrived late at work in the morning she would have to leave later in the afternoon and this means that the teacher at the crèche would have to wait for her and when this happens the teacher will tell her off. Rita keeps this rhythm up from Monday to Friday. She usually also works on Saturdays for different employers in order to have some extra income. The crèche is closed on that day so if she is allowed she takes her baby with her to work, if not she leaves her with her sister, if she is available. On Sundays she rests, plays with the baby and, as she told me, she gathers the strength to last for another week.

She stressed that it is really hard to raise a child all on her own but she feels that her life was much worse before she had her baby.

> It's hard but you know ... I can cope. When I didn't have the baby yet ... you know ... when you are all alone it's the loneliness that kills you.

But now Rita is terrified that they will take her baby away from her. She fears that Claudine's father will abduct her to Nigeria and this is why on Saturdays she does not leave her with him any more when she has to work. She now wants to be present every time he comes to see the baby because she knows of many women to whom this has happened. She is also scared that Social Services might take Claudine away from her. Although she earns L 2,000,000 monthly (a good wage for a domestic), her employers only declare a wage of L 1,400,000 for tax purposes. She pays L 550,000 towards rent and she therefore fears that if they take into consideration her 'official' wage she could be seen as incapable of providing for her daughter.

Rita's short-term plans for the future are to help her two sisters-in-law to come to Italy so she will not have to support them any more. At that point she will have to send money 'only' to her mother and brothers. In the long run she intends to go back to the Philippines after she has saved enough, in order to start a small business over there, maybe a restaurant. She told me that her plans are to have a better life in the future and above all to secure a better future than hers for her daughter Claudine.

Saida

Saida is 39; she is divorced and has two teenage children, a girl of 13 and a boy of 15. She is illiterate and comes from a rural town in Morocco. Both her parents are now dead. Her mother died in 1992 when Saida had already come to Italy. She arrived in Italy in 1990 as a *clandestina*, after having worked – illegally – for six months in the south of Spain. After six years of marriage she decided to run away from her husband, who was violent and regularly beat her up. She left her house and took refuge at her mother's place with her two small children. She then decided to leave the children there and go abroad in search of a job. When I asked her how she came to that decision she told me that she followed the example of a woman in her family who had done the same in the past.

Saida returned to Morocco from Spain six months later to give some money to her children. She then found a letter informing her that her husband had divorced her. She was relieved. She then left again, this time for Italy. On the train to Italy she heard from fellow-Moroccans that Bologna was a good place to find employment and so she decided to go there. She did in fact find a job as live-in carer for an elderly person almost immediately. She got the job through Caritas, the Catholic charity which is very active in helping immigrants. She says that the pay was low but at least there was a possibility of getting started.

> The wage was low ... L 600,000 ... 500,000 you know, because Caritas wants to help people, but they also want to help the people where you go to work, you know ... an old lady, poor thing, does not have the money ... poor thing I and poor things both of us ... anyway it's fine like that because one goes there 4 months, 6 months, 3 months and in the meantime you start to know the country well, the job and everything .... then little by little... It doesn't happen that you go to work with full pay immediately, you know.

In the summer of her first year in Bologna Saida went to Sicily in order to obtain a 'permit to stay':

> Down in Sicily it's very easy to obtain a permit to stay... Here in
> Bologna they want a lot of things ... they want the house, a job with a
> legal contract ... in Sicily they don't want all these things ... they just do
> it.

Today, almost ten years after her arrival, Saida has a stable job in a
cleaning co-operative, both her children are living with her, the boy has
completed the compulsory cycle of education and the girl is about to
complete it and they are all living in a council flat. She is one among the
few immigrants who have managed to obtain a council flat in Bologna.[3]
She is now paying L 200,000 inclusive. Her flat consists of a spacious
living room, a kitchen and two bedrooms. She lives there with her
children and with a female cousin whom she is temporarily hosting. Her
cousin too had to flee Morocco because of a man and Saida is doing all
she can to help her relative.

In spite of her low rent Saida has to work really hard at the cooperative in order to pay for all the expenses and for everything her
children need. She does a lot of overtime and she also works on
Saturdays, including heavy jobs such as de-greasing kitchens, cleaning
windows etc. She says that it is really hard to raise two children without
economic – or any other kind of – support from anybody else. This is
why she thinks that many women stay in unhappy or abusive marriages.
She thinks that it takes a lot of courage for a woman with children to
decide to leave a husband and start a new life independently.

> It is a problem if she has children, where does she go? It's better to shut
> up, isn't it? These children, where do you send them? They have to go to
> school, they need books, they need clothes ... it is better to leave them
> with their father and shut up ... this is a real problem... Now I'm fine, I
> work, I don't need him... Because the problem of my children ... now
> I'm lucky that they have grown up ... now that problem is not there any
> more.

Saida had always had to work full-time in order to be able to support
her children. Her mother looked after them for two years but then she
fell ill and eventually died. Saida then had to look for a house to be able
to get her children to Italy. She went to the Immigration Service of
Bologna City Council but they did not help her to find accommodation.
But it was there that she heard that some Moroccans were going to
occupy illegally an empty school and transform it into temporary
accommodation. She decided to go along with them and she secured a
place for her and her children. Ironically the first immigrants to be

housed by the council in the city's first 'centre of first shelter' for families (as opposed to single male workers) were those who carried out the illegal occupations.[4] Saida was among them so she got a place in the shelter. By occupying the empty school and living in the centre of first shelter she was able to reduce the cost of housing to a minimum and was therefore able to provide for herself and her two children. She proudly told me that she was never helped by Social Services.

Saida told me that she had a partner for seven years while living in Bologna but in the end it did not work out. He was a cousin of hers. The relationship started when she decided to host him in the flat she had obtained in centre of first shelter. At the time he was working in a factory and sleeping in his car. The problems arose because he was younger than her and he had never been married. His mother was putting pressure on him to go back to Morocco and marry a young woman instead of living with a divorcee with two children. Eventually, he did what his mother wanted and married a young woman during a summer holiday in Morocco. He wanted to continue the relationship with Saida back in Bologna, but she refused to accept this new situation and forced him to leave the house and never to see her again. She told me that initially she suffered but now she is fine and she does not think that she wants to get into a relationship ever again.

Saida hopes that the worst part of her life is now over. Now she has a job, a house and above all her children are more or less grown up. She says that they are very well integrated in Italy, all their friends are Italian and they are used to living here. She says – with a slight sense of sadness – that they speak excellent Italian because they have always spent very little time with her since she has been working all the time.

> They only come to my house to sleep ... all day they are in school ... in the morning they leave at 8.00 and they stay there until 4.00, I come back from work at 7.00, I prepare the dinner then they go to bed straight away ... they never stay up with me and chat with me ... that's why they only speak Italian.

Sunday is the only free day for Saida. She says that she uses it to do things in the house, since during the week she does not have any time. She never goes out on Sundays, normally she stays at home and, after she has done her domestic chores, she rests. Often people come to visit her so she spends some time chatting with them. When I visited her on a Sunday her Italian neighbour was there drinking coffee with her. Both her children were out with friends. Her cousin was also out with a Moroccan boyfriend she had recently met in Bologna. Saida told me that they are going to get married. She sadly commented that it is easier for her cousin to find a new partner because she has not got any children. Saida feels that if she did not have the children she would also have been able to remarry. She sees her future and that of her children in Italy:

> Now I'm used to being here. I want to go to Morocco only to have a look, to have a tour, I go as a tourist and that is enough, yes I like it here. Before I didn't like it but now it is already ten years that I'm here ... day after day now I like it here ... when somebody does something for the first time it's hard but now I'm happy here.

Similarities and differences

The stories of Rita and Saida present similarities as well as differences. They are both very strong women who are capable of balancing different roles and coping with difficulties very well. Rita did not choose to come to Italy but was told to emigrate by her eldest sister in order to do her share for the survival of her Filipino household. For Saida emigration to Italy was her last hope to escape a situation of violence; she came against the will of other members of her family and she feels quite proud of what she did. In the future Rita hopes to go back to the Philippines whereas Saida is aware of the fact that for a divorcee like her Italy offers greater chances than Morocco. Both women had hoped to find a husband in Italy but had bad experiences and are now saying that they are not prepared to enter into a relationship anymore. Rita experimented with both a fellow-countryman and a foreigner but in both cases they had other relationships and did not want to marry her. Saida does not even consider the possibility of having a relationship with a non-Moroccan, and above all with a non-Muslim. Her long-term relationship with her cousin ended because he gave in to family pressure and 'ideological' predicaments, such as those concerning the age of the bride (she has to be younger than the groom) or the ideal of virginity (because of which divorcees are not desired brides).

For different reasons both women found themselves alone with children. Because of that they both have to work extremely hard. Their life is difficult since they have to fulfil both the role of provider and that of carer, without any help. On top of these pressures, Rita is responsible for her Filipino household; she is in fact still sending money to her mother, brothers and sisters-in-law. Saida does not have to send money to Morocco; she devotes her income to her teenage children. She does, however, feel morally obliged to provide help and hospitality to her relatives who came to Bologna, like her cousins.

Both women hardly have any free time at all. They invest all their time in work and in caring for their children, although Saida feels that maybe they do not entirely appreciate what she is doing for them.

Married women with children

My last two case-studies are married women with children. Gina is married to a fellow Filipino and Ilham – who is Moroccan – to a Tunisian. Another element that distinguishes Ilham's situation is that this is her second marriage; in fact, like Saida, she came to Italy when her first marriage collapsed, but unlike her she did not take her son with her to Italy and in so doing she increased her chances of remarriage.

Gina

Gina is 46, is married and has a son called Paolo who is now 14. She arrived in Italy in 1982 with a legal contract to work as a live-in maid for a family in Salerno. She has five brothers and sisters. Her mother remarried after her first husband died. She had two children from the first marriage and five from the second one (one has since died). Gina is the eldest from the second marriage. All her brothers and sisters are still in the Philippines. Her parents are both farmers and live in a remote part of the country. She was raised by her unmarried aunt who was living in Manila and was working as a cashier in a hospital where Gina was also working before she came to Italy.

Today she works as a part-time maid. She works for four hours per day and earns L 1,300,000 (£420). She has been with this employer for 11 years. She sometimes works two afternoons a week for her old employer for whom she worked as live-in domestic before she had her baby. She considers herself really lucky because she has had two employers who are 'human' and who helped her on different occasions.

> I'm lucky to have found this *signora* ... she is a social worker, maybe this is why she understands ... she knows what other people's problems are. Even if I don't go to work for a week, at the end of the month my wage is still the same.

Although she is happy with her employer, Gina is thinking about the possibility of changing job. A friend told her of the possibility of working for an old people's home. She does not think that this job will be an improvement in terms of tasks nor in economic terms; in fact she would earn the same as she is earning now and be working two more hours per day. The reason why she is seriously considering it is for the possibility of getting a better pension.

Today Gina is living in a beautiful – although very small – flat in the centre of Bologna with her husband and their son. She is renting the place from her former employer and – unlike what happens to most of her compatriots – she got a good deal. She pays L 700,000 monthly, which in Bologna is below the average. She owns all the furniture in the flat. When I visited her at home everything was perfectly tidy and spotless. Her son was in his room doing his homework and her husband was at work. He has changed from being a domestic help like Gina to become a factory worker in pasta production because this is a more regular job and above all it has better provisions in terms of rights and pension entitlements.

Gina had met her husband in 1983 when she was still working as a live-in maid in Salerno (a town near Naples) and went to visit a friend in Florence. It was he who told her about the possibility of finding employment in Bologna. She came to Bologna both because she was not happy in the South of Italy and also because she 'followed her boyfriend' as she told me, slightly embarrassed. They got married in Milan in 1985 at the Filipino Embassy. Their son was born in 1986.

> Paolo was born in '86 ... life was difficult for us then ... there was a baby... I left my employment as live-in maid immediately before he was born, I asked a friend of mine if I could stay at her place until the baby was born, so I went to live with her... I asked her to stay there only for two months because also there one couldn't keep babies ... then he was born, we baptised him and when he was one month old I took him back to the Philippines because I didn't have a house. In Italy this is the problem number one: housing.

A year and a half later Gina and her husband managed to find a house and they brought Paolo back to Italy. He is now finishing intermediate school and will enrol at high school next academic year. Since he came back to Italy, he has been back to the Philippines only once, when he was six. He considers himself Italian, all his friends are Italian and he has no intention of going back to a country that he does not consider his own. In Gina's words,

> He told me you are Filipina, I'm Italian ... then ... well then I left things as they were, he has his own friends, he can choose who they are ... he is settled very well here.

Gina now feels she is trapped in Italy. She never thought that she would stay in Italy forever but she is now realising that this is becoming a very distinct possibility. She was initially hoping that an aunt (who had originally called her to Italy) would get her to the United States where she is now living, but now she is aware that without the relevant documents this is almost impossible and above all she would have to abandon her son.

Gina's husband, like the son, does not want to go back to the Philippines. All his family are also abroad and they have already sold everything they had back home. Only one of his brothers is still there but he is also planning to go to Italy to work. On the contrary, all of Gina's relatives are still in the Philippines and she suffers from the fact of not having anybody from the family around. It is particularly hard, she says, at times when you are in difficulty because you do not have anybody to turn to. That was the case when Paolo was little and she had to cope with everything all on her own. That is why she did not want to have other children. If she cannot go to the States, once she retires she would like to go back to the Philippines. The problem is that her son will not follow her.

> I'm thinking of going back one day, when I'm old. But my son does not want to go there, he has already told me that if I go I have to leave him here. To cut it short ... he was born here, he grew up here, so I have to leave him here ... but I ... maybe if I cannot work anymore, if I cannot walk anymore ... then I would prefer to go back there, but if it happens that I'm here and I can't move anymore ... well if I die here I die here.

Gina tried to convince one of her sisters to join her in Bologna but she refused, saying that she could not survive away from her five children. Gina understands her position but was slightly complaining about the fact that since she is the only one abroad everybody expects money from her. In fact, she has helped economically all the members of her family. She sends money regularly to her elderly parents and also she has given them money to build a new house; she gave money to her sister to buy a jeepney; to her brother and sister to start a business raising pigs and at present she sends a considerable sum of money – L 4,500,000 – every year to help her nephews to go to school.

Ilham

Ilham is 28, married with two sons. She arrived in Italy in 1991 as a *clandestina* after her first marriage ended. She comes from a middle-class family; her father is a policeman and her mother a hairdresser working in her own shop with one of Ilham's sisters. There are six brothers and sisters. Two of her brothers and one sister are living in Italy. In Morocco there are still the youngest sister who is 13 and the sister who is working with her mother. Ilham complains that while the women in her family are all very serious, the men are not. She is particularly resentful about her eldest brother who lives near Verona and is at present unemployed. She says that he has just lost his 'permit to stay' and she attributes this to the fact that he was staying with an Italian girlfriend who was buying everything for him. Ilham thinks that because of that he did not try hard enough to keep a job and as a result he lost his permit. The other brother has just arrived as a clandestine immigrant and is temporarily living with Ilham while looking for a job. Her sister lives near Rimini and is married to a Moroccan man. Ilham told me that she is not as close to her sister as she used to be although she does not live far from her. The reason is her sister's husband. Years ago her sister had left him because he was seeing another woman. Ilham helped her a lot in that period, but then she felt betrayed when the sister went back to him.

Today Ilham lives in a one-bedroom flat in Casalecchio, half an hour from the centre of Bologna. She pays L 800,000 monthly. Her husband works in a factory and earns L 1,500,000. The first time I interviewed her this was the only income of the family. On top of the expenses related to the flat she also had to pay L 300,000 monthly towards the crèche fee for her two-year-old son. When I asked her how she could cope she replied:

> We are always in debt ... we are always overdrawn ... this is also why I'm looking for a job so I can pay off some of the debt.

Until ten months before the interview Ilham was working as a carer looking after an old person. This person eventually died and so she lost her job. I met her the first time in the office of a small charity which helps immigrant women to find employment, usually as domestic helpers and carers for old people. She told me that at first she was only looking for a couple of hours of work per day, just 'to help out', but now, because their debt has increased, she is prepared to work much more. She also told me that because of their present financial situation she was unable to send money to her nine-year-old son whom she had with her first husband and who is now in Morocco living with Ilham's parents. When we had our first interview she told me that she was hoping to get a job so that she could get her son to Italy.

When I had the second interview with Ilham she had managed to find a job. She was working as a cleaner for a bank. She told me that her life was really hard at the moment. She had to get up at 5.45 am to go to the centre of Bologna to clean the bank, and then come back to Casalecchio to take Mustapha – her son – to the crèche. After that she went to do a couple of hours' cleaning for a family who lived nearby. She has not told her husband about this second job because she uses this income to send money to her other son. Her husband must not find out about it so she has to keep her own flat perfectly clean otherwise he will become suspicious and he will make a big scene. This already happened once when he found that the bathroom had not been cleaned on that day. 'It's a shame to have our house in this condition ... I don't want to live like an immigrant', he apparently said to Ilham.

On the day of my second visit to her house she had just come back from her second job after having worked in the bank early in the morning. At 4.00 pm we went together to pick up Mustapha from the crèche. We went by moped, which is the means of transport that allows her to commute between Casalecchio and Bologna in a limited time. She was then in a rush to feed her son and finish tidying up the flat before her husband arrived at 6.30 pm.

The first time I visited Ilham there were five people and the child living in her one-bedroom place. Apart from her husband there was her brother who had just arrived from Morocco and wanted to find a job in Bologna. He did not have a permit to stay. There were also two women, Fatima and Amina, who were not related to Ilham. She had met both of them while visiting the usual places in Bologna that offer jobs to immigrant women. They both had terrible stories and both did not know where to go since they had had disagreements with the few relatives they had in Bologna. Ilham decided to put both of them up in her flat and spent a month taking them around Bologna in search of a job or at least a place to sleep. Finding a bed for them turned out to be more difficult than finding a job. Most of the Council's centres for immigrants are for males only and the few public or religious institutions that there are for women give priority to those with children or who had been victims of violence.

The presence of these two guests provoked endless quarrels between Ilham and her husband. The situation degenerated week after week; at first he was only complaining, later on he stopped talking to Ilham altogether and refused to eat at home. But she was determined not to give in and be forced to tell them to leave.

> I do that because before I had also been without a husband, without a house, without a job. If an elderly person dies, people cry for her... I cry because I don't know where I'm going to go. From tomorrow they send me away, but where shall I go? I had already been through these things, you know? This is why I always used to say that if one day I get married and have my own house, if I find one woman outside I'll take her to my place. Even if we

have to sleep all in one room I don't care, the only important thing is that she doesn't spend the night out like a....

Ilham had these experiences when she came to Italy to look for a way of supporting her first son after divorcing her previous husband. She worked in several places in the north of Italy before meeting her husband while she was in Pordenone working as a live-in maid. He was the uncle of one of her friends in Pordenone. One day on a trip to Naples to buy gold with her friend they stopped in Bologna to visit the uncle. He then started to court Ilham via phone. She told me that she did not want to go out with another man then but he was a serious man who had studied and so she agreed to become engaged to him. They got married in 1996 at the Registry Office in Bologna Town Hall. In December 1997 their son Mustapha was born.

Although Ilham has another son in Morocco whom she cannot manage to bring over to Italy, she confided that she was currently thinking of having another baby. When I asked her if a baby at that particular time would not have complicated her situation further she replied that she had the feeling that if she did not have another baby her husband would leave her. She had consulted with her mother who shared her fears. Her mother offered to help her if she decides to have another baby; she volunteered to keep the child in Morocco for a while. Ilham confessed to me that the reason why she does not bring her other son to Bologna is not only economic. It also has to do with the fact that he is not the son of her husband. Although she misses him a lot, sometimes she is happy that he is not there because she fears that her husband would make his life too difficult. She thinks that he is happier with the grandparents. The only thing she regrets is that one day he might hate her for having abandoned him, but she feels she has no choice.

Ilham sees her future life in Italy. She is happy to go back to Morocco once or twice a year on holidays to see her family but she has no desire to go back there for good: 'I don't think I have a life there anymore, never again. My life is here.' Her husband is expecting a large sum of money from his insurance for a work-related incident he had a few years ago. Ilham was hoping that with this money they would be able to pay the deposit for buying a house. Having her own house will mean for Ilham no longer having to worry about the possibility of finding herself on the street again without anywhere to go.

Similarities and differences

Both Gina and Ilham decided to migrate independently, although as a divorcee Ilham did not have many alternatives. After a period of great sacrifices, both managed to find a certain degree of stability in Bologna, both married and got a flat (which both value highly), and by having a husband in employment achieved the possibility of working fewer hours, although for Ilham this is more an ideal than the reality.

Marriage and children also brought new responsibilities and commitments for both of them. Gina realised that now that she has a son who feels Italian it will be very difficult for her to achieve her dream to go to the US or even to go back to the Philippines. Ilham has to fulfil well her role as mother and housekeeper (although she is also a worker), otherwise she will lose her husband, and also a certain degree of security.

Both Gina and Ilham have responsibilities for other members of their families. Like most Filipinas, Gina is still helping economically various members of her Filipino household, whereas Ilham is responsible for the child that she had from her previous marriage. The difference is that in a Filipino household it is accepted that both husband and wife (particularly the wife) have duties towards their family of origin; in Ilham's case she has to send the money secretly because her husband would never accept that. Like Saida, Ilham has a moral obligation to host members of her family who come to Bologna in search of jobs, though she has extended this obligation to also include other Moroccan women not related to her who are in need of help. In order to fulfil this desire she is even prepared to oppose her husband.

Conclusions

Although the question of the impact of transnationalism and migration on women occupies an important position in the literature on gender and migration, there seems to be no clear-cut answer. The case-studies dealing with immigration in the southern European context all mention the stretching of immigrant women's responsibilities brought about by transnationalism. Many authors have noted how familial relationships and responsibilities of female migrants span more than one country, indeed sometimes more than two countries, as with the Cape Verdean women interviewed by Andall (1999) who were found to have family responsibilities in Italy, Cape Verde, Portugal and the Netherlands. The Moroccan and Filipina women I interviewed in Bologna likewise were required to discharge their financial and moral obligations to family members both in Italy and in their countries of origin. Hence, migration can be seen as having given both new possibilities and more control to women, in many cases making them the major earner of the family (as was the case for Maria, Rita and Saida), but also as something that has not changed their role as those who have to sacrifice themselves (through international migration) for the good of the family and their children (as have Maria, Rita and, to an extent also, Saida and Ilham). Ribas-Mateos (2000) has noted the same outcomes for the Filipina women in Spain. Moreover, having to be both wage earners and responsible for maintaining a transnational family may be seen as a further burden for immigrant women.

In this chapter I have told the stories of six different women united by their experience of migration to the city of Bologna. As we have seen, their biographies present both similarities and differences that cut across the nationality boundary of the two groups. For instance, most of the women I have interviewed are confined to the same types of jobs in the care and domestic sector and are limited in their agency by their roles as members of households and families.[5] But a job as a domestic in Italy can be both an extension of such roles, as is the case for some of the Filipino women – like Maria and Rita – who have to work to remit money to other members of their families, and an escape route and a way of achieving economic (and other forms of) independence, as is the case for many Moroccan women – like Saida and Ilham – who decided to run away from their homes and make a new start abroad. Hence the cases I have presented are, in various combinations, migrations of obligation, of opportunity, of escape and of self-discovery. Their cultural encounters and cultural negotiations are as much with the households and societies of their countries of origin as with the host society in Italy.

In this account I have also exemplified the multi-faceted meanings of family formation in migrant groups and what the role of women is in contributing both to their households of origin and to the creation of new ones in the context of emigration. Through the six biographies I have selected it also emerges how such roles shape and influence these women's agency. By choosing families at different stages of their developmental cycle I also wanted to show how constraints and opportunities change at different stages of these women's lives.

Many feminist scholars (Anthias and Yuval Davis 1992; Lutz 1997; Yuval Davis 1997) believe that, in the debate about multiculturalism, too much attention has been given to cultural rights. In their view, the key issue for many migrant women is their access to formal and substantive rights. They believe that often it is migrant women's precarious position within receiving societies that poses obstacles to their incorporation. At the same time, denying the existence of differences between 'majority' and 'minority' women is also problematic, for it assumes the values and norms of the majority (in this case women) as the norm to which migrant women have to comply. Both Lutz (1997) and Morokvasic (1991) argue that, in order to understand migrant women's agency, instead of focusing on their unconditioned adoption of specific (Western) values and behaviours, a more fruitful approach for a feminist analysis would be one that looks at their resistance and at change that is produced by it. Lutz talks about a feminist analysis based on the idea of a 'differentiated' universalism, meaning an approach that neither denies difference nor reifies it. She believes that:

> It is no longer possible to make claims from a feminist perspective without recognising that (groups of) women are positioned differently towards each other and that they face different opportunities as well as structural constraints in performing their agency (Lutz 1997, p. 107).

I agree with this analysis since I believe that making reference to culture alone is not sufficient to understand the role and status of immigrant women in Bologna. In fact, the values present in the host society and, above all, the possibilities offered by the local context of arrival also play a significant role. These possibilities for the most part remain heavily constrained within those parts of the segmented Italian labour market which are available to immigrant women from poor countries, but nevertheless possibilities for change and improvement are not entirely absent, as some of my case-histories have shown. What this analysis has also demonstrated is the complexity of the intersections between work possibilities, stage in the life and family cycle, policy and legislative factors regarding residence rights and access to housing and welfare, and cultural values of the societies of origin.

Notes

1 This chapter is based on fieldwork carried out as part of my ongoing doctoral research at the University of Sussex; my DPhil is provisionally entitled 'Family Formation in Gendered Migrations in Southern Europe: A Comparative Ethnographic Study in Bologna and Barcelona'. The research is supported by an ESRC Research Studentship. I did fieldwork in Bologna between August 1999 and January 2000, employing typical ethnographic research methods such as participant observation, semi-structured interviews and life-histories of immigrants, other interviews with key informants, and document analysis of printed material produced by local institutions and NGOs dealing with immigrants.

2 I have translated all interview quotes and conversations into English. Although in many cases my informants spoke imperfect Italian, I have not tried to render their imperfections into English.

3 On the issue of housing policies for immigrants in Bologna see Bernardotti and Mottura (1999); also Però (1997).

4 'Centre of first shelter' is the rather clumsy English translation of the Italian term *centro di prima accoglienza* – temporary reception accommodation for immigrants when they arrive in Italy. Although such accommodation is meant to be temporary, often the occupants end up by staying a long time because of their inability to access other types of housing. Again see Bernardotti and Mottura (1999) and Però (1997) for details.

5   As shown by other studies of female migrants in southern Europe: see Andall (1998, 1999), Chell (1997) and the case-studies collected in Anthias and Lazaridis (2000).

References

Andall, J. (1998) Catholic and state constructions of domestic workers: the case of Cape Verdean women in Rome in the 1970s, in Koser, K. and Lutz, H. (eds) *The New Migration in Europe: Social Construction and Social Realities*. London: Macmillan, pp. 124–41.

Andall, J. (1999) Cape Verdean women on the move: 'immigration shopping' in Italy and Europe, *Modern Italy*, 4(2), pp. 241–57.

Anthias, F. and Yuval Davis, N., eds (1992) *Racialised Boundaries. Race, Nation, Gender, Colour, Class and the Anti-Racist Struggle*. London and New York: Routledge.

Anthias, F. and Lazaridis, G., eds (2000) *Gender and Migration in Southern Europe*. Oxford: Berg.

Bernardotti, A. and Mottura, G. (1999) *Il Gioco delle Tre Case. Immigrazione e politiche abitative a Bologna dal 1990 al 1999*. Turin: L'Harmattan Italia.

Bjerén, G. (1997) Gender and reproduction, in Hammar, T., Brochmann, G., Tamas, K. and Faist, T. (eds) *International Migration, Immobility and Development*. Oxford: Berg, pp. 219–46.

Boyd, M. (1989) Family and personal networks in international migration: recent development and new agendas, *International Migration Review*, 23(3), pp. 638–70.

Buijs, G., ed. (1993) *Migrant Women: Crossing Boundaries and Changing Identities*. Oxford: Berg.

Chell, V. (1997) Gender-selective migration: Somalian and Filipina women in Rome, in King, R. and Black, R. (eds) *Southern Europe and the New Immigrations*. Brighton: Sussex Academic Press, pp. 75–92.

Escrivà, A. (1997) Control, composition and character of new migration to south-west Europe: the case of Peruvian women in Barcelona, *New Community*, 23(1), pp. 43–57.

Goddard, V. (1996) *Gender, Family and Work in Naples*. Oxford: Berg.

Lutz, H. (1997) The limits of European-ness: immigrant women in Fortress Europe, *Feminist Review*, 57, pp. 93–111.

Maffioli, D. (1994) Il matrimonio e la nascita dei figli, in Vicarelli, G. (ed.) *Le Mani Invisibili. La vita e il lavoro delle donne immigrate*. Rome: Ediesse, pp. 110–27.

Maher, V. (1996) Immigration and social identities, in Forgacs, D. and Lumley, R. (eds) *Italian Cultural Studies*. Oxford: Oxford University Press, pp. 160–77.

Morokvasic, M.. (1991) Fortress Europe and migrant women, *Feminist Review*, 39, pp. 69–84.

Però, D. (1997) Immigrants and politics in left-wing Bologna: results from Participatory Action Research, in King, R. and Black, R. (eds) *Southern Europe and the New Immigrations*. Brighton: Sussex Academic Press, pp. 158–81.

Phizacklea, A., ed. (1983) *One Way Ticket: Migration and Female Labour*. London: Routledge and Kegan Paul.

Ribas-Mateos, N. (2000) Female birds of passage: living and settling in Spain, in Anthias, F. and Lazaridis, G. (eds) *Gender and Migration in Southern Europe*. Oxford: Berg, pp. 173–98.

Vicarelli, G., ed. (1994) *Le Mani Invisibili. La vita e il lavoro delle donne immigrate*. Rome: Ediesse.

Yuval Davis, N. (1997) Women, citizenship, difference, *Feminist Review*, 57, pp. 4–27.

Zontini, E. (2000) Immigrazione al femminile e domanda abitativa. Donne filippine nella città di Bologna, in Bernardotti, A. (ed.) *Con la Valigia Accanto al Letto. Immigrati e casa a Bologna*. Milan: Franco Angeli, in press.

12

Transforming traditions: a critical analysis of the trafficking and exploitation of young Albanian girls in Italy

Nicola Mai

Introduction

The aim of this chapter is to contextualise the phenomenon of international trafficking and sexual exploitation of young Albanian girls in Italy within the socio-cultural environment that produced it historically. I argue that it is only by starting from an in-depth analysis of the social and cultural dynamics which characterise contemporary Albanian society that an explanation of the phenomenon can be found which moves beyond the reductive tales of criminalisation and victimisation made constantly available by both Italian and Albanian media. These patronising and sensationalist stories of cruelty and ruthless exploitation provide, in fact, a stigmatising description of Albanian migrants in terms that ultimately end up by legitimising and reinforcing their actual condition of social exclusion.

This chapter therefore takes a different stance to the other contributions to this book. Instead of documenting a cultural encounter in the destination country, I examine a very specific form of migration – that of the trafficking of young Albanian women to Italy – and attempt to provide an explanation for this tragic human movement by exploring the social, cultural and historical context in the sending country. For these girls, the 'Mediterranean passage' is likely to be a short and speedy boat-ride across the Adriatic and a lot of furtive activity on the part of their traffickers and pimps. The fact that some of these 'migration agents' are actually their relatives and 'friends' is a telling preliminary comment on the peculiar nature of contemporary Albanian society, which will be expanded on in the pages that follow.

This chapter arises as an offshoot of fieldwork I have been conducting in Albania since 1998. The initial focus of this research was the impact of Italian television on Albanians' views of the outside world, their self-perceptions and their migration behaviour; see Mai (2001) for a preliminary account of this. As the focus of my work in Albania broadened, partly because of my involvement in the Kosovan refugee crisis and my work for an Italian NGO, I came to be in a position to observe and document other forms of migration and social behaviour in Albania, including the subject of the present contribution.

My account is structured in five main parts. First, I review the scale and nature of the phenomenon of the trafficking of Albanian girls for prostitution in Italy. Given the limitations of the few scattered data available, I concentrate on the qualitative aspects of the phenomenon, including regional variations within Albania, the social origins of the traffickers and the media reaction in Italy. The next section of the chapter enters into a brief discussion about the definition of prostitution and makes the link with forms of sexual exploitation which have been endemic to Albanian society. The third and fourth parts of the chapter are a more extended discussion of the historical conditions of patriarchy and the position of women in Albanian society, tracing linkages between Albanian customary law, the communist period, and (in the fourth section) the chaotic post-communist transition of the last ten years when people (males) attempted a reinvention of some strategic aspects of their traditional (patriarchal) cultural heritage in order to serve their own needs – exercise of power and acquisition of capital in a situation of mounting economic and social chaos. The conclusion draws the historical analysis and the contemporary scene together within a partial theoretical framework.

Before we begin the main part of the analysis, three important preliminary points must be made. First of all, it is important to underline that the Albanian State, starting from the mid–late 1980s and continuing through to the dramatic events of 1997,[1] underwent a process of gradual and systematic dissolution both as the institution regulating the legitimate use of authority and force in the Albanian territory and as the institution promoting and sustaining Albanian national culture, its values, roles and models. Second, the vacuum left by the progressive collapse of the state over the approximately ten-year period defined above has been accompanied by a re-emergence and re-elaboration of patriarchal values, roles and practices. These have always been part of the Albanian cultural heritage, but have recently been revitalised by new social actors in order to respond to the new social needs which emerged in relation to the access to social and economic resources which became available after the collapse of the communist state. In the light of these changes it is also important to analyse some specific aspects of Albanian culture with particular reference to the condition and status of women in an historical perspective.

Finally, in these introductory remarks, trafficking and migration must be analysed jointly as two different but tightly related aspects of the complex process of transformation in which Albania finds itself after the collapse of the communist state. This process has been characterised by dynamics of removal and idealisation. On the one hand some of the values, rules and models which have belonged historically to Albanian culture have in fact been refused because of their symbolic association with the coercion and violence of the communist state. On the other hand the process of social construction of a new nexus of local culture started from narrative and visual material coming from very different social, cultural and economic contexts, whose own contradictions and predicaments have not been understood in an emancipatory and empowering perspective. In this respect the past, both because of the continuity of discourses and practices belonging to the traditional cultural heritage in the present and because of the symmetrical refusal and reactive opposition to values and roles associated with the communist experience, is still a driving force in the present and future development of Albanian culture and society. Having said this, it is very important to consider trafficking in people as a completely new social phenomenon, which is based on a process of appropriation and transformation of some selected aspects of the Albanian cultural tradition to serve new emerging social needs and in relation to new social actors.

Nature and scale of the phenomenon

Although the phenomenon of the international trafficking of Albanian girls for sexual exploitation started with the first mass exoduses which took place after the collapse of the communist state in 1991,[2] it became a subject of public awareness only in 1993, the date of the first influx recorded in Italy of Albanian women engaged as sexual workers. In general the trafficking is more developed in Albania's neighbouring countries such as Italy and Greece, but more recently many other European countries (Austria, Holland, Switzerland, UK) have been targeted, according to research undertaken by the NGO 'Useful to Albanian Women' (Ballauri 1997, p. 18). Although this activity rather quickly became an important source of income for a growing number of Albanians, there are no accurate data on the actual number of people involved.

Nevertheless, there are some indicative figures available. In early 1998 the Italian Home Office estimated that Albanian sexual workers in Italy numbered between 10,000 and 15,000, representing two-thirds of all foreign sexual workers in Italy. This cross-checks reasonably well with Campani's (2000, p. 155) estimate that Italy contains between 18,800 and 25,100 foreign prostitutes. As of early 1998, an Albanian girl was worth between 20 and 25 million lire (11,000–14,000 dollars). The protector would keep the totality of her earnings in the street until her full cost is recovered, the lowest charge for one performance being around 50,000 lire (about 25 dollars); girls can make as much as 600,000 or even 1 million lire per night (UNICEF 1998, p. 86).

Beyond its quantitative dimension, the phenomenon can be contextualised within some specific aspects of the Albanian socio-cultural environment. In 1996 IOM (International Organisation for Migration) carried out a study on the trafficking and sexual exploitation of foreign girls in Italy (IOM 1996). Of the 50 women interviewed, 26 were Albanian. According to the results of this research, the typical profile of the Albanian trafficked woman is that of a very young, unmarried girl who was taken to Italy by a male relative, often a fiancé, under the promise of marriage or of a good working opportunity. In comparison with sexual workers coming from other countries, Albanians were amongst the youngest, the majority being between 14 and 18 years old. According to interviews carried out in Italy, the large majority of the trafficked girls were not aware that they were going to be sexual workers in Italy. Even those who knew were totally unaware of the conditions of aggressive and violent exploitation that they would have to face once there (Campani 1998 and 2000).

Perhaps the most characteristic aspect of the phenomenon of the trafficking of young Albanian girls for the purposes of exploitation is the degree of their physical and psychological subjection to their protectors and exploiters. Compared to sexual workers of other nationalities, Albanian women are the group the most strongly subjected to the power of their protectors and exploiters. They are in fact followed at a distance even when they are with a customer, and are subject to constant threats addressed both to their own lives and towards their family back in Albania (UNICEF 1998, p. 86). Compared to girls coming from other countries, Albanian sex workers are also by far the ones with the highest level of psychological dependence. According to an enquiry made in 1995 by the Department of Social Affairs of the Municipality of Venice, 'the majority of Albanian women left Albania with only a vague idea about the actual purpose of the migration. Their relationship with their exploiters is very complex, as it seems to be tied both to a romantic dream and to a relation of psychological dependence on men. They seem to delegate to the man (the dealer) the necessity of taking care of themselves. Even when they are facing systematic physical or psychological violence, when they are forced to work the streets, they end up by accepting their fate in order not to lose the entitlement to male protection' (Brussa 1996). In all these respects summarised in this quote, Albanian girls were found to be in a more vulnerable, exploited and dependent position than those from other countries.

According to a recent World Bank report on Albania which analyses 'the new conditions of social weakness suddenly created by the turmoil in society, which are qualitatively different from poverty', the examination of the process of post-communist transformation in Albania has identified two main conditions of vulnerability: social exclusion, which marginalises people via the mechanism of rejection from mainstream society; and gender abuse which marginalises women via the threat and use of violence (World Bank 1999, pp. i–ii). The phenomenon of trafficking is a social dynamic that emerges at the encounter between two social groups who found themselves in a condition of vulnerability in the process of cultural and social transformation which characterised post-communist Albania: young men at risk of criminal behaviour and young women at risk of sexual exploitation (World Bank 1999, pp. 8–9).

Although trafficking in people is now a widespread phenomenon within Albania, the way in which the implicated vulnerable groups get involved in it and its intensity varies across different regional areas. Trafficking is in fact stronger from two main areas, corresponding to two different socio-cultural situations: the rural and peri-urban villages of the interior of central and southern Albania, and the towns and rural communities of the mountainous north and north-east.

Historically, compared to the more austere and isolated northern regions, central and southern Albania have enjoyed a higher level of social and economic development which in turn has made it relatively more free from patriarchal and conservative values. After the collapse of the communist state, cultural and social changes there have been both sharper and faster and have led to the most dramatic consequences; this is especially the case in the districts around the towns of Berat, Lushnjë, Fier, Korça and Pogradec in the south and Tirana, Elbasan, Kavajë and Durrës in the centre. To the south Vlorë, Albania's third largest town, surpassed Durrës, which now is more controlled by the state forces, being only about 40 km away from the capital city, as the most important harbour in Albania for the illegal traffic of people and goods. In the towns and rural communities of the middle and coastal regions facing Italy, the massive and uncontrolled migratory flow accelerated the breakdown both of rural traditional extended family networks and of already existing urban or peri-urban nuclear families, leaving many young women and men unprotected and disoriented. The lack of a coherent and satisfactory set of values and roles in the aftermath of the collapse of the communist system and the general increase in criminal activities are producing a very dangerous social situation, in which younger generations are increasingly at risk of criminal activities which victimise other vulnerable social groups (World Bank 1999, p. ii). It is true that in the south and south-east regions, much of the migration is temporary due to the proximity to Greece; this means that here young men are at lesser risk of criminal behaviour and young women of being trafficked. However, the production and trafficking of drugs and people involves an increasing number of young men, while young women are in a very weak position because their male relatives are usually working in Greece or elsewhere and cannot protect them.

In the towns and rural communities of the north and north-east, young women are increasingly at risk of being trafficked as a consequence of the return, in mutated forms, of the traditional cultural and social norms related to the practice of betrothal and because of the migration abroad of the male members of their families, who leave them unprotected. In fact, young women are initiated into prostitution almost exclusively by close friends or boyfriends, many of them linked to organised crime. The girls' families, even though they may be aware of what awaits their daughters or sisters, are sometimes complicit in their departures, as the local version of the Albanian customary law prescribes that, according to the tradition of the betrothal, the bride should move into the husband's house (World Bank 1999, p. iv). Moreover, because of the level of social stigmatisation of prostitution in Albania, trafficked girls, whether they were active participants or not in their exploitative migration, are usually afraid to return to Albania, as they fear the reaction of their relatives and parents (Ballauri 1997, p. 23). This is equally true in the southern regions of Albania so that, whilst the north–south regional differences have to be kept in mind, most of the contextual factors for the trafficking and exploitation of young women are present in all parts of the country, varying regionally only in intensity.

Whereas the scientific literature and the very few data available on the phenomenon focus on the features and life-histories of trafficked subjects (Campani 2000), very little is usually said about the role and conditions of the traffickers and exploiters. These are an emerging group which arises from the fusion of traditional models and the uncertainties and opportunities created by transition and the weakness of the state in enforcing the law. The rejection of traditional Albanian values of honesty and morality (because of their association with the communist heritage), the lack of economic opportunities, the loss of many families' savings,[3] and the corruption of state officials who control access to limited public and private resources are some of the key factors which impel many young men, who have very low expectations for their economic futures and very little faith in the state's ability to solve their problems, to see criminal behaviour as a positive way to help themselves and their families. Conservative estimates consider that at least 25 per cent of young men aged between 18 and 25 years of age are engaged in criminal activities (World Bank 1999, p. 20). At highest risk are uneducated young men in the peri-urban areas of coastal cities and the capital, where drug smuggling and trafficking in women and children are concentrated. Another category of people at high risk of being attracted to the possibility of making fast money through trafficking human beings and weapons are uneducated and unemployed young men in the mountainous interior. In these areas the state is absolutely unable to control criminal activity, because the well-established 'defensive suzerainties' controlling local 'manipulative resources' (cf Humphrey 1991, p. 10) and traffickable goods (mainly drugs, people and weapons) have an almost complete control over the use of force. Beyond these regional differences, one should not forget that one of the main predicaments of the process of post-communist transformation is poverty. This must be considered as one of the main general reasons for the existence of trafficking in people in Albania. Moreover poverty has affected women in the first place, as a consequence of female unemployment, as we shall see later in the chapter.

Sex workers have also appeared in the main Albanian cities. Having said this, there is very little information available on the hidden domestic market. Although by 1997 the police had discovered 48 flats used as illegal brothels, only 14 people have been accused and convicted for the organisation and exploitation of prostitution, according to Albanian Ministry of Justice data. Nobody has been convicted for running a brothel. These figures appear very low when compared to the number of Albanians condemned in Italy. Out of the 4,376 accusations of sexual exploitation filed by the Italian police in 1997, two thirds were reportedly against Albanians (UNICEF 1998, pp. 85–6). Behind these differences one can easily see the higher level of social stigmatisation confronting sex workers in Albania, which makes even recording it or talking about it openly in terms of its damage to vulnerable women highly problematic.

The invisibility and under-representation of the phenomenon in the Albanian public sphere contrasts sharply with the visibility and prominence it is given in Italian media, where it is usually associated with broader and heavily politicised issues related to migration and the integration of foreign people into Italian society. According to a survey carried out on behalf of the business association Confcommercio in 1996, 70 per cent of Italians believed that migrants from developing countries (usually described as *extracomunitari*, meaning non-EU people) were responsible for an increase in criminality. What is even more telling is that 80 per cent of the police officers and magistrates interviewed also thought that the increasing presence of foreigners in Italy was linked to a rise in criminal activities. A poll carried out, again by Confcommercio, in all its associate bodies nationwide, showed that 94 per cent of those interviewed felt immigrants had aggravated the problem of criminality, particularly with regard to prostitution, but also in relation to drug dealing, petty burglary, racketeering and illegal work (Confcommercio surveys, quoted in Jamieson and Silj 1997).

In 1997 the 'Ethnobarometer' international institute of social research carried out a survey of the relation between the actual deviancy ratio, as far as petty criminality is concerned, among Albanian immigrants in Italy and the association between Albanian immigration flows and Albanian and Italian organised crime. With respect to petty or 'micro-criminality', the research concludes that the proportion of crimes committed by Albanian people living in Italy is 'relatively small, both in relation to total crimes perpetrated in Italy and in relation to crimes committed by other country nationals' (Jamieson and Silj 1997, p. 26). As far as the relation between the Albanian migratory flow and both the spread of organised crime and the increase in the exploitation of sexual workers are concerned, the report shows that if it is true that Albanian criminal groups are a growing force within the Italian organised crime scene, this could not but happen through the co-operation with local and already existing Italian criminal organisations. This is hardly surprising if one keeps in mind that it is actually in Italy that the network of social phenomena now generally known as mafia, currently the epithet *par excellence* for any network of organised crime world-wide, has historically emerged.

Analysts of the press coverage given in Italy to the periodic Albanian crises of the 1990s have blamed Italian national media for introducing and promoting an unquestioned association between Albanian migrants and potential criminals and for having contributed to marginalisation and social exclusion (Cotesta 1999; Vehbiu and Devole 1996). It is important to underline how these dynamics of criminalisation are very powerful agents of marginalisation as they provide the host communities with stigmatising prejudices which, by preventing Albanian migrants from accessing legal sources of income, relegate them to a condition of illegality and vulnerability from which it is increasingly difficult to exit. This has particularly negative consequences for Albanian trafficked and exploited girls who, having been associated with prostitution, find themselves increasingly marginalised both at home, on the basis of their moral corruption, and in Italy, where their supposed condition of immorality is also associated with their ethnic identity.

Trafficking or prostitution?

According to IOM, the general concept of international trafficking can be defined as any illicit transporting of migrant men, women and children and/or trading them in for economic or other personal gain. This may include facilitating the illegal movement of migrant women to other countries, with or without their consent or knowledge, deceiving migrant women about the purpose (legal or illegal) of the migration, physically or sexually abusing migrant women for the purpose of trafficking them, and finally selling women for the purpose of employment, marriage, prostitution or other forms of profit-making abuse (IOM 1996).

In Albania the difference between 'sexual work', defined as the free and voluntary exercise of a profession, and trafficking or exploitation is not clear. Even concepts such as sexual harassment or sexual abuse are currently confused and commonly associated with the idea of 'prostitution', which is usually seen as a condition reflecting the immorality and lust of the people involved. Albanian law forbids prostitution, condemning both sexual workers and people exploiting or favouring prostitution; the term of imprisonment is three years. Although formally forbidden during the communist regime, some forms of sexual exploitation of women have always existed in Albania (Ballauri 1997). Today, however, the phenomenon confronts Albanian society 'with a magnitude that could not have been imagined 10 years ago' (UNDP 1998, p. 51). It has become an important social problem, even though public opinion does not seem to be ready to acknowledge its relevance for Albanian contemporary society and its future development. Above all, because of the prejudices stemming from hegemonic patriarchal values and models, social stigmatisation and exclusion tend to fall on exploiters and trafficked people alike.

Although any discussion of prostitution is replete with controversies and difficulties, it is very important to offer a general definition and an interpretative framework which can highlight the social and political relevance of the emergence of the trafficking and exploitation of young Albanian girls within contemporary Albania. In her essay 'What's wrong with prostitution?' Carole Pateman, an American feminist sociologist, discarding any reduction of the political and ideological relevance of prostitution in terms of a deal by which a prostitute 'contracts out a certain form of labour power for a given period in exchange for money', defines prostitution as a social institution which is an integral part of patriarchal capitalism and patriarchal civil society. Prostitution, far from being a 'mutual, pleasurable exchange of the use of bodies', is the 'unilateral use of a woman's body by a man in exchange for money' (Pateman 1988, p. 198) and therefore it acknowledges and legitimises a relationship of symbolic and political subordination of the female to the male. What is important in analysing prostitution is that the prostitution contract is entered into by a female subject with a male subject and not with some abstract and non-gendered customer, the object of the contract being in fact the access to the feminine body by a man, not a de-gendered transaction. Even though the body and the self are not identical, selves are inseparable from bodies and there is an integral relationship between them. Civil mastery in fact is not exercised on exclusively rational or biological identities (Pateman 1988, p. 207). Moreover although the self is not completely subsumed in its sexuality, identity is inseparable from the social construction of the self and masculinity and femininity are central elements in the definition of one's identity, beyond one's sexual orientation (Pateman 1988, p. 207). Prostitution, then, is a patriarchal institution because it is based on a form of contract by which a man 'contracts to buy sexual use of a *woman* for a certain period', and on an ideological construction of the difference between masculinity and femininity in terms of subjection and subordination. The most important aspect of an analysis of prostitution in these terms is that it highlights its political and cultural relevance, beyond any speculation on the many different combinations of agency, empowerment, passivity and coercion that can be involved in this social dynamic.

Returning to the specific issue of trafficking, young Albanian girls who are being sexually exploited in Italy are denied their agency and dignity in three different respects: in being forced into sexual work by deception and abuse; in taking part in a social practice that reinforces their condition of subordination and psychological and cultural dependency on males (whether they actually do it by choice or out of coercion); and in being denied access, once in Italy, to any alternative and socially accepted source of income. Paradoxically, they end up by being excluded and stigmatised by those very values, discourses and forces which actually constructed them socially as prostitutes.

A brief historical outline of the condition of Albanian women

Because of its historical condition of marginality and isolation and of its recent communist past, Albania never actually disenfranchised itself completely from the values and traditions of a pre-modern society. These stem from an agro-pastoral mode of production and from a related model of conceptualisation and organisation of social relations and power structured rigidly around a central male leading figure. Such a model was necessarily personalistic and authoritarian in its very conception. Albanian traditional values have in fact been historically consistent with the life-cycle of the extended patriarchal family, characterised by the supremacy of the adult male as the moral authority over all other members of the family. In particular this meant the utmost submission of women to men. As pointed out above, this historical ultra-patriarchal social model was most typical of the northern part of the country.

Although the most extreme implications of these values and traditions were challenged and partially changed by the communist regime, it is undeniably true that their main features still shape the most meaningful aspects of contemporary Albanian culture, which is still characterised by the overwhelming supremacy of the institution of the family and its patriarchal values over all other social institutions and values. The communist ideology of Enver Hoxha, the man who ruled Albania undisputed for more than 40 years, must be seen as stemming from the very features of Albanian traditional culture it actually wanted to move against at first. The fact that Albanian communism was substantially the dictatorship of one man over all Albanian men and women can be understood by locating him as father-figure and moral guide of the nation-family within the values of obeisance and submission that stem from the cultural background of the whole of Albanian society. The result was to reinforce rather than break the isolation of Albania from the rest of the world, with Enver Hoxha succeeding in sealing and ruling the country despotically until the year of his death.

Historically, then, violence and abuse against women have easily found legitimisation in Albania, a country whose traditional culture has always been characterised by the strong presence of patriarchal values and practices. In order to further understand the Albanian mentality it is important to briefly analyse some aspects of a specific version of the Albanian customary law, which has historically been in use in the northern regions of the country (Hall 1994, pp. 26–8). This set of rules and prescriptions is known as the Kanun of Lek Dukajini, the person who put it in a written form in the fifteenth century.

My reference to a code which is more than six centuries old and which was in use in a specific area of Albania, an area of Catholic influence known for its conservatism and isolation, to explain contemporary phenomena which occur across the whole of Albania is problematic and needs some justification and clarification. First of all it is important to say that the Kanun is a geographically specific sedimentation of practices and values which were shared in part with other local versions of customary law practised in other regions of the country. The Kanun is a particularly conservative and patriarchal version, stemming from the conditions of hardship and cultural isolation of the specific environment that produced it. Keeping this in mind, one could say that some of the patriarchal values and institutions that are at its core have been at the basis of the historical continuity of Albanian culture as a whole, right down to the present time. Moreover, notwithstanding the efforts of the communist apparatuses, the Kanun never completely lost its influence in the areas where it originated (Hall 1994, p. 28), and recently it has been revitalised and 'modernised' in the aftermath of the collapse of the communist state (Schwandner-Sievers 1999, p. 141; Vickers and Pettifer 1997, pp. 132–5). Even though the relevance of this text is more symbolic than actual in order to understand the condition of women in contemporary

Albania, some of its rules and definitions are worth examining in some detail (Hall 1994, pp. 82–90).

Firstly, the Kanun bases its strength not on individual responsibility, but on the institution of the extended family clan, with authority the exclusive prerogative of men. Within this ideological framework males dominate private as well as social life: they enjoy civil and political rights while females are relegated to a subordinated and instrumental role. The Kanun's definition of a woman is self-explanatory: according to Article XXIX, 'A woman is known as a sack, made to endure as long as she lives in her husband's house.' Customary law denies freedom to women by imposing very strict discipline, while men are called to be the guardians of women's will and behaviour. Accordingly, the husband has the right to advise and correct his wife, and to beat her when she does not abide by his orders. And the wife has the duty 'to submit to his domination' (Article XIII).[4] Moreover, according to tradition, the husband is entitled to kill his wife for adultery or refusal to attend to some sacred duties, such as honouring guests. The parents of the bride used to give the husband a bullet during the ceremony of marriage to express their giving away their daughter's life (UNICEF 1998, p. 83). According to the Kanun, daughters are actually sold to their future husband, who is entitled to reimbursement if the wife dies within two years of the date of the marriage without bearing a child.

In the remaining parts of the country women were subject to similar conditions. For instance, in the Orthodox south they could not participate in any social activity without the consent of their husbands. In the Muslim central region they were confined to the home and had to wear veils, while men were allowed to practise polygamy (Hall 1994, pp. 82–3). This being the situation it is not surprising that the first Civil Code of 1929 merely formalised and legitimised already existing practices of discrimination and exclusion, by requesting the husband's approval for the woman to access the labour market (UNICEF 1998, p. 66).

Immediately after the Second World War, although formal equality between women and men was legally sanctioned, the relationship between the Party of Labour of Albania (the official name of the ruling party after 1948) and women remained deeply ambivalent and contradictory. Although during the 45-year-long communist regime women were gradually granted entitlement to equal education and employment, it is also true that the hegemonic patriarchal mentality was never really undermined. During the Cultural Revolution of the 1960s, when new ideological roles and models were forged out of the destruction of old traditions in the name of the empowerment of underprivileged social groups, the institution of the patriarchal family was attacked, since 'clan identity was seen as a major impediment to the creation of a truly communist state' (Vickers and Pettifer

1997, p. 138). Although this attack led to the destruction of the big (extended family) rural mansions and their replacement with small (nuclear family) flats, because the ideological campaign against clans was seen as a campaign against class (Vickers and Pettifer 1997, p. 138), nevertheless the cognitive framework of patriarchy remained unchallenged. Moreover, by imposing from above the replacement of the patriarchal extended family clan by the new nuclear family, Enver Hoxha left unquestioned both the patriarchal ethic and model, according to which decisions can be taken only from a male central authoritarian figure. And of course at the national level of the Albanian family that figure was none other than Hoxha himself!

The economic crisis which hit Albania at the end of the 1980s and which culminated in 1991 with the collapse of the communist state and of its juridical and economic foundations, brought with it widespread unemployment, which has affected women much more than men (Vickers and Pettifer 1997, pp. 132–41). Collective services, such as kindergartens, canteens, laundries and bakeries, which used to support women's reproductive burden, were closed down (UNICEF 1998, p. 67). In today's chaotic and rapidly urbanising market economy, both men and women are experiencing uncertainty about their respective roles and a consequent loss of self-esteem. Households now include varying family structures, based on their location and on the ages and migration history of family members. In general, the disintegration or re-composition in new forms of the traditional or the nuclear family structure is intensifying conflict within the family environment (World Bank 1999, p. 13).

In such a situation it is easy to understand how women tend to be particularly and increasingly vulnerable. In 1995, Refleksione, an Albanian NGO, first attempted to document violence against women. The study, which was carried out through interviews with people of both sexes, living in both rural and urban areas and belonging to all of the three main religions present in the country (Muslim, Roman Catholic, Christian Orthodox), revealed that, while 64 per cent of the Albanians interviewed did not see family violence as a social issue, around the same percentage admitted to having experienced some form of violence, either psychological or physical, either at home or abroad. Moreover around 34 per cent of respondents admitted that serious physical or psychological violence had taken place within their families of origin. Since the majority of the people interviewed were female (but interviews were not designated by sex), it is reasonable to assume that women were the targets of most of this violence. In Albania, staying at home for a woman is actually more dangerous than going out; of the interviewed women who actually admitted to having been raped, only in 14 per cent of the cases was the abuser unknown to the victim. The abuser was the partner in 40 per cent of the cases, a family member in 29 per cent and a known person in the remaining 15 per cent (Miria *et al.* 1995).

Analysis of the Albanian post-communist transformation

Finally, in order to contextualise the trafficking of young Albanian girls into Italy for sexual exploitation within contemporary Albanian society, it is very important to try and analyse some features of the Albanian post-communist transformation. More specifically, there are three main features of Albanian communism which have important implications for the nature of Albania's current situation:

- the lack of contact with the outside world;
- the systematic stigmatisation of popular pleasures in everyday life;
- the subversive meaning which consumption acquired in the Enverist state.

As far as the lack of contact with the outside world is concerned, suffice it to say that bureaucratic, social and border controls were brutally efficient in rendering it absolutely impossible for Albanians to leave, both physically and metaphorically, their own country for 45 years.[5] The diffusion of a very efficient system of social surveillance, through the establishment of a capillary network of informers at every level and sector of social life, both public and private, made it extremely dangerous for any Albanian to transgress the regime's many rules and prescriptions, which covered many aspects of private life and individual freedom. All this assisted the regime's claims that Albania was close to paradise on earth, because it prevented Albanians from accessing any other source of information about the outside world, apart from the propagandistic stories about the bad old days of pre-communist times and about the moral depravation of the West, which were made constantly available by the national cultural agencies. The only meaningful exception to this rule has been the unauthorised watching of Italian television, which started in the late 1970s and which played a major role in providing information about an alternative way of life (Mai 2001).

Regarding the mortification and denial of pleasure as an important and meaningful factor in people's lives, it is important to underline how Albanian traditional culture stemmed from the difficulties and hardships of an economic context characterised by extreme scarcity of goods and fierce competition for resources. It should come as no surprise that in a social and economic environment in which culture and social life have been historically structured around the mere necessity of reproduction and survival of families and their individual members, very little room has been left for the ephemeral or the pleasurable. Most of the songs, tales and objects which are expressions of Albanian traditional culture seem to refer to a cultural environment in which the individual is conceived of exclusively as part of a family network and its perceived priorities and needs. Moreover, and perfectly in line with this conservative and patriarchal cultural heritage, under the communist regime of Enver Hoxha the very search for an aesthetic dimension was equated to an anti-communist and subversive stance – a bourgeois act of contempt for the working class.[6]

Finally, it is important to understand how in Albania, as in other socialist regimes, consumption came to acquire a central role within the emergence of a political opposition and how this has influenced the nature of the Albanian transition to democracy. Paradoxically socialist regimes, by insisting that under socialism the actual material living standards would improve, and by failing to meet these expectations, ended up by arousing the desire to consume and kept it alive by deprivation. Since material plenty was a basic indicator of the level of advancement of the whole system, this desire was understood and constituted as a right. Within socialist countries, the combination of the dynamics of arousal and yet frustration of the desire to consume and people's consequent resistance to their regimes led them to build their social identities specifically through consuming. To acquire foreign consumption goods became a strategy of constituting a selfhood against a regime, its set of rules, its laws and values (Humphrey 1995, pp. 55–6).

Moreover in Albania, as in many other states which have experienced a socialist totalitarian regime, the process of social construction of the individual occurred through an oscillation between a public moralised identity based on an ideal model of a communist citizen and an alternative private space of consumption and pleasure. Because of the fact that many Albanian people, at least in the conclusive phase of the Enverist regime, discovered themselves by retreating from the communist faith (whilst pretending still to be following it), their life came to be organised through the alternation between the mundane space of their households and the heroic and ethicised space of their public person. This schizophrenic switching between a public space of pretension and heroism and a private space of leisure and mundanity has very important implications for how capitalism and democracy came to be understood under and immediately after communism in Albania. The centrality of consumption within the emergence of political opposition in Albania is also central to an understanding of its nature, as this opposition has stemmed from a non-heroic, non-moralised private and individualised dimension in which leisure and desire were free from the need to be publicly acknowledged as ethic (Kharkhordin 1995, pp. 214–15).

As a consequence of all of these changes and tensions, freedom and democracy in Albania have come to be associated primarily with a higher level of material wealth, more specifically with the possibility to purchase

Western commodities, and also, in particular as far as the first post-communist years were concerned, with the possibility to transgress and ignore rules, indeed any rule, whose observance came to be identified with the communist past. The most striking aspect of contemporary Albanian culture is in fact its chaotic fragmentation. The contemporary presence of conflicting and contradictory systems of management of power, from revitalised elements harking back to the never-forgotten tradition to the recently introduced democratic model, generates confusion and unrest at every level of Albanian society.

It is very easy to notice the existence within contemporary Albanian society of a profound crisis of individuals in relation to their social function and the models of identification available to them; above all this is because the country lacks a new shared, organic, ontological foundation to fill the vacuum left by the vanishing of the collective and the public as meaningful dimensions at the basis of culture and society. What is going on today in Albania is a phase of reaction to the obsessive collectivisation of public and private life which characterised Enverist times; the country is witnessing a counter-process of anarchic and individualistic privatisation of life in all of its aspects, from politics to public spaces and public behaviour.[7]

This is full of dramatic implications in a cultural context such as the Albanian one, in which individual actions, desires and thoughts have historically found a legitimisation almost exclusively within a collective or semi-collective dimension, related first to the patriarchal and authoritative values and models at work in the extended family networks and then to the communist state. The vanishing of this fundamental ethical and collective dimension potentially frees onto the social scene a new model of the individual, who shares the patriarchal, aggressive and authoritarian values at work within traditional Albanian culture and potentially needs to find only in himself and in his perceived needs the ultimate moral legitimisation of his actions and thoughts (Fuga 1998, p. 151). Moreover Western capitalism and democracy were initially learned through the consumption of foreign television and, because of the lack of knowledge of the contradictions and actual functioning of capitalist democracies, they have come to be conceived primarily in terms of a utopian and a-moral world of unrestricted fulfilment of the consumerist imagination (Mai 2001). In particular, the representation of Italian society given by Italian television, by referring predominantly to the pleasures of consumption, has emphasised practices and discourses of social inclusion, linked to the access to Western consumer goods, while at the same time underplaying the existence of a system of rules regulating the use of force and restricting the entitlement to rights and the access to resources within capitalist societies.

Conclusion

This attempt to contextualise the phenomenon of the trafficking of young Albanian girls into Italy for sexual exploitation within the socio-cultural environment that historically produced it is based on a definition of culture as a local process of reconstruction through time of a knowing subject and its knowable environment (Appadurai 1995, p. 206). It is also necessary to underline how material products are culturally embedded. They 'represent' culture, not because they are merely there as the environment in which we operate, but because they are an integral part of that project of objectification by which we create ourselves as an industrial society: our identities, our social affiliations, our lived everyday practices (Miller 1987, p. 215). Cultural products in turn are very complex 'social forms of construction and distribution of knowledge' that 'acquire especially intense, new and striking qualities when the spatial, cognitive, or institutional distances between production, distribution, and consumption are great' (Appadurai 1986, pp. 41–8). This is particularly true if we consider the reception of cultural constructs from the West in the rest of the world, particularly in post-socialist states like Albania, where consumption of Western products acquired a politically subversive function. Finally this analysis is based on a definition of memory in terms of a creative and subjective practice which constantly re-interprets past events, practices and traditions through time in relation to the overarching social needs of the present (Passerini 1988).

Following this perspective in Albania violence and tradition can be seen as 'strategic tools for defining exclusion and inclusion in the access to new resources ... which became accessible after the breakdown of earlier Albanian isolationism' (Schwandner-Sievers 2000, p. 256). The trafficking in Albanian girls is a phenomenon that is both deeply embedded within some of the values and specific social practices which have been historically hegemonic within Albanian culture, and completely new, as it is related to the emergence of new social subjects and opportunities within the recent phase of post-communist transformation. The discourses and values of customary law, in its various local versions, have been interpreted in order to legitimate the use of violence for unprecedented aims and on the part of new social actors, starting from the elements referring to the patriarchal institutions characteristic of Albania's most peripheral and isolated communities.

As we have seen, the Albanian post-communist transformation has been characterised by the disappearance of the state as the institution which both regulates the legitimate use of force and promotes and sustains Albanian national culture. This process has been accompanied on the one hand by the rejection, together with the entire communist ideology, of values and practices related to a collective ethical dimension, and on the other hand by the absence of a coherent and alternative system of knowledge and an uninformed idealisation of the West, associated with a universe of material plenty and luxury. As a consequence of this situation in many peripheral areas of the country, people experienced a 're-traditionalisation', a reinvention of some strategic aspects of the traditional cultural heritage in order to serve new ends, corresponding to the emerging social needs of new social identities (Schwandner-Sievers 2000, p. 256). These emerged in reaction against the world of hardship and violence provided by the communist state and in relation to the access to the world of material superiority which became at first visible through Italian and other foreign television channels, and then potentially available through migration and other means after the collapse of the isolationism and repression that had characterised life under communism.

It is important to underline the novel character of these new social practices. Whereas the Kanun legitimated the power of domination by the adult male within the institution of the family, it most certainly did not authorise fathers and brothers to sell and sexually exploit their children, sisters and wives for profit. Today, in contexts which are at the margins of the process of elaboration and deployment of a new Albanian democratic culture, in peri-urban areas and in isolated rural places where the presence of the state is now and has always been very weak, new institutions have been established which are based on 'modernised' codes of honour (Schwandner-Sievers 1999). There are gangs of young men, unemployed and virtually illiterate, who are directly involved in new kinds of violence such as the trafficking of drugs, weapons and people into neighbouring countries. There are families, shaken by economic hardship and bewildered by the collapse of a moral and ethical order, who can, with varying degrees of awareness, end up by trading their daughters for sexual exploitation. There are isolated and repressed young girls who want to break free from the submission and violence they experience at home, stimulated by the world of emancipation, freedom and wealth they see on Italian or other foreign television channels. These girls may consciously decide to be sex workers abroad, underestimating the level of brutality and annihilation they are going to face once there; they may be easily deceived by the false promise of a good job abroad or seduced by the possibility of marrying somebody who might allow them to leave the family; or they might be traded directly by their own family members.

Interviews with Albanian traffickers have shown that they simply consider trafficking and exploiting their young wives, fiancées and relatives their own private business. Most of them fail to understand why the police should be interested in their private economic activities at all (Ballauri 1997). This is because their re-interpretation and re-adaptation of practices and values belonging to a distant past in the light of their own cultural construction of capitalist democracy fully authorises and legitimises them to dispose of women as sources of income for the accumulation of their own capital.

Notes

1   In 1997, following the collapse of unofficially state-endorsed pyramid-selling financial schemes, Albania has been on the verge of civil war, which has caused a massive flow of refugees from Albania into Italy and whose handling by the Italian and international authorities and institutions has produced many controversies. For further information see Morozzo della Rocca (1997).

2   Between 7 and 10 March 1991, as the 45-year-old Albanian communist regime was disintegrating, some 25,700 Albanians crossed the Otranto Channel between Albania and Italy; in August 1991, another 20,000 arrived. At the end of 1997, 83,807 Albanian immigrants were officially living and working in Italy (Caritas di Roma 1998, p. 79), although it is estimated that the actual figure, including so-called irregular immigrants, may be as high as 150,000 people (UNDP 1998, p. 36). Zinn (1996) has documented the ambivalent, but ultimately negative reaction of the Italian government and media to the influx of Albanian migrants in the early 1990s.

3   In 1997, the network of private pyramid-selling investment schemes collapsed and bankrupted at least 70 per cent of Albanian families (UNICEF 1998, p. 24) as well as wiping out the savings and remittances earned by migrants abroad.

4   These quotations from the Kanun are given in UNICEF (1998, p. 66).

5   Until 1991, it had been literally impossible for any Albanian citizen to leave the country, every kilometre of borderline being guarded obsessively day and night. Even internal migration has been very limited and people were strictly forbidden from coming in contact, without official permission, with the very few foreigners visiting the country. Until 1985, the year of the death of Enver Hoxha, mail and telephones were very carefully checked and Albanians were forbidden to watch foreign television. No foreign literature was available, apart from some classic works belonging to the tradition of popular realism and naturalism, and the monopoly press was state-run, with specific journals and newspapers for groups such as the youth and trade unions, which were seen as evidently needing further surveillance. Moreover the isolationist paranoia of the Enverist regime has left omnipresent marks on the whole of the Albanian territory. For instance Hoxha ordered the construction of over 600,000 bunkers, one for every family, in case of military aggression from a foreign power. The road network has never been rationalised, in order to make it more difficult for the enemy to occupy the country in case of invasion (Vickers 1995). As a result, the country is densely sprinkled with bunkers and it still takes more than 18 hours to drive the 350 km that separate the northern from the southern extremities of Albania.

6   In communist times Albanian women and men were forced to wear mortifying grey and standardised uniform-like clothes. Jewels, make-up, non-'popular' (i.e. folkloristic) music, in short anything which could be seen as not strictly functional and directed to the satisfaction of Albanian people's basic needs, which had to be identified and acknowledged as such by the directors of the national cultural and political apparatuses, was banned. For instance in both rural and urban areas both concrete and brick-built houses were very seldom faced, leaving a very shoddy outward impression of

most residential units. This was because, according to official policies and propaganda, houses had to be comfortable inside, but their external decoration would both have been a betrayal of popular values and would surely have aroused foreign nations' desire to occupy the country. For further information, see Hall (1994, pp. 153–5).

7 The labyrinth of kiosks which has replaced the Youth Park and partially occupied the pavements of the main boulevards and squares in central Tirana is a very telling testimony of how a public space of relaxation and leisure has been fragmented and replaced by privatised and unregulated spaces of consumption, by a chaotic assembly of clothes shops, record shops, bars and restaurants whose cultural universe of reference is evident from their names: Bar Amerika, Pizzeria Santa Lucia, Bar Soros, Bar Marlboro, Bar West, Bar Lady Diana, etc. In Berat, the hall in which the Provisional Government of Albania was first created on 20 October 1944, a small building positioned right in the centre of the town, once an important national monument, has been transformed into a 'Tele Bingo', where many unemployed young men spend their days betting, smoking and drinking.

References

Appadurai, A. (1986) Introduction: commodities and the politics of value, in Appadurai, A. (ed.) *The Social Life of Things*. Cambridge: Cambridge University Press, pp. 3–64.

Appadurai, A. (1995) The production of locality, in Fardon, R. (ed.) *Counterworks: Managing the Diversity of Knowledge*. London: Routledge, pp. 204–25.

Ballauri, E. (1997) Prostitution, history, causes, reality, in *Prostitution – Society in Dilemma*. Tirana: Useful to Albanian Women, pp. 1–31.

Brussa, L. (1996) *Progetto Città e Prostituzione. Analisi del primo anno di lavoro*. Venice : Comune di Venezia, Assessorato Politiche Sociali.

Campani, G. (1998) Trafficking for sexual exploitation and the sex business in the new context of international migration: the case of Italy, *South European Society and Politics*, 3(3), pp. 230–61.

Campani, G. (2000) Immigrant women in southern Europe: social exclusion, domestic work and prostitution in Italy, in King, R., Lazaridis, G. and Tsardanidis, C. (eds) *Eldorado or Fortress? Migration in Southern Europe*. London: Macmillan, pp. 145–69.

Caritas di Roma (1998) *Immigrazione Dossier Statistico '98*. Rome: Anterem.

Cotesta, V. (1999) Mass media, conflitti etnici e immigrazione, *Studi Emigrazione*, 135, pp. 387–497.

Fuga, A. (1998) *L'Albanie entre la Pensée Totalitaire et la Raison Fragmentaire*. Paris: L'Harmattan.

Hall, D. (1994) *Albania and the Albanians*. London: Pinter Reference.

Humphrey, C. (1991) 'Icebergs', barter, and the Mafia in provincial Russia, *Anthropology Today*, 7(2), pp. 8–13.

Humphrey, C. (1995) A culture of disillusionment, in Miller, D. (ed.) *World Apart: Modernity through the Prism of the Local*. London: Routledge, pp. 43–68.

Jamieson, A. and Silj, A. (1997) *Migration and Criminality: the Case of Albanians in Italy*. Rome: Ethnobarometer Working Paper 1.

Kharkhordin, O. (1995) The Soviet individual: genealogy of a dissimulating animal, in Featherstone, M., Lash, S. and Robertson, R. (eds) *Global Modernities*. London: Sage, pp. 209–26.

IOM (1996) *Trafficking in Women to Italy for Sexual Exploitation*. Online. Available HTTP: http://www.iom.int/iom/Publications/entry.htm (June 1996).

Mai, N. (2001) 'Italy is beautiful': the role of Italian television in Albanian migration, in King, R. and Wood, N. (eds) *Media and Migration*. London: Routledge, in press.

Miller, D. (1987) *Material Culture and Mass Consumption*. Oxford: Blackwell.

Miria, S., Valdet, S. and Fico, D. (1995) *Violence Against Women and the Psychosocial Taboos Favouring Violence.* Tirana: Women's Association Refleksione.

Morozzo della Rocca, M. (1997) *Albania. Le Radici della Crisi.* Milan: Guerini.

Passerini, L. (1988) *Storia e Soggettività. Le fonti orali, la memoria.* Florence: La Nuova Italia Editrice.

Pateman, C. (1988) What is wrong with prostitution? in *The Sexual Contract.* Cambridge: Cambridge University Press, pp. 189–218.

Schwandner-Sievers, S. (1999) Humiliation and reconciliation in northern Albania. The logic of feuding in symbolic and diachronic perspectives, in Feuchtwang, S., Elwert, S. and Neubert, D. (eds) *Dynamics of Violence. Processes of Escalation and De-escalation in Violent Group Conflicts.* Berlin: Duncker and Humbolt, pp. 134–52.

Schwandner-Sievers, S. (2000) The enactment of 'tradition': Albanian constructions of identity, violence and power in times of crisis, in Schmidt, B. and Schroeder, I. (eds) *Anthropology of Violence and Conflict.* London and New York: Routledge, pp. 235–61.

UNDP (1998) *Albanian Human Development Report 1998.* Tirana: UNDP.

UNICEF (1998) *Situation Analysis 1998: Children's and Women's Rights in Albania.* Tirana: UNICEF.

Vehbiu, A. and Devole, R. (1996) *La Scoperta dell'Albania. Gli Albanesi secondo i Mass-Media.* Milan: Paoline.

Vickers, M. (1995) *The Albanians: a Modern History.* London: I.B. Tauris.

Vickers, M. and Pettifer, J. (1997) *Albania: From Anarchy to a Balkan Identity.* London: Hurst.

World Bank (1999) *Albania: Filling the Vulnerability Gap.* Tirana: The World Bank.

Zinn, D. L. (1996) Adriatic brethen or black sheep? Migration in Italy and the Albanian crisis, *European Urban and Regional Studies,* 3(3), pp. 241–9.

13

Deconstructing naturalism: the racialisation of ethnic minorities in Greece

Gabriella Lazaridis and Maria Koumandraki

Introduction

Observing the growing racist tendencies that affect Europe today, an increasing number of scholars have tried to analyse contemporary racism (and racisms) and to develop a set of hypotheses that would account for racialised social relations in various national and local settings, at a time of social and cultural change (Solomos and Wrench 1993; Wieviorka 1994). Although these studies cover several European countries, one finds very little acknowledgement of racism in the literature on migration into Greece, with the exception of a survey by the Eurobarometer (EEC 1989) and a number of small-scale studies (Lazaridis 1999, 2000; Lazaridis and Wickens 1999; Triandafyllidou *et al.* 1997).

How are we to understand racism in the Greek context? How are we to interpret the racialisation of 'others' and their experiences of discrimination and exclusion? This chapter attempts to answer these questions in the context of recent migration into the country and the racist abuse suffered not only by black minority groups but also by members of the 'white minority' who have migrated to Greece (and specifically Athens) from non-EU member states. It draws on research carried out by the authors on the self-employment of ethnic minority groups in what has now become a multi-racial city.[1]

In an attempt to contextualise the study within existing theoretical approaches to racism, the first section of the chapter looks at the shift from the old certainties of 'colour' as the primary indicator of social exclusion to more complex processes of inclusion and exclusion that vary across time and space. Section two looks at methodological issues. Trying to grasp the interviewee's experience of 'inter-ethnic social relationships and their engagement with shifting meanings about racial difference at a time of wider rapid social change' (Mac an Ghaill 1999, p. 4), the remainder of the chapter presents empirical work to provide a critical reflection on the relative adequacy of the various theoretical approaches to explain the situation in Greece. We suggest explanations which may be helpful in understanding processes of racialisation of different ethnic minority groups in the Greek context. Life stories are used to show how crude stereotypes racialise different groups of migrant men and women and reflect socially constructed hierarchies of nation, ethnicity, religion and 'colour'. All groups experience discrimination but in different degrees; 'invisible others', once not excluded on the basis of membership of race groups, are now becoming subject to different forms and degrees of prejudice, discrimination, disadvantage and racialised exclusion.

We argue that one should move away from 'colour' racism (black–white model) as a single overarching factor shaping racial and ethnic relations in Greece and try to understand what is going on through the kaleidoscope of difference, diversity and cultural pluralism. In questioning the fixed boundaries around 'colour' racism established by earlier race-relations and class-based perspectives, we follow the argument of Mac an Ghaill (1999, p. 7) that 'contemporary conditions are helping to produce multiple forms of racism and new ethnic identifications'. Institutional racism (here understood as the systematic exclusion not only of black people but also of other racialised ethnic minority groups from and within institutions) will also be looked at. We argue that in Greece today, biological notions of racial difference seem to co-exist with cultural notions, where the cultural visibility of the object of racism may or may not be that distinct. Hence, within the study of racism, one may find various versions and permutations of the association between cultural differentialism and social inegalitarianism. Racism based on cultural differentialism considers the 'other' different, and thus to be avoided; racism based on social inegalitarianism considers the 'other' as an inferior being to be exploited (Wieviorka 1994, pp. 182–3).

Theoretical context: rethinking the black–white dualism

Race has been traditionally defined narrowly on the basis of inherent biological/physical characteristics shared by a human grouping (Van de Berghe 1978, p. 10). The term 'race' denoted a categorisation of human groupings on the basis of biological differences (phenotypical or genotypical), thus viewing race as a natural, rather than socially constructed category (Guillaumin 1995). Broader definitions, borrowing elements from ethnicity, use both biological and cultural characteristics (language, religion etc.) and see race as being a social and ideological construct, lacking any 'scientific' basis for categorisation and hierarchisation of people based on a genetic stock.

Some argue that, in spite of the above-mentioned criticisms, race has to be retained as an analytical category for the purposes of sociological analysis, provided that it is incorporated within the more inclusive category of 'ethnos', i.e. nation and ethnicity. For Anthias race has no analytical validity in its own right but, as she puts it, 'is a social construction with its own representational, organisational and experiential forms linking it ontologically to the wider category of ethnos which provides its analytical axis... Its placement within the category of ethnos ... is not in terms of cultures of difference but in terms of the specific positioning of boundaries' (Anthias 1990, pp. 21–2). She differentiates her position from that of Gilroy (1987) and Omi and Winant (1986) who do not locate race within the ethnic, national and class formations. She argues that 'race denotes a particular way in which communal or collective differences come to be constructed and understood ... a particular articulation of where and how the boundary [between those who belong to a particular ethnic group and those who do not] is to be constructed' (Anthias 1990, p. 22). For Anthias the acknowledgement of 'race' does not suggest any kind of racial hierarchy and identification of superior and inferior races; 'race' is not a presupposition for 'racism'.

Unlike Anthias, who retains race as an analytical category, others (e.g. Miles 1982, 1989) have argued that there are no races in the biological sense of there being distinct and discrete biological groups, distinguished by genetic and physical characteristics organised in some hierarchical fashion; and moreover that there is no case for attributing these supposedly biological groups with fixed cultural attributes. Hence any racial categorisation of human populations is scientifically invalid and therefore the race category should be totally dispensed with. Retaining the concept reinforces arguments of 'scientific racism' which make use of the alleged existence of superior and inferior races, which is the first step towards proceeding into arguments on the inherent biological inferiority of particular human groups to justify the exclusion and/or extermination of such groups. The retention of the concept even for sociological analysis implies that race has a valid status. Hence race and racism are connected in that 'without racism physical characteristics are devoid of social significance' (Van de Berghe 1978, p. 11). Husband (1982) and Mason (1994) share a similar point of view. As Husband (1982, p. 325) puts it, 'to believe that races are valid categories is to endorse an ideology that is racism'.

Therefore, the key debate in the theorisation of race has been concerned with the validity of race as an analytical category. Some authors have argued that race is not 'a material fact which produces social consequences', (Guillaumin 1995, p. 61); they view race as a social and political construct which has to be understood within a particular time and space setting and are interested in examining the way in which this social construct has been created and why and how this is changing and what purposes it serves (Guillaumin 1995; Solomos and Back 1996). Others, like Cohen for example, have argued that race is an ideological construct, the object of racist discourse; 'it signifies a set of imaginary properties of inheritance which fix and legitimate real positions of social domination or subordination in terms of genealogies of genetic difference' (Cohen 1988, p. 23).

It is nowadays widely accepted that race *is* a social construct. However, unlike ethnicity, the association of race with physical difference leads it to be used to refer to divisions between black and white. 'Current debates between anti-racists and cultural theorists are providing a limited discussion, with the former emphasising common experiences of racism and the latter focusing on the differentiated experiences of different ethnic groups and subgroups in ethnic minority communities' (Mac an Ghaill 1999, p. 8). The terms race and ethnicity are often used interchangeably to refer to similar processes and groupings (Bradley 1996, p. 122; Mason 1999). Moreover, 'there has been a marked tendency in recent years to elevate the conflation of the concepts of race and ethnicity into a theoretical principle by invoking the concept of racialisation. The notion seeks to identify the processes by which ethnic and other differences are naturalised' (Mason 1999, p. 22).

A further distinction is being made in the literature between 'old' and 'new' racism. 'Old racism' arguments have been used to justify discrimination, exclusion and extermination of particular human groupings on the supposedly biological/genetic differences shared by these human groupings. 'New racism', on the other hand, looks at discrimination policies and exclusion of migrants and minority groups on the basis of cultural characteristics (religion, language and other cultural differences). A main element of 'new racism' is the deracialisation of race 'involving the displacement of an older racial vocabulary in public arenas, in which explicit references to race are now coded in the language of culture' (Mac an Ghaill 1999, p. 71). For some, 'the two logics of racism', that is the 'old' and the 'new', coexist. As Wieviorka (1994, p. 183) argues, 'there are not two racisms, but one, with various versions of the association of cultural differentialism and social inegalitarianism'. Hence 'new racism' or 'cultural racism' is not that new. This view is shared by Brah *et al.* (1999), Mason (1994), Rattansi (1994) and others. Husband (1982, p. 319), for example, argues that such ideas 'refer back to notions that already exist in common sense, taken for granted, popular belief that enables the elements of the new racism to cohere in a seemingly rational, and more importantly *reasonable*, package'. Hence there is nothing new about cultural differentiation as a basis for racist discourse. Brah *et al.* (1999, pp. 5–6) have argued that the study of racism within the race relations approach led to the concentration of research on the black–white divide and hence obscured the multi-dimentional character of exclusion and inclusion and generated the view that colour was the predominant signifier of 'race', resulting in the non-colour racisms being overlooked. As shown in the sections that follow, the people we interviewed were victims of racism not only because of their phenotypical characteristics, but also because of their religious affiliation (Muslims) or cultural affinity. Therefore, in the Greek context, 'colour racism' is only one form of racism. As Anthias (1992, pp. 431–2) argues, treating blacks as victims and whites as racists results in an homogenisation of both the subjects and objects of racism and obscures the differential impact of racisms along gender, class and ethnic divisions.

Post-modernists have pointed out that racism is not a static, unitary and homogeneous phenomenon but is historically specific and takes different forms both within a given society and in different countries (see Cohen and Bains 1988; Goldberg 1990a and 1990b; Rattansi and Westood 1994; Silverman and Yuval-Davis 1999). According to Goldberg (1990a, p. xiii), for example, 'the presumption of a single monolithic racism is being displaced by a mapping of the multifarious historical formulations of *racisms*'. Also, its subjects vary, in that it is not directed only towards 'black people' but also towards a variety of 'white' minority groups. It is therefore important to examine how national, public racist discourses interrelate with practices in specific settings, such as the Greek one. In addition, a stress on difference and diversity, with each group experiencing different patterns of disadvantage, allows us to better understand the experiences of some of the groups within the patchwork of heterogeneous ethnic groups that Greece is today.

Methods

Our empirical material is based on qualitative research grounded in individuals' accounts from selected ethnic minority groups, namely Africans and East-Central Europeans. In making this choice, we avoided the pitfall of either over-racialising selected groups of non-whites or de-racialising white minorities.

A variety of methods have been used to refer to the biographical approach, such as life-story approach, life history, the (auto)biographical perspective, the narrative approach etc. (Miller 2000, p. 1). Most American texts speak of the 'personal documents' composing a life history: letters, diaries, personal records, open interviews, autobiographies and tape-recorded life stories. Bertaux and Kohli (1984) are critical of this since 'no systematic distinction is drawn between the broader conception of personal documents on the one hand, and life stories on the other'. These authors argue that, although both of these sources give us access to the actor's perspective, 'if one takes the dimension of personal history seriously, it is appropriate to insist on a more specific characterisation: the life-story approach should be based on narratives about one's life or relevant parts thereof'(Bertaux and Kohli 1984, pp. 216–17). We chose the biographical method as this gives voice to our marginalised and socially excluded subjects and gives them the chance to narrate their experiences and life-styles. But how does the biographical interview differ from a semi-structured or an open-ended interview schedule?

According to Miller (2000, pp. 8, 18), two distinguishing features of biographical research differentiate it from other qualitative methods. First, its 'holistic' character and breadth of coverage implies, in one sense, that it can cover the totality of a person's life. However, as Rosenthal (1993, p. 62) points out, this 'cannot be taken to mean simply a review of every single event that ever took place in a person's life. It must rather be interpreted in a gestalt sense of biography as a comprehensive, general pattern of orientation that is selective in separating the relevant from the irrelevant.' The oral account is thus selective, with biographically relevant experiences linked up in a temporally and thematically consistent pattern. The second feature which distinguishes the biographical approach from other related methods is the 'process'. To quote Rosenthal again, 'the individual has their own history of personal development and change as they "process" along their life course... [In addition], historical events and social change at the societal level impinge upon the individual's own unique life history' (Rosenthal 1993, p. 63).

In the interviews we carried out, although the emphasis was on the individual as 'a unique entity located in a complex network of social relationships that change and evolve over historical time' (Miller 2000, p. 10), we did not aim at individual particularities, but sought to unravel common elements that allowed us to gain access to 'the reality of life of social aggregates' (Kohli 1981, p. 63).

We conducted 18 narrative interviews with a heterogeneous group of migrant individuals living and working in Athens since the early 1990s, approximately the time when Greece changed from being an emigration country to a country receiving large numbers of 'third-country' migrants. We interviewed people of varying nationalities (7 Nigerians, 3 Ghanaians, 3 Sierra Leoneans, 3 ethnic-Greek Albanians, 1 Egyptian and 1 Ethiopian), 14 men and 4 women, with ages ranging from 24 to 48. About half were married with small children, one was a single mother and the rest were single. The sample was chosen not in terms of county of origin, but in terms of work they did. At the time we interviewed them, they were all engaged in self-employment activities (decorator, street-hawker, publisher, and owners of a variety of shops, restaurants, beauty parlours and hairdressing salons). In other words, each person was chosen for interview because they were deemed to represent a certain type of self-employment activity that was considered to be important in the new multi-ethnic economy of Athens. Our goal was to secure a spread of individuals who represent all types that are significant for the phenomenon under consideration. The snow-balling technique was adopted for gaining access to interviewees who were reluctant to be interviewed due to their illegal or semi-legal status as well as their fear of being reported to the authorities for lacking the necessary documents. Thus, initial contacts were established with some key informants who introduced us to other respondents. All the people interviewed were willing to narrate their life story (including their experiences of racism and xenophobia) and to allow the interview to be tape-recorded. The duration of the interviews varied from one to several hours. The thematic focus specified was that of self-employment. The material on experiences of racism presented below represents a general construct of biographical experiences derived from 'past interactional episodes and future expectations' (Rosenthal 1993, p. 65). From this coagulate of past and future, a creation of the lived present was obtained in the form of a narration, based on the narrator's choice of stories and/or memories to be narrated and the way in which s/he perceived them at the time of the interview.

The interviews consist of two parts: the main narration, during which the interviewer was a listener, and the questioning part. The main narration varied in length from one interview to another, depending on the willingness of the interviewee to speak. The interviewee was given the chance to elaborate on the life experiences that s/he considered to be important or worth sharing with the interviewer. As Rosenthal (1993) puts it, it is then the interviewer's task to explain, via hermeneutic case reconstruction, why the interviewee reflects on particular topics and elaborates on particular events of their life and not others. Thus, the non-directiveness of this approach is its main strength. The interviewees were asked by means of an initial opening question to give a full narration (as opposed to an argument) of events and experiences from their own lives, encouraged by non-verbal and paralinguistic expressions of interest and attention. In this way, we provided the interviewees with 'a framework for selecting the stories to be included' (Rosenthal 1993, p. 65). But it was up to them to narrate and talk about what they considered important and crucial.

When the narrative part of the interview was completed, the questioning part followed. During this part we tried to be as non-directive as possible, initially asking the interviewee to elaborate only on topics or themes s/he had introduced in the narrative part, followed by a focused interview technique whereby the interviewee was asked to elaborate on themes which were of particular interest to us, such as migration history, work history, life experiences in Greece, experiences of racism, discrimination etc. Our main aim was to ask questions that would produce further narration rather than argumentation, and as a result we tried to be as non-directive as possible. We collected information from a cross-section of individuals, trying to understand the respondent's viewpoint during the telling of his/her story, at the same time being aware that this was mediated by the individual's social positioning and the time and the social context of the interview itself.

Racism experienced by ethnic minorities in Greece: attitudes, perceptions and ascriptions

Throughout the 1990s a large number of people emigrated from less affluent parts of the world to the comparatively rich member states of the EU. A high proportion entered the EU via its 'soft underbelly', as southern Europe has come to be known (Anthias and Lazaridis 1999), the 'softer of the soft' arguably being Greece's extended and permeable coastline and mountainous borders. The country's geographical position in the 'passage' between Western Europe on the one hand and, on the other, North Africa and Greece's poor Balkan neighbours, also makes it particularly susceptible to migrant traffic, including trafficked sex-workers (Lazaridis 2001).

Although 'third-country' migrants can be found in every class group, the great majority are undocumented, fulfilling specific roles within the Greek parallel economy.[2] They do not form a single niche but rather cluster in particular niches, undertaking a variety of low-skilled, low-paid jobs (Lazaridis and Romaniszyn 1998). Some are self-employed, having generally higher economic power relative to other groups. The feminisation of entire sectors of the labour market is of particular importance. Filipinas, Albanians and East Africans dominate the domestic work and nursing sectors; most women from East-Central Europe and Russia work in the so-called 'entertainment industry'. For a closer examination of the sectors employing women migrant workers, one must consider the connection between gender and race, and racism and sexism, if one is to understand the position of migrant women and the kind of racialisation they face (Lazaridis 2000, 2001).

Undocumented migrants, irrespective of their gender, age or occupation, are exposed to pressures and antagonism both from above (where the Greek government tries to comply with the Schengen requirements and be seen to respond to worries about the heavy burden migrants may eventually impose on an already rudimentary and underdeveloped welfare state) and from below (where they represent to the Greeks the 'other'). Immigration law No. 1975 introduced in 1991, and the lack of race relations legislation to combat xenophobia and racial discrimination, can be seen as articulations of Greek racism, justifying the exclusion and expulsion of 'third-country' migrants and constructing categorical boundaries between those who are 'in' and whose who are 'out'. The law – the first on immigration since 1929 – homogenised undocumented migrants and failed to display a recognition of 'difference'. Amongst other things, the 1991 law foresees a number of financial and punitive sanctions for those facilitating the entry, stay or employment of undocumented/illegal immigrants, and provides for mass deportations (Lazaridis 1996). Until the present day, Greece has not developed institutional apparatus to advance the interests of its minorities and to safeguard against the *de facto* reality of discrimination. At the same time, there is a 'silent' policy of tolerance towards the entry of cheap foreign labour due to pressures from employers of small labour-intensive units, trying to survive the pressures of competition through numerical flexibilisation, or from farmers needing extra seasonal labour. Hence we have the development of a discourse on 'desirable' and 'undesirable' third-country undocumented migrants where, seasonally, the 'undesirable' become 'desirable' and vice-versa according to the needs of the economy – as for instance when extra hands are needed during the olive and tomato harvests in the south, for the cotton and tobacco harvests in central and northern Greece, or during the tourist period.

As stated elsewhere (Lazaridis and Wickens 1999), immigration has evoked a variety of negative reactions among the Greeks, including stereotyped and stigmatic labelling. Anti-immigration agitation has meant that the use of the word *xenos* to identify the non-Europeans has been replaced by the word *kafros*, especially when trying to identify those with dark skin such as Africans. The word 'Filipina' has become synonymous with domestic worker, the word 'Pole' denotes a decorator. At the centre-stage of racialised discourses about the 'other' one finds the Albanians. On the one hand, the word 'Albanian' has become synomymous with 'a hard-working man'; one often hears people saying *'san Albanos doulevi'* (he works like an Albanian – meaning, he is hard-working). On the other hand, the word 'Albanian' has come to mean 'vagabond, someone who is likely to cheat or steal', 'untrustworthy', 'rogue'. Abusive terms like *kleftis* (thief) or *pseftis* (liar) are indiscriminately applied to all Albanians. Such stereotypical images or metaphors, which by and large portray the Albaninas as ruthless 'barbarians', hold the key to understanding people's emotions and, at the same time, are likely to have serious consequences in shaping racist attitudes and practices. For example an older woman, who was looking to let a flat in Athens, quoted a higher price to Albanians so as to avoid letting it to them. When she was asked why, she replied, 'I am not a fool, I do not want to take the risk of being found strangled in the cupboard one day; Albanians are bad people; they are not to be trusted.' A child aged three, when she heard her mother looking for her purse, said: 'An Albanian must have nicked it.' In other words, Albanians have been ascribed characteristics which inferiorise them in the eyes of the 'majority'. Such ascriptions or expressions 'do not merely propose racial differences; they assign racial preferences, and they express desired, intended or actual inclusions or exclusions, entitlements or restrictions' (Goldberg 1990b, p. 266). Racist acts which follow are based on such beliefs; these may fall under the general principle of discriminatory behaviour against the 'other', by virtue of them being constructed as 'a source of trouble, a *classe dangereuse*' (Lazaridis and Wickens 1999, p. 646). In other cases, behaviour is racist on the basis of its outcome.

Anti-immigrant sentiment is also very much shaped by representations in the Greek media discourse encouraging the perception of some migrant groups as 'dangerous to the public' (Lazaridis and Wickens 1999). Migrants are portrayed as 'the problem' for every evil in society, including the rise in crime, thus presenting a threat to the fabric of society as a whole. Thus the 'other' is fixed in public imagination as the irredeemably 'different'. Anti-immigrant slogans are common. Muslims have been stereotyped for being *allothriski* ('of other religion') and in major cities like Athens have failed to build a mosque and a Muslim cemetery. Scapegoating of Albanians in particular has been a regular feature of the media. They are discriminated against on a number of grounds other than race, such as religion (most are Muslims) and historico-political factors (part of Albania was once Greek territory and a sizeable Greek minority is currently living in that area and allegedly suffers discrimination and oppression by the Albanian authorities). The Albanian is not of course 'in' the 'black category'; they have however emerged as a separate racialised grouping, moving in other words from an 'invisible' minority to a 'visible' one. Their religion and culture (rather than their 'colour') constitute the main signifiers of their racialisation. Such signifiers have been used to construct racialised boundaries; individuals are either included or excluded, depending on whether they 'belong' or 'do not belong'. The demarcation line between 'belonging' and 'not belonging' can be described as a *'muro di gomma'*, a 'rubber wall' whose position is not static, but changes depending on the 'interplay between different social divisions enacted within the context of historically produced economic, political and cultural relations' (Anthias 1990, p. 24). The discourse on Albanians is different to that on black minority groups; these latter have been constructed as the 'exotic' rather than the 'dangerous' 'others'. Nevertheless, a similarity exists between the two in terms of status: the majority are undocumented. The construction of the 'problem of illegal immigration' constitutes a major leverage for the emergence of anti-immigrant sentiment, which is often used to justify the government's *'skoupa'* or 'sweeping' operations, as the massive forced deportations of Albanians have become known. What is interesting here is that there is no conflation of Albanians, Africans and other illegal migrants.

Having looked briefly at ways in which racism is interwoven into the fabric of everyday living in Greece, and the ways in which it is reproduced, we examine in the next section the experiences of some migrants in Greece. We focus on the general processes through which racism is expressed and the specific problems that the migrants encountered. We consider the conditions under which the self-employment idea arose as a response to or a specific strategy towards encountering these adverse conditions. We will also look at strategies developed in order to cope with problems after starting the business. What will appear from these accounts is that individuals make choices, but within a framework of constraints.

Migrant stories

Five case-histories have been selected from our data. To guarantee anonymity, some changes have been made to the personal details. The interviews with the three West Africans were conducted in English, those with the Albanians in Greek. In the interview quotes that follow, the Africans' imperfect English is left as it was spoken, whereas the Albanians' Greek has been translated into English.

Wilson

The first story is that of Wilson, a 30-year-old man from Nigeria. He is from a middle-class family and is highly educated, with a degree in economics and a further qualification in health administration. Prior to becoming self-employed he worked for some years in Greece as manual worker. He saved some money and started working as a street-hawker, which is what most Nigerian men do in Greece. He now runs an electronics shop in Athens, and acts as the middle-man in the trading chain between the wholesalers and the street-hawkers. Community networks are crucial for the survival of his business. He came to Greece in the 1980s to study, at a time when the Nigerian government encouraged studies abroad by granting scholarships, and he stayed ever since. He stressed the role of ethnic networks in facilitating his stay and 'integration' into the host society. After he graduated he tried to get a job which would match his qualifications but this was difficult as his permit had expired; he eventually got an unskilled low-paid job in an aluminium factory. He was unhappy in that job because,

> They were never calling me with my name ... and the employer instead of calling me with my name he called me '*mavre*' (black)... Because of the unemployment problem one is subjected to such conditions... The bad experience I had was not paying me Christmas bonus. He only paid the Greeks.

He quit this job when he was refused his entitled Christmas bonus and set up his own business – a shop where he stores and trades electronic goods. Interestingly, when Wilson was asked to recount his life story, he *chose* to start by producing a long narrative on the racial discrimination that 'foreigners' and especially 'black people' encountered in public places and various institutions in Greece. He started by saying:

> Foreigners generally, foreigners are really confronting a lot of problems. Firstly foreigners – especially Africans – the black people, black people I can say, they are not ... they don't have comfort in public places ... attitude from the Greeks against the black people in public places, like restaurants, shops, post office, they create inequality. The way the services are for the Greeks is not the way they are for blacks, to Africans, to black Africans... Another example is [when] you go to the Greek hospitals. The medical care that is given to the Greeks is not the same. They are very different. Before the Greek doctor will respond to a black man he will be reluctant... Most of the Greek doctors don't even care as such to respond to black patients... In addition, also for us to get accommodation here, this is another problem... The minute they hear, that they understand that you are not – from your accent – that you are not a Greek it might influence the price or they will tell you no. 'Not for foreigners'... People are discriminated because they are black... In getting [a] house, in getting accommodation we are being discriminated, in the labour market we observe a lot of discriminations. Yes totally... [In] restaurants, they delay to serve... And they are not serving black men well. They serve you food that is not eatable, that you cannot eat ... it is cooked yesterday... They cannot give it to a Greek man, but they give it to a black man.

Wilson's experience suggests that there is a markedly differential provision of services towards black people. Black people are racialised because they are 'different'. The 'other' is inferior; s/he may have a place in Greek society, but it is an inferior one. This falls under what Wieviorka (1994, p. 182) calls 'classical inegalitarian racism'. Wilson went on to argue that as a result of this behaviour, foreigners like him often feel scared. He argued that when he came to study law in Greece he hoped that he would be able to get a job after he graduated. At one point he mentioned that when he first arrived, in the 1980s, he would hear people in the streets commenting: 'Oh Mother Christ, he is *a black man*' (he stresses the last three words). This suggests that, although back then Greek society had not yet formed an opinion on immigration issues *per se* and public opinion had not yet expressed feelings of opposition, there was a kind of measured reaction towards the 'other', based on assumptions concerning the natural boundaries between Greeks and the 'other', on the basis of 'race'. Black people like Wilson were defined as 'different' and this was accompanied by practices of inferiorisation, subordination and exploitation.

> The Greeks naturally, they are racists... I am telling you this, the truth ... naturally the Greeks they are racists. The Greek people discriminate, their way of discrimination is they discriminate civilisedly ... by not beating us on the street... They leave you, they don't talk to you, they humiliate you, they discriminate you... For example... I enter a store to buy things from the supermarket, I will be in a queue and he will neglect me and attend the Greek people... Do you understand me? You know nature, you know nature is the colour and the body... You know every creature is proud, proud. A Greek man entered the shop after me, instead of attending to me, he attended the Greek man... I was very angry. I hate to observe that discrimination.

Later, when asked to elaborate, he adds:

> There are many forms of discrimination ... in the labour market, in the Greek bureaucratic system, in government offices... Greek people they hate black, they don't like our colour, they don't like black people ... in this country there are many forms of discrimination ... but the Greek people believe that they are not racists. But me as a black person looking at them they are racists. Educate the people on how to handle foreigners.

In these extracts above, Wilson describes the form and degree of racism he has experienced at the level of intersubjective relations and also at the institutional level. Elsewhere in the interview he stressed the point that, unlike other countries in southern Europe, in Greece there is no racist violence in the streets. He argued that Greece should follow the example of other European countries and develop anti-discrimination policies and change attitudes towards black people.

He then moved on to the issue of self-employment and explained the path through which he was driven into becoming self-employed. When he was asked why he decided to become self-employed, he said, 'Because of the exploitation, because of the labour market, people do not accept foreigners, they call you black. So … I decided to work for myself …' In other words, running a business was the best way to make a living, earn more money and have some control over the work situation. It was his attempt to carve out spaces of control.

How does he cope? 'The best thing I do is that I ignore Greek people… I pretend I do not know.' When asked to narrate his experiences with various institutions he said, 'the Greek people when they know that they will gain from us … [and] earn money … they treat us fine'.

Anestis and Giannis

Anestis is an ethnic-Greek Albanian. He is 37 years old. A skilled worker, he lives and works in Athens as a decorator. He is married with two young children. Like many other Albanians, he migrated to Greece because of lack of work after the drastic political and economic changes which took place in Albania in the early 1990s; the factory he was working at closed down. When he came to Greece he started working as a builder. He was paid £10 for a day's work (from 7 am to 6 pm) and was expected also to work at weekends, without a break. The fact that he had a family to support made him decide to become self-employed. He represents an example of a migrant entrepreneur who moved from being a manual worker to becoming self-employed, still in the informal economy, in order to avoid the exploitative conditions under which he was previously working, to control his work conditions as far as this was possible, and to make a better living. His success is based first on the competitive prices he can offer because of his illegal status in a market where the demand for informal, individualised, poorly-paid services is growing; and second, on the informal networks (relatives, neighbours, friends, acquaintances) which helped him develop a clientele. He said: 'You cannot trust people, because there is racism, a lot of racism. Especially here in Greece, it is a lot… You have to work many hours, many hours to earn money'.

Giannis is an ethnic-Greek Albanian who came to Greece via the mountains in 1991. He first worked in the olive harvest and other agricultural activities. Then he worked in a canteen, serving drinks to the personnel of a nearby factory, before moving on to join his brothers in

Athens. There he started cleaning offices at night, then moved on to an off-licence and a petrol station, little by little accumulating capital to buy a kiosk with his brother. Giannis recounted the racism and discrimination he encountered in the Greek labour market and in his contacts with the police. He provided the following account of his experiences with the police:

> They could keep someone in prison for two–three days in order to check your papers, that is for an unimportant reason. The police were stopping us in the middle of the street, 'Where are you from?' 'Albanian?' 'Come with us, stay in prison, wait until we check your papers, see who you are.' OK, but [they treat us] with hatred and with racism ... the way they treat you is often bad...

Both Anestis and Giannis make references to the racism they have experienced in Greece. Their experience illustrates the fact that the signifiers that racism uses are not always those of biology or phenotypical characteristics.

Adama

The fourth story is of a 27-year-old single mother from Sierra Leone, Adama. She migrated to Greece as a student in 1991, but dropped out of the university because of difficulties with the language. She worked for some years cleaning houses and later in a hairdressing salon. She gathered some capital and in 1997 she set up her own business – a hairdressing salon. The choice of this enterprise obviously reflected her previous work experience but was also because her former Greek husband did not want her to work outside the home. The first racist experience she had was within her own household. She describes this as follows:

> The mother [his mother] was ... a big problem. You are black, you are foreigner ... my son wants to use you... [she] hit me everywhere in my breasts... They were always abusing me that I am black, I am foreigner. Even the mum told me once that she will pay me my ticket to go back to my country, make me run away. I tell her, look I didn't come here, to Greece, [for] your son. I came on my own. Just happened that when I came I met your son... Please don't disturb me. But she was still doing the same... So the woman was interfering in my life until I say to my husband 'I can't stand it any more... I have to start working [again]'.

She left the house and went to stay with some of her relatives. She identified a niche in the market for a hairdressing salon catering for African hair styles; she soon developed a clientlele.

She also made some remarks on the way in which Greek men see foreign women:

> If see Greek man on the road I don't even want to talk to them, because I know all they talk to you is come with me for a coffee, from coffee they will ask when we are going to go out, go out for what? Only because they want to sleep with you if you give them chance. For me I don't have time for that... I used to get annoyed ... people they think you are a whore, because you are a foreigner.

When asked whether she has Greek friends, she narrated an episode with some neighbours who were trying to fix a problem in their central heating system. They needed to get access to the pipes through her flat, repaired the heating fault but did not redecorate her flat, leaving it in a mess. She attributed this lack of respect to her being discriminated against because she is a foreigner.

Here racialisation is intensified and interwoven with sexism. As Anthias (1998, p. 529) has put it, 'there are two sets of gender relations that are involved, those of the minority and those of the dominant majority. These gender relations then produce a particular class structuration for different migrant and ethnic minority groups in conjunction with labour market processes and racialisation'. Moreover, as the women we interviewed pointed out, racialised sexual violence against migrant women is common. The latter is often justified in terms of the lure of the exotic sexuality of the black woman or the control of the 'superior' Greek over the 'backward' Albanian whose sexuality can be 'owned' by the Greek male.

Juliana

Racist experiences were also narrated by another woman we interviewed, Juliana, a 37-year-old woman from Sierra Leone.

> When I was working in one house ... my employer's mother did not like me. She used to say bad things about me ... look, look, how she is eating ... she will tell all the bad words, you understand... I am not staying with you black in the house – and she would laugh – I will call the police now... I was working for a family. They abused me. They boy would call me a bitch.

Her young daughter is laughed at in school.

> Sometimes I have to go to the school to warn them, to tell them, to tell the teacher to tell the parent – so teach your children how to behave in school ... tell them don't mind the colour, they should not teach the children to be racists... Maria [her daughter] is black, they are white... Sometimes she will come and tell me 'mum they tell me I am a *mavri* [black]'.

Juliana decided to become self-employed when one employer refused to pay any national insurance contributions.

Discussion

As can be seen from the above five cases, these migrants generally agree that racism in Greece is a given fact. Their testimonies show that it is intricately woven in the fabric of everyday living and transcends other group divisions, such as class, age and gender. Interview texts provide commentaries on the processes through which racism is being expressed. One of the most persistent themes in our interviews was that of covert racism – victimisation integrated into the subtleties of everyday interaction rather than expressed by violent attacks, while at the same time Greeks continue to pride themselves on how hospitable and tolerant they are. Yet the myth of Greek hospitality and of tolerance is contradicted by ample evidence of verbal aggression, such as calling migrants 'blacks' in a derogatory tone. Most of our African interviewees spoke with bitterness about this: they feel that 'Greeks are not to be trusted'. Another form of aggression lies with the police, who pursue a policy of criminalising the Albanians and to a lesser extent black migrants. Recipients of this agression feel powerless against the practices of the dominant group. Opposition to racism takes place on an individual basis rather than in an organised fashion. In a country where racism has only recently become a topic of public discussion, there is a lack of any sanctions against racism.

Our African interviewees see racism articulated as a 'colour' hierarchy. This confirms that in Greece the notion of race is often used to represent a complex system of biological differentiation. Albanians put more emphasis on cultural marginalisation. They try to deny their culture and to assimilate, as they believe that the Greeks will never accept them as they are (Lazaridis 1999). As we have seen, rejection often takes the form of social segregation, in particular in housing and in social life. We have also shown above how the use of stereotypes by the media and public discourse has been used to rationalise the marginalisation and 'demonisation' of the Albanians in Greece and their exclusion from access to material and non-material resources. Questioning their presence and pathologising them as prone to criminality legitimises their consistent marginalisation.

How to deal with racism? The Albanians have adopted 'voluntary assimilation', trying to fit in by changing their names to Greek ones, denying their Albanian identity, baptising themselves Christian Orthodox etc. (Lazaridis and Romaniszyn 1998; Lazaridis and Wickens 1999). On the labour market front, the people we interviewed tried to develop constructive strategies and empower themselves by becoming self-employed. Black women invested their money and energy in serving the needs of the black communities. This may prove in the future to be an important way of increasing group power. At the same time the perpetuation of the myth of Greek tolerance and hospitality means that migrants do not have much room for a legitimate basis of opposition to racism. In this fashion, racism is rejected but not problematised in Greek public discourse and dominant thinking.

Concluding remarks

Racism has taken a particular form in Greece in the 1990s. It is not directed only towards 'black people' *per se*, but towards a variety of groups including 'white' minorities. It cannot therefore be interpreted solely on the basis of 'colour prejudice' based on the experiences of 'black people'. Other groups such as the Albanians in Greece cannot be ignored, as the problems they nowadays face (discrimination and exclusions) are expressions or outcomes of racialised social relations. Some argue that the anti-Albanian sentiment is a special case.[3] We would suggest that racism in Greece is constituted by a set of overlapping and interrelated ideologies and practices that severely affect the life-chances of most immigrant groups in the country. In Greece racist ideologies and practices deploy both biological and cultural characteristics to discriminate against specific groups. Hence colour racism is one form of racism where phenotypical characteristics are used to inferiorise. However, treating blacks as victims and whites as racists obscures the specific racism experiences of different ethnic groups and the differential impact of racism along gender, class and ethnic divisions. Treating for example the Albanians as 'dangerous others' constructs the 'white' as the 'other'. In the case of Albanians, a variety of cultural characteristics have been deployed to mark their inferior status. Racist public discourses (the media in particular) have used various stereotypes for the ideological purpose of legitimising and justifying social relations of power and domination, resulting in the inferiorisation of this group.

It is therefore clear that we should not talk about Greek racism but about Greek racisms. The case studies we have looked at support Husband's (1982, p. 326) argument that 'the elements of the dominant ideology (top-down) mesh differently with the existential consciousness of people in different material conditions'. Hence the subjective personal experiences may have a differential impact on individuals depending on one's class, gender and race, resulting in different outcomes. In the above cases we have shown the variety of ways in which racisms are integrated into personal biographies and consciousness, which are determined by people's structured material existences. Thus, while racism, as a dominant ideology, *should* possess common core features, 'the unique multiple social identity of individuals makes the incorporation of the different elements of racist ideologies a unique configuration' for Nigerian men, Sierra Leonean women and ethnic-Greek and other Albanians (Husband 1982, p. 329).

Racism as a set of ideologies, leading to humiliation, discrimination and racist acts, gathered momentum in the context of immense changes which have taken place in Greece since the late 1980s. It developed further within the context of large flows of migrants from East-Central Europe, increasing unemployment and a national identity crisis. Migrant groups have become the target of a rising insecurity, accused of potentially becoming a burden by claiming benefits from the state.

Common explanations for arguing against migrants centre around the dubious starting-point that Greece needs to protect its national heritage and culture. In this context the migrants are seen as 'contaminating' Greek culture. This particular origin of racism can be traced within the Greek model of the nation, comprised only of ethnic Greeks, leading to the rejection of difference. The strategic manipulation of nationalist feelings by Greek politicians based on an ethnically and culturally defined model of nationality, highlights the power of political and cultural myths in sensitising the Greeks to the alleged peril of the 'other'. The implications of an ethnically or culturally defined model of nationality justifies the ethnic majority campaigning over the control of symbols, traditions and glorious ancestors. Hence anti-migrant nationalists are seen as patriots who 'protect' the country from a co-ordinated plan by the West's main opponent, Islam, to Islamise Europe and from Greece's main opponent, Turkey, to take over Greece both territorially and symbolically.

Traditions, myths and collective memories associated with national struggles against 'invaders' or 'enemies' have played a prominent role in the formation of the Greek nation (Triandafyllidou *et al.* 1997). The nation is represented as an homogeneous and compact unit, its ethnic origins being in antiquity. The glorious past of classical Greek culture and Orthodox religion distinguishes Greeks from the Turks and neighbouring Slavs. The integration of the past in the present within the Greek concept of national identity is manifested also in the Greek language, where the Greek concept of an ethnic group and a nation is described by the term *ethnos* which combines the pre-modern concept of an homogeneous ethnic community with the modern notion of the nation as a political entity; hence ethnic customs, linguistic ties and religious beliefs are transformed into national sentiments. The nationalist feelings of the population are often manipulated by political parties as a campaigning device, whereby the glories of the past are used to compensate for the failures and dissatisfactions of the present. Such manipulations unite people in the face of a common threat, and national pride is often emphasised in political discourse 'which concentrates on the injustice caused by foreigners' (Triandafyllidou *et al.* 1997).

The modern history of Greece has been marked by the collapse of the Ottoman Empire, the accession of Greece to the EEC in 1981, and the dismantling of communist regimes in Eastern Europe. The contemporary question of Greek national identity has to be seen in its specific historical context, namely the shifting boundaries, between east and west, where politics, culture and religion are inextricably interlinked. The relationship between the Greeks and the ethnic-Greek Albanians is characterised by a religious affinity, in that they share a common Christian Orthodox tradition. However, the common religion shared by those two also involves a potential for conflict with respect to the Muslim populations residing in the area. The idea of 'difference' becomes horribly salient within the Balkan context, as we have seen in Bosnia, Kosovo and elsewhere. Greeks have distinct symbols, language and culture from the Slavic populations and to a certain extent from the Turkish populations. The dichotomy between the Greeks and the non-Greeks (or the 'barbarians', as those not enlightened by the Greek thought were characterised) is currently being played out within a new context. Migrants have now been identified as the 'other'; the supposedly homogeneous composition of the Greek nation, in response to the pressure from an external threat, has led to neglect of social and cultural diversity existing among people living within the national territory and to the suppression of minority religious rights (Pollis 1992).

The dominant culture is perceived as superior whereas 'other' cultures are problematised. This leads Greek people to define their sense of the 'we' in contrast to a 'they' which becomes manifest in a number of racist practices. There is a strong tendency to assume the superiority of Greek traditions, values and religion and the hidden expectation that minority ethnic groups must accept this and eventually adapt. For those who are not black, and therefore do not 'look different', there is a culturally defined standard compared to which the 'other' is different. However, Greece has not encouraged or moved towards either the enforcement of cultural assimilation, nor ethnicisation,[4] let alone favouring a policy of multiculturalism or pluralism.

In this chapter we have looked at questions of migration, nation and ethnic belonging, which are key elements of the rapid social transformations Greece has been going through since the late 1980s; questions about race and ethnicity are of major significance when trying to explain the complex configurations of contemporary social change in Greece. The country is experiencing a cultural shift from hospitality and a tradition of welcoming strangers, to a nation marked by racism and discriminatory attitudes towards the 'other'. This is marked by uncertainty as to whether the country belongs to the 'west' or to the 'east'. The failure to resolve the issue of cultural belonging is reflected in issues of migration and of difference. It seems that Greeks have not yet understood that ethnic purity and the search for roots are delusions; we are all mongrels. Following Mac an Ghaill (1998, p. 8), the question remains: at a time of increased anti-Islamic feelings, can Greece develop a new civic nationalism for the 2000s which challenges the racist and nationalist exclusions currently experienced by ethnic minority groups and at the same time addresses the fears of the majority of the members of Greek society?

Notes

1 This chapter is an offshoot of a project funded by the EU's TSER (Targeted Socio-Economic Research) initiative. The project is on 'Self-employment practices in relation to women and minorities: their success and failure in relation to social citizenship policies'. Gabriella Lazaridis and Maria Koumandraki are respectively Director and Research Assistant on the Greek part of the project. The authors acknowledge the financial contribution of the European Commission on this project (grant no. CEC: SOE2–CT97–3042).

2 The Ministry of Public Security indicated that in 1992 there were around 500,000 foreigners in Greece. By the mid–1990s, the number of undocumented migrants was estimated at around 600,000 – 5 per cent of the total population, 12 per cent of the active population and 15 per cent of the labour force.

3 The complexity of the Albanian question is due to the intertwining of cultural, political and geographical issues. There is also a once-Greek part of Albania, Northern Epirus, which formed an integral part of the Greek state and nation. According to many, the inhabitants of this region define themselves as Greeks; certainly they have been highly prone to migrate to Greece.

4 According to Philomena Essed (1991, p. 189), ethnicisation is 'the activation of the ideal of tolerance, which involves the redefinition of specific areas of the system on the basis of "ethnic" criteria (e.g. ethnic policy, ethnic business, ethnic jobs) and the concomitant creation of specific functions to control these "ethnic" niches'.

References

Anthias, F. (1990) Race and class revisited – conceptualising race and racisms, *The Sociological Review*, 38(1), pp. 19–42.

Anthias, F. (1992) Connecting race and ethnic phenomena, *Sociology*, 26(3), pp. 421–38.

Anthias, F. (1998) Rethinking social divisions: some notes towards a theoretical framework, *The Sociological Review*, 46(3), pp. 505–35.

Anthias, F. and Lazaridis, G. (eds) (1999) *Into the Margins: Migration and Exclusion in Southern Europe*. Aldershot: Ashgate.

Bertaux, D. and Kohli, M. (1984) The life story approach: a continental view, *Annual Review of Sociology*, 10, pp. 215–37.

Bradley, H. (1996) *Fractured Identities*. Oxford: Blackwell.

Brah, A., Hickman, M. and Mac an Ghaill, M. (1999) Thinking identities: ethnicity, racims and culture, in Brah, A., Hickman, M. and Mac an Ghaill, M. (eds) *Thinking Identities:*

Ethnicity, Racisms and Culture. Basingstoke: Macmillan, pp. 1–21.

Cohen, P. (1988) The perversions of inheritance: studies in the making of multi-racist Britain, in Cohen, P. and Bains, H. (eds) *Multi-Racist Britain.* Basingstoke: Macmillan, pp. 9–18.

Cohen, P. and Bains, H. (eds) (1988) *Multi-Racist Britain.* Basingstoke: Macmillan.

EEC (1989) *Eurobarometer: Public Opinion in the European Community.* Brussels: Commission of the European Communities.

Essed, P. (1991) *Understanding Everyday Racism: An Interdisciplinary Theory.* London: Sage.

Gilroy, P. (1987) *There Ain't No Black in the Union Jack.* London: Hutchinson.

Goldberg, D.T. (1990a) *Anatomy of Racism.* Minneapolis: University of Minnesota Press.

Goldberg, D. T. (1990b) The social formation of racist discource, in Goldberg, D. T. (ed.) *Anatomy of Racism.* Minneapolis: University of Minnesota Press, pp. 295–318.

Guillaumin, C. (1995) The idea of race and its elevation to autonomous scientific and legal status, in Guillaumin, C. (ed.) *Racism, Sexism, Power and Ideology.* London: Routledge, pp. 61–98.

Husband, C. (1982) British racisms: the construction of racial ideologies, in Husband, C. (ed.) *'Race' in Britain: Continuity and Change.* London: Routledge, pp. 319–31.

Kohli, M. (1981) Biography: account, text, method, in Bertaux, D. (ed.) *Biography and Society.* Beverly Hills: Sage, pp. 61–75.

Lazaridis, G. (1996) Immigration to Greece: a critical evaluation of Greek policy, *New Community*, 22(2), pp. 335–48.

Lazaridis, G. (1999) The helots of the new millennium: ethnic-Greek Albanians and 'other' Albanians in Greece, in Anthias, F. and Lazaridis, G. (eds) *Into the Margins: Migration and Exclusion in Southern Europe.* Aldershot: Ashgate, pp. 105–21.

Lazaridis, G. (2000) Filipino and Albanian women migrant workers in Greece: multiple layers of oppression, in Anthias, F. and Lazaridis, G. (eds) *Gender and Migration in Southern Europe: Women on the Move.* Oxford: Berg, pp. 49–79.

Lazaridis, G. (2001) Trafficking and prostitution: the growing exploitation of migrant women in Greece, *European Journal of Women's Studies*, 8(1), pp. 67–102.

Lazaridis, G. and Romaniszyn, C. (1998) Albanian and Polish undocumented workers in Greece: a comparative analysis, *Journal of European Social Policy*, 8(1), pp. 5–22.

Lazaridis, G. and Wickens, E. (1999) 'US' and the 'OTHERS': ethnic minorities in Greece, *Annals of Tourism Research*, 26(3), pp.623–55.

Mac an Ghaill, M. (1999) *Contemporary Racisms and Ethnicities.* Buckingham: Oxford University Press.

Mason, D. (1994) On the dangers of disconnecting race and racism, *Sociology*, 28(4), pp. 845–58.

Mason, D. (1999) The continuing significance of race? Teaching ethnic and racial studies in sociology, in Bulmer, M. and Solomos, J. (eds) *Ethnic and Racial Studies Today.* London: Routledge, pp. 13–28.

Miles, R. (1982) Racism and nationalism in Britain, in Husband, C. (ed.) *'Race' in Britain: Continuity and Change.* London: Routledge, pp. 292–315.

Miles, R. (1989) *Racism.* London: Routledge.

Miller, R.L. (2000) *Researching Life Stories and Family Histories.* London: Sage.

Omi, M. and Winant, H. (1986) *Racial Formation in the United States.* London: Routledge.

Pollis, A. (1992) Greek national identity: religious minorities, rights and European norms, *Journal of Modern Greek Studies*, 10, pp. 171–95.

Rattansi, A. (1994) Western racisms, ethnicities and identities in a 'postmodern' frame, in Rattansi, A. and Westood, S. (eds) *Racism, Modernity, Identity: On the Western Front.*

Cambridge: Cambridge University Press, pp. 15–86.

Rattansi, A. and Westood, S. (1994) (eds) *Racism, Modernity, Identity: On the Western Front*. Cambridge: Cambridge University Press.

Rosenthal, G. (1993) Reconstructing life stories: principles of selection in generating stories for narrative biographical interview, in Josselson, R. and Lieblich, A. (eds) *The Narrative Study of Lives*. London: Sage, pp. 59–91.

Silverman, M. and Yuval-Davis, N. (1999) Jews, Arabs and the theorisation of racism in Britain and France, in Brah, A., Hickman, M. and Mac an Ghaill, M. (eds) *Thinking Identities: Ethnicity, Racism and Culture*. London: Macmillan, pp. 25–48.

Solomos, J. (1993) *Race and Racism in Britain*. Basingstoke: Macmillan.

Solomos, J. and Back, L. (1996) *Racism and Society*. Basingstoke: Macmillan.

Triandafyllidou, A., Calloni, M. and Mikrakis, A. (1997) New Greek nationalism, *Sociological Research Online*, 2(1), http://www.socresonline.org.uk/socresonline/2/1/7

Van de Berghe, P. (1978) *Race and Racism: A Comparative Perspective*. New York: John Wiley and Sons.

Wieviorka, M. (1994) Racism in Europe: unity and diversity, in Rattansi, A. and Westwood, S. (eds) *Racism, Modernity and Identity on the Western Front*, Cambridge: Cambridge University Press, pp. 173–88.

Index

Information in notes is indexed in the form 117n8, ie note 8 on page 117